ACCA

PAPER F7

FINANCIAL REPORTING (INTERNATIONAL)

In this June 2007 new edition

- We discuss the **best strategies** for revising and taking your ACCA exams

- We show you how to be well prepared for the **December 2007 exam**

- We give you **lots of great guidance** on tackling questions

- We show you how you can **build your own exams**

- We provide you with **three** mock exams including the **Pilot paper**

- We provide the **ACCA examiner's answers** as well as our own to key exam questions and the Pilot Paper as an additional revision aid

Our **i-Pass** product also supports this paper.

FOR EXAMS IN DECEMBER 2007

PRACTICE & REVISION KIT

LEARNING MEDIA

First edition June 2007

ISBN 9780 7517 3364 8

British Library Cataloguing-in-Publication Data
A catalogue record for this book
is available from the British Library

Published by

BPP Learning Media Ltd
BPP House, Aldine Place
London W12 8AA

www.bpp.com/learningmedia

Printed in Great Britain by
Ashford Colour Press Ltd
Unit 600
Fareham Reach, Fareham Road
Gosport
PO13 0FW

We are grateful to the Association of Chartered
Certified Accountants for permission to reproduce past
examination questions. The answers to past
examination questions have been prepared by BPP
Learning Media Ltd.

Contents

Question index

The headings in this checklist/index indicate the topics of questions. Most questions are marked 2.5, which means they were examination questions under the previous Financial Reporting syllabus. Some have since been amended or split into shorter questions on different topics.

Preparation questions, listed in italics, provide you with a firm foundation for attempts at exam-standard questions.

Examiners answers. For any 2006 questions (6/06 or 12/06) the examiners answers can be found at the end of the kit.

BPP LEARNING MEDIA

Mock exam 2

Mock exam 3 (Pilot paper)

Planning your question practice

Our guidance from page 27 shows you how to organise your question practice, either by attempting questions from each syllabus area or **by building your own exams** – tackling questions as a series of practice exams.

BPP)))
LEARNING MEDIA

Using your BPP Practice and Revision Kit

Tackling revision and the exam

You can significantly improve your chances of passing by tackling revision and the exam in the right ways. Our advice is based on recent feedback from ACCA examiners.

- We look at the dos and don'ts of revising for, and taking, ACCA exams
- We focus on Paper F7; we discuss revising the syllabus, what to do (and what not to do) in the exam, how to approach different types of question and ways of obtaining easy marks

Selecting questions

We provide signposts to help you plan your revision.

- A full **question index**
- **BPP's question plan** highlighting the most important questions and explaining why you should attempt them
- **Build your own exams**, showing how you can practise questions in a series of exams

Making the most of question practice

At BPP we realise that you need more than just questions and model answers to get the most from your question practice.

- Our **Top tips** provide essential advice on tackling questions, presenting answers and the key points that answers need to include
- We show you how you can pick up **Easy marks** on questions, as we know that picking up all readily available marks often can make the difference between passing and failing
- We summarise **Examiner's comments** to show you how students who sat the exam coped with the questions
- We include ACCA's **marking guides** to show you what the examiner rewards
- We refer to the **BPP 2007 Study Text** for detailed coverage of the topics covered in each question
- A number of questions include **Analysis** and **Helping hands** attached to show you how to approach them if you are struggling
- In a bank at the end of this Kit we include the **examiner's answers** to the Pilot paper and other questions. Used in conjunction with our answers they provide an indication of all possible points that could be made, issues that could be covered and approaches to adopt.

Attempting mock exams

There are three mock exams that provide practice at coping with the pressures of the exam day. We strongly recommend that you attempt them under exam conditions. **Mock exams 1 and 2** reflect the question styles and syllabus coverage of the exam; **Mock exam 3** is the Pilot paper. To help you get the most out of doing these exams, we not only provide help with each answer, but also guidance on how you should have approached the whole exam.

Passing ACCA exams

Revising and taking ACCA exams

To maximise your chances of passing your ACCA exams, you must make best use of your time, both before the exam during your revision, and when you are actually doing the exam.

- Making the most of your revision time can make a big, big difference to how well-prepared you are for the exam

- Time management is a core skill in the exam hall; all the work you've done can be wasted if you don't make the most of the three hours you have to attempt the exam

In this section we simply show you what to do and what not to do during your revision, and how to increase and decrease your prospects of passing your exams when you take them. Our advice is grounded in feedback we've had from ACCA examiners. You may be surprised to know that much examiner advice is the same whatever the exam, and the reasons why many students fail don't vary much between subjects and exam levels. So if you follow the advice we give you over the next few pages, you will **significantly** enhance your chances of passing **all** your ACCA exams.

How to revise

☑ Plan your revision

At the start of your revision period, you should draw up a **timetable** to plan how long you will spend on each subject and how you will revise each area. You need to consider the total time you have available and also the time that will be required to revise for other exams you're taking.

☑ Practise Practise Practise

The **more exam-standard questions** you do, the **more likely you are to pass** the exam. Practising full questions will mean that you'll get used to the time pressure of the exam. When the time is up, you should note where you've got to and then try to complete the question, giving yourself practice at everything the question tests.

☑ Revise enough

Make sure that your revision covers the breadth of the syllabus, as in most papers most topics could be examined in a compulsory question. However it is true that some topics are **key** – they often appear in compulsory questions or are a particular interest of the examiner – and you need to spend sufficient time revising these. Make sure you also know the **basics** – the fundamental calculations, proformas and report layouts.

☑ Deal with your difficulties

Difficult areas are topics you find dull and pointless, or subjects that you found problematic when you were studying them. You mustn't become negative about these topics; instead you should build up your knowledge by reading the **Passcards** and using the **Quick quiz** questions in the Study Text to test yourself. When practising questions in the Kit, go back to the Text if you're struggling.

☑ Learn from your mistakes

Having completed a question you must try to look at your answer critically. Always read the **Top tips guidance** in the answers; it's there to help you. Look at **Easy marks** to see how you could have quickly gained credit on the questions that you've done. As you go through the Kit, it's worth noting any traps you've fallen into, and key points in the **Top tips** or **Examiner's comments** sections, and referring to these notes in the days before the exam. Aim to learn at least one new point from each question you attempt, a technical point perhaps or a point on style or approach.

☑ Read the examiners' guidance

We refer throughout this Kit to **Examiner's comments**; these are available on ACCA's website. As well as highlighting weaknesses, examiners' reports as often provide clues to future questions, as many examiners will quickly test again areas where problems have arisen. ACCA's website also contains articles by examiners which you **must** read, as they may form the basis of questions on any paper after they've been published.

Read through the examiner's answers to key exam questions and the Pilot paper included at the back of the Kit. In general these are far longer and more comprehensive than any answer you could hope to produce in the exam, but used in conjunction with our more realistic solutions, they provide a useful revision tool, covering all possible points and approaches.

☑ Complete all three mock exams

You should attempt the **Mock exams** at the end of the Kit under **strict exam conditions**, to gain experience of selecting questions, managing your time and producing answers.

How NOT to revise

☒ Revise selectively

Examiners are well aware that some students try to forecast the contents of exams, and only revise those areas that they think will be examined. Examiners try to prevent this by doing the unexpected, for example setting the same topic in successive sittings or setting topics in compulsory questions that have previously only been examined in optional questions.

☒ Spend all the revision period reading

You cannot pass the exam just by learning the contents of Passcards, Course Notes or Study Texts. You have to develop your **application skills** by practising questions.

☒ Audit the answers

This means reading the answers and guidance without having attempted the questions. Auditing the answers gives you **false reassurance** that you would have tackled the questions in the best way and made the points that our answers do. The feedback we give in our answers will mean more to you if you've attempted the questions and thought through the issues.

☒ Practise some types of question, but not others

Although you may find the numerical parts of certain papers challenging, you shouldn't just practise calculations. These papers will also contain written elements, and you therefore need to spend time practising written question parts.

☒ Get bogged down

Don't spend a lot of time worrying about all the minute detail of certain topic areas, and leave yourself insufficient time to cover the rest of the syllabus. Remember that a key skill in the exam is the ability to **concentrate on what's important** and this applies to your revision as well.

☒ Overdo studying

Studying for too long without interruption will mean your studying becomes less effective. A five minute break each hour will help. You should also make sure that you are leading a **healthy lifestyle** (proper meals, good sleep and some times when you're not studying).

How to PASS your exams

☑ Prepare for the day

Make sure you set at least one alarm (or get an alarm call), and allow plenty of time to get to the exam hall. You should have your route planned in advance and should listen on the radio for potential travel problems. You should check the night before to see that you have pens, pencils, erasers, watch, calculator with spare batteries, also exam documentation and evidence of identity.

☑ Select the right questions

You should select the optional questions you feel you can answer **best**, basing your selection on the topics covered, the requirements of the question, how easy it will be to apply the requirements and the availability of easy marks.

☑ Plan your three hours

You need to make sure that you will be answering the correct number of questions, and that you spend the right length of time on each question – this will be determined by the number of marks available. Each mark carries with it a **time allocation** of **1.8 minutes**. A 25 mark question therefore should be selected, completed and checked in 45 minutes. With some papers, it's better to do certain types of question first or last.

☑ Read the questions carefully

To score well, you must follow the requirements of the question, understanding what aspects of the subject area are being covered, and the tasks you will have to carry out. The requirements will also determine what information and examples you should provide. Reading the question scenarios carefully will help you decide what **issues** to discuss, **techniques** to use, **information** and **examples** to include and how to **organise** your answer.

☑ Plan your answers

Five minutes of planning plus twenty-five minutes of writing is certain to earn you more marks than thirty minutes of writing. Consider when you're planning how your answer should be **structured, w**hat the **format** should be and **how long** each part should take.

Confirm before you start writing that your plan makes **sense,** covers **all relevant points** and does not include **irrelevant material.**

☑ Show evidence of judgement

Remember that examiners aren't just looking for a display of knowledge; they want to see how well you can **apply** the knowledge you have. Evidence of application and judgement will include writing answers that only contain **relevant** material, using the material in scenarios to **support** what you say, **criticising** the **limitations** and **assumptions** of the techniques you use and making **reasonable recommendations** that follow from your discussion.

☑ Stay until the end of the exam

Use any spare time to **check and recheck** your script. This includes checking you have filled out the candidate details correctly, you have labelled question parts and workings clearly, you have used headers and underlining effectively and spelling, grammar and arithmetic are correct.

How to FAIL your exams

☒ Don't do enough questions

If you don't attempt sufficient questions on the paper, you are making it harder for yourself to pass the questions that you do attempt. If for example you don't do a 20 mark question, then you will have to score 50 marks out of 80 marks on the rest of the paper, and therefore have to obtain 63% of the marks on the questions you do attempt. Failing to attempt all of the paper is symptomatic of poor time management or poor question selection.

☒ Include irrelevant material

Markers are given detailed mark guides and will not give credit for irrelevant content. Therefore you should **NOT** braindump all you know about a broad subject area; the markers will only give credit for what is **relevant**, and you will also be showing that you lack the ability to **judge what's important.**

☒ Fail to use the details in the scenario

General answers or reproductions of old answers that don't refer to what is in the scenario in **this** question won't score enough marks to pass.

☒ Copy out the scenario details

Examiners see **selective** use of the right information as a key skill. If you copy out chunks of the scenario which aren't relevant to the question, or don't use the information to support your own judgements, you won't achieve good marks.

☒ Don't do what the question asks

Failing to provide all the examiner asks for will limit the marks you score. You will also decrease your chances by not providing an answer with enough **depth** – producing a single line bullet point list when the examiner asks for a discussion.

☒ Present your work poorly

Markers will only be able to give you credit if they can read your writing. There are also plenty of other things that will make it more difficult for markers to reward you. Examples include:

- Not using black or blue ink
- Not showing clearly which question you're attempting
- Scattering question parts from the same question throughout your answer booklet
- Not showing clearly workings or the results of your calculations

Paragraphs that are too long or which lack headers also won't help markers and hence won't help you.

Using your BPP products

This Kit gives you the question practice and guidance you need in the exam. Our other products can also help you pass:

- **Learning to Learn Accountancy** gives further valuable advice on revision

- **Passcards** provide you with clear topic summaries and exam tips

- **Success CDs** help you revise on the move

- **i-Pass CDs** offer tests of knowledge against the clock

- **Learn Online** is an e-learning resource delivered via the Internet, offering comprehensive tutor support and featuring areas such as study, practice, email service, revision and useful resources

You can purchase these products by visiting www.bpp.com/mybpp.

Visit our website www.bpp.com/acca/learnonline to sample aspects of Learn Online free of charge. Learn Online is hosted by BPP Professional Education.

Passing F7

Revising F7

F7 is a demanding and time-pressured paper. However, you can pass by learning the basics really well and then keeping your head and producing sensible, readable answers. This does not mean that you only revise certain topics. The examiner warns against 'question spotting' and he will produce questions which cover a wide range of the syllabus. You are very unlikely to pass this paper on three questions.

Topics to revise

What we do know about F7 is that there will be a compulsory consolidation question. This can be a balance sheet or income statement or both, and it will probably include an associate, so be prepared for all of this. Therefore you must revise all the consolidation workings, and you must know how to account for an associate.

Question 2 will be a single company accounts preparation question. This allows the examiner to bring in more complex issues that he would not test in the consolidation question. Make sure you can deal with finance leases, deferred tax, calculating finance costs using the effective interest rate, prior period adjustments, discontinued operations and construction contracts.

Question 3 will be on cash flow statements or interpretation of accounts. You have studied both of these at 1.1, so make sure you can do them well. Other recent questions have involved non-current assets and impairment, intangible assets, EPS, provisions and regulatory issues. These are all likely topics for questions 4 and 5.

There will be a certain amount of discussion in some of the questions, so be prepared to write about financial reporting topics, such as the *Framework* or specific accounting standards.

Question practice

This is the most important thing to do if you want to get through. All of the most up-to-date exam questions from the previous syllabus are in this kit. Practice doing them under timed conditions, then go through the answers and go back to the study text for any topic you are really having trouble with. Come back to a question week later and try it again – you will be surprised at how much better you are getting. Be very ruthless with yourself at this stage – you have to do the question in the time, without looking at the answer. This will really sharpen your wits and make the exam experience less worrying. Just keep doing this and you will get better at doing questions and you will really find out what you know and what you don't know.

Passing the F7 exam

If you have honestly done your revision then you can pass this exam. What you must do is remain calm and tackle it in a professional manner. The examiner stresses a number of points which you should bear in mind.

- You must read the question properly. Students often fail to read the question properly and miss some of the information. Time spent reading the question a second time would be time well spent. Make yourself do this, don't just rush into it in a panic.

- Workings must be clear and cross-referenced. If the marker can read and understand your workings they can give you credit for using the right method, even if your answer is wrong. If your answer is wrong and there are no workings, or they are illegible and incomprehensible, you will get no marks for that part of the question.

- Stick to the timings and answer all questions. Do not spend too long on one question at the expense of others. The number of extra marks you will gain on that question will be minimal, and you could have at least obtained the easy marks on the next question.

- Do not neglect the short parts of the question. If you get a 20-mark consolidation with a 5-mark discussion topic at the end, leave time for that last part. You can't afford to throw away 5 marks.

- Make sure you get the easy marks. If an accounts preparation question contains something that you are unable to do, just ignore it and do the rest. You will probably only lose a few marks and if you start trying to puzzle it out you might waste a lot of minutes.

- Answer the question. In a discussion-type question you may be tempted to just write down everything you know about the topic. This will do you no good. The marking parameters for these questions are quite precise. You will only get marks for making points that answer the question exactly as it has been set. So don't waste your time waffling – you could be scoring marks somewhere else.

Gaining the easy marks

The first point to make is that you do not get any marks for just writing down the formats for a financial statement. But, once you have put the formats down, you are then in a position to start filling in the numbers and getting the easy marks. Also, correct formats will give you a guide so that you don't miss things. For instance, it's easy to forget about the minority interest in a group income statement. So that's a good place to start.

Having put down the formats, then go through the workings and slot in the figures. Make sure you get in all the ones you can do easily. Complicated parts are well worth doing if you are able to do them – there will be marks for those. Complicated parts which you don't know how to do are best left alone.

If you have an interpretation question, you will not get many marks for just producing lots of ratios or restating information you have already been given in the question. You have to be able to evaluate the information and see what judgements can be made. So go through the information critically and see which ratios are actually relevant. Then calculate them and say something sensible about them.

Exam information

Format of the exam

All questions are compulsory.

	Number of marks
Questions 1-3; 25 marks each	75
Question 4	15
Question 5	10
	100

Time allowed: 3 hours

Additional information

The Study Guide provides more detailed guidance on the syllabus.

Pilot paper

		Marks
1	Consolidated balance sheet including associate	25
2	Single company accounts preparation question	25
3	Performance appraisal including calculation of ratios	25
4	Discursive question on qualitative characteristics of financial information including short scenario	15
5	Construction contract	10
		100

Useful websites

The websites below provide additional sources of information of relevance to your studies for *Financial Reporting*.

- www.ft.com

  This website provides information about current international business. You can search for information and articles on specific industry groups as well as individual companies.

- www.bpp.com

  Our website provides information about BPP products and services, with a link to the ACCA website.

- www.invweek.co.uk

- www.accaglobal.com

  ACCA's website. Includes student section.

Planning your question practice

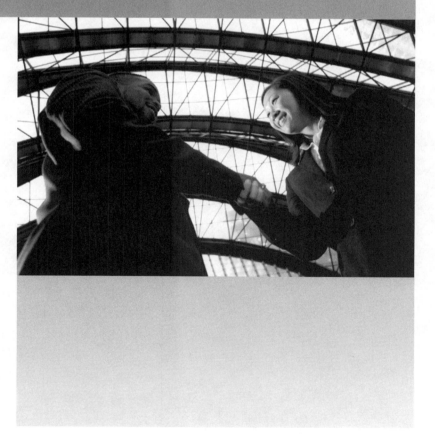

BPP
LEARNING MEDIA

Planning your question practice

We have already stressed that question practice should be right at the centre of your revision. Whilst you will spend some time looking at your notes and Paper F7 Passcards, you should spend the majority of your revision time practising questions.

We recommend two ways in which you can practise questions.

- Use **BPP's question plan** to work systematically through the syllabus and attempt key and other questions on a section-by-section basis

- **Build your own exams** – attempt questions as a series of practice exams

These ways are suggestions and simply following them is no guarantee of success. You or your college may prefer an alternative but equally valid approach.

BPP's question plan

The BPP plan below requires you to devote a **minimum of 45 hours** to revision of Paper F7. Any time you can spend over and above this should only increase your chances of success.

Step 1   **Review your notes** and the chapter summaries in the Paper F7 **Passcards** for each section of the syllabus.

Step 2   **Answer the key questions** for that section. These questions have boxes round the question number in the table below and you should answer them in full. Even if you are short of time you must attempt these questions if you want to pass the exam. You should complete your answers without referring to our solutions.

Step 3   **Attempt the other questions** in that section.

Step 4   Attempt **Mock exams 1, 2 and 3** under strict exam conditions.

Syllabus section	2007 Passcards chapters	Questions in this Kit	Comments	Done ☑
The conceptual framework	1	1, 2	Peterlee is a straightforward question on the *Framework* and Derringdo gets you to apply the *Framework* to the issue of revenue recognition.	☐
The regulatory framework	2	3	This question covers a lot of material and is good revision.	☐
Presentation of published financial statements	3	4	All of these questions are good. Do as many as you can. Winger is a good all-round example.	☐
Non-current assets	4	10	Broadoak is a full question on IAS 16, so make sure you do it. The other questions reflect what you may see for a 10 or 15-mark question.	☐
Intangible assets	5	15	Dexterity is a 25-mark on goodwill and intangible assets, so it covers a lot of ground.	☐
Impairment of assets	6	17	Wilderness is an excellent question on impairment. See if you can do it in the time.	☐
Reporting financial performance	7	19, 23	Research Co is a good preparation question and Partway is a recent question on discontinued operations.	☐
Introduction to groups	8	24, 25	Question 24 is a good preparation question on the basics. Question 25 looks at the effect of related parties on group accounts. This is the context within which the examiner will examine related parties.	☐
The consolidated balance sheet	9	27, 28	Hample is a straightforward consolidated balance sheet. Highveldt does not require the whole balance sheet, but gets you to produce the key workings.	☐
The consolidated income statement	10	29, 30, 31, 32	Start with the preparation question, and then do Hydan, which is a recent question.	☐
Accounting for associates	11	33, 34, 39	Do the two preparation questions first and then question 39, which is the latest exam question.	☐
Inventories and construction contracts	12	40, 41	Start with the preparation question and make sure you also do Merryview.	☐
Provisions, contingent liabilities and contingent assets	13	44	Make sure you do Bodyline, which is a full question on provisions.	☐
Financial assets and financial liabilities	14	46, 47	Both of these questions cover calculation of interest costs. Make sure you can do them.	☐
The legal versus the commercial view of accounting	15	50, 51	These are good questions on the application of substance over form. Do both of them.	☐
Leasing	16	52, 53, 54	These are all short questions. Do them all.	☐
Accounting for taxation	17	56, 57	Do the preparation question. Question 57 is good practice for a discursive question on deferred tax.	☐

BPP LEARNING MEDIA

Syllabus section	2007 Passcards chapters	Questions in this Kit	Comments	Done ☑
Earnings per share	18	59, 60	Question 60 is part of a recent exam question, so good practice.	☐
Analysing and interpreting financial statements	19	63	Boston is a good question on ratio analysis.	☐
Limitations of financial statements and interpretation techniques	20	65, 66	Breadline is a good question on these issues.	☐
Cash flow statements	21	67, 72	Do the preparation question and Minster, which is the most recent question.	☐
Alternative models and practices	22	73	Update is a typical question on this area.	☐
Specialised, not-for-profit and public sector entities	23	Pilot paper 3(c)	You will not get a full question on this. The examiner has stated that this part-question in the pilot paper is typical of how it will be examined.	☐

Build your own exams

Having revised your notes and the BPP Passcards, you can attempt the questions in the Kit as a series of practice exams. This is our suggestion:

	Practice exams					
	1	2	3	4	5	6
1	26	29	30	34	35	36
2	5	6	7	21	22	23
3	68	69	70	71	62	63
4	10	15	17	49	48	44

We have selected these questions on the following basis:

- Question 1 will be a consolidation
- Question 2 will be an accounts preparation question
- Question 3 will be a cash flow statement or an interpretation of accounts question
- Questions 4 and 5 will test other areas of the syllabus

In your exam Question 4 will be 15 marks and Question 5 will be 10 marks. In our selections we have given you a 25-mark Question 4 instead.

BPP
LEARNING MEDIA

Questions

1 Peterlee (2.5 6/06)

23 mins

(a) The IASB's *Framework for the preparation and presentation of financial statements* (Framework) sets out the concepts that underlie the preparation and presentation of financial statements that external users are likely to rely on when making economic decisions about an enterprise.

Required

Explain the purpose and authoritative status of the Framework. **(5 marks)**

(b) Of particular importance within the Framework are the definitions and recognition criteria for assets and liabilities.

Required

Define assets and liabilities and explain the important aspects of their definitions. Explain why these definitions are of particular importance to the preparation of an entity's balance sheet and income statement.

(8 marks)

(Total = 13 marks)

2 Derringdo (2.5 6/03)

20 mins

Revenue recognition is the process by which companies decide when and how much income should be included in the income statement. It is a topical area of great debate in the accounting profession. The IASB looks at revenue recognition from conceptual and substance points of view. There are occasions where a more traditional approach to revenue recognition does not entirely conform to the IASB guidance; indeed neither do some International Accounting Standards.

Required

(a) Explain the implications that the IASB's Framework for the Preparation and Presentation of Financial Statements (Framework) and the application of substance over form have on the recognition of income. Give examples of how this may conflict with traditional practice and some accounting standards. **(6 marks)**

(b) Derringdo sells goods supplied by Gungho. The goods are classed as A grade (perfect quality) or B grade, having slight faults. Derringdo sells the A grade goods acting as an agent for Gungho at a fixed price calculated to yield a gross profit margin of 50%. Derringdo receives a commission of 12·5% of the sales it achieves for these goods. The arrangement for B grade goods is that they are sold by Gungho to Derringdo and Derringdo sells them at a gross profit margin of 25%. The following information has been obtained from Derringdo's financial records:

		$'000
Inventory held on premises 1 April 20X2	– A grade	2,400
	– B grade	1,000
Goods from Gungho year to 31 March 20X3	– A grade	18,000
	– B grade	8,800
Inventory held on premises 31 March 20X3	– A grade	2,000
	– B grade	1,250

Required

Prepare the income statement extracts for Derringdo for the year to 31 March 20X3 reflecting the above information. **(5 marks)**

(Total = 11 marks)

3 Regulatory framework (2.5 12/04)   45 mins

Historically financial reporting throughout the world has differed widely. The International Accounting Standards Committee Foundation (IASCF) is committed to developing, in the public interest, a single set of high quality, understandable and enforceable global accounting standards that require transparent and comparable information in general purpose financial statements. The various pronouncements of the IASCF are sometimes collectively referred to as International Financial Reporting Standards (IFRS) GAAP.

Required

(a)   Describe the functions of the various internal bodies of the IASCF, and how the IASCF interrelates with other national standard setters.   **(10 marks)**

(b)   Describe the IASCF's standard setting process including how standards are produced, enforced and occasionally supplemented.   **(10 marks)**

(c)   Comment on whether you feel the move to date towards global accounting standards has been successful.
                                                                                                      (5 marks)

                                                                                                (Total = 25 marks)

4 Winger (2.5 pilot paper amended)   45 mins

The following list of account balances relates to Winger at 31 March 20X1.

	$'000	$'000
Sales revenue (note a)		358,450
Cost of sales	185,050	
Distribution costs	28,700	
Administration expenses	15,000	
Lease rentals (note b)	20,000	
Loan interest paid	2,000	
Dividend paid	12,000	
Property at cost (note c)	200,000	
Plant and equipment cost	154,800	
Depreciation 1 April 20X0 - plant and equipment		34,800
Development expenditure (note d)	30,000	
Profit on disposal of non-current assets		45,000
Trade accounts receivable	55,000	
Inventories: 31 March 20X1	28,240	
Cash and bank	10,660	
Trade accounts payable		29,400
Taxation: over provision in year to 31 March 20X0		2,200
Equity shares of 25c each		150,000
8% loan notes (issued in 20W8)		50,000
Retained earnings 1 April 20X0		71,600
	741,450	741,450

The following notes are relevant.

(a)   Included in sales revenue is $27 million, which relates to sales made to customers under sale or return agreements. The expiry date for the return of these goods is 30 April 20X1. Winger has charged a mark-up of 20% on cost for these sales.

(b)   A lease rental of $20 million was paid on 1 April 20X0. It is the first of five annual payments in advance for the rental of an item of equipment that has a cash purchase price of $80 million. The auditors have advised that this is a finance lease and have calculated the implicit interest rate in the lease as 12% per annum. Leased assets should be depreciated on a straight-line basis over the life of the lease.

(c)   On 1 April 20X0 Winger acquired a new property at a cost of $200 million. For the purpose of calculating depreciation only, the asset has been separated into the following elements.

Separate asset	Cost	Life
	$'000	
Land	50,000	freehold
Heating system	20,000	10 years
Lifts	30,000	15 years
Building	100,000	50 years

The depreciation of the elements of the property should be calculated on a straight-line basis. The new property replaced an existing one that was sold on the same date for $95 million. It had cost $50 million and had a carrying value of $80 million at the date of sale. The profit on this property has been calculated on the original cost. It had not been depreciated on the basis that the depreciation charge would not be material.

Plant and machinery is depreciated at 20% on the reducing balance basis.

(d)   The figure for development expenditure in the list of account balances represents the amounts deferred in previous years in respect of the development of a new product. Unfortunately, during the current year, the government has introduced legislation which effectively bans this type of product. As a consequence of this the project has been abandoned. The directors of Winger are of the opinion that writing off the development expenditure, as opposed to its previous deferment, represents a change of accounting policy and therefore wish to treat the write off as a prior period adjustment.

(e)   A provision for income tax for the year to 31 March 20X1 of $15 million is required.

Required

(a)   Prepare Winger's income statement for the year to 31 March 20X1, along with the changes in retained earnings from the statement of changes in equity.   **(9 marks)**

(b)   A balance sheet as at 31 March 20X1 in accordance with International Financial Reporting Standards as far as the information permits.   **(11 marks)**

(c)   Discuss the acceptability of the company's previous policy in respect of non-depreciation of property.
                                                                                                                              (5 marks)

                                                                                                                      (Total = 25 marks)

4 Question with analysis: Winger (2.5 pilot paper amended)

45 mins

The following list of account balances relates to Winger at 31 March 20X1.

	$'000	$'000
Sales revenue **(note a)**		358,450
Cost of sales	185,050	
Distribution costs	28,700	
Administration expenses	15,000	
Lease rentals **(note b)**	20,000	
Loan interest paid	2,000	
Dividend paid	12,000	
Property at cost **(note c)**	200,000	
Plant and equipment cost	154,800	
Depreciation 1 April 20X0 - plant and equipment		34,800
Development expenditure **(note d)**	30,000	
Profit on disposal of non-current assets		45,000
Trade accounts receivable	55,000	
Inventories: 31 March 20X1	28,240	
Cash and bank	10,660	
Trade accounts payable		29,400
Taxation: over provision in year to 31 March 20X0		2,200
Equity shares of 25c each		150,000
8% loan notes (issued in 20W8)		50,000
Retained earnings 1 April 20X0		71,600
	741,450	741,450

> i.e 3 years before 20X1

(annotation pointing to "8% loan notes (issued in 20W8)": i.e 3 years before 20X1)

The following notes are relevant.

> **Consider IAS 18. Can we take these sales as final before 30/04/X1?**

(a)   Included in sales revenue is $27 million, which relates to sales made to customers under sale or return agreements. The expiry date for the return of these goods is 30 April 20X1. Winger has charged a mark-up of 20% on cost for these sales.

(b)   A lease rental of $20 million was paid on 1 April 20X0. It is the first of five annual payments **in advance** for the rental of an item of equipment that has a cash purchase price of $80 million. The auditors have advised that this is a **finance lease** and have calculated the implicit interest rate in the lease as 12% per annum. Leased assets should be depreciated on a straight-line basis over the life of the lease.

(c)   On 1 April 20X0 Winger acquired a new property at a cost of $200 million. For the purpose of calculating depreciation only, the asset has been separated into the following elements.

> **No depreciation on land**

Separate asset	Cost	Life
	$'000	
Land	50,000	freehold
Heating system	20,000	10 years
Lifts	30,000	15 years
Building	100,000	50 years

The depreciation of the elements of the property should be calculated on a straight-line basis. The new property replaced an existing one that was sold on the same date for $95 million. It had cost $50 million and had a carrying value of $80 million at the date of sale. The profit on this property has been calculated on the original cost. It had not been depreciated on the basis that the depreciation charge would not be material.

Plant and machinery is depreciated at 20% on the reducing balance basis.

BPP
LEARNING MEDIA

(d)   The figure for development expenditure in the list of account balances represents the amounts deferred in previous years in respect of the development of a new product. Unfortunately, during the current year, the government has introduced legislation which effectively bans this type of product. As a consequence of this the project has been abandoned. The directors of Winger are of the opinion that writing off the development expenditure, as opposed to its previous deferment, represents a change of accounting policy and therefore wish to treat the write off as a prior period adjustment.

(e)   A provision for income tax for the year to 31 March 20X1 of $15 million is required.

> Is this treatment correct?

Required

(a)   Prepare Winger's income statement for the year to 31 March 20X1, along with the changes in retained earnings from the statement of changes in equity.   **(9 marks)**

(b)   A balance sheet as at 31 March 20X1 in accordance with International Financial Reporting Standards as far as the information permits.   **(11 marks)**

(c)   Discuss the acceptability of the company's previous policy in respect of non-depreciation of property.   **(5 marks)**

(Total = 25 marks)

5 Harrington (2.5 6/05)   45 mins

Reproduced below are the draft financial statements of Harrington, a public company, for the year to 31 March 20X5:

INCOME STATEMENT - YEAR TO 31 MARCH 20X5

	$'000
Sales revenue (note (i))	13,700
Cost of sales (note (ii))	(9,200)
Gross profit	4,500
Operating expenses	(2,400)
Loan note interest paid (refer to balance sheet)	(25)
Profit before tax	2,075
Income tax expense (note (vi))	(55)
Profit for the period	2,020

BALANCE SHEET AS AT 31 MARCH 20X5	$'000	$'000
Property, plant and equipment (note (iii))		6,270
Investments (note (iv))		1,200
		7,470
Current assets		
Inventory	1,750	
Trade receivables	2,450	
Bank	350	
		4,550
Total assets		12,020
Equity and liabilities:		
Ordinary shares of 25c each (note (v))		2,000
Reserves:		
Share premium		600
Retained earnings – 1 April 20X4	2,990	
– Year to 31 March 20X5	2,020	
– dividends paid	(500)	
		4,510
		7,110
Non-current liabilities		
10% loan note (issued 20X2)	500	
Deferred tax (note (vi))	280	
		780
Current liabilities		
Trade payables		4,130
		12,020

The company policy for ALL depreciation is that it is charged to cost of sales and a full year's charge is made in the year of acquisition or completion and none in the year of disposal.

The following matters are relevant:

(i)   Included in sales revenue is $300,000 being the sale proceeds of an item of plant that was sold in January 20X5. The plant had originally cost $900,000 and had been depreciated by $630,000 at the date of its sale. Other than recording the proceeds in sales and cash, no other accounting entries for the disposal of the plant have been made. All plant is depreciated at 25% per annum on the reducing balance basis.

(ii)   On 31 December 20X4 the company completed the construction of a new warehouse. The construction was achieved using the company's own resources as follows:

	$'000
Purchased materials	150
Direct labour	800
Supervision	65
Design and planning costs	20

Included in the above figures are $10,000 for materials and $25,000 for labour costs that were effectively lost due to the foundations being too close to a neighbouring property. All the above costs are included in cost of sales. The building was brought into immediate use on completion and has an estimated life of 20 years (straightline depreciation).

(iii)   Details of the other property, plant and equipment at 31 March 20X5 are:

	$'000	$'000
Land at cost		1,000
Buildings at cost	4,000	
Less accumulated depreciation at 31 March 20X4	(800)	3,200
Plant at cost	5,200	
Less accumulated depreciation at 31 March 20X4	(3,130)	
		2,070
		6,270

At the beginning of the current year (1 April 20X4), Harrington had an open market basis valuation of its properties (excluding the warehouse in note (ii) above). Land was valued at $1·2 million and the property at $4·8 million. The directors wish these values to be incorporated into the financial statements. The properties had an estimated remaining life of 20 years at the date of the valuation (straight-line depreciation is used). Harrington makes a transfer to realised profits in respect of the excess depreciation on revalued assets. Note: depreciation for the year to 31 March 20X5 has not yet been accounted for in the draft financial statements.

(iv)   The investments are in quoted companies that are carried at their stock market values with any gains and losses recorded in the income statement. The value shown in the balance sheet is that at 31 March 20X4 and during the year to 31 March 20X5 the investments have risen in value by an average of 10%. Harrington has not reflected this increase in its financial statements.

(v)   On 1 October 20X4 there had been a fully subscribed rights issue of 1 for 4 at 60c. This has been recorded in the above balance sheet.

(vi)   Income tax on the profits for the year to 31 March 20X5 is estimated at $260,000. The figure in the income statement is the underprovision for income tax for the year to 31 March 20X4. The carrying value of Harrington's net assets is $1·4 million more than their tax base at 31 March 20X5. The income tax rate is 25%.

Required

(a)   Prepare a restated income statement for the year to 31 March 20X5 reflecting the information in notes (i) to (vi) above.   **(9 marks)**

(b)   Prepare a statement of changes in equity for the year to 31 March 20X5.   **(6 marks)**

(c)   Prepare a restated balance sheet at 31 March 20X5 reflecting the information in notes (i) to (vi) above.   **(10 marks)**

(Total = 25 marks)

6 Petra (2.5 12/05)

45 mins

The following trial balance relates to Petra, a public listed company, at 30 September 2005:

	$'000	$'000
Revenue (note (i))		197,800
Cost of sales (note (i))	114,000	
Distribution costs	17,000	
Administration expenses	18,000	
Loan interest paid	1,500	
Ordinary shares of 25 cents each fully paid		40,000
Share premium		12,000
Retained earnings 1 October 2004		34,000
6% Redeemable loan note (issued in 2003)		50,000
Land and buildings at cost (land element $40 million) note (ii))	100,000	
Plant and equipment at cost (note (iii))	66,000	
Deferred development expenditure (note (iv))	40,000	
Accumulated depreciation at 1 October 2004 – buildings		16,000
– plant and equipment		26,000
Accumulated amortisation of development expenditure at 1 October 2004		8,000
Income tax (note (v))	1,000	
Deferred tax (note (v))		15,000
Trade receivables	24,000	
Inventories – 30 September 2005	21,300	
Cash and bank	11,000	
Trade payables		15,000
	413,800	413,800

The following notes are relevant.

(i)   Included in revenue is $12 million for receipts that the company's auditors have advised are commission sales. The costs of these sales, paid for by Petra, were $8 million. $3million of the profit of $4 million was attributable to and remitted to Sharma (the auditors have advised that Sharma is the principal for the transactions). Both the $8 million cost of sales and the $3 million paid to Sharma have been included in cost of sales.

(ii)   The buildings had an estimated life of 30 years when they were acquired and are being depreciated on the straight–line basis.

(iii)   Included in the trial balance figures for plant and equipment is plant that had cost $16 million and had accumulated depreciation of $6 million at 1 October 2004. Following a review of the company's operations this plant was made available for sale at the beginning of the year. Negotiations with a broker have concluded that a realistic selling price of this plant will be $7.5 million and the broker will charge a commission of 8% of the selling price. The plant had not been sold by the year end. Plant is depreciated at 20% per annum using the reducing balance method. Depreciation of buildings and plant is charged to cost of sales.

(iv)   The development expenditure relates to the capitalised cost of developing a product called the Topaz. It had an original estimated life of five years. Production and sales of the Topaz started in October 2003. A review of the sales of the Topaz in late September 2005, showed them to be below forecast and an impairment test concluded that the fair value of the development costs at 30 September 2005 was only $18 million and the expected period of further sales (from this date) was only a further two years.

(v)   The balance on the income tax account in the trial balance is the under–provision in respect of the income tax liability for the year ended 30 September 2004. The directors have estimated the provision for income tax for the year ended 30 September 2005 to be $4 million and the required balance sheet provision for deferred tax at 30 September 2005 is $17.6 million.

Required

Prepare for Petra:

(a) An income statement for the year ended 30 September 2005; and   **(10 marks)**
(b) A balance sheet as at 30 September 2005   **(10 marks)**

Note. A statement of changes in equity is NOT required. Disclosure notes are NOT required.

(c) The directors hold options to purchase 24 million shares for a total of $7.2 million. The options were granted two years ago and have been correctly accounted for. The options do not affect your answer to (a) and (b) above. The average stock market value of Petra's shares for the year ended 30 September 2005 can be taken as 90 cents per share.

Required

A calculation of the basic and diluted earnings per share for the year ended 30 September 2005 (comparatives are not required)   **(5 marks)**

(Total = 25 marks)

7 Allgone (2.5 6/03)   45 mins

The following trial balance relates to Allgone at 31 March 20X6:

	$'000	$'000
Sales revenue (note (i))		236,200
Purchases	127,850	
Operating expenses	12,400	
Loan interest paid	2,400	
Preference dividend	1,000	
Land and buildings – at valuation (note (ii))	130,000	
Plant and equipment – cost	84,300	
Software – cost 1 April 20X3	10,000	
Stock market investments – cost 1 April 20X5 (note (iii))	12,000	
Depreciation 1 April 20X5 – plant and equipment		24,300
Depreciation 1 April 20X5 – software		6,000
Costs of fraud (note (iv))	32,000	
Trade receivables	23,000	
Inventory – 1 April 20X5	19,450	
Bank		350
Trade payables		15,200
Ordinary shares of 25c each		60,000
10% Preference shares (redeemable)		20,000
12% Loan note (issued 1 July 20X5)		40,000
Deferred tax		3,000
Revaluation reserve (relating to land and buildings and the investments)		45,000
Retained earnings – 20X5		4,350
	454,400	454,400

The following notes are relevant:

(i) Sales include $8 million for goods sold in March 20X6 for cash to Funders, a merchant bank. The cost of these goods was $6 million. Funders has the option to require Allgone to repurchase these goods within one month of the year-end at their original selling price plus a facilitating fee of $250,000.

Inventory at 31 March 20X6 was counted at a cost value of $8·5 million. This includes $500,000 of slow moving inventory that is expected to be sold for a net $300,000.

(ii)   *Non-current assets*

On 1 April 20X5 Allgone revalued its land and buildings. The details are:

	Cost 1 April 20X0	Valuation 1 April 20X5
	$'000	$'000
Land	20,000	25,000
Building	80,000	105,000

The building had an estimated life of 40 years when it was acquired and this has not changed as a result of the revaluation. Depreciation is on a straight-line basis. The surplus on the revaluation has been added to the revaluation reserve, but no other movements on the revaluation reserve have been recorded.

Plant and equipment is depreciated at 20% per annum on the reducing balance basis.

Software is depreciated by the sum of the digits method over a 5-year life.

(iii) The investment represents 7·5% of the ordinary share capital of Wondaworld. Allgone has a policy of revaluing its investments at their market price at each year-end. Changes in value are taken to the revaluation reserve which at 1 April 20X5 contained a surplus of $5 million for previous revaluations of the investments. The stock market price of Wondaworld's ordinary shares was $2·50 each on 1 April 20X5 and by 31 March 20X6 this had fallen to $2·25.

(iv)   A $32m fraud was discovered during this financial year. A senior employee of the company, who left in January 20X5, had diverted investment funds into his private bank account. The fraud was discovered by the employee's replacement in April 20X5. It is unlikely that any of the funds will be recovered. Allgone has now implemented tighter procedures to prevent such a fraud recurring. The company has been advised that this loss will not qualify for any tax relief. The directors have asked if this loss can be treated as an extraordinary item.

(v)   The directors have estimated the provision for income tax for the year to 31 March 20X6 at $11·3 million. The deferred tax provision at 31 March 20X6 is to be adjusted to reflect the tax base of the company's net assets being $16 million less than their carrying values. The rate of income tax is 30%. The movement on deferred tax should be charged to the income statement.

(vi)   The finance charge relating to the preference shares is $2,000,000 per annum.

Required

In accordance with International Accounting Standards and International Financial Reporting Standards as far as the information permits, prepare:

(a)	the income statement of Allgone for the year to 31 March 20X6	**(7 marks)**
(b)	the statement of Changes in Equity for the year to 31 March 20X6	**(5 marks)**
(c)	a balance sheet as at 31 March 20X6	**(13 marks)**

Notes to the financial statements are not required.   **(Total = 25 marks)**

8 Tadeon (2.5 12/06)

45 mins

The following trial balance relates to Tadeon, a publicly listed company, at 30 September 2006:

	$'000	$'000
Revenue		277,800
Cost of sales	118,000	
Operating expenses	40,000	
Loan interest paid (note (i))	1,000	
Rental of vehicles (note (ii))	6,200	
Investment income		2,000
25 year leasehold property at cost (note (iii))	225,000	
Plant and equipment at cost	181,000	
Investments at amortised cost	42,000	
Accumulated depreciation at 1 October 2005 – leasehold property		36,000
– plant and equipment		85,000
Equity shares of 20 cents each fully paid		150,000
Retained earnings at 1 October 2005		18,600
2% Loan note (note (i))		50,000
Deferred tax balance 1 October 2005 (note (iv))		12,000
Trade receivables	53,500	
Inventories at 30 September 2006	33,300	
Bank		1,900
Trade payables		18,700
Suspense account (note (v))		48,000
	700,000	700,000

The following notes are relevant:

(i)   The loan note was issued on 1 October 2005. It is redeemable on 30 September 2010 at a large premium (in order to compensate for the low nominal interest rate). The finance department has calculated that the effective interest rate on the loan is 5.5% per annum.

(ii)   The rental of the vehicles relates to two separate contracts. These have been scrutinised by the finance department and they have come to the conclusion that $5 million of the rentals relate to a finance lease. The finance lease was entered into on 1 October 2005 (the date the $5 million was paid) for a four year period. The vehicles had a fair value of $20 million (straight-line depreciation should be used) at 1 October 2005 and the lease agreement requires three further annual payments of $6 million each on the anniversary of the lease. The interest rate implicit in the lease is to be taken as 10% per annum. (Note: you are not required to calculate the present value of the minimum lease payments.) The other contract is an operating lease and should be charged to operating expenses.

Other plant and equipment is depreciated at 12 1/2% per annum on the reducing balance basis.

All depreciation of property, plant and equipment is charged to cost of sales.

(iii)   On 30 September 2006 the leasehold property was revalued to $200 million. The directors wish to incorporate this valuation into the financial statements.

(iv)   The directors have estimated the provision for income tax for the year ended 30 September 2006 at $38 million. At 30 September 2006 there were $74 million of taxable temporary differences, of which $20 million related to the revaluation of the leasehold property (see (iii) above). The income tax rate is 20%.

(v)   The suspense account balance can be reconciled from the following transactions:

The payment of a dividend in October 2005. This was calculated to give a 5% yield on the company's share price of 80 cents as at 30 September 2005.

The net receipt in March 2006 of a fully subscribed rights issue of one new share for every three held at a price of 32 cents each. The expenses of the share issue were $2 million and should be charged to share premium.

Note. The cash entries for these transactions have been correctly accounted for.

Required

Prepare for Tadeon:

(a)	An income statement for the year ended 30 September 2006; and	**(8 marks)**
(b)	A balance sheet as at 30 September 2006.	**(17 marks)**

Note. A statement of changes in equity is not required. Disclosure notes are not required.   **(Total = 25 marks)**

9 Derringdo (2.5 6/03)   16 mins

Derringdo acquired an item of plant at a gross cost of $800,000 on 1 October 20X2. The plant has an estimated life of 10 years with a residual value equal to 15% of its gross cost. Derringdo uses straight-line depreciation on a time apportioned basis. The company received a government grant of 30% of its cost price at the time of its purchase. The terms of the grant are that if the company retains the asset for four years or more, then no repayment liability will be incurred. If the plant is sold within four years a repayment on a sliding scale would be applicable. The repayment is 75% if sold within the first year of purchase and this amount decreases by 25% per annum. Derringdo has no intention to sell the plant within the first four years. Derringdo's accounting policy for capital based government grants is to treat them as deferred credits and release them to income over the life of the asset to which they relate.

Required

(a) Discuss whether the company's policy for the treatment of government grants meets the definition of a liability in the IASB's Framework; and   **(3 marks)**

(b) Prepare extracts of Derringdo's financial statements for the year to 31 March 20X3 in respect of the plant and the related grant:

- applying the company's policy;

- in compliance with the definition of a liability in the Framework. Your answer should consider whether the sliding scale repayment should be used in determining the deferred credit for the grant.
                                                                                                  (6 marks)

                                                                                            (Total = 9 marks)

10 Broadoak (2.5 12/01)   45 mins

The broad principles of accounting for property, plant and equipment involve distinguishing between capital and revenue expenditure, measuring the cost of assets, determining how they should be depreciated and dealing with the problems of subsequent measurement and subsequent expenditure. IAS 16 Property, plant and equipment has the intention of improving consistency in these areas.

Required

(a) Explain:

(i) How the initial cost of property, plant and equipment should be measured   **(4 marks)**

(ii) The circumstances in which subsequent expenditure on those assets should be capitalised
                                                                                                  (3 marks)

(b) Explain IAS 16's requirements regarding the revaluation of non-current assets and the accounting treatment of surpluses and deficits on revaluation and gains and losses on disposal. **(8 marks)**

(c) (i) Broadoak has recently purchased an item of plant from Plantco, the details of this are:

	$	$
Basic list price of plant		240,000
Trade discount applicable to Broadoak		12.5% on list price
Ancillary costs:		
Shipping and handling costs		2,750
Estimated pre-production testing		12,500
Maintenance contract for three years		24,000
Site preparation costs:		
electrical cable installation	14,000	
concrete reinforcement	4,500	
own labour costs	7,500	
		26,000

Broadoak paid for the plant (excluding the ancillary costs) within four weeks of order, thereby obtaining an early settlement discount of 3%.

Broadoak had incorrectly specified the power loading of the original electrical cable to be installed by the contractor. The cost of correcting this error of $6,000 is included in the above figure of $14,000.

The plant is expected to last for 10 years. At the end of this period there will be compulsory costs of $15,000 to dismantle the plant and $3,000 to restore the site to its original use condition.

Required

Calculate the amount at which the plant will be measured at recognition. (Ignore discounting.)

(5 marks)

(ii) Broadoak acquired a 12 year lease on a property on 1 October 20X0 at a cost of $240,000. The company policy is to revalue its properties to their market values at the end of each year. Accumulated amortisation is eliminated and the property is restated to the revalued amount. Annual amortisation is calculated on the carrying values at the beginning of the year. The market values of the property on 30 September 20X1 and 20X2 were $231,000 and $175,000 respectively. The existing balance on the revaluation surplus at 1 October 20X0 was $50,000. This related to some non-depreciable land whose value had not changed significantly since 1 October 20X0.

Required

Prepare extracts of the financial statements of Broadoak (including the movement on the revaluation reserve) for the years to 30 September 20X1 and 20X2 in respect of the leasehold property.

(5 marks)

(Total = 25 marks)

11 Elite Leisure (2.5 12/05)   22 mins

Elite Leisure is a private limited liability company that operates a single cruise ship. The ship was acquired on 1 October 20W6. Details of the cost of the ship's components and their estimated useful lives are:

Component	Original cost ($ million)	Deprecation basis
Ship's fabric (hull, decks etc)	300	25 years straight–line
Cabins and entertainment area fittings	150	12 years straight–line
Propulsion system	100	Useful life of 40,000 hours

At 30 September 20X4 no further capital expenditure had been incurred on the ship.

In the year ended 30 September 20X4 the ship had experienced a high level of engine trouble which had cost the company considerable lost revenue and compensation costs. The measured expired life of the propulsion system at 30 September 20X4 was 30,000 hours. Due to the unreliability of the engines, a decision was taken in early October 20X4 to replace the whole of the propulsion system at a cost of $140 million. The expected life of the new propulsion system was 50,000 hours and in the year ended 30 September 20X5 the ship had used its engines for 5,000 hours.

At the same time as the propulsion system replacement, the company took the opportunity to do a limited upgrade to the cabin and entertainment facilities at a cost of $60 million and repaint the ship's fabric at a cost of $20 million. After the upgrade of the cabin and entertainment area fittings it was estimated that their remaining life was five years (from the date of the upgrade). For the purpose of calculating depreciation, all the work on the ship can be assumed to have been completed on 1 October 20X4. All residual values can be taken as nil.

Required

Calculate the carrying amount of Elite Leisure's cruise ship at 30 September 20X5 and its related expenditure in the income statement for the year ended 30 September 20X5. Your answer should explain the treatment of each item.

(12 marks)

12 Myriad (2.5 12/01)   16 mins

Myriad owns several properties which are revalued each year. Three of its properties are rented out under annual contracts. Details of these properties and their valuations are as follows.

Property type/life

	Cost	Value 30 September 20X1	Value 30 September 20X2
	$'000	$'000	$'000
A freehold 50 years	150	240	200
B freehold 50 years	120	180	145
C freehold 15 years	120	140	150

All three properties were acquired on 1 October 20X0. The valuations of the properties are based on their age at the date of the valuation. Myriad's policy is to carry all non-investment properties at cost. Annual depreciation, where appropriate, is based on the carrying value of assets at the beginning of the relevant period.

Property A is let to a subsidiary of Myriad on normal commercial terms. The other properties are let on normal commercial terms to companies not related to Myriad.

Myriad adopts the fair value model of accounting for investment properties in IAS 40 *Investment property*, and the cost model for owner-occupied properties in IAS 16 *Property, plant and equipment*.

Required

(a)   Describe the possible accounting treatments for investment properties under IAS 40 and explain why they may require a different accounting treatment to owner-occupied properties.   **(4 marks)**

(b)   Prepare extracts of the consolidated financial statements of Myriad for the year to 30 September 20X2 in respect of the above properties assuming the company adopts the fair value method in IAS 40.   **(5 marks)**

(Total = 9 marks)

13 Merryview (2.5 6/02)

18 mins

Merryview conducts its activities from two properties, a head office in the city centre and a property in the countryside where staff training is conducted. Both properties were acquired on 1 April 20X0 and had estimated lives of 25 years with no residual value. The company has a policy of carrying its land and buildings at current values. However, until recently property prices had not changed for some years. On 1 October 20X2 the properties were revalued by a firm of surveyors. Details of this and the original costs are:

	Land $	Buildings $
Head office: cost 1 April 20X0	500,000	1,200,000
revalued 1 October 20X2	700,000	1,350,000
Training premises: cost 1 April 20X0	300,000	900,000
revalued 1 October 20X2	350,000	600,000

The fall in the value of the training premises is due mainly to damage done by the use of heavy equipment during training. The surveyors have also reported that the expected life of the training property in its current use will only be a further 10 years from the date of the valuation. The estimated life of the head office remained unaltered.

Note: Merryview treats its land and its buildings as separate assets. Depreciation is based on the straight-line method from the date of purchase or subsequent revaluation.

Required

Prepare extracts of the financial statements of Merryview in respect of the above properties for the year to 31 March 20X3. **(10 marks)**

14 Myriad II (2.5 12/01)

18 mins

You have been asked to assist the financial accountant of Myriad in preparing the company's financial statements for the year to 30 September 20X2. The financial accountant has asked for your advice in the following matters.

Myriad's new auditors have recently pointed out that Myriad's policy of prudently writing off all development expenditure is not acceptable for development expenditure meeting the capitalisation criteria of IAS 38 *Intangible assets*. The corrected policy, to be first applied for the financial statements to 30 September 20X2, is to recognise development costs as an intangible asset where they comply with the requirements of IAS 38. Amortisation of all 'qualifying' development expenditure is on a straight-line basis over a four-year period (assuming a nil residual value). Recognised development expenditure 'qualifies' for amortisation when the project starts commercial production of the related product. The amount of recognised development expenditure, and the amount qualifying for amortisation each year is as follows.

	Amount recognised as an asset $'000	Amount qualifying for amortisation $'000
In the year to 30 September 20X0	420	300
In the year to 30 September 20X1	250	360
In the year to 30 September 20X2	560	400
	1,230	1,060

No development costs were incurred by Myriad prior to 20X0.

Required

(a)   Explain the circumstances when a company should change its accounting policies. Is the correction required as above a change of accounting policy? **(4 marks)**

(b)   Prepare extracts of Myriad's financial statements for the year to 30 September 20X2 including the comparatives following the error correction.   **(6 marks)**

Note. Ignore taxation.   **(Total = 10 marks)**

15 Dexterity (2.5 6/04)   45 mins

(a)   During the last decade it has not been unusual for the premium paid to acquire control of a business to be greater than the fair value of its tangible net assets. This increase in the relative balance sheet proportions of intangible assets has made the accounting practices for them all the more important. During the same period many companies have spent a great deal of money internally developing new intangible assets such as software and brands. IAS 38 'Intangible Assets' was issued in September 1998 and prescribes the accounting treatment for intangible assets.

Required

In accordance with IAS 38, discuss whether intangible assets should be recognised, and if so how they should be initially recorded and subsequently amortised in the following circumstances:

–   when they are purchased separately from other assets;
–   when they are obtained as part of acquiring the whole of a business; and
–   when they are developed internally.   **(10 marks)**

Note: your answer should consider goodwill separately from other intangibles.

(b)   Dexterity is a public listed company. It has been considering the accounting treatment of its intangible assets and has asked for your opinion on how the matters below should be treated in its financial statements for the year to 31 March 20X4.

(i)   On 1 October 20X3 Dexterity acquired Temerity, a small company that specialises in pharmaceutical drug research and development. The purchase consideration was by way of a share exchange and valued at $35 million. The fair value of Temerity's net assets was $15 million (excluding any items referred to below). Temerity owns a patent for an established successful drug that has a remaining life of 8 years. A firm of specialist advisors, Leadbrand, has estimated the current value of this patent to be $10 million, however the company is awaiting the outcome of clinical trials where the drug has been tested to treat a different illness. If the trials are successful, the value of the drug is then estimated to be $15 million. Also included in the company's balance sheet is $2 million for medical research that has been conducted on behalf of a client.   **(4 marks)**

(ii)   Dexterity has developed and patented a new drug which has been approved for clinical use. The costs of developing the drug were $12 million. Based on early assessments of its sales success, Leadbrand have estimated its market value at $20 million.   **(3 marks)**

(iii)   Dexterity's manufacturing facilities have recently received a favourable inspection by government medical scientists. As a result of this the company has been granted an exclusive five-year licence to manufacture and distribute a new vaccine. Although the licence had no direct cost to Dexterity, its directors feel its granting is a reflection of the company's standing and have asked Leadbrand to value the licence. Accordingly they have placed a value of $10 million on it.   **(3 marks)**

(iv)   In the current accounting period, Dexterity has spent $3 million sending its staff on specialist training courses. Whilst these courses have been expensive, they have led to a marked improvement in production quality and staff now need less supervision. This in turn has led to an increase in revenue and cost reductions. The directors of Dexterity believe these benefits will continue for at least three years and wish to treat the training costs as an asset.   **(2 marks)**

(v)   In December 20X3, Dexterity paid $5 million for a television advertising campaign for its products that will run for 6 months from 1 January 20X4 to 30 June 20X4. The directors believe that increased sales as a result of the publicity will continue for two years from the start of the advertisements.

(3 marks)

Required

Explain how the directors of Dexterity should treat the above items in the financial statements for the year to 31 March 20X4. **(15 marks as indicated)**

Note: The values given by Leadbrand can be taken as being reliable measurements. You are not required to consider depreciation aspects. **(Total = 25 marks)**

16 Derwent (2.5 12/04 amended)   23 mins

Advent is a publicly listed company.

Details of Advent's non-current assets at 1 October 20X8 were:

	Land and building $m	Plant $m	Telecommunications licence $m	Total $m
Cost/valuation	280	150	300	730
Accumulated depreciation/amortisation	(40)	(105)	(30)	(175)
Net book value	240	45	270	555

The following information is relevant:

(i)   The land and building were revalued on 1 October 20X3 with $80 million attributable to the land and $200 million to the building. At that date the estimated remaining life of the building was 25 years. A further revaluation was not needed until 1 October 20X8 when the land and building were valued at $85 million and $180 million respectively. The remaining estimated life of the building at this date was 20 years.

(ii)   Plant is depreciated at 20% per annum on cost with time apportionment where appropriate. On 1 April 20X9 new plant costing $45 million was acquired. In addition, this plant cost $5 million to install and commission. No plant is more than four years old.

(iii)   The telecommunications licence was bought from the government on 1 October 20X7 and has a 10 year life. It is amortised on a straight line basis. In September 20X9, a review of the sales of the products related to the licence showed them to be very disappointing. As a result of this review the estimated recoverable amount of the licence at 30 September 20X9 was estimated at only $100 million.

There were no disposals of non-current assets during the year to 30 September 20X9.

Required

(a)   Prepare balance sheet extracts of Advent's non-current assets as at 30 September 20X9 (including comparative figures), together with any disclosures (other than those of the accounting policies) under current International Financial Reporting Standards. **(9 marks)**

(b)   Explain the usefulness of the above disclosures to the users of the financial statements. **(4 marks)**

(Total = 13 marks)

17 Wilderness (2.5 12/05)   45 mins

(a)   IAS 36 *Impairment of assets* was issued in June 1998 and subsequently amended in March 2004. Its main objective is to prescribe the procedures that should ensure that an entity's assets are included in its balance sheet at no more than their recoverable amounts. Where an asset is carried at an amount in excess of its recoverable amount, it is said to be impaired and IAS 36 requires an impairment loss to be recognised.

Required

(i)   Define an impairment loss explaining the relevance of fair value less costs to sell and value in use; and state how frequently assets should be tested for impairment;   **(6 marks)**

Note: your answer should NOT describe the possible indicators of an impairment.

(ii)   Explain how an impairment loss is accounted for after it has been calculated.   **(5 marks)**

(b)   The assistant financial controller of the Wilderness group, a public listed company, has identified the matters below which she believes may indicate an impairment to one or more assets:

(i)   Wilderness owns and operates an item of plant that cost $640,000 and had accumulated depreciation of $400,000 at 1 October 2004. It is being depreciated at $12\frac{1}{2}\%$ on cost. On 1 April 2005 (exactly half way through the year) the plant was damaged when a factory vehicle collided into it. Due to the unavailability of replacement parts, it is not possible to repair the plant, but it still operates, albeit at a reduced capacity. Also it is expected that as a result of the damage the remaining life of the plant from the date of the damage will be only two years. Based on its reduced capacity, the estimated present value of the plant in use if $150,000. The plant has a current disposal value of $20,000 (which will be nil in two years' time), but Wilderness has been offered a trade–in value of $180,000 against a replacement machine which has a cost of $1 million (there would be no disposal costs for the replaced plant). Wilderness is reluctant to replace the plant as it is worried about the long–term demand for the produce produced by the plant. The trade–in value is only available if the plant is replaced.

Required

Prepare extracts from the balance sheet and income statement of Wilderness in respect of the plant for the year ended 30 September 2005. Your answer should explain how you arrived at your figures.
                                                                              (7 marks)

(ii)   On 1 April 2004 Wilderness acquired 100% of the share capital of Mossel, whose only activity is the extraction and sale of spa water. Mossel had been profitable since its acquisition, but bad publicity resulting from several consumers becoming ill due to a contamination of the spa water supply in April 2005 has led to unexpected losses in the last six months. The carrying amounts of Mossel's assets at 30 September 2005 are:

	$'000
Brand (Quencher – see below)	7,000
Land containing spa	12,000
Purifying and bottling plant	8,000
Inventories	5,000
	32,000

The source of the contamination was found and it has now ceased.

The company originally sold the bottled water under the brand name of 'Quencher', but because of the contamination it has rebranded its bottled water as 'Phoenix'. After a large advertising campaign, sales are now starting to recover and are approaching previous levels. The value of the brand in the balance sheet is the depreciated amount of the original brand name of 'Quencher'.

The directors have acknowledged that $1.5 million will have to be spent in the first three months of the next accounting period to upgrade the purifying and bottling plant.

Inventories contain some old 'Quencher' bottled water at a cost of $2 million; the remaining inventories are labeled with the new brand 'Phoenix'. Samples of all the bottled water have been tested by the health authority and have been passed as fit to sell. The old bottled water will have to be relabeled at a cost of $250,000, but is then expected to be sold at the normal selling price of (normal) cost plus 50%.

Based on the estimated future cash flows, the directors have estimated that the value in use of Mossel at 30 September 2005, calculated according to the guidance in IAS 36, is $20 million. There is no reliable estimate of the fair value less costs to sell of Mossel.

Required

Calculate the amounts at which the assets of Mossel should appear in the consolidated balance sheet of Wilderness at 30 September 2005. Your answer should explain how you arrive at your figures. **(7 marks)**

(Total = 25 marks)

18 Multiplex   11 mins

On 1 January 20X2 Multiplex acquired Steamdays, a company that operates a scenic railway along the coast of a popular tourist area. The summarised balance sheet at fair values of Steamdays on 1 January 20X2, reflecting the terms of the acquisition was:

	$'000
Goodwill	200
Operating licence	1,200
Property - train stations and land	300
Rail tack and coaches	300
Two steam engines	1,000
Purchase consideration	3,000

The operating licence is for ten years. It was renewed on 1 January 20X0 by the transport authority and is stated at the cost of its renewal. The carrying values of the property and rail track and coaches are based on their value in use. The engines are valued at their fair values less costs to sell.

On 1 February 20X2 the boiler of one of the steam engines exploded, completely destroying the whole engine. Fortunately no one was injured, but the engine was beyond repair. Due to its age a replacement could not be obtained. Because of the reduced passenger capacity the estimated value in use of the whole of the business after the accident was assessed at $2 million.

Passenger numbers after the accident were below expectations even allowing for the reduced capacity. A market research report concluded that tourists were not using the railway because of their fear of a similar accident occurring to the remaining engine. In the light of this the value in use of the business was re-assessed on 31 March 20X2 at $1.8 million. On this date Multiplex received an offer of $900,000 in respect of the operating licence (it is transferable). The realisable value of the other net assets has not changed significantly.

Required

Calculate the carrying value of the assets of Steamdays (in Multiplex's consolidated balance sheet) at 1 February 20X2 and 31 March 20X2 after recognising the impairment losses. **(6 marks)**

19 Preparation question: Research Co

Research Co for a number of years capitalised all expenditure on a development project. It was discovered that this was a mistake as one of the criteria for the capitalisation of the expenses had never been met. The directors consider this a material error.

Balance sheet extracts are as follows:

	20X1	20X0
	$'000	$'000
Development costs	680	460
Amortisation	(150)	(100)
	530	360
Other assets	3,300	2,240
	3,830	2,600
Share capital	550	500
Revaluation surplus (properties)	120	–
Retained earnings	2,130	1,460
	2,800	1,960
Liabilities	1,030	640
	3,830	2,600

During 20X0 the company made a profit of $410,000 after charging $50,000 for amortisation of development costs and incurring development costs of $180,000.

No dividends were paid in either year.

Required

Prepare extracts after adjusting for the error for the revised:

(a) balance sheet;
(b) statement of recognised income and expense;
(c) statement of changes in equity.

20 Derringdo (2.5 6/03 amended)   9 mins

Derringdo sells carpets from several retail outlets. In previous years the company has undertaken responsibility for fitting the carpets in customers' premises. Customers pay for the carpets at the time they are ordered. The average length of time from a customer ordering a carpet to its fitting is 14 days. In previous years, Derringdo had not recognised a sale in income until the carpet had been successfully fitted as the rectification costs of any fitting error would be expensive. From 1 April 20X2 Derringdo changed its method of trading by sub-contracting the fitting to approved contractors. Under this policy the sub-contractors are paid by Derringdo and they (the subcontractors) are liable for any errors made in the fitting. Because of this Derringdo is proposing to recognise sales when customers order and pay for the goods, rather than when they have been fitted. Details of the relevant sales figures are:

	$'000
Sales made in retail outlets for the year to 31 March 20X3	23,000
Sales value of carpets fitted in the 14 days to 14 April 20X2	1,200
Sales value of carpets fitted in the 14 days to 14 April 20X3	1,600

Note: the sales value of carpets fitted in the 14 days to 14 April 20X2 are not included in the annual sales figure of $23 million, but those for the 14 days to 14 April 20X3 are included.

Required

Discuss whether the above represents a change of accounting policy, and, based on your discussion, calculate the amount that you would include in sales revenue for carpets in the year to 31 March 20X3.   **(5 marks)**

21 Telenorth (2.5 12/01)

45 mins

The following trial balance relates to Telenorth at 30 September 20X1.

	$'000	$'000
Sales revenue		283,460
Inventory 1 October 20X0	12,400	
Purchases	147,200	
Distribution expenses	22,300	
Administration expenses	34,440	
Loan note interest paid	300	
Interim dividends: ordinary	2,000	
preference	480	
Investment income		1,500
25 year leasehold building – cost	56,250	
Plant and equipment – cost	55,000	
Computer system – cost	35,000	
Investments at valuation	34,500	
Depreciation 1 October 20X0 (note (b))		
Leasehold building		18,000
Plant and equipment		12,800
Computer system		9,600
Trade accounts receivable (note (c))	35,700	
Bank overdraft		1,680
Trade accounts payable		17,770
Deferred tax (note (d))		5,200
Ordinary shares of $1 each		20,000
Suspense account (note (e))		26,000
6% loan notes (issued 1 October 20X0)		10,000
8% preference shares (redeemable)		12,000
Revaluation surplus (note (d))		3,400
Retained earnings 1 October 20X0		14,160
	435,570	435,570

The following notes are relevant.

(a)   An inventory count was not conducted by Telenorth until 4 October 20X1 due to operational reasons. The value of the inventory on the premises at this date was $16 million at cost. Between the year-end and the inventory count the following transactions have been identified.

	$
Normal sales at a mark up on cost of 40%	1,400,000
Sales on a sale or return basis at a mark up on cost of 30%	650,000
Goods received at cost	820,000

All sales and purchases had been correctly recorded in the period in which they occurred.

(b)   Telenorth has the following depreciation policy.

Leasehold building – straight-line

Plant and equipment – five years straight line with residual values estimated at $5,000,000

Computer system – 40% per annum reducing balance

Depreciation of the leasehold building and plant is treated as cost of sales; depreciation of the computer system is an administration cost.

(c)   The outstanding account receivable of a major customer amounting to $12 million was factored to Kwikfinance on 1 September 20X1. The terms of the factoring were as follows.

    (i)   Kwikfinance paid 80% of the outstanding account to Telenorth immediately

    (ii)   The balance will be paid (less the charges below) when the account is collected in full. Any amount of the account outstanding after four months will be transferred back to Telenorth at its full book value.

    (iii)   Kwikfinance will charge 1.0% per month of the net amount owing from Telenorth at the beginning of each month. Kwikfinance had not collected any of the amounts receivable by the year end.

Telenorth debited the cash from Kwikfinance to its bank account and removed the account receivable from its sales ledger. It has prudently charged the difference as an administration cost.

(d)   A provision for income tax of $23.4 million for the year to 30 September 20X1 is required. The deferred tax liability is to be increased by $2.2 million, of which $1 million is to be charged direct to the revaluation surplus.

(e)   The suspense account contains the proceeds of two share issues.

    (i)   The exercise of all the outstanding directors' share options of four million shares on 1 October 20X0 at $2 each

    (ii)   A fully subscribed rights issue on 1 July 20X1 of 1 for 4 held at a price of $3 each. The stock market price of Telenorth's shares immediately before the rights issue was $4.

(f)   The finance charge relating to the preference shares is equal to the dividend payable.

Required

(a)   (i)   The income statement of Telenorth for the year to 30 September 20X1   **(8 marks)**

    (ii)   A balance sheet as at 30 September 20X1 in accordance with International Financial Reporting Standards as far as the information permits.   **(12 marks)**

Notes to the financial statements are not required.

(b)   Calculate the earnings per share in accordance with IAS 33 for the year to 30 September 20X1 (ignore comparatives).   **(5 marks)**

(Total = 25 marks)

22 Tourmalet (2.5 12/03)   45 mins

The following extracted balances relate to Tourmalet at 30 September 20X4:

	$000	$000
Ordinary shares of 20 cents each		50,000
Retained earnings at 1 October 20X3		47,800
Revaluation reserve at 1 October 20X3		18,500
6% Redeemable preference shares 20X6		30,000
Trade accounts payable		35,300
Tax		2,100
Land and buildings – at valuation (note (iii))	150,000	
Plant and equipment – cost (note (v))	98,600	
Investment property – valuation at 1 October 20X3 (note (iv))	10,000	
Depreciation 1 October 20X3 – land and buildings		9,000
Depreciation 1 October 20X3 – plant and equipment		24,600
Trade accounts receivable	31,200	
Inventory – 1 October 20X3	26,550	
Bank	3,700	
Sales revenue (note (i))		313,000
Investment income (from properties)		1,200
Purchases	158,450	
Distribution expenses	26,400	
Administration expenses	23,200	
Interim preference dividend	900	
Ordinary dividend paid	2,500	
	531,500	531,500

The following notes are relevant:

(i)   Sales revenue includes $50 million for an item of plant sold on 1 June 20X4. The plant had a book value of $40 million at the date of its sale, which was charged to cost of sales. On the same date, Tourmalet entered into an agreement to lease back the plant for the next five years (being the estimated remaining life of the plant) at a cost of $14 million per annum payable annually in arrears. An arrangement of this type is deemed to have a financing cost of 12% per annum. No depreciation has been charged on the item of plant in the current year.

(ii)   The inventory at 30 September 20X4 was valued at cost of $28·5 million. This includes $4·5 million of slow moving goods. Tourmalet is trying to sell these to another retailer but has not been successful in obtaining a reasonable offer. The best price it has been offered is $2 million.

(iii)   On 1 October 20X0 Tourmalet had its land and buildings revalued by a firm of surveyors at $150 million, with $30 million of this attributed to the land. At that date the remaining life of the building was estimated to be 40 years. These figures were incorporated into the company's books. There has been no significant change in property values since the revaluation. $500,000 of the revaluation reserve will be realised in the current year as a result of the depreciation of the buildings and should be transferred to retained earnings.

(iv)   Details of the investment property are:

Value – 1 October 20X3 $10 million
Value – 30 September 20X4 $9·8 million

The company adopts the fair value method in IAS 40 'Investment Property' of valuing its investment property.

(v)   Plant and equipment (other than that referred to in note (i) above) is depreciated at 20% per annum on the reducing balance basis. All depreciation is to be charged to cost of sales.

(vi) The above balances contain the results of Tourmalet's car retailing operations which ceased on 31 December 20X3 due to mounting losses. The results of the car retailing operation, which is to be treated as a discontinued operation, for the year to 30 September 20X4 are:

	$000
Sales	15,200
Cost of sales	16,000
Operating expenses (4,000 less 800 tax repayment due)	3,200

The operating expenses are included in administration expenses in the trial balance. Tourmalet is still paying rentals for the lease of its car showrooms. The rentals are included in operating expenses. Tourmalet is hoping to use the premises as an expansion of its administration offices. This is dependent on obtaining planning permission from the local authority for the change of use, however this is very difficult to obtain. Failing this, the best option would be early termination of the lease which will cost $1·5 million in penalties. This amount has not been provided for.

(vii) The balance on the taxation account in the trial balance is the result of the settlement of the previous year's tax charge. The directors have estimated the provision for income tax for the year to 30 September 20X4 at $9·2 million.

(viii) The preference shares will be redeemed at par. The finance cost is equivalent to the annual dividend.

Required

(a) Comment on the substance of the sale of the plant and the directors' treatment of it. **(5 marks)**

(b) Prepare the income statement. **(17 marks)**

(c) A statement of changes in equity for Tourmalet for the year to 30 September 20X4 in accordance with current International Accounting Standards. **(3 marks)**

Note: A balance sheet is NOT required. Disclosure notes are NOT required. **(Total = 25 marks)**

23 Partway (2.5 12/06) 45 mins

(a) (i) State the definition of both non-current assets held for sale and discontinued operations and explain the usefulness of information for discontinued operations. **(4 marks)**

Partway is in the process of preparing its financial statements for the year ended 31 October 2006. The company's main activity is in the travel industry mainly selling package holidays (flights and accommodation) to the general public through the Internet and retail travel agencies. During the current year the number of holidays sold by travel agencies declined dramatically and the directors decided at a board meeting on 15 October 2006 to cease marketing holidays through its chain of travel agents and sell off the related high-street premises. Immediately after the meeting the travel agencies' staff and suppliers were notified of the situation and an announcement was made in the press. The directors wish to show the travel agencies' results as a discontinued operation in the financial statements to 31 October 2006. Due to the declining business of the travel agents, on 1 August 2006 (three months before the year end) Partway expanded its Internet operations to offer car hire facilities to purchasers of its Internet holidays.

The following are Partway's summarised income statement results – years ended:

	31 October 2006				31 October 2005
	Internet	travel agencies	car hire	total	total
	$'000	$'000	$'000	$'000	$'000
Revenue	23,000	14,000	2,000	39,000	40,000
Cost of sales	(18,000)	(16,500)	(1,500)	(36,000)	(32,000)
Gross profit/(loss)	5,000	(2,500)	500	3,000	8,000
Operating expenses	(1,000)	(1,500)	(100)	(2,600)	(2,000)
Profit/(loss) before tax	4,000	(4,000)	400	400	6,000

The results for the travel agencies for the year ended 31 October 2005 were: revenue $18 million, cost of sales $15 million and operating expenses of $1.5 million.

Required

(ii) Discuss whether the directors' wish to show the travel agencies' results as a discontinued operation is justifiable. **(4 marks)**

(iii) Assuming the closure of the travel agencies is a discontinued operation, prepare the (summarised) income statement of Partway for the year ended 31 October 2006 together with its comparatives.

Note. Partway discloses the analysis of its discontinued operations on the face of its income statement. **(6 marks)**

(b) (i) Describe the circumstances in which an entity may change its accounting policies and how a change should be applied. **(5 marks)**

The terms under which Partway sells its holidays are that a 10% deposit is required on booking and the balance of the holiday must be paid six weeks before the travel date. In previous years Partway has recognised revenue (and profit) from the sale of its holidays at the date the holiday is actually taken. From the beginning of November 2005, Partway has made it a condition of booking that all customers must have holiday cancellation insurance and as a result it is unlikely that the outstanding balance of any holidays will be unpaid due to cancellation. In preparing its financial statements to 31 October 2006, the directors are proposing to change to recognising revenue (and related estimated costs) at the date when a booking is made. The directors also feel that this change will help to negate the adverse effect of comparison with last year's results (year ended 31 October 2005) which were better than the current year's.

Required

(ii) Comment on whether Partway's proposal to change the timing of its recognition of its revenue is acceptable and whether this would be a change of accounting policy. **(6 marks)**

(Total = 25 marks)

24 Preparation question with helping hands: Simple consolidation

Boo Co has owned 80% of Goose's equity since its incorporation. On 31 December 20X8 it despatched goods which cost $80,000 to Goose, at an invoiced cost of $100,000. Goose received the goods on 2 January 20X9 and recorded the transaction then. The two companies' draft accounts as at 31 December 20X8 are shown below.

INCOME STATEMENT FOR THE YEAR ENDED 31 DECEMBER 20X8

	Boo	Goose
	$'000	$'000
Revenue	5,000	1,000
Cost of sales	2,900	600
Gross profit	2,100	400
Other expenses	1,700	320
Profit before tax	400	80
Income tax expense	130	25
Profit for the period	270	55

BALANCE SHEETS AT 31 DECEMBER 20X8

	$'000	$'000
Assets		
Non-current assets	2,000	200
Current assets		
Inventories	500	120
Trade receivables	650	40
Bank and cash	390	35
	1,540	195
Total assets	3,540	395
Equity and liabilities		
Equity		
Share capital	2,000	100
Retained earnings	500	240
	2,500	340
Current liabilities		
Trade payables	910	30
Tax	130	25
	1,040	55
Total equity and liabilities	3,540	395

Required

Prepare a draft consolidated balance sheet and income statement.

Helping hands

1   This is a very easy example to ease you into the technique of preparing consolidated accounts. There are a number of points to note.

2   Inventory in transit should be included in the balance sheet and deducted from cost of sales at cost to the group.

3   Similarly, the intra-group receivable and sale should be eliminated as a consolidation adjustment.

4   Boo Co must have included its inter-company account in trade receivables as it is not specifically mentioned elsewhere in the accounts.

5   Remember that only the parent's issued share capital is shown in the group accounts.

6   The minority interest in the income statement is easily calculated as 20% of post-tax profit for the year as shown in Goose's accounts. In the balance sheet, the minority interest represents the minority interest in retained earnings and share capital only.

7   Don't forget that Boo's accounts must somewhere contain a balance for its investment in Goose (its holding of shares in Goose, at par value since no share premium is shown in Goose's books). Non-current assets must therefore be reduced by this amount to correspond to the cancellation of Goose's share capital.

25 Hideaway (2.5 12/05 amended)

23 mins

Related party relationships are a common feature of commercial life. The objective of IAS 24 *Related party disclosures* is to ensure that financial statements contain the necessary disclosures to make users aware of the possibility that financial statements may have been affected by the existence of related parties.

Required

(a)   Describe the main circumstances that give rise to related parties.   **(4 marks)**

(b)   Explain why the disclosure of related party relationships and transactions may be important.

(3 marks)

(c)   Hideaway is a public listed company that owns two subsidiary company investments. It owns 100% of the equity shares of Benedict and 55% of the equity shares of Depret. During the year ended 30 September 20X5 Depret made several sales of goods to Benedict. These sales totaled 415 million and had cost Depret $14 million to manufacture. Depret made these sales on the instruction of the Board of Hideaway. It is known that one of the directors of Depret, who is not a director of Hideaway, is unhappy with the parent company's instruction as he believes the goods could have been sold to other companies outside the group at the far higher price of $20 million. All directors within the group benefit from a profit sharing scheme.

Required

Describe the financial effect that Hideaway's instruction may have on the financial statements of the companies within the group and the implications this may have for other interested parties.   **(6 marks)**

(Total = 13 marks)

26 Highveldt (2.5 6/05)

45 mins

Highveldt, a public listed company, acquired 75% of Samson's ordinary shares on 1 April 20X4. Highveldt paid an immediate $3·50 per share in cash and agreed to pay a further amount of $108 million on 1 April 20X5. Highveldt's cost of capital is 8% per annum. Highveldt has only recorded the cash consideration of $3·50 per share.

The summarised balance sheets of the two companies at 31 March 20X5 are shown below:

| | Highveldt | | Samson | |
	$million	$million	$million	$million
Tangible non-current assets (note (i))		420		320
Development costs (note (iv))		nil		40
Investments (note (ii))		300		20
		720		380
Current assets		133		91
Total assets		853		471
Equity and liabilities				
Ordinary shares of $1 each		270		80
Reserves:				
Share premium		80		40
Revaluation reserve		45		nil
Retained earnings – 1 April 20X4	160		134	
– year to 31 March 20X5	190		76	
		350		210
		745		330
Non-current liabilities				
10% inter company loan (note (ii))		nil		60
Current liabilities		108		81
Total equity and liabilities		853		471

The following information is relevant:

(i)   Highveldt has a policy of revaluing land and buildings to fair value. At the date of acquisition Samson's land and buildings had a fair value $20 million higher than their book value and at 31 March 20X5 this had increased by a further $4 million (ignore any additional depreciation).

(ii)   Included in Highveldt's investments is a loan of $60 million made to Samson at the date of acquisition. Interest is payable annually in arrears. Samson paid the interest due for the year on 31 March 20X5, but Highveldt did not receive this until after the year end. Highveldt has not accounted for the accrued interest from Samson.

(iii)   Samson had established a line of products under the brand name of Titanware. Acting on behalf of Highveldt, a firm of specialists, had valued the brand name at a value of $40 million with an estimated life of 10 years as at 1 April 20X4. The brand is not included in Samson's balance sheet.

(iv)   Samson's development project was completed on 30 September 20X4 at a cost of $50 million. $10 million of this had been amortised by 31 March 20X5. Development costs capitalised by Samson at the date of acquisition were $18 million. Highveldt's directors are of the opinion that Samson's development costs do not meet the criteria in IAS 38 'Intangible Assets' for recognition as an asset.

(v)   Samson sold goods to Highveldt during the year at a profit of $6 million, one-third of these goods were still in the inventory of Highveldt at 31 March 20X5.

(vi)   An impairment test at 31 March 20X5 on the consolidated goodwill concluded that it should be written down by $22 million. No other assets were impaired.

Required

(a)   Calculate the following figures as they would appear in the consolidated balance sheet of Highveldt at 31 March 20X5:

        (i)   Goodwill   **(8 marks)**

        (ii)   Minority interest   **(4 marks)**

        (iii)   The following consolidated reserves

                share premium, revaluation reserve and retained earnings.   **(8 marks)**

                Note: Show your workings

(b)   Explain why consolidated financial statements are useful to the users of financial statements (as opposed to just the parent company's separate (entity) financial statements).   **(5 marks)**

                                                                                                    (Total = 25 marks)

27 Hample (2.5 6/99 part)   36 mins

Hample is a small publicly listed company. On 1 April 20X8 it acquired 90% of the equity shares in Sopel, a private limited company. On the same day Hample accepted a 10% loan note from Sopel for $200,000 which was repayable at $40,000 per annum (on 31 March each year) over the next five years. Sopel's retained earnings at the date of acquisition were $2,200,000.

BALANCE SHEETS AS AT 31 MARCH 20X9

	Hample		Sopel	
	$'000	$'000	$'000	$'000
Assets				
Non-current assets				
Property, plant and equipment		2,120		1,990
Intangible: Software		-		1,800
Investments: equity in Sopel		4,110		-
10% loan note Sopel		200		-
others		65		210
		6,495		4,000
Current assets				
Inventories	719		560	
Trade receivables	524		328	
Sopel current account	75		-	
Cash	20		-	
		1,338		888
Total assets		7,833		4,888
Equity and liabilities				
Equity				
Equity shares of $1 each	2,000		1,500	
Share premium	2,000		500	
Retained earnings	2,900		1,955	
		6,900		3,955
Non-current liabilities				
10% loan from Hample	-		160	
Government grant	230		40	
		230		200
Current liabilities				
Trade payables	475		472	
Hample current account	-		60	
Income taxes payable	228		174	
Operating overdraft	–		27	
		703		733
Total equity and liabilities		7,833		4,888

The following information is relevant.

(a)   Included in Sopel's property at the date of acquisition was a leasehold property recorded at its depreciated historical cost of $400,000. On 1 April 20X8 the leasehold was sublet for its remaining life of four years at an annual rental of $80,000 *payable in advance* on 1 April each year. The directors of Hample are of the opinion that the fair value of this leasehold is best reflected by the present value of its future cash flows. An appropriate cost of capital for the group is 10% per annum.

The present value of a $1 annuity received at the end of each year where interest rates are 10% can be taken as:

	$
3 year annuity	2.50
4 year annuity	3.50

(b)   The software of Sopel represents the depreciation cost of the development of an integrated business accounting package. It was completed at a capitalised cost of $2,400,000 and went on sale on 1 April 20X7. Sopel's directors are depreciating the software on a straight-line basis over an eight-year life (ie $300,000 per annum). However, the directors of Hample are of the opinion that a five-year life would be more appropriate as sales of business software rarely exceed this period.

(c) The inventory of Hample on 31 March 20X9 contains goods at a transfer price of $25,000 that were supplied by Sopel who had marked them up with a profit of 25% on cost. Unrealised profits are adjusted for against the profit of the company that made them.

(d) On 31 March 20X9 Sopel remitted to Hample a cash payment of $55,000. This was not received by Hample until early April. It was made up of an annual repayment of the 10% loan note of $40,000 (the interest had already been paid) and $15,000 off the current account balance.

(e) Goodwill is reviewed for impairment annually. At 31 March 20X9 there had been an impairment loss of $120,000 in the value of goodwill since acquisition.

Required

Prepare the consolidated balance sheet of Hample as at 31 March 20X9. **(20 marks)**

28 Preparation question: Acquisition during the year

Port has many investments, but before 20X4 none of these investments met the criteria for consolidation as a subsidiary. One of these older investments was a $2.3m 12% loan to Alfred which was made in 20W1 and is not due to be repaid until 20Y6.

On 1st November 20X4 Port purchased 75% of the equity of Alfred for $650,000. The consideration was 35,000 $1 equity shares in Port with a fair value of $650,000.

Noted below are the draft income statements and movement in retained earnings for Port and its subsidiary Alfred for the year ending 31st December 20X4 along with the draft balance sheets as at 31st December 20X4.

INCOME STATEMENTS FOR THE YEAR ENDING 31 DECEMBER 20X4

	Port $'000	Alfred $'000
Revenue	100	996
Cost of sales	(36)	(258)
Gross profit	64	738
Interest on loan to Alfred	276	-
Other investment income	158	-
Operating expenses	(56)	(330)
Finance costs	-	(276)
Profit before tax	442	132
Income tax expense	(112)	(36)
Profit after tax	330	96

CHANGES IN RETAINED EARNINGS FOR THE YEAR-ENDING 31 DECEMBER 20X4

	Port $'000	Alfred $'000
Opening retained earnings	2,640	235
Profit for the year	330	96
Dividends paid	(70)	–
Closing retained earnings	2,900	331

BALANCE SHEETS AS AT 31 DECEMBER 20X4

	Port $'000	Alfred $'000
Assets		
Non-current assets		
Property, plant and equipment	100	3,000
Investments		
Loan to Alfred	2,300	-
Other investments	600	-
	3,000	3,000
Current assets	800	139
Total assets	3,800	3,139
Equity and liabilities		
Equity		
$1 Equity shares	200	100
Share premium	500	85
Retained earnings	2,900	331
	3,600	516
Non-current liabilities		
Loan from Port	-	2,300
Current liabilities		
Sundry	200	323
Total equity and liabilities	3,800	3,139

Notes

(a) Port has not accounted for the issue of its own shares or for the acquisition of the investment in Alfred.

(b) There has been no impairment in the value of the goodwill.

Required

(a) Prepare the income statement for the Port Group for the year-ending 31 December 20X4, along with a balance sheet at that date.

(b) Prepare a statement of changes in equity for the Port Group for the year-ending 31 December 20X4.

Approaching the question

1 Establish the **group structure**, noting for how long Alfred was a subsidiary.

2 Adjust Port's balance sheet for the issue of its own shares and the cost of the investment in Alfred.

3 Sketch out the **format** of the group income statement and balance sheet, and then fill in the amounts for each company directly from the question. (Note, sub-totals are not normally needed when you do this.)

4 **Time apportion** the income, expenditure and taxation for the subsidiary acquired.

5 Calculate the **goodwill**.

6 Remember to time-apportion the minority interest in Alfred.

29 Hillusion (2.5 6/03)   45 mins

In recent years Hillusion has acquired a reputation for buying modestly performing businesses and selling them at a substantial profit within a period of two to three years of their acquisition. On 1 July 20X2 Hillusion acquired 80% of the ordinary share capital of Skeptik at a cost of $10,280,000. On the same date it also acquired 50% of Skeptik's 10% loan notes at par. The summarised draft financial statements of both companies are:

INCOME STATEMENTS: YEAR TO 31 MARCH 20X3

	Hillusion	Skeptik
	$'000	$'000
Sales revenue	60,000	24,000
Cost of sales	(42,000)	(20,000)
Gross profit	18,000	4,000
Operating expenses	(6,000)	(200)
Loan interest received (paid)	75	(200)
Profit before tax	12,075	3,600
Income tax expense	(3,000)	(600)
Profit for the year	9,075	3,000

BALANCE SHEETS: AS AT 31 MARCH 20X3

	Hillusion	Skeptik
	$'000	$'000
Assets		
Tangible non-current Assets	19,320	8,000
Investments	11,280	Nil
	30,000	8,000
Current assets	15,000	8,000
Total assets	45,600	16,000
Equity and liabilities		
Equity		
Ordinary shares of $1 each	10,000	2,000
Accumulated profits	25,600	8,400
	35,600	10,400
Non-current liabilities		
10% loan notes	Nil	2,000
Current liabilities	10,000	3,600
Total equity and liabilities	45,600	16,000

The following information is relevant:

(i) The fair values of Skeptik's assets were equal to their book values with the exception of its plant, which had a fair value of $3·2 million in excess of its book value at the date of acquisition. The remaining life of all of Skeptik's plant at the date of its acquisition was four years and this period has not changed as a result of the acquisition. Depreciation of plant is on a straight-line basis and charged to cost of sales. Skeptik has not adjusted the value of its plant as a result of the fair value exercise.

(ii) In the post acquisition period Hillusion sold goods to Skeptik at a price of $12 million. These goods had cost Hillusion $9 million. During the year Skeptik had sold $10 million (at cost to Skeptik) of these goods for $15 million.

(iii) Hillusion bears almost all of the administration costs incurred on behalf of the group (invoicing, credit control etc.). It does not charge Skeptik for this service as to do so would not have a material effect on the group profit.

(iv) Revenues and profits should be deemed to accrue evenly throughout the year.

(v) The current accounts of the two companies were reconciled at the year-end with Skeptik owing Hillusion $750,000.

(vi) The goodwill was reviewed for impairment at the balance sheet date and had suffered an impairment loss of $300,000, which is to be treated as an operating expense.

(vii) Hillusion's opening retained earnings were $16,525,000 and Skeptik's were $5,400,000. No dividends were paid or declared by either entity during the year.

Required

(a)   Prepare a consolidated income statement and balance sheet for Hillusion for the year to 31 March 20X3

(20 marks)

(b)   Explain why it is necessary to eliminate unrealised profits when preparing group financial statements; and how reliance on the entity financial statements of Skeptik may mislead a potential purchaser of the company.

(5 marks)

(Total = 25 marks)

Note. Your answer should refer to the circumstances described in the question.

30 Hydan (2.5 6/06)   45 mins

On 1 October 20X5 Hydan, a publicly listed company, acquired a 60% controlling interest in Systan paying $9 per share in cash. Prior to the acquisition Hydan had been experiencing difficulties with the supply of components that it used in its manufacturing process. Systan is one of Hydan's main suppliers and the acquisition was motivated by the need to secure supplies. In order to finance an increase in the production capacity of Systan, Hydan made a non-dated loan at the date of acquisition of $4 million to Systan that carried an actual and effective interest rate of 10% per annum. The interest to 31 March 20X6 on this loan has been paid by Systan and accounted for by both companies. The summarised draft financial statements of the companies are:

INCOME STATEMENTS FOR THE YEAR ENDED 31 MARCH 20X6

	Hydan	Systan pre-acquisition	Systan post-acquisition
	$'000	$'000	$'000
Revenue	98,000	24,000	35,200
Cost of sales	(76,000)	(18,000)	(31,000)
Gross profit	22,000	6,000	4,200
Operating expenses	(11,800)	(1,200)	(8,000)
Interest income	350	nil	nil
Finance costs	(420)	nil	(200)
Profit/(loss) before tax	10,130	4,800	(4,000)
Income tax (expense)/relief	(4,200)	(1,200)	1,000
Profit/(loss) for the period	5,930	3,600	(3,000)

BALANCE SHEETS AS AT 31 MARCH 2006

	Hydan	Systan
	$'000	$'000
Non-current assets		
Property, plant and equipment	18,400	9,500
Investments (including loan to Systan)	16,000	nil
	34,400	9,500
Current assets	18,000	7,200
Total assets	52,400	16,700

	Hydan $'000	Systan $'000
Equity and liabilities		
Ordinary shares of $1 each	10,000	2,000
Share premium	5,000	500
Retained earnings	20,000	6,300
	35,000	8,800
Non-current liabilities		
7% Bank loan	6,000	nil
10% loan from Hydan	nil	4,000
Current liabilities	11,400	3,900
Total equity and liabilities	52,400	16,700

The following information is relevant:

(i)   At the date of acquisition, the fair values of Systan's property, plant and equipment were $1·2 million in excess of their carrying amounts. This will have the effect of creating an additional depreciation charge (to cost of sales) of $300,000 in the consolidated financial statements for the year ended 31 March 20X6. Systan has not adjusted its assets to fair value.

(ii)   In the post acquisition period Systan's sales to Hydan were $30 million on which Systan had made a consistent profit of 5% of the selling price. Of these goods, $4 million (at selling price to Hydan) were still in the inventory of Hydan at 31 March 20X6. Prior to its acquisition Systan made all its sales at a uniform gross profit margin.

(iii)   Included in Hydan's current liabilities is $1 million owing to Systan. This agreed with Systan's receivables ledger balance for Hydan at the year end.

(iv)   An impairment review of the consolidated goodwill at 31 March 20X6 revealed that its current value was $375,000 less than its carrying amount.

(v)   Neither company paid a dividend in the year to 31 March 20X6.

Required

(a)   Prepare the consolidated income statement for the year ended 31 March 20X6 and the consolidated balance sheet at that date. **(20 marks)**

(b)   Discuss the effect that the acquisition of Systan appears to have had on Systan's operating performance.

(5 marks)

(Total = 25 marks)

31 Hydrate (2.5 12/02 amended)   36 mins

Hydrate is a public company operating in the industrial chemical sector. In order to achieve economies of scale, it has been advised to enter into business combinations with compatible partner companies. As a first step in this strategy Hydrate acquired all of the ordinary share capital of Sulphate by way of a share exchange on 1 April 20X2. Hydrate issued five of its own shares for every four shares in Sulphate. The market value of Hydrate's shares on 1 April 20X2 was $6 each. The share issue has not yet been recorded in Hydrate's books. The summarised financial statements of both companies for the year to 30 September 20X2 are:

INCOME STATEMENT – YEAR TO 30 SEPTEMBER 20X2

	Hydrate	Sulphate
	$'000	$'000
Sales revenue	24,000	20,000
Cost of sales	(16,600)	(11,800)
Gross profit	7,400	8,200
Operating expenses	(1,600)	(1,000)
Profit before tax	5,800	7,200
Taxation	(2,000)	(3,000)
Profit for the period	3,800	4,200

BALANCE SHEET – AS AT 30 SEPTEMBER 20X2

	$'000	$'000	$'000	$'000
Non-current assets				
Property, plant and equipment		64,000		35,000
Investment		nil		12,800
		64,000		47,800
Current Assets				
Inventory	22,800		23,600	
Trade receivables	16,400		24,200	
Bank	500	39,700	200	48,000
Total assets		103,700		95,800
Equity and liabilities				
Ordinary shares of $1 each		20,000		12,000
Reserves:				
Share premium	4,000		2,400	
Retained earnings	57,200		42,700	
		61,200		45,100
		81,200		57,100
Non-current liabilities				
8% loan rate		5,000		18,000
Current liabilities				
Trade payables	15,300		17,700	
Taxation	2,200		3,000	
		17,500		20,700
		103,700		95,800

The following information is relevant.

–   The fair value of Sulphate's investment was $5 million in excess of its book value at the date of acquisition. The fair values of Sulphate's other net assets were equal to their book values.

–   Goodwill was reviewed at 30 September 20X2. A $3m impairment loss is to be recognised.

–   No dividends have been paid or proposed by either company.

Required

Prepare the consolidated income statement, statement of changes in equity, and balance sheet of Hydrate for the year to 30 September 20X2.   **(20 marks)**

32 Preparation question: Laurel Co

Laurel Co acquired 80% of the ordinary share capital of Hardy Co for $160,000 and 40% of the ordinary share capital of Comic Co for $70,000 on 1 January 20X7 when the retained earnings balances were $64,000 in Hardy Co and $24,000 in Comic Co.

The balance sheets of the three companies at 31 December 20X9 are set out below:

	Laurel Co $'000	Hardy Co $'000	Comic Co $'000
Non-current assets			
Property, plant and equipment	220	160	78
Investments	230		
	450	160	78
Current assets			
Inventories	384	234	122
Trade receivables	275	166	67
Cash at bank	42	10	34
	701	410	223
	1,151	570	301
Equity			
Share capital – $1 ordinary shares	400	96	80
Share premium	16	3	-
Retained earnings	278	128	97
	694	227	177
Current liabilities			
Trade payables	457	343	124
	1,151	570	301

You are also given the following information:

1   On 30 November 20X9 Laurel Co sold some goods to Hardy Co for cash for $32,000. These goods had originally cost $22,000 and none had been sold by the year-end. On the same date Laurel Co also sold goods to Comic Co for cash for $22,000. These goods originally cost $10,000 and Comic had sold half by the year end.

2   On 1 January 20X7 Hardy Co owned some items of equipment with a book value of $45,000 that had a fair value of $57,000. These assets were originally purchased by Hardy on 1 January 20X5 and are being depreciated over 6 years.

3   Cumulative impairment losses on recognised goodwill amounted to $15,000 at 31 December 20X9. No impairment losses have been necessary to date relating to the investment in the associate.

Required

Prepare a consolidated balance sheet for Laurel Co and its subsidiary, incorporating its associate in accordance with IAS 28.

33 Preparation question: Tyson Co

Below are the income statements of Tyson Co, its subsidiary and associate at 31 December 20X8.

	Tyson Co $'000	Douglas Co $'000	Frank Co $'000
Revenue	500	150	70
Cost of sales	(270)	(80)	(30)
Gross profit	230	70	40
Other expenses	(150)	(20)	(15)
Finance income	15	10	–
Finance costs	(20)	–	(10)
Profit before tax	75	60	15
Income tax expense	(25)	(15)	(5)
Profit for the period	50	45	10

You are also given the following information:

1 Tyson Co acquired 80,000 shares in Douglas Co for $188,000 3 years ago when Douglas Co had a credit balance on its retained earnings of $40,000. Douglas Co has 100,000 $1 ordinary shares.

2 Tyson Co acquired 40,000 shares in Frank Co for $60,000 2 years ago when that company had a credit balance on its retained earnings of $20,000. Frank Co has 100,000 $1 ordinary shares.

3 During the year Douglas Co sold some goods to Tyson Co for $66,000 (cost $48,000). None of the goods had been sold by the year end.

4 An impairment test carried out at the year end resulted in half of the recognised goodwill relating to Douglas being written off and recognition of impairment losses of $2,400 relating to the investment in Frank.

Required

Prepare the consolidated income statement for the year ended 31 December 20X8 for Tyson Co, incorporating its associate.

34 Hepburn   45 mins

(a) On 1 October 20X0 Hepburn acquired 80% of the equity share capital of Salter by way of a share exchange. Hepburn issued five of its own shares for every two shares in Salter. The market value of Hepburn's shares on 1 October 20X0 was $3 each. The share issue has not yet been recorded in Hepburn's books. The summarised financial statements of both companies are:

INCOME STATEMENTS
YEAR TO 31 MARCH 20X1

	Hepburn $'000	Salter $'000
Sales revenues	1,200	1,000
Cost of sales	(650)	(660)
Gross profit	550	340
Operating expenses	(120)	(88)
Debenture interest	Nil	(12)
Profit before tax	430	240
Income tax expense	(100)	(40)
Profit for the period	330	200

BALANCE SHEETS
AS AT 31 MARCH 20X1

	Hepburn		Salter	
	$'000	$'000	$'000	$'000
Assets				
Non-current assets				
Property, plant and equipment		620		660
Investments		20		10
		640		670
Current assets				
Inventory	240		280	
Accounts receivable	170		210	
Bank	20		40	
		430		530
Total assets		1,070		1,200
Equity and liabilities				
Equity				
Equity shares of $1 each		400		150
Retained earnings		450		700
		850		850
Non-current liabilities				
8% debentures		nil		150
Current liabilities				
Trade accounts payable	170		155	
Current tax payable	50		45	
		220		200
Total equity and liabilities		1,070		1,200

The following information is relevant:

(i) The fair values of Salter's assets were equal to their book values with the exception of its land, which had a fair value of $125,000 in excess of its book value at the date of acquisition.

(ii) In the post acquisition period Hepburn sold goods to Salter at a price of $100,000, this was calculated to give a mark-up on cost of 25% to Hepburn. Salter had half of these goods in inventory at the year end.

(iii) Consolidated goodwill is reviewed annually for impairment. At 31 March 20X1 its impaired value was $180,000.

(iv) The current accounts of the two companies disagreed due to a cash remittance of $20,000 to Hepburn on 26 March 20X1 not being received until after the year end. Before adjusting for this, Salter's debit balance in Hepburn's books was $56,000.

Required

Prepare a consolidated income statement and balance sheet for Hepburn for the year to 31 March 20X1.

(20 marks)

(b) At the same date as Hepburn made the share exchange for Salter's shares, it also acquired 6,000 'A' shares in Woodbridge for a cash payment of $20,000. The share capital of Woodbridge is made up of:

Equity voting A shares   10,000
Equity non-voting B shares   14,000

All of Woodbridge's equity shares are entitled to the same dividend rights; however during the year to 31 March 20X1 Woodbridge made substantial losses and did not pay any dividends.

Hepburn has treated its investment in Woodbridge as an ordinary long-term investment on the basis that:

(i)   It is only entitled to 25% of any dividends that Woodbridge may pay
(ii)   It does not have any directors on the board of Woodbridge
(iii)   It does not exert any influence over the operating policies or management of Woodbridge

Required

Comment on the accounting treatment of Woodbridge by Hepburn's directors and state how you believe the investment should be accounted for.   **(5 marks)**

Note. You are not required to amend your answer to part (a) in respect of the information in part (b).

(Total = 25 marks)

35 Holdrite (2.5 12/04)   45 mins

Holdrite purchased 75% of the issued share capital of Staybrite and 40% of the issued share capital of Allbrite on 1 April 20X4.

Details of the purchase consideration given at the date of purchase are:

Staybrite: a share exchange of 2 shares in Holdrite for every 3 shares in Staybrite plus an issue to the shareholders of Staybrite 8% loan notes redeemable at par on 30 June 20X6 on the basis of $100 loan note for every 250 shares held in Staybrite.

Allbrite: a share exchange of 3 shares in Holdrite for every 4 shares in Allbrite plus $1 per share acquired in cash. The market price of Holdrite's shares at 1 April 20X4 was $6 per share.

The summarised income statements for the three companies for the year to 30 September 20X4 are:

	Holdrite	Staybrite	Allbrite
	$000	$000	$000
Revenue	75,000	40,700	31,000
Cost of Sales	(47,400)	(19,700)	(15,300)
Gross Profit	27,600	21,000	15,700
Operating expenses	(10,480)	(9,000)	(9,700)
Operating Profit	17,120	12,000	6,000
Interest expense	(170)		
Profit before tax	16,950	12,000	6,000
Income tax expense	(4,800)	(3,000)	(2,000)
Profit for period	12,150	9,000	4,000

The following information is relevant:

(i)   A fair value exercise was carried out for Staybrite at the date of its acquisition with the following results:

	Book value	Fair value
	$'000	$'000
Land	20,000	23,000
Plant	25,000	30,000

The fair values have not been reflected in Staybrite's financial statements. The increase in the fair value of the plant would create additional depreciation of $500,000 in the post acquisition period in the consolidated financial statements to 30 September 20X4.

Depreciation of plant is charged to cost of sales.

(ii) The details of each company's share capital and reserves at 1 October 20X3 are:

	Holdrite $'000	Staybrite $'000	Allbrite $'000
Equity shares of $1 each	20,000	10,000	5,000
Share premium	5,000	4,000	2,000
Retained earnings	18,000	7,500	6,000

(iii) In the post acquisition period Holdrite sold goods to Staybrite for $10 million. Holdrite made a profit of $4 million on these sales. One-quarter of these goods were still in the inventory of Staybrite at 30 September 20X4.

(iv) Impairment tests on the goodwill of Staybrite and Allbrite at 30 September 20X4 resulted in the need to write down Staybrite's goodwill by $750,000.

(v) Holdrite paid a dividend of $5 million on 20 September 20X4. Staybrite and Allbrite did not make any dividend payments.

Required

(a) Calculate the goodwill arising on the purchase of the shares in both Staybrite and Allbrite at 1 April 20X4.

(8 marks)

(b) Prepare a consolidated income statement for the Holdrite Group for the year to 30 September 20X4.

(15 marks)

(c) Show the movement on the consolidated retained earnings attributable to Holdrite for the year to 30 September 20X4.

(2 marks)

(Total = 25 marks)

Note. The additional disclosures in IFRS 3 *Business Combinations* relating to a newly acquired subsidiary are not required.

36 Hapsburg (2.5 6/04)   45 mins

(a) Hapsburg, a public listed company, acquired the following investments:

– On 1 April 20X3, 24 million shares in Sundial. This was by way of an immediate share exchange of 2 shares in Hapsburg for every 3 shares in Sundial plus a cash payment of $1 per Sundial share payable on 1 April 20X6. The market price of Hapsburg's shares on 1 April 20X3 was $2 each.

– On 1 October 20X3, 6 million shares in Aspen paying an immediate $2·50 in cash for each share.

Based on Hapsburg's cost of capital (taken as 10% per annum), $1 receivable in three years' time can be taken to have a present value of $0·75.

Hapsburg has not yet recorded the acquisition of Sundial but it has recorded the investment in Aspen.

The summarised balance sheets at 31 March 20X4 are:

	Hapsburg		Sundial		Aspen	
	$'000	$'000	$'000	$'000	$'000	$'000
Non-current assets		41,000		34,800		37,700
Property, plant and equipment		15,000		3,000		nil
Investments		56,000		37,800		37,700
Current assets						
Inventory	9,900		4,800		7,900	
Trade and other receivables	13,600		8,600		14,400	
Cash	1,200		3,800		Nil	
		24,700		17,200		22,300
Total assets		80,700		55,000		60,000
Equity and liabilities						
Equity						
Ordinary shares $1 each		20,000		30,000		20,000
Reserves:						
Share premium	8,000		2,000		Nil	
Retained earnings	10,600		8,500		8,000	
		18,600		10,500		8,000
		38,600		40,500		28,000
Non-current liabilities						
10% loan note		16,000		4,200		12,000
Current liabilities						
Trade and other payables	16,500		6,900		13,600	
Bank overdraft	Nil		Nil		4,500	
Taxation	9,600		3,400		1,900	
		26,100		10,300		20,000
Total equity and liabilities		80,700		55,000		60,000

The following information is relevant:

(i) Below is a summary of the results of a fair value exercise for Sundial carried out at the date of acquisition:

Asset	Carrying value at acquisition	Fair value at acquisition	Notes
	$'000	$'000	
Plant	10,000	15,000	Remaining life at acquisition four years
Investments	3,000	4,500	No change in value since acquisition

The book values of the net assets of Aspen at the date of acquisition were considered to be a reasonable approximation to their fair values.

(ii) The profits of Sundial and Aspen for the year to 31 March 20X4, as reported in their entity financial statements, were $4·5 million and $6 million respectively. No dividends have been paid by any of the companies during the year. All profits are deemed to accrue evenly throughout the year.

(iii) In January 20X4 Aspen sold goods to Hapsburg at a selling price of $4 million. These goods had cost Aspen $2·4 million. Hapsburg had $2·5 million (at cost to Hapsburg) of these goods still in inventory at 31 March 20X4.

(iv) Impairment losses recognised for group purposes since acquisition are $3,200,000 on the recognised goodwill of Sundial and $750,000 on the investment in Aspen.

(v) Depreciation is charged on a straight-line basis.

Required

Prepare the Consolidated Balance Sheet of Hapsburg as at 31 March 20X4. **(20 marks)**

(b) Some commentators have criticised the use of equity accounting on the basis that it can be used as a form of off balance sheet financing.

Required

Explain the reasoning behind the use of equity accounting and discuss the above comment. **(5 marks)**

(Total = 25 marks)

37 Hedra (2.5 12/05)   45 mins

Hedra, a public listed company, acquired the following investments:

(i) On 1 October 2004, 72 million shares in Salvador for an immediate cash payment of $195 million. Hedra agreed to pay further consideration on 30 September 2005 of $49 million if the post acquisition profits of Salvador exceeded an agreed figure at that date. Hedra has not accounted for this deferred payment as it did not believe it would be payable, however Salvador's profits have now exceeded the agreed amount (ignore discounting). Salvador also accepted a $50 million 8% loan from Hedra at the date of its acquisition.

(ii) On 1 April 2005, 40 million shares in Aragon by way of a share exchange of two shares in Hedra for each acquired share in Aragon. The share market value of Hedra 's shares at the date of this share exchange was $2.50. Hedra has not yet recorded the acquisition of the investment in Aragon.

The summarised balance sheets of the three companies as at 30 September 2005 are:

	Hedra		Salvador		Aragon	
	$m	$m	$m	$m	$m	$m
Non–current assets						
Property, plant and equipment		358		240		270
Investments – in Salvador		245		nil		nil
– other		45		nil		nil
		648		240		270
Current assets						
Inventories	130		80		110	
Trade receivables	142		97		70	
Cash and bank	nil		4		20	
		272		181		200
		920		421		470

	Hedra		Salvador		Aragon	
	$m	$m	$m	$m	$m	$m
Equity and liabilities						
Ordinary share capital ($1 each)		400		120		100
Reserves:						
Share premium	40		50		nil	
Revaluation	15		nil		nil	
Retained earnings	240		60		300	
		295		110		300
		695		230		400
Non–current liabilities						
8% loan note	nil		50		nil	
Deferred tax	45	45	nil	50	nil	nil
Current liabilities						
Trade payables	118		141		40	
Bank overdraft	12		nil		nil	
Current tax payable	50		nil		30	
		180		141		70
Total equity and liabilities		920		421		470

The following information is relevant.

(a)   Fair value adjustments and revaluations:

(i)   Hedra's accounting policy for land and buildings is that they should be carried at their fair values. The fair value of Salvador's land at the date of acquisition was $20 million in excess of its carrying value. By 30 September 2005 this excess had increased by a further $5 million. Salvador's buildings did not require any fair value adjustments. The fair value of Hedra's own land and buildings at 30 September 2005 was $12 million in excess of its carrying value in the above balance sheet.

(ii)   The fair value of some of Salvador's plant at the date of acquisition was $20 million in excess of its carrying value and had a remaining life of four years (straight–line depreciation is used).

(iii)   At the date of acquisition Salvador had unrelieved tax losses of $40 million from previous years. Salvador had not accounted for these as a deferred tax asset as its directors did not believe the company would be sufficiently profitable in the near future. However, the directors of Hedra were confident that these losses would be utilised and accordingly they should be recognised as a deferred tax asset. By 30 September 2005 the group had not yet utilised any of these losses. The income tax rate is 25%.

(b)   The retained earnings of Salvador and Aragon at 1 October 2004, as reported in their separate financial statements, were $20 million and $200 million respectively. All profits are deemed to accrue evenly throughout the year.

(c)   An impairment test on 30 September 2005 showed that consolidated goodwill should be written down by $20million. Hedra has applied IFRS 3 *Business combinations* since the acquisition of Salvador.

(d)   The investment in Aragon has not suffered any impairment.

Required

Prepare the consolidated balance sheet of Hedra as at 30 September 2005.   **(25 marks)**

38 Hosterling (2.5 12/06)

45 mins

Hosterling purchased the following equity investments:

On 1 October 2005: 80% of the issued share capital of Sunlee. The acquisition was through a share exchange of three shares in Hosterling for every five shares in Sunlee. The market price of Hosterling's shares at 1 October 2005 was $5 per share.

On 1 July 2006: 6 million shares in Amber paying $3 per share in cash and issuing to Amber's shareholders 6% (actual and effective rate) loan notes on the basis of $100 loan note for every 100 shares acquired.

The summarised income statements for the three companies for the year ended 30 September 2006 are:

	Hosterling	Sunlee	Amber
	$'000	$'000	$'000
Revenue	105,000	62,000	50,000
Cost of sales	(68,000)	(36,500)	(61,000)
Gross profit/(loss)	37,000	25,500	(11,000)
Other income (note (i))	400	nil	nil
Distribution costs	(4,000)	(2,000)	(4,500)
Administrative expenses	(7,500)	(7,000)	(8,500)
Finance costs	(1,200)	(900)	nil
Profit/(loss) before tax	24,700	15,600	(24,000)
Income tax (expense)/credit	(8,700)	(2,600)	4,000
Profit/(loss) for the period	16,000	13,000	(20,000)

The following information is relevant:

(i)   The other income is a dividend received from Sunlee on 31 March 2006.

(ii)   The details of Sunlee's and Amber's share capital and reserves at 1 October 2005 were:

	Sunlee	Amber
	$'000	$'000
Equity shares of $1 each	20,000	15,000
Retained earnings	18,000	35,000

(iii)   A fair value exercise was carried out at the date of acquisition of Sunlee with the following results:

	Carrying amount	Fair value	Remaining life (straight line)
	$'000	$'000	
Intellectual property	18,000	22,000	still in development
Land	17,000	20,000	not applicable
Plant	30,000	35,000	five years

The fair values have not been reflected in Sunlee's financial statements.

Plant depreciation is included in cost of sales.

No fair value adjustments were required on the acquisition of Amber.

(iv)   In the year ended 30 September 2006 Hosterling sold goods to Sunlee at a selling price of $18 million. Hosterling made a profit of cost plus 25% on these sales. $7.5 million (at cost to Sunlee) of these goods were still in the inventories of Sunlee at 30 September 2006.

(v)   Impairment tests for both Sunlee and Amber were conducted on 30 September 2006. They concluded that the goodwill of Sunlee should be written down by $1.6 million and, due to its losses since acquisition, the investment in Amber was worth $21.5 million.

(vi)   All trading profits and losses are deemed to accrue evenly throughout the year.

Required

(a)   Calculate the goodwill arising on the acquisition of Sunlee at 1 October 2005.   **(5 marks)**

(b)   Calculate the carrying amount of the investment in Amber at 30 September 2006 under the equity method prior to the impairment test.   **(4 marks)**

(c)   Prepare the consolidated income statement for the Hosterling Group for the year ended 30 September 2006.
   (16 marks)

(Total = 25 marks)

39 Preparation question: Contract

The following details are as at the 31 December 20X5.

	Contract 1	Contract 2	Contract 3	Contract 4
Contract value	$120,000	$72,000	$240,000	$500,000
Costs to date	$48,000	$8,000	$103,200	$299,600
Estimated costs to completion	$48,000	$54,000	$160,800	$120,400
Progress payments received and receivable	$50,400	–	$76,800	$345,200
Date started	1.3.20X5	15.10.20X5	1.7.20X5	1.6.20X4
Estimated completion date	30.6.20X6	15.9.20X6	30.11.20X6	30.7.20X6
% complete	45%	10%	35%	70%

You are to assume that profit accrues evenly over the contract.

The income statement for the previous year showed revenue of $225,000 and expenses of $189,000 in relation to contract 4.

The company considers that the outcome of a contract cannot be estimated reliably until a contract is 25% complete. It is, however, probable that the customer will pay for costs incurred so far.

Required

Calculate the amounts to be included in the income statement for the year ended 31 December 20X5 and the balance sheet as at that date.

40 Merryview (2.5 6/02)   27 mins

Merryview specialises in construction contracts. One of its contracts, with Better Homes, is to build a complex of luxury flats. The price agreed for the contract is $40 million and its scheduled date of completion is 31 December 20X3. Details of the contract to 31 March 20X2 are:

Commencement date	1 July 20X1

CONTRACT COSTS:

	$'000
Architects' and surveyors' fees	500
Materials delivered to site	3,100
Direct labour costs	3,500
Overheads are apportioned at 40% of direct labour costs	
Estimated cost to complete (excluding depreciation – see below)	14,800

Plant and machinery used exclusively on the contract cost $3,600,000 on 1 July 20X1. At the end of the contract it is expected to be transferred to a different contract at a value of $600,000. Depreciation is to be based on a time apportioned basis.

Inventory materials on site at 31 March 20X2 is $300,000

Better Homes paid a progress payment of $12,800,000 to Merryview on 31 March 20X2.

At 31 March 20X3 the details for the construction contract have been summarised as:

	$'000
Contract cost to date (ie since the start of the contact) excluding all depreciation	20,400
Estimated cost to complete (excluding deprecation)	6,600

A further progress payment of $16,200,000 was received on 31 March 20X3.

Merryview accrues profit on its construction contracts using the percentage of completion basis as measured by the percentage of the cost to date compared to the total estimated contract cost.

Required

Prepare extracts of the financial statements of Merryview for the construction contract with Better Homes for:

(a)   The year to 31 March 20X2   **(8 marks)**

(b)   The year to 31 March 20X3   **(7 marks)**

(Total = 15 marks)

41 Linnet (2.5 6/04)   23 mins

(a)   Linnet is a large public listed company involved in the construction industry. Revenue on construction contracts is normally recognised by reference to the stage of completion of the contract. However, in certain circumstances, revenue is only recognised to the extent that it does not exceed recoverable contract costs.

   Required

   Discuss the principles that underlie each of the two methods and describe the circumstances in which their use is appropriate.   **(5 marks)**

(b)   Linnet is part way through a contract to build a new football stadium at a contracted price of $300 million. Details of the progress of this contract at 1 April 20X3 are shown below:

	$ million
Cumulative sales revenue recognised	150
Cumulative cost of sales to date	112
Profit to date	38

   The following information has been extracted from the accounting records at 31 March 20X4:

	$ million
Total progress payment received for work certified at **29 February 20X4**	180
Total costs incurred to date (excluding rectification costs below)	195
Rectification costs	17

   Linnet has received progress payments of 90% of the work certified at 29 February 20X4. Linnet's surveyor has estimated the sales value of the further work completed during March 20X4 was $20 million.

   At 31 March 20X4 the estimated remaining costs to complete the contract were $45 million.

   The rectification costs are the costs incurred in widening access roads to the stadium. This was the result of an error by Linnet's architect when he made his initial drawings.

   Linnet calculates the percentage of completion of its contracts as the proportion of sales value earned to date compared to the contract price.

   All estimates can be taken as being reliable.

BPP
LEARNING MEDIA

Required

Prepare extracts of the financial statements for Linnet for the above contract for the year to 31 March 20X4.

(8 marks)

(Total = 13 marks)

42 Torrent (2.5 6/06)   22 mins

Torrent is a large publicly listed company whose main activity involves construction contracts. Details of three of its contracts for the year ended 31 March 20X6 are:

Contract	Alfa	Beta	Ceta
Date commenced	1 April 20X4	1 October 20X5	1 October 20X5
Estimated duration	3 years	18 months	2 years
	$m	$m	$m
Fixed contract price	20	6	12
Estimated costs at start of contract	15	7.5 (note (iii))	10
Cost to date:			
At 31 March 20X5	5	Nil	Nil
At 31 March 20X6	12.5 (note (ii))	2	4
Estimated costs at 31 March 20X6 to complete	3.5	5.5 (note (iii))	6
Progress payments received at 31 March 20X5 (note (i))	5.4	Nil	Nil
Progress payments received at 31 March 20X6 (note (i))	12.6	1.8	nil

Notes

(a)   The company's normal policy for determining the percentage completion of contracts is based on the value of work invoiced to date compared to the contract price. Progress payments received represent 90% of the work invoiced. However, no progress payments will be invoiced or received from contract Ceta until it is completed, so the percentage completion of this contract is to be based on the cost to date compared to the estimated total contract costs.

(b)   The cost to date of $12·5 million at 31 March 20X6 for contract Alfa includes $1 million relating to unplanned rectification costs incurred during the current year (ended 31 March 20X6) due to subsidence occurring on site.

(c)   Since negotiating the price of contract Beta, Torrent has discovered the land that it purchased for the project is contaminated by toxic pollutants. The estimated cost at the start of the contract and the estimated costs to complete the contract include the unexpected costs of decontaminating the site before construction could commence.

Required

Prepare extracts of the income statement and balance sheet for Torrent in respect of the above construction contracts for the year ended 31 March 20X6.

(12 marks)

43 Multiplex II (2.5 pilot paper part)   16 mins

Multiplex is in the intermediate stage of a construction contract for the building of a new privately owned road bridge over a river estuary. The original details of the contract are:

Approximate duration of contract: 3 years

Date of commencement:	1 October 20X0
Total contract price:	$40 million
Estimated total cost:	$28 million

An independent surveyor certified the value of the work in progress as follows:

- on 31 March 20X1 $12 million
- on 31 March 20X2 $30 million (including the $12 million in 20X1

Total costs incurred at:

- 31 March 20X1 $9 million
- 31 March 20X2 $28.5 million (including the $9 million in 20X1

Progress billings at 31 March 20X2 were $25 million

On 1 April 20X1 Multiplex agreed to a contract variation that would involve an additional $5 million revenues with associated additional estimated costs of $2 million.

The costs incurred during the year to 31 March 20X2 include $2.5 million relating to the replacement of some bolts which had been made from material that had been incorrectly specified by the firm of civil engineers who were contracted by Multiplex to design the bridge. These costs were not included in the original estimates, but Multiplex is hopeful that they can be recovered from the firm of civil engineers.

Multiplex calculates profit on construction contracts using the percentage of completion method. The percentage of completion of the contract is based on the value of the work certified to date compared to the total contract price.

Required

Prepare the income statement and balance sheet extracts in respect of the contract for the year to 31 March 20X2 only. **(9 marks)**

44 Bodyline (2.5 12/03)   45 mins

IAS 37 *Provisions, contingent liabilities and contingent assets* was issued in 1998. The Standard sets out the principles of accounting for these items and clarifies when provisions should and should not be made. Prior to its issue, the inappropriate use of provisions had been an area where companies had been accused of manipulating the financial statements and of creative accounting.

Required

(a)   Describe the nature of provisions and the accounting requirements for them contained in IAS 37. **(6 marks)**

(b)   Explain why there is a need for an accounting standard in this area. Illustrate your answer with three practical examples of how the standard addresses controversial issues. **(6 marks)**

(c)   Bodyline sells sports goods and clothing through a chain of retail outlets. It offers customers a full refund facility for any goods returned within 28 days of their purchase provided they are unused and in their original packaging. In addition, all goods carry a warranty against manufacturing defects for 12 months from their date of purchase. For most goods the manufacturer underwrites this warranty such that Bodyline is credited with the cost of the goods that are returned as faulty. Goods purchased from one manufacturer, Header, are sold to Bodyline at a negotiated discount which is designed to compensate Bodyline for manufacturing defects. No refunds are given by Header, thus Bodyline has to bear the cost of any manufacturing faults of these goods.

     Bodyline makes a uniform mark up on cost of 25% on all goods it sells, except for those supplied from Header on which it makes a mark up on cost of 40%. Sales of goods manufactured by Header consistently account for 20% of all Bodyline's sales.

     Sales in the last 28 days of the trading year to 30 September 20X3 were $1,750,000. Past trends reliably indicate that 10% of all goods are returned under the 28-day return facility. These are not faulty goods. Of these 70% are later resold at the normal selling price and the remaining 30% are sold as 'sale' items at half the normal retail price.

In addition to the above expected returns, an estimated $160,000 (at selling price) of the goods sold during the year will have manufacturing defects and have yet to be returned by customers. Goods returned as faulty have no resale value.

Required

Describe the nature of the above warranty/return facilities and calculate the provision Bodyline is required to make at 30 September 20X3:

    (i)   For goods subject to the 28 day returns policy

    (ii)   For goods that are likely to be faulty   **(8 marks)**

(d)   Rockbuster has recently purchased an item of earth moving plant at a total cost of $24 million. The plant has an estimated life of 10 years with no residual value, however its engine will need replacing after every 5,000 hours of use at an estimated cost of $7.5 million. The directors of Rockbuster intend to depreciate the plant at $2.4 million ($24 million/10 years) per annum and make a provision of $1,500 ($7.5 million/5,000 hours) per hour of use for the replacement of the engine.

Required

Explain how the plant should be treated in accordance with International Accounting Standards and comment on the Directors' proposed treatment.   **(5 marks)**

                                                (Total = 25 marks)

45 Myriad II (2.5 12/01)   **11 mins**

Myriad manufactures and sells high quality printing paper. The auditor has drawn the company's attention to the sale of some packs of paper on 20 October 20X2 at a price of $45 each. These items were included in closing inventory on 30 September 20X2 at their manufactured cost of $48 each. Further investigations revealed that during the inventory count on 30 September 20X2 a quantity of packs of A3 size paper had been damaged by a water leak. The following week the company removed the damage by cutting the paper down to A4 size (A4 size is smaller than A3). The paper was then repackaged and put back into inventory. The cost of cutting and repackaging was $4 per pack. The normal selling price of the paper is $75 per pack for the A3 and $50 per pack for the A4. However on 12 October 20X2 the company reduced the selling prices of all its paper by 10% in response to similar price cuts by its competitors.

Securiprint, one of the customers that bought some of the 'damaged' paper had used it to print some share certificates for a customer. Securiprint informed Myriad that these share certificates had been returned by the customer because they contained marks that were not part of the design. Securiprint believes the marks were part of a manufacturing flaw on the part of Myriad and is seeking appropriate compensation.

Required

Discuss the impact the above information may have on the draft financial statements of Myriad for the year to 30 September 20X2.   **(6 marks)**

46 Peterlee II (2.5 6/06 part)   **22 mins**

Peterlee is preparing its financial statements for the year ended 31 March 20X6. The following items have been brought to your attention:

(a)   Peterlee acquired the entire share capital of Trantor during the year. The acquisition was achieved through a share exchange. The terms of the exchange were based on the relative values of the two companies obtained by capitalising the companies' estimated future cash flows. When the fair value of Trantor's identifiable net assets was deducted from the value of the company as a whole, its goodwill was calculated at $2·5 million.

A similar exercise valued the goodwill of Peterlee at $4 million. The directors wish to incorporate both the goodwill values in the companies' consolidated financial statements. **(4 marks)**

(b) During the year Peterlee acquired an iron ore mine at a cost of $6 million. In addition, when all the ore has been extracted (estimated in 10 years time) the company will face estimated costs for landscaping the area affected by the mining that have a present value of $2 million. These costs would still have to be incurred even if no further ore was extracted. The directors have proposed that an accrual of $200,000 per year for the next ten years should be made for the landscaping. **(4 marks)**

(c) On 1 April 20X5 Peterlee issued an 8% $5 million convertible loan at par. The loan is convertible in three years time to ordinary shares or redeemable at par in cash. The directors decided to issue a convertible loan because a non-convertible loan would have required an interest rate of 10%. The directors intend to show the loan at $5 million under non-current liabilities. The following discount rates are available:

	8%	10%
Year 1	0·93	0·91
Year 2	0·86	0·83
Year 3	0·79	0·75

(4 marks)

Required

Describe (and quantify where possible) how Peterlee should treat the items in (a) to (b) in its financial statements for the year ended 31 March 20X6 commenting on the directors' views where appropriate.

The mark allocation is shown against each of the three items above. **(Total = 12 marks)**

47 Jedders   27 mins

Your assistant at Jedders, a small listed company, has been preparing the financial statements for the year ended 31 December 20X0 and has raised the following queries.

(a) The company has three long leasehold properties in different parts of the region. The leases were acquired at different times, and the lease terms are all for fifty years. As at 1 January 20X0, their original cost, accumulated depreciation to date and carrying (book) values were as follows.

	Cost	Depreciation	Carrying value 1.1.20X0
	$'000	$'000	$'000
Property in North	3,000	1,800	1,200
Property in Central	6,000	1,200	4,800
Property in South	3,750	1,500	2,250

On 1 January an independent surveyor provided valuation information to suggest that the value of the South property was the same as book value, the North property had fallen against carrying value by 20% and the Central property had risen by 40% in value against the carrying value.

The directors of the company wish to include the revaluation of the Central property in the accounts to 31 December 20X0, whilst leaving the other properties at their depreciated historical cost.

The directors believe that this treatment of the North property is prudent and can be justified because property prices are expected to recover within the next few years so that this fall in value will be entirely reversed.

Required

(i) Advise the directors whether their proposal is acceptable, assuming they are committed to the use of current value for the Central property. **(2 marks)**

(ii) Assuming that all of the properties are revalued, calculate the income statement charges and the non-current asset balance sheet extracts for all the properties for the year ended 31 December 20X0. You should follow the requirements of IAS 16 Property, plant and equipment. **(3 marks)**

(b) On 1 October 20X0, Jedders signed a debt factoring agreement with a company Fab Factors. Jedders' trade receivables are to be split into three groups, as follows.

- *Group A* receivables will not be factored or administered by Fab Factors under the agreement, but instead will be collected as usual by Jedders.

- *Group B* receivables are to be factored and collected by Fab Factors on a 'with recourse' basis. Fab Factors will charge a 1% per month finance charge on the balance outstanding at the beginning of the month. Jedders will reimburse in full any individual balance outstanding after three months.

- *Group C* receivables will be factored and collected by Fab Factors 'without recourse'; Fab Factors will pay Jedders 95% of the book value of the debtors.

Jedders has a policy of making a receivables allowance of 20% of a trade receivable balance when it becomes three months old.

The receivables groups have been analysed as follows.

| | Balance @ 1 Oct 20X0 | % of 1 October 20X0 balance collected in: | | |
		October	November	December
	$'000			
Group A	1,250	30%	30%	20%
Group B	1,500	40%	30%	20%
Group C	2,000	50%	25%	22%

Required

For the accounts of Jedders, calculate the finance costs and receivables allowance for each group of trade receivables for the period 1 October - 31 December 20X0 and show the balance sheet values for those trade receivables as at 31 December 20X0. **(5 marks)**

(c) On 1 January 20X0, Jedders issued $15m of 7% convertible loan notes at par. The loan notes are convertible into equity shares in the company, at the option of the note holders, five years after the date of issue (31 December 20X4) on the basis of 25 shares for each $100 of loan stock. Alternatively, the loan notes will be redeemed at par.

Jedders has been advised by Fab Factors that, had the company issued similar loan notes without the conversion rights, then it would have had to pay interest of 10%; the rate is thus lower because the conversion rights are favourable.

Fab Factors also suggest that, as some of the loan note holders will choose to convert, the loan notes are, in substance, equity and should be treated as such on Jedders' balance sheet. Thus, as well as a reduced finance cost being achieved to boost profitability, Jedders' gearing has been improved compared to a straight issue of debt.

The present value of $1 receivable at the end of each year, based on discount rates of 7% and 10% can be taken as:

End of year	7%	10%
1	0.93	0.91
2	0.87	0.83
3	0.82	0.75
4	0.76	0.68
5	0.71	0.62

Required

In relation to the 7% convertible loan notes, calculate the finance cost to be shown in the income statement and the balance sheet extracts for the year to 31 December 20X0 for Jedders and comment on the advice from Fab Factors. **(5 marks)**

(Total = 15 marks)

48 Triangle (2.5 6/05)   45 mins

Triangle, a public listed company, is in the process of preparing its draft financial statements for the year to 31 March 20X5. The following matters have been brought to your attention:

(i)   On 1 April 20X4 the company brought into use a new processing plant that had cost $15 million to construct and had an estimated life of ten years. The plant uses hazardous chemicals which are put in containers and shipped abroad for safe disposal after processing. The chemicals have also contaminated the plant itself which occurred as soon as the plant was used. It is a legal requirement that the plant is decontaminated at the end of its life. The estimated present value of this decontamination, using a discount rate of 8% per annum, is $5 million. The financial statements have been charged with $1·5 million ($15 million/10 years) for plant depreciation and a provision of $500,000 ($5 million/10 years) has been made towards the cost of the decontamination. **(8 marks)**

(ii)   On 15 May 20X5 the company's auditors discovered a fraud in the material requisitions department. A senior member of staff who took up employment with Triangle in August 20X4 had been authorising payments for goods that had never been received. The payments were made to a fictitious company that cannot be traced. The member of staff was immediately dismissed. Calculations show that the total amount of the fraud to the date of its discovery was $240,000 of which $210,000 related to the year to 31 March 20X5. (Assume the fraud is material). **(5 marks)**

(iii)   The company has contacted its insurers in respect of the above fraud. Triangle is insured for theft, but the insurance company maintains that this is a commercial fraud and is not covered by the theft clause in the insurance policy. Triangle has not yet had an opinion from its lawyers. **(4 marks)**

(iv)   On 1 April 20X4 Triangle sold maturing inventory that had a carrying value of $3 million (at cost) to Factorall, a finance house, for $5 million. Its estimated market value at this date was in excess of $5 million. The inventory will not be ready for sale until 31 March 20X8 and will remain on Triangle's premises until this date. The sale contract includes a clause allowing Triangle to repurchase the inventory at any time up to 31 March 20X8 at a price of $5 million plus interest at 10% per annum compounded from 1 April 20X4. The inventory will incur storage costs until maturity. The cost of storage for the current year of $300,000 has been included in trade receivables (in the name of Factorall). If Triangle chooses not to repurchase the inventory, Factorall will pay the accumulated storage costs on 31 March 20X8. The proceeds of the sale have been debited to the bank and the sale has been included in Triangle's sales revenue. **(8 marks)**

Required

Explain how the items in (i) to (iv) above should be treated in Triangle's financial statements for the year to 31 March 20X5 in accordance with current international accounting standards. Your answer should quantify the amounts where possible.

The mark allocation is shown against each of the four matters above. **(Total = 25 marks)**

49 Forest

45 mins

The overriding requirement of a company's financial statements is that they should represent faithfully the underlying transactions and other events that have occurred. To achieve this transactions have to be accounted for in terms of their 'substance' or economic reality rather than their legal form. This principle is included in the IASB Framework for the Preparation and Presentation of Financial Statements, and is also used in many standards, in particular IAS 17 Accounting for leases and IAS 18 Revenue.

Required

(a) Describe why it is important that substance rather than legal form is used to account for transactions, and describe how financial statements can be adversely affected if the substance of transactions is not recorded.

(5 marks)

(b) Describe, using examples, how the following features may indicate that the substance of a transaction is different from its legal form.

(i) Separation of ownership from beneficial use
(ii) The linking of transactions including the use of option clauses
(iii) When an asset is sold at a price that differs from its fair value **(9 marks)**

(c) On 1 April 20X1 Forest had an inventory of cut seasoning timber which had cost $12 million two years ago. Due to shortages of this quality of timber its value at 1 April 20X1 had risen to $20 million. It will be a further three years before this timber is sold to a manufacturer of high-class furniture. On 1 April 20X1 Forest entered into an arrangement to sell Barret Bank the timber for $15 million. Forest has an option to buy back the timber at any time within the next three years at a cost of $15 million plus accumulated interest at 2% per annum above the base rate. This will be charged from the date of the original sale. The base rate for the period of the transaction is expected to be 8%. Forest intends to buy back the timber on 31 March 20X4 and sell it the same day for an expected price of $25 million.

Note. Ignore any storage costs and capitalisation of interest that may relate to inventories.

Required

Assuming the above transactions take place as expected, prepare extracts to reflect the transactions in the income statements for the years to 31 March 20X2, 20X3 and 20X4 and the balance sheets (ignore cash) at those year ends:

(i) If Forest treated the transactions in their legal form
(ii) If the substance of the transactions is recorded

Comment briefly on your answer to (c) above. **(11 marks)**

(Total = 25 marks)

50 Atkins (2.5 12/02)

27 mins

The principle of recording the substance or economic reality of transactions rather than their legal form lies at the heart of the *Framework for Preparation and Presentation of Financial Statements* and several International Financial Reporting Standards. The development of this principle was partly in reaction to a minority of public interest companies entering into certain complex transactions. These transactions sometimes led to accusations that company directors were involved in 'creative accounting'.

(i) Atkins's operations involve selling cars to the public through a chain of retail car showrooms. It buys most of its new vehicles directly from the manufacturer on the following terms:

– Atkins will pay the manufacturer for the cars on the date they are sold to a customer or six months after they are delivered to its showrooms whichever is the sooner.

– The price paid will be 80% of the retail list price as set by the manufacturer at the date that the goods are delivered.

– Atkins will pay the manufacturer 1.5% per month (of the cost price to Atkins) as a 'display charge' until the goods are paid for.

– Atkins may return the cars to the manufacturer any time up until the date the cars are due to be paid for. Atkins will incur the freight cost of any such returns. Atkins has never taken advantage of this right of return.

– The manufacturer can recall the cars or request them to be transferred to another retailer any time up until the time they are paid for by Atkins.

Required

Discuss which party bears the risks and rewards in the above arrangement and come to a conclusion on how the transactions should be treated by each party. **(6 marks)**

(ii) Atkins bought five identical plots of development land for $2 million in 20X0. On 1 October 20X2 Atkins sold three of the plots of land to an investment company, Landbank, for a total of $2.4 million. This price was based on 75% of the fair market value of $3.2 million as determined by an independent surveyor at the date of sale. The terms of the sale contained two clauses:

– Atkins can re-purchase the plots of land for the full fair value of $3.2 million (the value determined at the date of sale) any time until 30 September 20X5; and

– On 1 October 20X5, Landbank has the option to require Atkins to re-purchase the properties for $3.2 million. You may assume that Landbank seeks a return on its investments of 10% per annum.

Required

Discuss the substance of the above transactions; and **(3 marks)**

Prepare extracts of the income statement and balance sheet (ignore cash) of Atkins for the year to 30 September 20X3:

– If the plots of land are considered as sold to Landbank; and **(2 marks)**
– Reflecting the substance of the above transactions. **(4 marks)**

(Total = 15 marks)

51 Angelino (2.5 12/06)   45 mins

(a) Recording the substance of transactions, rather than their legal form, is an important principle in financial accounting. Abuse of this principle can lead to profit manipulation, non-recognition of assets and substantial debt not being recorded on the balance sheet.

Required

Describe how the use of off balance sheet financing can mislead users of financial statements.

Note. Your answer should refer to specific user groups and include examples where recording the legal form of transactions may mislead them. **(9 marks)**

(b) Angelino has entered into the following transactions during the year ended 30 September 2006:

(i) In September 2006 Angelino sold (factored) some of its trade receivables to Omar, a finance house. On selected account balances Omar paid Angelino 80% of their book value. The agreement was that Omar would administer the collection of the receivables and remit a residual amount to Angelino depending upon how quickly individual customers paid. Any balance uncollected by Omar after six months will be refunded to Omar by Angelino. **(5 marks)**

(ii) On 1 October 2005 Angelino owned a freehold building that had a carrying amount of $7.5 million and had an estimated remaining life of 20 years. On this date it sold the building to Finaid for a price of $12 million and entered into an agreement with Finaid to rent back the building for an annual rental of $1.3 million for a period of five years. The auditors of Angelino have commented that in their opinion the building had a market value of only $10 million at the date of its sale and to rent an equivalent building under similar terms to the agreement between Angelino and Finaid would only cost $800,000 per annum. Assume any finance costs are 10% per annum. **(6 marks)**

(iii) Angelino is a motor car dealer selling vehicles to the public. Most of its new vehicles are supplied on consignment by two manufacturers, Monza and Capri, who trade on different terms.

Monza supplies cars on terms that allow Angelino to display the vehicles for a period of three months from the date of delivery or when Angelino sells the cars on to a retail customer if this is less than three months. Within this period Angelino can return the cars to Monza or can be asked by Monza to transfer the cars to another dealership (both at no cost to Angelino). Angelino pays the manufacturer's list price at the end of the three month period (or at the date of sale if sooner). In recent years Angelino has returned several cars to Monza that were not selling very well and has also been required to transfer cars to other dealerships at Monza's request.

Capri's terms of supply are that Angelino pays 10% of the manufacturer's price at the date of delivery and 1% of the outstanding balance per month as a display charge. After six months (or sooner if Angelino chooses), Angelino must pay the balance of the purchase price or return the cars to Capri. If the cars are returned to the manufacturer, Angelino has to pay for the transportation costs and forfeits the 10% deposit. Because of this Angelino has only returned vehicles to Capri once in the last three years. **(5 marks)**

Required

Describe how the above transactions and events should be treated in the financial statements of Angelino for the year ended 30 September 2006. Your answer should explain, where relevant, the difference between the legal form of the transactions and their substance.

Note. The mark allocation is shown against each of the three transactions above. **(Total = 25 marks)**

52 Preparation question: Branch Co

Branch Co acquired an item of plant and equipment on a finance lease on 1 January 20X1. The terms of the agreement were as follows:

Deposit : $1,150 (non-refundable)
Instalments : $4,000 pa for seven years payable in arrears
Cash price : $20,000

The asset has useful life of four years and the interest rate implicit in the lease is 11%.

Required

Prepare extracts from the income statement and balance sheet for the year ending 31 December 20X1.

(Notes to the financial statements are not required.)

53 Evans

22 mins

On 1 October 20X3 Evans Co entered into a non-cancellable agreement whereby Evans Co would lease a new rocket booster. The terms of the agreement were that Evans Co would pay 26 rentals of $3,000 quarterly in advance commencing on 1 October 20X3, and that after this initial period Evans Co could continue, at its option, to use the rocket booster for a nominal rental which is not material. The cash price of this asset would have been $61,570 and the asset has a useful life of 10 years. Evans Co considers this lease to be a finance lease and charges a full year's depreciation in the year of purchase of an asset. The rate of interest implicit in the lease is 2% per quarter.

On 1 July 20X2 Evans Co entered into another non-cancellable agreement to lease a Zarkov rocket for a period of 10 years at a rental of $5,000 half-yearly to be paid in advance, commencing on 1 July 20X2. Evans Co considers this lease to be an operating lease.

Required

Show how these transactions would be reflected in the financial statements for the year ended 31 December 20X3.

(12 marks)

(Total = 12 marks)

54 Bowtock (2.5 12/03 amended)

9 mins

Bowtock has leased an item of plant under the following terms:

Commencement of the lease was **1 January 20X2**

Term of lease 5 years

Annual payments in advance $12,000

Cash price and fair value of the asset – $52,000 at 1 January 20X2 – equivalent to the present value of the minimum lease payments.

Implicit interest rate within the lease (as supplied by the lessor) 8% per annum (to be apportioned on a time basis where relevant).

The company's depreciation policy for this type of plant is 20% per annum on cost (apportioned on a time basis where relevant).

Required

Prepare extracts of the income statement and balance sheet for Bowtock for the year to 30 September 20X3 for the above lease.

(5 marks)

55 Preparation question: Julian Co

Julian Co recognised a deferred tax liability for the year end 31 December 20X3 which related solely to accelerated tax depreciation on property, plant and equipment at a rate 30%. The net book value of the property, plant and equipment at that date was $310,000 and the tax written down value was $230,000.

The following data relates to the year ended 31 December 20X4:

(i)   At the end of the year the carrying value of property, plant and equipment was $460,000 and their tax written down value was $270,000. During the year some items were revalued by $90,000. No items had previously required revaluation. In the tax jurisdiction in which Julian operates revaluations of assets do not affect the tax base of an asset or taxable profit. Gains due to revaluations are taxable on sale.

(ii)   Julian began development of a new product during the year and capitalised $60,000 in accordance with IAS 38. The expenditure was deducted for tax purposes as it was incurred. None of the expenditure had been amortised by the year end.

(iii) Julian's income statement showed interest income receivable of $55,000, but only $45,000 of this had been received by the year end. Interest income is taxed on a receipts basis.

(iv)   During the year, Julian made a provision of $40,000 to cover an obligation to clean up some damage caused by an environmental accident. None of the provision had been used by the year end. The expenditure will be tax deductible when paid.

The corporate income tax rate recently enacted for the following year is 30% (unchanged from the previous year).

The current tax charge was calculated for the year as $45,000.

Current tax is settled on a net basis with the national tax authority.

Required

(a)   Prepare a table showing the carrying values, tax bases and temporary differences for each for the items above at 31 December 20X4.

(b)   Prepare the income statement and balance sheet notes to the financial statements relating to deferred tax for the year ended 31 December 20X4.

56 Deferred taxation   27 mins

(a)   Explain, with examples, the nature and purpose of deferred taxation.   **(10 marks)**

(b)   The information below relates to G Co for the year ended 31 March 20X3.

The balance on the provision for deferred taxation account at 1 April 20X2 was $35,000. This represented taxation at 35% on cumulative timing differences of $100,000 at 1 April 20X2. Capital allowances (tax depreciation) and depreciation for the year ending 31 March 20X3 are as follows.

	Capital allowances	*Depreciation*
	$'000	*$'000*
20X3 (actual)	100	90

The income tax rate for 20X3 is 30% and is expected to remain at this level for the for the foreseeable future.

Required

State, with reasons, how to account for deferred tax in the year ended 31 March 20X3.   **(5 marks)**

(Total = 15 marks)

57 Bowtock (2.5 12/03 amended)   20 mins

(a)   IAS 12 *Income Tax* was issued in 1996 and revised in 2000. It details the requirements relating to the accounting treatment of deferred tax.

Required

Explain why it is considered necessary to provide for deferred tax and briefly outline the principles of accounting for deferred tax contained in IAS 12 *Income Tax*.   **(5 marks)**

(b)   Bowtock purchased an item of plant for $2,000,000 on 1 October 20X0. It had an estimated life of eight years and an estimated residual value of $400,000. The plant is depreciated on a straight-line basis. The tax authorities do not allow depreciation as a deductible expense. Instead a tax expense of 40% of the cost of this type of asset can be claimed against income tax in the year of purchase and 20% per annum (on a reducing balance basis) of its tax base thereafter. The rate of income tax can be taken as 25%.

Required

In respect of the above item of plant, calculate the deferred tax charge/credit in Bowtock's income statement for the year to 30 September 20X3 and the deferred tax balance in the balance sheet at that date. **(6 marks)**

Note: work to the nearest $'000. **(Total = 11 marks)**

58 Preparation question: Fenton Co

(a) Fenton Co had 5,000,000 ordinary shares in issue on 1 January 20X1.

On 31 January 20X1, the company made a rights issue of 1 for 4 at $1.75. The cum rights price was $2 per share.

On 30 June 20X1, the company made an issue at full market price of 125,000 shares.

Finally, on 30 November 20X1, the company made a 1 for 10 bonus issue.

Profit for the year was $2,900,000.

The reported EPS for year ended 31 December 20X0 was 46.4c.

Required

What was the earnings per share figure for year ended 31 December 20X1 and the restated EPS for year ended 31 December 20X0?

(b) Sinbad Co had the same 10 million ordinary shares in issue on both 1 January 20X1 and 31 December 20X1. On 1 January 20X1 the company issued 1,200,000 $1 units of 5% convertible loan stock. Each unit of stock is convertible into 4 ordinary shares on 1 January 20X9 at the option of the holder. The following is an extract from Sinbad Co's income statement for the year ended 31 December 20X1:

	$'000
Profit before interest and tax	980
Interest payable on 5% convertible loan stock	(60)
Profit before tax	920
Income tax expense (at 30%)	(276)
Profit for the period	644

Required

What was the basic and diluted earnings per share for the year ended 31 December 20X1?

(c) Talbot Co has in issue 5,000,000 50c ordinary shares throughout 20X3.

During 20X1 the company had given certain senior executives options over 400,000 shares exercisable at $1.10 at any time after 31 May 20X4. None were exercised during 20X3. The average market value of one ordinary share during the period was $1.60. Talbot Co had made a profit after tax of $540,000 in 20X3.

Required

What is the basic and diluted earnings per share for the year ended 31 December 20X3?

59 Savoir (2.5 6/06 part)

23 mins

(a)   The issued share capital of Savoir, a publicly listed company, at 31 March 20X3 was $10 million. Its shares are denominated at 25 cents each. Savoir's earnings attributable to its ordinary shareholders for the year ended 31 March 20X3 were also $10 million, giving an earnings per share of 25 cents.

Year ended 31 March 20X4

On 1 July 20X3 Savoir issued eight million ordinary shares at full market value. On 1 January 20X4 a bonus issue of one new ordinary share for every four ordinary shares held was made. Earnings attributable to ordinary shareholders for the year ended 31 March 20X4 were $13,800,000.

Year ended 31 March 20X5

On 1 October 20X4 Savoir made a rights issue of shares of two new ordinary shares at a price of $1·00 each for every five ordinary shares held. The offer was fully subscribed. The market price of Savoir's ordinary shares immediately prior to the offer was $2·40 each. Earnings attributable to ordinary shareholders for the year ended 31 March 20X5 were $19,500,000.

Required

Calculate Savoir's earnings per share for the years ended 31 March 20X4 and 20X5 including comparative figures.   **(9 marks)**

(b)   On 1 April 20X5 Savoir issued $20 million 8% convertible loan stock at par. The terms of conversion (on 1 April 20X8) are that for every $100 of loan stock, 50 ordinary shares will be issued at the option of loan stockholders. Alternatively the loan stock will be redeemed at par for cash. Also on 1 April 20X5 the directors of Savoir were awarded share options on 12 million ordinary shares exercisable from 1 April 20X8 at $1·50 per share. The average market value of Savoir's ordinary shares for the year ended 31 March 20X6 was $2·50 each. The income tax rate is 25%. Earnings attributable to ordinary shareholders for the year ended 31 March 20X6 were $25,200,000. The share options have been correctly recorded in the income statement.

Required

Calculate Savoir's basic and diluted earnings per share for the year ended 31 March 20X6 (comparative figures are not required).

You may assume that both the convertible loan stock and the directors' options are dilutive.   **(4 marks)**

(Total = 13 marks)

60 Niagara (2.5 6/03 part)

23 mins

Extracts of Niagara's consolidated income statement for the year to 31 March 20X3 are:

	$'000
Revenue	36,000
Cost of sales	(21,000)
Gross profit	15,000
Other operating expenses	(6,200)
Interest payable	(800)
Impairment of non-current assets	(4,000)
Share of profit of associates	1,500
Profit before tax	5,500
Income tax expense	(2,800)
Profit for the year	2,700

Attributable to:

Equity holders of the parent	2,585
Minority interest	115
	2,700

This draft income statement does **not** include any amounts in respect of the preference dividends or equity dividends for the year.

The impairment of non-current assets attracted tax relief of $1 million which has been included in the tax charge.

Niagara paid an interim ordinary dividend of 3c per share in June 20X2 and declared a final dividend on 25 March 20X3 of 6c per share.

The issued share capital of Niagara on **1 April 20X2** was:

Ordinary shares of 25c each	$3 million
8% Preference shares	$1 million

The preference shares are non-redeemable.

The company also had an issue $2 million 7% convertible loan stock dated 20X5. The loan stock will be redeemed at par in 20X5 or converted to ordinary shares on the basis of 40 new shares for each $100 of loan stock at the option of the stockholders. Niagara's income tax rate is 30%.

There are also in existence directors' share warrants (issued in 20X1) which entitle the directors to receive 750,000 new shares in total in 20X5 at no cost to the directors.

The following share issues took place during the year to 31 March 20X3:

- 1 July 20X2; a rights issue of 1 new share at $1·50 for every 5 shares held. The market price of Niagara's shares the day before the rights was $2·40.

- 1 October 20X2; an issue of $1 million 6% non-redeemable preference shares at par.

Both issues were fully subscribed.

Niagara's basic earnings per share in the year to 31 March 20X2 was correctly disclosed as 24c.

Required

Calculate for Niagara for the year to 31 March 20X3:

(a) the dividend cover and explain its significance; **(3 marks)**

(b) the basic earnings per share including the comparative; **(4 marks)**

(c) the fully diluted earnings per share (ignore comparative); and advise a prospective investor of the significance of the diluted earnings per share figure. **(6 marks)**

(Total = 13 marks)

61 Preparation question: Analytical review

As internal auditor of AB Co, a limited liability company, you are conducting an investigation of the company's trading results. Your directors believe a further issue of debentures is needed to fund both the repayment of the 10% inventory due for repayment in 20X9 and for investment in new plant and machinery. The industry in which AB Co operates is, and is likely to remain, highly competitive.

Note. 'Now' is November 20X8.

The following financial information has been provided.

BALANCE SHEETS AS AT 31 DECEMBER

	20X7	20X6	20X5	20X4	20X3
Assets	$m	$m	$m	$m	$m
Non-current assets					
Land and buildings	3.0	2.5	2.4	1.6	1.5
Plant and machinery	3.2	2.0	1.2	0.8	0.6
	6.2	4.5	3.6	2.4	2.1
Current assets					
Inventories	5.0	4.7	3.0	2.4	1.9
Receivables	2.6	2.0	1.9	1.5	1.4
Total assets	13.8	11.2	8.5	6.3	5.4
Equity and liabilities					
Equity					
$1 equity shares fully paid	1.5	1.5	1.5	1.5	1.0
Retained earnings	4.5	2.2	2.0	1.1	0.9
	6.0	3.7	3.5	2.6	1.9
*Current liabilities**	4.3	4.0	3.5	2.2	2.0
Non-current liabilities					
10% loan stock 20X9	1.5	1.5	1.5	1.5	1.5
12% loan stock 20Y5	2.0	2.0	-	-	-
	13.8	11.2	8.5	6.3	5.4
*Includes bank overdraft	1.9	1.3	0.6	0.8	0.9

EXTRACTS FROM INCOME STATEMENT

Net sales	16.4	13.5	10.0	8.5	7.3
Cost of sales	8.9	7.1	6.1	5.5	4.8
Profit before tax	3.0	1.5	1.4	0.8	0.5

Some average statistics for the industry as a whole in 20X7 are given as follows.

Net profit before tax: sales	14%
Net profit before tax: total assets less current liabilities	18%
Working capital (current) ratio	2.2:1
Liquidity ratio	0.75:1
Sales: non-current assets	3.0
Turnover of inventory	2.8
Receivables collection period (based on average receivables)	45 days
Age of inventory	120 days

Required

(a)   Present a schedule of data derived from the financial information provided for AB Co which would be used as the basis of an analytical review.

(b)   Use the data from (a) above:

    (i)   To analyse the financing proposals and

    (ii)   To assess the reasonableness of the figures in the five-year statement of results.

Approaching the question

1   Do not calculate too many ratios: the question itself gives you a big hint as to those you should provide.

2   Your analysis must be as good as your calculations, as well as being supported by them.

3   Make sensible points and do not be afraid to state the obvious.

62 Rytetrend (2.5 6/03)

45 mins

Rytetrend is a retailer of electrical goods. Extracts from the company's financial statements are set out below:

Income statement for the year ended 31 March:

		20X3		20X2
	$'000	$'000	$'000	$'000
Sales revenue		31,800		23,500
Cost of sales		(22,500)		(16,000)
Gross profit		9,300		7,500
Other operating expense		(5,440)		(4,600)
Interest payable – loan notes	(260)		(500)	
– overdraft	(200)	(460)	Nil	(500)
Profit before taxation		3,400		2,400
Income tax expense		(1,000)		(800)
Profit for the year		2,400		1,600

Balance Sheets as at 31 March

		20X3		20X2
Assets	$'000	$'000	$'000	$'000
Non-current assets (note (i))		24,500		17,300
Current assts				
Inventory	2,650		3,270	
Receivables	1,100		1,950	
Bank	Nil	3,750	400	5,620
Total assets		28,250		22,920
Equity and liabilities				
Equity				
Ordinary capital ($1 shares)		11,500		10,000
Share premium		1,500		Nil
Retained earnings		8,130		6,160
		21,130		16,160
Non-current liabilities				
10% loan notes		Nil		4,000
6% loan notes		2,000		Nil
Current liabilities				
Bank overdraft	1,050		Nil	
Trade payables	2,850		1,980	
Taxation	720		630	
Warranty provision (note (ii))	500	5,120	150	2,760
Total equity and liabilities		28,250		22,920

Notes

(i)   The details of the non-current assets are:

	Cost	Accumulated depreciation	Net book value
	$'000	$'000	$'000
At 31 March 20X2	27,500	10,200	17,300
At 31 March 20X3	37,250	12,750	24,500

During the year there was a major refurbishment of display equipment. Old equipment that had cost $6 million in September 20W8 was replaced with new equipment at a gross cost of $8 million. The equipment manufacturer had allowed Rytetrend a trade in allowance of $500,000 on the old display equipment. In addition to this Rytetrend used its own staff to install the new equipment. The value of staff time spent on the installation has been costed at $300,000, but this has not been included in the cost of the asset. All staff costs have been included in operating expenses. All display equipment held at the end of the financial year is depreciated at 20% on its cost. No equipment is more than five years old.

(ii)   Operating expenses contain a charge of $580,000 for the cost of warranties on the goods sold by Rytetrend. The company makes a warranty provision when it sells its products and cash payments for warranty claims are deducted from the provision as they are settled.

(iii)   Dividends paid in the year ended 31 March 20X3 were $430,000.

Required

(a)   Prepare a cash flow statement for Rytetrend for the year ended 31 March 20X3.   **(12 marks)**

(b)   Write a report briefly analysing the operating performance and financial position of Rytetrend for the years ended 31 March 20X2 and 20X3.   **(13 marks)**

Your report should be supported by appropriate ratios.   **(Total = 25 marks)**

63 Harper (2.5 12/02)   45 mins

You are a partner in a small audit and accounting practice. You have just completed the audit and finalised the financial statements of a small family owned company in discussion with its managing director Mrs Harper. After the meeting Mrs Harper has asked for your help. She has obtained the published financial statements of several quoted companies in which she is considering buying some shares as a personal investment. She presents you with the following information:

(a)   In the year to 30 September 20X2, two companies, Gamma and Toga, reported identical profits before tax of $100 million. Information in the Chairmen's reports said both companies also expected profits from their core activities (to be interpreted as from continuing operations) to grow by 10% in the following year. Mrs Harper has extracted information from the income statements and made the following summary:

	Gamma	Toga
	$ million	*$ million*
Operating profit:		
Continuing activities	70	1,000
Acquisitions	nil	50
Discontinued activities	30	(40)
	100	100

A note to the financial statements of Toga said that both the discontinuation and acquisition occurred on 1 April 20X2 and were part of an overall plan to focus on its traditional core activities after incurring large losses on a new foreign venture.

Required

(i)   Briefly explain to Mrs Harper why information on discontinued operations is useful;   **(3 marks)**

(ii)   Calculate the expected operating profit for both companies for the year to 30 September 2003 (assuming the Chairmen's growth forecasts are correct):

    –   in the absence of information of the discontinued operations; and

    –   based on the information provided above.   **(4 marks)**

(b)   Taylor is another company about which Mrs Harper has obtained the following information from its published financial statements:

Earnings per share:

Year to 30 September	*20X2*	*20X1*
Basic earnings per share	25 cents	20 cents

The earnings per share is based on attributable earnings of $50 million ($30 million in 20X1) and 200 million ordinary shares in issue throughout the year (150 million weighted average number of ordinary shares in 20X1).

Balance sheet extracts:	$ million	$ million
8% Convertible loan stock	200	200

The loan stock is convertible to ordinary shares in 20X4 on the basis of 70 new shares for each $100 of loan stock.

Note to the financial statements:

There are directors' share options (in issue since 20W9) that allow Taylor's directors to subscribe for a total of 50 million new ordinary shares at a price of $1·50 each.

(Assume the current rate of income tax for Taylor is 25% and the market price of its ordinary shares throughout the year has been $2·50)

Mrs Harper has read that the trend of the earnings per share is a reliable measure of a company's profit trend. She cannot understand why the increase in profits is 67% ($30 million to $50 million), but the increase in the earnings per share is only 25% (20 cents to 25 cents). She is also confused by the company also quoting a diluted earnings per share figure, which is lower than the basic earnings per share.

Required

(i)   Explain why the trend of earnings per share may be different from the trend of the reported profit, and which is the more useful measure of performance;   **(3 marks)**

(ii)   Calculate the diluted earnings per share for Taylor based on the effect of the convertible loan stock and the directors' share options for the year to 30 September 20X2 (ignore comparatives); and
                                                                                                        (5 marks)

(iii)   Explain the relevance of the diluted earnings per share measure.   **(4 marks)**

(c)   Mrs Harper has noticed that the tax charge for a company called Stepper is $5 million on profits before tax of $35 million. This is an effective rate of tax of 14·3%. Another company Jenni has an income tax charge of $10 million on profit before tax of $30 million. This is an effective rate of tax of 33·3% yet both companies state the rate of income tax applicable to them is 25%. Mrs Harper has also noticed that in the cash flow statements each company has paid the same amount of tax of $8 million.

Required

Advise Mrs Harper of the possible reasons why the income tax charge in the financial statements as a percentage of the profit before tax may not be the same as the applicable income tax rate, and why the tax paid in the cash flow statement may not be the same as the tax charge in the income statement.   **(6 marks)**

(Total = 25 marks)

64 Comparator (2.5 12/03)   45 mins

Comparator assembles computer equipment from bought in components and distributes them to various wholesalers and retailers. It has recently subscribed to an interfirm comparison service. Members submit accounting ratios as specified by the operator of the service, and in return, members receive the average figures for each of the specified ratios taken from all of the companies in the same sector that subscribe to the service. The specified ratios and the average figures for Comparator's sector are shown below.

Ratios of companies reporting a full year's results for periods ending between 1 July 20X3 and 30 September 20X3

Return on capital employed	22·1%
Revenue/capital employed	1·8 times
Gross profit margin	30%
Net profit (before tax) margin	12·5%
Current ratio	1·6:1
Quick ratio	0·9:1
Inventory holding period	46 days
Accounts receivable collection period	45 days
Accounts payable payment period	55 days
Debt to equity	40%
Dividend yield	6%
Dividend cover	3 times

Comparator's financial statements for the year to 30 September 20X3 are set out below:

Income statement	$'000
Sales revenue	2,425
Cost of sales	(1,870)
Gross profit	555
Other operating expenses	(215)
Interest payable	(34)
Inventory write off due to obsolescence	(120)
Profit before taxation	186
Income tax expense	(90)
Profit for the year	96

Extracts of changes in equity	$'000
Retained earnings – 1 October 20X2	179
Net profit for the period	96
Dividends paid (interim $60,000; final $30,000)	(90)
Retained earnings – 30 September 20X3	185

Balance Sheet	$'000	$'000
Non-current assets (note (i))		540
Current assets		
Inventory	275	
Accounts receivable	320	
Bank	Nil	595
		1,135
Equity and liabilities		
Equity		
Ordinary shares (25 cents each)		150
Retained earnings		185
		335
Non-current liabilities		
8% loan notes		300
Current liabilities		
Bank overdraft	65	
Trade accounts payable	350	
Taxation	85	500
		1,135

Notes

(i)   The details of the non-current assets are:

	Cost	Accumulated depreciation	Net book value
	$'000	$'000	$'000
At 30 September 20X3	3,600	3,060	540

(ii)   The market price of Comparator's shares throughout the year averaged $6·00 each.

Required

(a)   Explain the problems that are inherent when ratios are used to assess a company's financial performance. Your answer should consider any additional problems that may be encountered when using interfirm comparison services such as that used by Comparator.   **(7 marks)**

(b)   Calculate the ratios for Comparator equivalent to those provided by the interfirm comparison service.   **(6 marks)**

(c)   Write a report analysing the financial performance of Comparator based on a comparison with the sector averages.   **(12 marks)**

(Total = 25 marks)

65 Breadline (2.5 6/02)   45 mins

You are the assistant financial controller of Judicious. One of your company's credit controllers has asked you to consider the account balance of one of your customers, Breadline. He is concerned at the pattern of payments and increasing size and age of the account balance. As part of company policy he has obtained the most recently filed financial statements of Breadline and these are summarised below. A note to the financial statements of Breadline states that it is a wholly owned subsidiary of Wheatmaster, and its main activities are the production and distribution of bakery products to wholesalers. By coincidence your company's Chief Executive has been made aware that Breadline may be available for sale. She has asked for your opinion on whether Breadline would make a suitable addition to the group's portfolio.

BREADLINE
INCOME STATEMENT YEAR TO:

	31 December 20X1		31 December 20X0	
	$'000	$'000	$'000	$'000
Sales revenue		8,500		6,500
Cost of sales		(5,950)		(4,810)
Gross profit		2,550		1,690
Operating expenses		(560)		(660)
Finance costs: loan note	10		nil	
overdraft	10		5	
		(20)		(5)
Profit before tax		1,970		1,025
Taxation		(470)		(175)
Profit for the period		1,500		850

BALANCE SHEETS AS AT:

	31 December 20X1		31 December 20X0	
	$'000	$'000	$'000	$'000
Non-current assets				
Freehold premises at valuation		nil		1,250
Leasehold premises		2,500		nil
Plant		1,620		750
		4,120		2,000
Current assets				
Inventory	370		240	
Accounts receivable	960		600	
Bank	nil		250	
		1,330		1,090
Total assets		5,450		3,090
Equity and liabilities				
Equity				
Ordinary shares of $1 each		500		100
Reserves				
Share premium	200		nil	
Revaluation surplus				
(re freehold premises)	nil		700	
Retained earnings	3,000		1,700	
		3,200		2,400
		3,700		2,500
Non-current liabilities				
2% loan note		500		nil
Current liabilities				
Accounts payable	1,030		590	
Overdraft	220		nil	
		1,250		590
Total equity and liabilities		5,450		3,090

From your company's own records you have ascertained that sales to Breadline for the year to 20X1 and 20X0 were $1,200,000 and $800,000 respectively and the year-end account balances were $340,000 and $100,000 respectively. Normal credit terms, which should apply to Breadline, are that payment is due 30 days after the end of the month of sale. You are also aware that the company has not changed its address and is trading from the same premises. A note to Breadline's financial statements says that the profit on the disposal of its freehold premises has been included in cost of sales as this is where the depreciation on the freehold was charged. Dividends of $900,000 were paid in 20X1. No dividends were paid in 20X0.

Note: a commercial rate of interest on the loan note of Breadline would be 8% per annum.

Required

(a) Describe the matters that may be relevant when entity financial statements are used to assess the performance of a company that is a wholly owned subsidiary. **(5 marks)**

Note: your answer should give attention to related party issues.

(b) From the information above and with the aid of suitable ratios, prepare a report for your Chief Executive on the overall financial position of Breadline. Your answer should include reference to matters in the financial statements of Breadline that may give you cause for concern or require further investigation. **(20 marks)**

(Total = 25 marks)

66 Preparation question: Dickson Co

Below are the balance sheets of Dickson Co as at 31 March 20X8 and 31 March 20X7, together with the income statement for the year ended 31 March 20X8.

	20X8 $'000	20X7 $'000
Non-current assets		
Property, plant and equipment	825	637
Goodwill	100	100
Development expenditure	290	160
	1,215	897
Current assets		
Inventories	360	227
Trade receivables	274	324
Investments	143	46
Cash	29	117
	806	714
	2,021	1,611
Equity		
Share capital – $1 ordinary shares	500	400
Share premium	350	100
Revaluation surplus	152	60
Retained earnings	237	255
	1,239	815
Non-current liabilities		
6% debentures	150	100
Finance lease liabilities	100	80
Deferred tax	48	45
	298	225
Current liabilities		
Trade payables	274	352
Finance lease liabilities	17	12
Current tax	56	153
Debenture interest	5	–
Bank overdraft	132	54
	484	571
	2,021	1,611

Income statement

	$'000
Revenue	1,476
Cost of sales	(962)
Gross profit	514
Other expenses	(157)
Finance costs	(15)
Profit before tax	342
Income tax expense	(162)
Profit for the period	180
Dividends paid during the period	156

Notes

(1)   Goodwill arose on the acquisition of unincorporated businesses. During 20X8 expenditure on development projects totalled $190,000.

(2)   During 20X8 items of property, plant and equipment with a net book value of $103,000 were sold for $110,000. Depreciation charged in the year on property, plant and equipment totalled $57,000. Dickson transfers extra depreciation on revalued property, plant and equipment to retained earnings as allowed by IAS 16. Depreciation based on historical cost in 20X8 is $49,000. Dickson purchased $56,000 of property, plant and equipment by means of finance leases, payments being made in arrears on the last day of each accounting period.

(3)   The current asset investments are government bonds and management has decided to class them as cash equivalents.

(4)   The new debentures were issued on 1.4.X7. Finance cost includes debenture interest and finance lease finance charges only.

(5)   During the year Dickson made a 1 for 8 bonus issue capitalising its retained earnings followed by a rights issue.

Required

Prepare a cash flow statement for Dickson Co in accordance with IAS 7 using the indirect method.

67 Planter (2.5 6/04)   45 mins

The following information relates to Planter, a small private company. It consists of an opening balance sheet as at 1 April 20X3 and a listing of the company's ledger accounts at 31 March 20X4 after the draft operating profit before interest and taxation (of $17,900) had been calculated.

PLANTER
BALANCE SHEET AS AT 1 APRIL 20X3

	$	$
Non-current assets		
Land and buildings (at valuation of $49,200 less accumulated depreciation of $5,000)		44,200
Plant (at cost of $70,000 less accumulated depreciation of $22,500)		47,500
Investments at cost		16,900
		108,600
Current assets		
Inventory	57,400	
Trade receivables	28,600	
Bank	1,200	87,200
Total assets		195,800
Equity and liabilities		
Equity		
Ordinary shares of $1 each		25,000
Share premium	5,000	
Revaluation reserve	12,000	
Retained earnings	70,300	
		87,300
		112,300
Non-current liabilities		
8% loan notes		43,200
Current liabilities		
Trade payables	31,400	
Taxation	8,900	40,300
		195,800

Ledger account listings at 31 March 20X4

	Dr $	Cr $
Ordinary shares of $1 each		50,000
Share premium		8,000
Retained earnings – 1 April 20X3		70,300
Profit before interest and tax – year to 31 March 20X4		17,900
Revaluation reserve		18,000
8% loan notes		39,800
Trade payables		26,700
Accrued loan interest		300
Taxation	1,100	
Land and buildings at valuation	62,300	
Plant at cost	84,600	
Buildings – accumulated depreciation 31 March 20X4		6,800
Plant – accumulated depreciation 31 March 20X4		37,600
Investments at cost	8,200	
Trade receivables	50,400	
Inventory – 31 March 20X4	43,300	
Bank		1,900
Investment income		400
Loan interest	1,700	
Ordinary dividend	26,100	
	277,700	277,700

Notes

(i)   There were no disposals of land and buildings during the year. The increase in the revaluation reserve was entirely due to the revaluation of the company's land.

(ii)   Plant with a net book value of $12,000 (cost $23,500) was sold during the year for $7,800. The loss on sale has been included in the profit before interest and tax.

(iii)   Investments with a cost of $8,700 were sold during the year for $11,000. The profit has been included in the profit before interest and tax. There were no further purchases of investments.

(iv)   On 10 October 20X3 a bonus issue of 1 for 10 ordinary shares was made utilising the share premium account. The remainder of the increase in ordinary shares was due to an issue for cash on 30 October 20X3.

(v)   The balance on the taxation account is after settlement of the provision made for the year to 31 March 20X3. A provision for the current year has not yet been made.

Required

From the above information, prepare a cash flow statement using the indirect method for Planter in accordance with IAS 7 'Cash Flow Statements' for the year to 31 March 20X4.   **(25 marks)**

68 Bigwood (2.5 12/04)

45 mins

Bigwood, a public company, is a high street retailer that sells clothing and food. The managing director is very disappointed with the current year's results. The company expanded its operations and commissioned a famous designer to restyle its clothing products. This has led to increased sales in both retail lines, yet overall profits are down.

Details of the financial statements for the two years to 30 September 20X4 are shown below.

Income statement:

	Year to 30 September 20X4		Year to 30 September 20X3	
	$'000	$'000	$'000	$'000
Revenue - clothing	16,000		15,600	
- food	7,000	23,000	4,000	19,600
Cost of sales - clothing	14,500		12,700	
- food	4,750	(19,250)	3,000	(15,700)
Gross profit		3,750		3,900
Other operating expenses		(2,750)		(1,900)
Operating profit		1,000		2,000
Interest expense		(300)		(80)
Profit before tax		700		1,920
Income tax expense		(250)		(520)
Profit for the period		450		1,400

Summarised changes in equity:

	Year to 30 September 20X4	Year to 30 September 20X3
	$'000	$'000
Retained profit b/f	1,900	1,100
Profit for the period	450	1,400
Dividends paid	(600)	(600)
Retained profit c/f	1,750	1,900

Balance sheets as at:

	30 September 20X4		30 September 20X3	
	$'000	$'000	$'000	$'000
Property, plant and equipment at cost		17,000		9,500
Accumulated depreciation		(5,000)		(3,000)
		12,000		6,500
Current assets				
Inventory – clothing	2,700		1,360	
– food	200		140	
Trade receivables	100		50	
Bank	Nil	3,000	450	2,000
Total assets		15,000		8,500
Equity and liabilities				
Issued ordinary capital ($1 shares)		5,000		3,000
Share premium		1,000		Nil
Retained earnings		1,750		1,900
		7,750		4,900
Non-current liabilities				
Long-term loans		3,000		1,000
Current liabilities				
Bank overdraft	930		nil	
Trade payables	3,100		2,150	
Current tax payable	220	4,250	450	2,600
		15,000		8,500

Note. The directors have signalled their intention to maintain annual dividends at $600,000 for the foreseeable future.

The following information is relevant:

(i)   The increase in property, plant and equipment was due to the acquisition of five new stores and the refurbishment of some existing stores during the year. The carrying value of fixtures scrapped at the refurbished stores was $1.2 million; they had originally cost $3 million. Bigwood received no scrap proceeds from the fixtures, but did incur costs of $50,000 to remove and dispose of them. The losses on the refurbishment have been charged to operating expenses. Depreciation is charged to cost of sales apportioned in relation to floor area (see below).

(ii)   The floor sales areas (in square metres) were:

	30 September 20X4	30 September 20X3
Clothing	48,000	35,000
Food	6,000	5,000
	54,000	40,000

(iii)   The share price of Bigwood averaged $6.00 during the year to 30 September 20X3, but was only $3.00 at 30 September 20X4.

(iv)   The following ratios have been calculated:

	20X4	20X3
Return on capital employed	9.3%	33.9%
Net assets turnover	2.1 times	3.3 times
Gross profit margin		
– clothing	9.4%	18.6%
– food	32.1%	25%
Net profit (after tax) margin	2.0%	7.1%
Current ratio	0.71:1	0.77:1
Inventory holding period		
– clothing	68 days	39 days
– food	15 days	17 days
Accounts payment period	59 days	50 days
Gearing	28%	17%
Interest cover	3.3 times	25 times

Required

(a)   Prepare, using the indirect method, a cash flow statement for Bigwood for the year to 30 September 20X4

(12 marks)

(b)   Write a report analysing the financial performance and financial position of Bigwood for the two years ended 30 September 20X4. **(13 marks)**

Your report should utilise the above ratios and the information in your cash flow statement. It should refer to the relative performance of the clothing and food sales and be supported by any further ratios you consider appropriate.

(Total = 25 marks)

69 Casino (2.5 6/05)   45 mins

(a)   Casino is a publicly listed company. Details of its balance sheets as at 31 March 20X5 and 20X4 are shown below together with other relevant information:

BALANCE SHEET AS AT	31 March 20X5		31 March 20X4	
Non-current assets (note (i))	$m	$m	$m	$m
Property, plant and equipment		880		760
Intangible assets		400		510
		1,280		1,270
Current assets				
Inventory	350		420	
Trade receivables	808		372	
Interest receivable	5		3	
Short term deposits	32		120	
Bank	15	1,210	75	990
Total assets		2,490		2,260
Share capital and reserves				
Ordinary shares of $1 each		300		200
Reserves				
Share premium	60		Nil	
Revaluation reserve	112		45	
Retained earnings	1,098		1,165	
		1,270		1,210
		1,570		1,410
Non-current liabilities				
12% loan note	Nil		150	
8% variable rate loan note	160		Nil	
Deferred tax	90	250	75	225
Current liabilities				
Trade payables	530		515	
Bank overdraft	125		Nil	
Taxation	15		110	
		670		625
Total equity and liabilities		2,490		2,260

The following supporting information is available:

(i)   Details relating to the non-current assets are:

Property, plant and equipment at:

	31 March 20X5			31 March 20X4		
	Cost/ valuation	Depreci- ation	Carrying value	Cost/ valuation	Depreci- ation	Carrying value
	$m	$m	$m	$m	$m	$m
Land & buildings	600	12	588	500	80	420
Plant	440	148	292	445	105	340
			880			760

Casino revalued the carrying value of its land and buildings by an increase of $70 million on 1 April 20X4. On 31 March 20X5 Casino transferred $3 million from the revaluation reserve to retained earnings representing the realisation of the revaluation reserve due to the depreciation of buildings.

During the year Casino acquired new plant at a cost of $60 million and sold some old plant for $15 million at a loss of $12 million.

There were no acquisitions or disposals of intangible assets.

(ii)   The following extract is from the draft income statement for the year to 31 March 20X5:

	$m	$m
Operating loss		(32)
Interest receivable		12
Finance costs		(24)
Loss before tax		(44)
Corporation tax repayment claim	14	
Deferred tax charge	(15)	
		(1)
Loss for the period		(45)

The finance costs are made up of:

	$m
Interest expense	(16)
Penalty cost for early redemption of fixed rate loan	(6)
Issue costs of variable rate loan	(2)
	(24)

(iii)   The short term deposits meet the definition of cash equivalents.

(iv)   Dividends of $25 million were paid during the year.

Required

As far as the information permits, prepare a cash flow statement for Casino for the year to 31 March 20X5 in accordance with IAS 7 *Cash flow statements*.   **(20 marks)**

(b)   In recent years many analysts have commented on a growing disillusionment with the usefulness and reliability of the information contained in some companies' income statements.

Required

Discuss the extent to which a company's cash flow statement may be more useful and reliable than its income statement.   **(5 marks)**

(Total = 25 marks)

70 Tabba (2.5 12/05)   45 mins

The following draft financial statements relate to Tabba, a private company.

Balance sheets as at:	30 September 2005		30 September 2005	
	$m	$m	$m	$m
Tangible non–current assets (note (ii))				15,800
Current assets				
Inventories	2,550		1,850	
Trade receivables	3,100		2,600	
Insurance claim (note (iii))	1,500		1,200	
Cash and bank	850		nil	
		8,000		5,650
Total assets		18,600		21,450
Equity and liabilities				
Share capital ($1 each)		6,000		6,000
Reserves:				
Revaluation (note (ii))	nil		1,600	
Retained earnings	2,550		850	
		2,550		2,450
				8,450
Non–current liabilities				
Finance lease obligations (note (ii))	2,000		1,700	
6% loan notes	800		nil	
10% loan notes	nil		4,000	
Deferred tax	200		500	
Government grants (note (ii))	1,400		900	
		4,400		7,100
Current liabilities				
Bank overdraft	nil		550	
Trade payables	4,050		2,950	
Government grants (note (ii))	600		400	
Finance lease obligations (note (ii))	900		800	
Current tax payable	100		1,200	
		5,650		5,900
Total equity and liabilities		18,600		21,450

The following additional information is relevant:

(i)   Income statement extract for the year ended 30 September 2005:

	$'000
Operating profit before interest and tax	270
Interest expense	(260)
Interest receivable	40
Profit before tax	50
Net income tax credit	50
Profit for the period	100

Note. The interest expense includes finance lease interest.

(ii)   The details of the tangible non–current assets are:

	Cost $'000	Acc'd deprecation $'000	Carrying value $'000
At 30 September 2004	20,200	4,400	15,800
At 30 September 2005	16,000	5,400	10,600

During the year Tabba sold its factory for its fair value $12 million and agreed to rent it back, under an operating lease, for a period of five years at $1 million per annum. At the date of sale it had a carrying value of $7.4 million based on a previous revaluating of $8.6 million less deprecation of $1.2 million since the revolution. The profit on the sale of the factory has been included in operating profit. The surplus on the revaluation reserve related entirely to the factory. No other disposals of non–current assets were made during the year.

Plant acquired under finance leases during the year was $1.5 million. Other purchases of plant during the year qualified for government grants of $950,000.

Amortisation of government grants has been credited to cost of sales.

(iii)   The insurance claim related to flood damage to the company's inventories which occurred in September 2004. The original estimate has been revised during the year after negotiations with the insurance company. The claim is expected to be settled in the near future.

Required

(a)   Prepare a cash flow statement using the indirect method for Tabba in accordance with IAS 7 *Cash flow statements* for the year ended 30 September 2005.   **(17 marks)**

(b)   Using the information in the question and your cash flow statement, comment on the change in the financial position of Tabba during the year ended 30 September 2005.   **(8 marks)**

Note. You are not required to calculate any ratios.   **(Total = 25 marks)**

71 Minster (2.5 12/06)   45 mins

Minster is a publicly listed company. Details of its financial statements for the year ended 30 September 2006, together with a comparative balance sheet, are:

BALANCE SHEET AT

	30 September 2006		30 September 2005	
	$'000	$'000	$'000	$'000
Non-current assets (note (i))				
Property, plant and equipment		1,280		940
Software		135		nil
Investments at fair value through				
profit and loss		150		125
		1,565		1,065
Current assets				
Inventories	480		510	
Trade receivables	270		380	
Amounts due from construction				
contracts	80		55	
Bank	nil		35	
		830		980
Total assets		2,395		2,045

	30 September 2006		30 September 2005	
	$'000	$'000	$'000	$'000
Equity and liabilities				
Equity shares of 25 cents each		500		300
Reserves				
Share premium (note (ii))	150		85	
Revaluation reserve	60		25	
Retained earnings	950		965	
		1,160		1,075
		1,660		1,375
Non-current liabilities				
9% loan note	120		nil	
Environmental provision	162		nil	
Deferred tax	18		25	
		300		25
Current liabilities				
Trade payables	350		555	
Bank overdraft	25		40	
Current tax payable	60		50	
Total equity and liabilities		435		645
		2,395		2,045

INCOME STATEMENT FOR THE YEAR ENDED 30 SEPTEMBER 2006

	$'000
Revenue	1,397
Cost of sales	(1,110)
Gross profit	287
Operating expenses	(125)
	162
Finance costs (note (i))	(40)
Investment income and gain on investments	20
Profit before tax	142
Income tax expense	(57)
Profit for the year	85

The following supporting information is available:

(i)   Included in property, plant and equipment is a coal mine and related plant that Minster purchased on 1 October 2005. Legislation requires that in ten years' time (the estimated life of the mine) Minster will have to landscape the area affected by the mining. The future cost of this has been estimated and discounted at a rate of 8% to a present value of $150,000. This cost has been included in the carrying amount of the mine and, together with the unwinding of the discount, has also been treated as a provision. The unwinding of the discount is included within finance costs in the income statement.

Other land was revalued (upward) by $35,000 during the year.

Depreciation of property, plant and equipment for the year was $255,000.

There were no disposals of property, plant and equipment during the year.

The software was purchased on 1 April 2006 for $180,000.

The market value of the investments had increased during the year by $15,000. There have been no sales of these investments during the year.

(ii)   On 1 April 2006 there was a bonus (scrip) issue of equity shares of one for every four held utilising the share premium reserve. A further cash share issue was made on 1 June 2006. No shares were redeemed during the year.

(iii) A dividend of 5 cents per share was paid on 1 July 2006.

Required

(a) Prepare a cash flow statement for Minster for the year to 30 September 2006 in accordance with IAS 7 Cash flow statements. **(15 marks)**

(b) Comment on the financial performance and position of Minster as revealed by the above financial statements and your cash flow statement. **(10 marks)**

(Total = 25 marks)

72 Preparation question: Changing prices

The following information has been extracted from the accounts of Norwich Co prepared under the historical cost convention for 20X6.

INCOME STATEMENT EXTRACTS 20X6

	$m
Revenue	200
Profit	15
Less finance costs	3
Profit for the period	12

SUMMARISED BALANCE SHEET AT 31 DECEMBER 20X6

Assets	$m	$m
Property, plant & equipment at cost less depreciation		60
Current assets		
Inventories	20	
Receivables	30	
Bank	2	
		52
Total assets		112
Equity and liabilities		
Equity		62
Non-current liabilities		20
Current liabilities		30
Total equity and liabilities		112

The company's accountant has prepared the following current cost data.

	$m
Current cost adjustments for 20X6	
Depreciation adjustment	3
Cost of sales adjustment	5
Replacement cost at 31 December 20X6	
Property, plant & equipment, net of depreciation	85
Inventories	21

Required

(a) Calculate the current cost operating profit of Norwich Co for 20X6 and the summarised current cost balance sheet of the company at 31 December 20X6, so far as the information permits.

(b) Calculate the following ratios from both the historical cost accounts and current cost accounts:

(i) Interest cover
(ii) Rate of return on shareholders' equity
(iii) Debt/equity ratio

(c)   Discuss the significance of the ratios calculated under (b) and of the reasons for differences between them.

Note. Ignore taxation.

Approaching the question

1   To save time in this question, the current cost adjustments are given to you. You should, of course, understand how they are calculated.

2   Part (b) is straightforward. Make sure you allow yourself time to give adequate weight to the discussion in part (c).

73 Update (2.5 6/03 part)   22 mins

Most companies prepare their financial statements under the historical cost convention. In times of rising prices it has been said that without modification such financial statements can be misleading.

Required

(a)   Explain the problems that can be encountered when users rely on financial statements prepared under the historical cost convention for their information needs.   **(6 marks)**

Note: your answer should consider problems with the income statement and the balance sheet.

(b)   Update has been considering the effect of alternative methods of preparing their financial statements. As an example they picked an item of plant that they acquired from Suppliers on 1 April 20X0 at a cost of $250,000.

The following details have been obtained:

–   the company policy is to depreciate plant at 20% per annum on the reducing balance basis.

–   the movement in the retail price index has been:

1 April 20X0	180
1 April 20X1	202
1 April 20X2	206
31 March 20X3	216

–   Suppliers' price catalogue at 31 March 20X3 shows an item of similar plant at a cost of $320,000. On reading the specification it appears that the new model can produce 480 units per hour whereas the model owned by Update can only produce 420 units per hour.

Required

Calculate for Update the depreciation charge for the plant for the year to 31 March 20X3 (based on year end values) and its balance sheet carrying value on that date using:

–   the historical cost basis;
–   a current purchasing power basis; and
–   a current cost basis.   **(6 marks)**

(Total = 12 marks)

Answers

1 Peterlee

(a) The primary purpose of the *Framework* is to provide a frame of reference to help the IASB itself in developing new accounting standards and reviewing existing ones. Its main impact on accounting practice is therefore through its influence on the standard-setting process. It also has the following purposes:

- To assist auditors in forming an opinion as to whether financial statements conform with accounting standards.

- To help preparers of financial statements and auditors faced with new or emerging accounting issues to carry out an initial analysis of the issues involved.

- To provide a common set of principles for use by standard setters which should reduce the number of alternative treatments allowed by IFRS and therefore facilitate harmonisation of accounting practice.

The *Framework* is not an accounting standard and does not contain requirements on how financial statements should be prepared or presented. This is governed by accounting standards and the overriding requirement of fair presentation. It is also not the only influence on standard setting. Factors such as legal requirements, implementation issues and industry-specific issues also play a part.

However, it is the frame of reference within which the standard-setting takes place and it contains the definitions and recognition criteria for assets, liabilities, income and expense. Fair presentation requires that these elements are accounted for in accordance with the criteria set out in the *Framework*.

(b) *Assets* are defined as 'a resource controlled by an entity as a result of past events and from which future economic benefits are expected to flow to the entity'. The use of 'controlled' agrees with the principle of substance over form in that where an entity may not legally 'own' an asset but has control of the rights to future economic benefits accruing from it, the asset should be recognised. The most obvious example of this is an asset held under a finance lease. This is not legally owned, but is shown on the balance sheet as a non-current asset. The emphasis on 'past transactions or events' prevents the recognition of contingent assets.

Liabilities are defined as 'a present obligation of the entity arising from past events, the settlement of which is expected to result in an outflow from the entity of resources embodying economic benefits'. This obligation may be legal or it may be constructive. For instance, a company may have no legal obligation to fulfil certain environmental requirements, but it may have created, by its previous actions, the expectation that it will do so. This will be regarded as a constructive obligation per IAS 37 and the cost of carrying it out will be provided for. Again, 'past transactions or events' prevents the use of liabilities for 'profit smoothing'. An entity cannot set up a provision for an obligation which has not yet been incurred, such as a restructuring which it intends to carry out in the following year.

The emphasis placed upon correctly defining and recognising assets and liabilities underlines the importance of the balance sheet. The elements of financial statements identified in the *Framework*, other than assets and liabilities themselves, are measured in terms of changes in assets and liabilities. Ownership interest is the excess of assets over liabilities and gains and losses are defined as increases or decreases in ownership interest, aside from contributions from and distributions to owners. So correct identification and measurement of assets and liabilities is crucial to the preparation of financial statements which present fairly the entity's position and results.

2 Derringdo

(a) *Framework*

The *Framework* states that "recognition of income occurs simultaneously with the recognition of increases in assets or decreases in liabilities". This implies that all gains reported in the balance sheet, whether realised or unrealised, should be claimed as income in the income statement. Traditionally, only realised gains have been recognised as income. IAS 18 *Revenue* follows the traditional approach, with revenue being measured as the consideration for a transaction rather than as the side affect of an asset revaluation. For example the profit on the sale of property is recognised as income, whereas the revaluation of the same item would be taken directly to the revaluation reserve. Some recent standards have followed the *Framework* rather than tradition; IAS 40 *Investment Property* and IAS 41 *Agriculture* require unrealised gains to be reported as income in the income statement.

Substance over form requires the commercial substance of a transaction to be reported, rather than its legal form. For example, if a manufacturer sells its factory to a Bank for $1m, and the Bank has the option to demand that the manufacturer buys it back a year later for $1.1m, then this is a secured loan, not a sale. The $1m cash received is treated as a liability, not as income.

(b) *Sale of goods*

When selling the A grade goods, Derringdo acts as an agent for Gungho. The goods never belong to Derringdo, and so they do not appear in the balance sheet as inventory or in the income statement as cost of sales. Instead Derringdo's revenue in the income statement will include the commissions earned on these sales.

The B grade goods are normal goods purchased for resale. The income statement will show the gross sales revenue and the related cost of sales.

		$'000
Revenues	(4,600 + 11,400)	16,000
Cost of sales		(8,550)
Gross profit		7,450

Workings

A grade goods		$'000	$'000
Revenues	(18,400 × 100 / 50)		36,800
Cost of sales	Opening inventory	2,400	
	Purchases	18,000	
	Closing inventory	(2,000)	
			18,400
Gross profit (25%)			18,400
Commission	36,800 @ 12.5%		4,600

B grade goods		$'000	$'000
Revenues	(8,550 × 100 / 75)		11,400
Cost of sales	Opening inventory	1,000	
	Purchases	8,800	
	Closing inventory	(1,250)	
			(8,550)
Gross profit (25%)			2,850

3 Regulatory framework

Text references. Chapter 2.

Top tips. A basic knowledge of the structure and processes of the IASCF would probably be enough to earn a pass mark, but parts of this question require a bit of thought. To earn a pass mark break each question down into its components and write a few lies on each. For example, in part (b) most people will sketch out the standard setting process, but make sure you also include a sentence or two on enforcing and on supplementing standards.

Easy marks. Part (a) is very straightforward and will earn you a maximum of ten easy marks. In part (b), five easy marks can be picked up by remembering the standard setting process.

Examiner's comments. Most answers were weak and very short. Enforcement issues were mostly ignored.

Marking scheme

		Marks
(a)	1 mark per relevant point to a **maximum**	10
(b)	1 mark per relevant point to a **maximum**	10
(c)	1 mark per relevant point to a **maximum**	5
	Maximum for question	**25**

(a)   Structure and function of IASCF

⇩   Appoints
↑   Reports to
☐   Advises
....   Membership links

IASCF International Accounting Standards Committee Foundation

The Trustees of the IASCF oversee the whole organisation. They arrange funding, appoint the IASB, IFRIC and SAC, and set the agenda for the IASB. The aims of the IASCF are:

* to develop a single set of high quality global accounting standards,
* to promote the use of these standards, and
* to bring about convergence of national and international accounting standards.

IASB International Accounting Standards Board

The IASB develops and issues International Financial Reporting Standards in its own right. It reports to the IASCF. Members of the IASB are appointed for their technical competence and independence.

IFRIC International Financial Reporting Interpretations Committee

IFRIC provides rapid guidance on accounting issues where divergent or unacceptable treatments are likely to arise. It reports to the IASB. Membership of IFRIC is drawn from a diverse range of geographical and professional backgrounds.

SAC Standards Advisory Council

The SAC provides a forum for organisations or individuals to take part in the standard setting process. It advises the IASB on agenda decisions, priorities, and its views on standard setting projects. Membership is drawn from a diverse range of geographical and professional backgrounds.

Advisory Committees

These are set up to advise the IASB on specific issues.

National Standard Setters

Although the IASCF is an independent organisation it works closely with national standard setters. The IASB, SAC and advisory committees draw heavily on personnel from national bodies. In return, many national standard setters incorporate IFRS's into their own accounting standards.

(b) **Setting, enforcing and supplementing standards**

Setting standards

The IASCF sets the agenda for producing accounting standards, but the IASB produces and issues these standards. The process is as follows:

1   The IASCF, taking into account advice from the SAC and others, identifies an issue requiring an accounting standard.

2   The IASB sets up an Advisory Committee to investigate the issue and report back to the IASB.

3   The IASB issues a Discussion Draft for public comment. A Discussion Draft needs a simple majority to be issued. Comments must be received within ninety days.

4   The IASB issues an Exposure Draft; comments must be received within ninety days. The Exposure Draft must be approved by 8 of the 14 members of the IASB.

5   The IASB issues an International Financial Reporting Standard on the internet. An IFRS must be approved by 8 of the 14 members of the IASB.

Public discussion is encouraged. The basis of conclusions for ED's and IFRS's are published, along with dissenting opinions. Most meetings of the IASB, IFRIC and SAC are open to the public, and they are exploring ways of using technology to make public access easier globally.

Enforcing standards

The IASB has no legal power to enforce adoption or compliance with standards, but enforcement of a sort is achieved (more or less successfully) in a number of ways:

•   Quoted companies within the European Union must comply with IFRS's, but it is up to each member state to police compliance. Some countries have a formal process to review published financial statements and punish non-compliance (for example the Financial Reporting Review Panel in the UK), but this is not universal. To a certain extent the onus is on the auditors to police compliance, but auditing standards themselves are not globally consistent.

- Companies using IFRS to obtain cross-border listings are required to have their financial statements audited in accordance with International Auditing Standards. This will help to ensure that these companies are complying with IFRS.

- Many countries are bringing their own standards into line with IFRS's, but again policing of national standards is inconsistent.

Supplementing standards

The IFRIC issues interpretations when divergent or unacceptable accounting treatments arise, whether through misinterpreting an existing standard or on an important issue not yet covered by a standard. Financial statements must comply with all of these interpretations if they claim to comply with International Financial Reporting Standards.

(c)   Has the move towards global accounting standards been successful?

On a practical level the move towards global accounting standards has been one of the accounting successes of the last decade. The standards themselves have improved, with the elimination of contradictory alternatives and the creation of an open and independent standard setting organisation. This in turn has lead to greater acceptance of these standards, culminating in 2005 with the adoption of IFRS for consolidated accounts by all quoted companies in the European Union and in many other countries. The on-going project with the International Organisation of Securities Commissions will encourage the use of IFRS for cross-border listings, and could even lead to the acceptance of IFRS in the USA.

However, as mentioned earlier, there is no global system of enforcement, and so it is too early to say if IFRS are being adopted properly.

Some countries with their own highly developed accounting standards see the adoption of IFRS as a backward step, whereas other countries see IFRS as unnecessarily complicated.

There is also the assumption that the globalisation of accounting standards is a good thing. Recent developments in IFRS have focussed on quoted companies in the western world; they may not be suitable for all types and sizes of business organisation, or for all stages of economic development.

4 Winger

Text reference. Chapter 3.

Top tips. As with consolidated accounts questions, a question on the preparation of a single company's accounts needs a methodical approach. Lay out proformas and fill the numbers in gradually by systematically working through the question.

(a)   WINGER
INCOME STATEMENT FOR THE YEAR ENDED 31 MARCH 20X1

	$'000
Sales revenues (358,450 – 27,000)	331,450
Cost of sales (W1)	(208,550)
Gross profit	122,900
Distribution expenses	(28,700)
Administration expenses	(15,000)
Profit on disposal of land and buildings (95,000 – 80,000)	15,000
Loss on abandonment of research project	(30,000)
Finance cost (W3)	(11,200)
Profit before tax	53,000
Income tax (15,000 – 2,200)	(12,800)
Profit for the year	40,200

ANSWERS

**These items could be included under the appropriate cost heading and then disclosed as exceptional items in the notes to the income statement.

STATEMENT OF CHANGES IN EQUITY

	Share capital $'000	Retained earnings $'000	Total $'000
Opening	150,000	101,600*	251,600
Profit for the year	-	40,200	40,200
Dividends paid	–	(12,000)	(12,000)
Closing	150,000	129,800	279,800

* Opening retained earnings

$71,600 from the trial balance, plus $30,000 from the revaluation reserve.

(b)   BALANCE SHEET AS AT 31 MARCH 20X1

	$'000	$'000
Assets		
Tangible non current assets		
Property (200,000 – 6,000 (W2))		194,000
Plant and equipment (W4)		160,000
		354,000
Current assets		
Inventories (28,240 + 22,500 (W1))	50,740	
Trade receivables (55,000 – 27,000 (W1))	28,000	
Cash	10,660	
		89,400
Total assets		443,400
Equity and liabilities		
Equity		
Equity shares 25c each		150,000
Retained earnings (see (a))		129,800
		279,800
Non-current liabilities		
Leasing liabilities (W5)	47,200	
8% loan notes	50,000	
		97,200
Current liabilities		
Trade and other accounts payable (W6)	51,400	
Income tax	15,000	
		66,400
Total equity and liabilities		443,400

Workings

1	Cost of sales	$'000
	Per question	185,050
	Less sale/return goods (27,000 × 100/120)	(22,500)
	Add depreciation (W2)	46,000
		208,550

120

2	*Depreciation*	$'000
	Building (100,000 ÷ 50)	2,000
	Heating system (20,000 ÷ 10)	2,000
	Lifts (30,000 ÷ 15)	2,000
		6,000
	Leased plant (80,000 × 20%)	16,000
	Owned plant (154,800 – 34,800) × 20%	24,000
		46,000

3	*Finance costs*	$'000
	Loan interest (50,000 × 8%)	4,000
	Finance lease (80,000 – 20,000) × 12%	7,200
		11,200

4	*Plant and equipment*	$'000
	Cost: owned plant	154,800
	leased plant	80,000
		234,800
	Depreciation: owned plant (34,800 + 24,000 (W2))	(58,800)
	leased plant (80,000 × 20%)	(16,000)
		160,000

5	*Leasing liabilities*	$'000
	Total capital due	80,000
	Less amount paid	(20,000)
		60,000
	Add accrued interest (60,000 × 12%)	7,200
	Total creditor	67,200
	Due within one year	20,000
	Due after one year	47,200

6	*Trade and other payables*	$'000
	Trial balance	29,400
	Lease creditor (W5)	20,000
	Accrued loan interest (4,000 – 2,000)	2,000
		51,400

(c)   Companies often used to justify the non-depreciation of buildings on several grounds, including:

(i)   That the current value of the buildings was **higher than cost**.

(ii)   That the level of **maintenance** meant that no deterioration or consumption had taken place.

(iii)   That the depreciation charge would **not be material**.

However, IAS 16 requires the **depreciable amount** of an asset to be charged against profit over its useful life. Using the cost model, the depreciable amount is obtained by comparing the cost of the asset with its **estimated residual value** at the end of its useful life. By requiring the residual value to be estimated at **current prices**, the standard removes any **potential inflationary effects** which would otherwise increase the residual value and hence reduce, even to zero, the depreciable amount. This overcomes the argument that high residual values remove the need for depreciation, unless the value of a second-hand asset has greater value than the same asset new – an unlikely proposition.

The argument regarding **immateriality** of the depreciation charge because of a long economic life may have some validity. Although it is not addressed directly by IAS 16, accounting standards generally only apply to **material items,** according to the *Framework.* However, under this principle, it will be necessary to consider not only each year's potential depreciation charge, but also the **accumulated depreciation** that would need to be provided against the asset. Over time, this latter amount would inevitably become material and the 'long life' argument would cease to hold.

Thus, Winger's **previous policy** was not appropriate and the change to depreciate assets was necessary to comply with IAS 16.

The directors' treatment of the deferred development expenditure is also incorrect. It needs to be written off because its **value** has become **impaired due to adverse legislation, not a change of accounting policy**. It now has no effective value. There has therefore not been a change of accounting policy, so it cannot be treated as a prior period adjustment. It must be written off to the income statement.

4 Question with analysis: Winger

(a)

WINGER

INCOME STATEMENT FOR THE YEAR ENDED 31 MARCH 20X1

> 't forget to
> uct the sale or
> rn items, as
> could be
> rned on
> /X1

	$'000
Sales revenues (358,450 – 27,000)	331,450
Cost of sales **(W1)**	(208,550)
Gross profit	122,900
Distribution expenses	(28,700)
Administration expenses	(15,000)
Profit on disposal of land and buildings** (95,000 – 80,000)	15,000
Loss on abandonment of research project***	(30,000)
Finance cost **(W3)**	(11,200)
Profit before tax	53,000
Income tax (15,000 – 2,200)	(12,800)
Profit for the year	40,200

**These items could be included under the appropriate cost heading and then disclosed as exceptional items in the notes to the income statement.

STATEMENT OF CHANGES IN EQUITY

		Share capital	Retained earnings	Total
		$'000	$'000	$'000
Opening		150,000	101,600*	251,600
Profit for the year		-	40,200	40,200
Dividends	Paid	–	(12,000)	(12,000)
Closing		150,000	129,800	279,800

* *Opening retained earnings*

$71,600 from the trial balance, plus $30,000 from revaluation reserve.

**   The trial balance shows $45,000 profit on disposal of land and buildings. We are told that the property had an original cost of $50m and a carrying value of $80m. Therefore the revaluation reserve held $30m prior to the disposal. It is not correct to add this $30m to the profit on sale, making $45m. However, the gain is now realised, so it should be transferred from the revaluation reserve to retained earnings.

***   The loss on abandonment of the research project cannot be shown as a prior year adjustment; it is shown as an expense in the current year's income statement.

(b)   BALANCE SHEET AS AT 31 MARCH 20X1

	$'000	$'000
Assets		
Tangible non current assets		
Property (200,000 – 6,000 **(W2)**)		194,000
Plant and equipment **(W4)**		160,000
		354,000
Current assets		
Inventories (28,240 + 22,500 **(W1)**)	50,740	
Trade receivables (55,000 – 27,000 **(W1)**)	28,000	
Cash	10,660	
		89,400
Total assets		443,400
Equity and liabilities		
Equity		
Equity shares 25c each		150,000
Retained earnings (see (a))		129,800
		279,800
Non-current liabilities		
Leasing liabilities **(W5)**	47,200	
8% loan notes	50,000	
		97,200
Current liabilities		
Trade and other accounts payable **(W6)**	51,400	
Income tax	15,000	
		66,400
Total equity and liabilities		443,400

As note (e) in the question →

Workings

1	Cost of sales		$'000
	Per question		185,050
	Less sale/return goods (27,000 × 100/120)		(22,500)
	Add depreciation **(W2)**		46,000
			208,550

2	Depreciation	$'000
	Building (100,000 ÷ 50)	2,000
	Heating system (20,000 ÷ 10)	2,000
	Lifts (30,000 ÷ 15)	2,000
		6,000
	Leased plant (80,000 × 20%)	16,000
	Owned plant **(154,800 – 34,800)** × 20%	24,000
		46,000

Reducing balance method →

3	Finance costs	$'000
	Loan interest (50,000 × 8%)	4,000
	Finance lease **(80,000 – 20,000)** × 12%	7,200
		11,200

> Interest rate of 12% is given in part (b). It must be calculated on outstanding balance

BPP LEARNING MEDIA

4	Plant and equipment	$'000
	Cost: owned plant	154,800
	leased plant	80,000
		234,800
	Depreciation: owned plant (34,800 + 24,000 **(W2)**)	(58,800)
	leased plant (80,000 × 20%)	(16,000)
		160,000

5	Leasing liabilities	$'000
	Total capital due	80,000
	Less amount paid	(20,000)
		60,000
	Add accrued interest (60,000 × 12%)	7,200
	Total creditor	67,200
	Due within one year	20,000
	Due after one year	47,200

al interest
a (W3) less
$2m

6	Trade and other payables	$'000
	Trial balance	29,400
	Lease creditor **(W5)**	20,000
	Accrued loan interest (4,000 – 2,000)	2,000
		51,400

(c) Companies often used to justify the non-depreciation of buildings on several grounds, including:

(i) That the current value of the buildings was **higher than cost**.

(ii) That the level of **maintenance** meant that no deterioration or consumption had taken place.

(iii) That the depreciation charge would **not be material**.

However, IAS 16 requires the **depreciable amount** of an asset to be charged against profit over its useful life. Using the cost model, the depreciable amount is obtained by comparing the cost of the asset with its **estimated residual value** at the end of its useful life. By requiring the residual value to be estimated at **current prices**, the standard removes any **potential inflationary effects** which would otherwise increase the residual value and hence reduce, even to zero, the depreciable amount. This overcomes the argument that high residual values remove the need for depreciation, unless the value of a second-hand asset has greater value than the same asset new – an unlikely proposition.

The argument regarding **immateriality** of the depreciation charge because of a long economic life may have some validity. Although it is not addressed directly by IAS 16, accounting standards generally only apply to **material items,** according to the *Framework*. However, under this principle, it will be necessary to consider not only each year's potential depreciation charge, but also the **accumulated depreciation** that would need to be provided against the asset. Over time, this latter amount would inevitably become material and the 'long life' argument would cease to hold.

Thus, Winger's **previous policy** was not appropriate and the change to depreciate assets was necessary to comply with IAS 16.

The directors' treatment of the deferred development expenditure is also incorrect. It needs to be written off because its **value** has become **impaired due to adverse legislation, not a change of accounting policy.** It now has no effective value. There has therefore not been a change of accounting policy, so it cannot be treated as a prior period adjustment. It must be written off to the income statement.

5 Harrington

Text reference. Chapter 3.

Top tips. There is a lot to get through in this question. Work through the adjustments methodically, but keep an eye on the time. Make sure that you attempt all three statements.

Easy marks. If you work methodically through the information, you can easily obtain 13 marks.

Examiner's comments. Most candidates answered this question well. However many candidates ignored part (b).

Marking scheme

		Marks
(a)	Restated income statement	
	Sales revenue	1
	Cost of sales	5
	Operating expenses	1
	Investment income	1
	Loan interest	1
	Income tax	2
	Available	**11**
	Maximum	**9**
(b)	Statement of changes in equity	
	Brought forward figures	1
	Rights issue	1
	(restated) profit for the financial year	1
	Surplus on land and buildings	2
	Transfer to realised profits	1
	Dividend paid	1
	Available	**7**
	Maximum	**6**
(c)	Balance sheet	
	Land and buildings	1
	Plant	1
	Investments	1
	Inventory and trade receivables	1
	Bank and trade payables	1
	Accrued loan interest	1
	Current tax	1
	10% loan note	1
	Deferred tax	1
	Share capital and premium	1
	Revaluation reserve	1
	Retained earnings	1
	Available	**12**
	Maximum	**10**
	Maximum for question	**25**

(a) INCOME STATEMENT FOR THE YEAR ENDING 31 MARCH 20X5

	$'000
Revenue (13,700 – 300 proceeds)	13,400
Cost of sales (W1)	(8,910)
Gross profit	4,490
Investment income ($1.2m × 10%)	120
Operating expenses	(2,400)
Finance costs ($500m × 10%)	(50)
Profit before tax	2,160
Taxation (W5)	(385)
Profit for the year	1,775

(b) STATEMENT OF CHANGES IN EQUITY FOR THE YEAR ENDING 31 MARCH 20X5

	Share Capital $'000	Share Premium $'000	Revaluation Reserve $'000	Retained Earnings $'000	Total $'000
Opening (W6)	1,600	40	-	2,990	4,630
Share issue (W6)	400	560	-	-	960
Revaluation (W4)	-	-	1,800	-	1,800
Excess depreciation (W4)	-	-	(80)	80	-
Profit for the year	-	-	-	1,775	1,775
Dividends paid	-	-	-	(500)	(500)
Closing	2,000	600	1,720	4,345	8,665

(c) BALANCE SHEET AS AT 31 MARCH 20X5

	$'000
Assets	
Non-current assets	
Property, plant and equipment (W4)	8,060
Investments ($1.2m × 110%)	1,320
	9,380
Current assets	
Inventories	1,750
Trade receivables	2,450
Bank	350
	4,550
Total assets	13,930
Equity and liabilities	
Equity	
Share Capital	2,000
Share Premium	600
Revaluation reserve	1,720
Retained earnings	4,345
	8,665
Non-current liabilities	
Loan note	500
Deferred tax ($1.4m × 25%)	350
	850
Current liabilities	
Trade payables	4,130
Accrued Loan Note interest ($50m charged - $25m paid)	25
Income Tax	260
	4,415
Total equity and liabilities	13,930

Workings

1	Cost of sales		$'000
	From question		9,200
	Less: profit on disposal (W2)		(30)
	Less: capitalisation (W3)		(1,000)
	Add: depreciation (W4)		740
			8,910

2	Disposal		$'000
	Proceeds (transferred from sales)		300
	Carrying value (900 – 630)		(270)
	Profit on disposal		30

3	Capitalisation		$'000
	Total costs incurred (150+800+65+20)		9,200
	Less: rectification costs (10+25)		(35)
			1,000

4   *Property, plant and equipment*

		Land $'000		Buildings $'000		Plant $'000	Total $'000
Cost	Opening	1,000		4,000		5,200	
	Additions	-	W3	1,000		-	
	Disposals	-		-	W2	(900)	
	Revaluation	200		800		-	
	Closing	1,200		5,800		4,300	
Depreciation	Opening	-		800		3,130	
	Charge	-		290		450	
	Disposals	-		-	W2	(630)	
	Revaluation	-		(800)		-	
	Closing	-		290		2,950	
Carrying value		1,200		5,510		1,350	8,060

Total revaluation   200+800+800 = $1,800,000
Total depreciation   290+450 = $740,000

Buildings

Revaluation of building excludes the addition during the year.

Depreciation: $5.8m/20 years = $290,000

Excess depreciation on revaluation

		$'000
Revalued depreciation	$4.8m / 20 years	240
Historic cost depreciation	$3.2m / 20 years	160
Excess		80

Depreciation on plant

		$'000
Cost		4,300
Cumulative depreciation	(3,130 – 630)	(2,500)
Balance		1,800
25% depreciation		450

5   *Income tax*

		$'000	$'000
Estimate for current year	(current liability)		260
Under-provision for prior year			55
Deferred tax			
Provision required ($1.4m × 25%)	(non-current liability)	350	
Opening provision		(280)	
Increase			70
			385

6   *Share issue*

The 1 for 4 rights issue means that there are five shares in issue at the year-end for every four in issue at the start. Therefore the opening capital must have been $2m × $^4/_5$ = $1.6m.

	Capital $'000	Premium $'000
Opening balance		
6.4m shares @ 25 cents each	1,600	40
1 for 4 rights issue at 60 cents		
Capital: 1.6m shares @ 25 cents	400	-
Premium: 1.6m shares @ 35 cents	-	560
	2,000	600

(The opening share premium is a balancing figure.)

6 Petra

Text reference. Chapters 7 and 18.

Top tips. There are five marks for two straight forward EPS calculations in part (c). Do these straight after Part (a) otherwise you might run out of time.

The main complications in Part (a) involve the treatment of agency sales and the treatment of tangible and intangible non-current assets.

Easy marks. The EPS calculations were relatively easy marks and, once you had the proformas down, there were plenty of marks to be had on the income statement and balance sheet.

Examiners comments. This was a familiar question requiring the preparation of an income statement, balance sheet and two EPS calculations.

The main errors were:

- Failure to understand the nature of the agency sale.

- Errors in calculating cost of sales – such as deducting depreciation and impairment and deducting closing inventory twice.

- Errors in calculating the tax charge, including dealing with the movement on deferred tax.

Marking scheme

			Marks
(a)	Income statement		1
	Revenue		1
	Cost of sales 1 mark per each item	Maximum	6
	Commission		1
	Distribution and administration		1
	Interest expense		1
	Income tax		2
		Available	12
		Maximum	10
(b)	Balance sheet		
	Development costs		1
	Property, plant and equipment (held for continuing use)		2
	Plant held for sale (1 mark for separate presentation)		2
	Inventories		1
	Trade receivables and cash bank		1
	Ordinary shares and share premium		1
	Retained earnings		1
	6% loan note		1
	Deferred tax		1
	Trade payables		1
	Current tax		1
		Available	13
		Maximum	10
(c)	Basic EPS		2
	Diluted EPS		3
		Maximum	5
		Maximum for question	25

(a)   INCOME STATEMENT FOR THE YEAR ENDING 30 SEPTEMBER 20X5

	$'000
Revenue (W1)	185,800
Cost of sales (W1)	(128,100)
Gross profit	57,700
Other income (W1)	1,000
Distribution costs	(17,000)
Administration expenses	(18,000)
Finance costs ($50m × 6%)	(3,000)
Profit before tax	20,700
Income tax expense (W5)	(7,600)
Profit for the year	13,100

BPP
LEARNING MEDIA

(b) BALANCE SHEET AS AT 30 SEPTEMBER 20X5

	$'000	$'000
Assets		
Non-current assets		
Property, plant and equipment (W2)		106,000
Intangible assets (W4)		18,000
		124,000
Current assets		
Inventories	21,300	
Trade receivables	24,000	
Bank	11,000	
	56,300	
Non-current asset held for sale (W3)	6,900	
		63,200
Total assets		187,200
Equity and liabilities		
Equity		
Share Capital		40,000
Share Premium		12,000
Retained earnings (34,000 + 13,100)		47,100
		99,100
Non-current liabilities		
Loan note	50,000	
Deferred tax	17,600	
		67,600
Current liabilities		
Trade payables	15,000	
Accrued Loan Note interest ($50m × 6% × $^6/_{12}$)	1,500	
Current tax	4,000	
		20,500
Total equity and liabilities		187,200

Workings

1   *Revenues and cost of sales*

	Revenue	Cost of Sales
	$'000	$'000
From TB	197,800	114,000
Commission sales	(12,000)	-
Cost of commission sales	-	(8,000)
Revenues due to Sharma	-	(3,000)
Depreciation on property (W2a)	-	2,000
Depreciation on plant (W2b)	-	6,000
Loss on surplus asset (W3)	-	3,100
Impairment of intangible (W4)	-	14,000
	185,800	128,100

Petra earns $1m commission on the sales undertaken for Sharma. This is shown as other income (although it could also be included within revenue). Petra never owns or controls the goods that are being sold so the cost of these items should not be included in Petra's income statement.

2   *Property, plant and equipment*

	$'000
Property (W2a)	82,000
Plant (W2b)	24,000
	106,000

ANSWERS

2a Property

		$'000	$'000
Cost			100,000
Depreciation	Opening	16,000	
	Charge (100 -40) / 30 years	2,000	
			(18,000)
			82,000

2b Plant and equipment

	Cost $'000	Depreciation $'000
From TB	66,000	26,000
Available for sale (See W3)	(16,000)	(6,000)
	50,000	20,000
Depreciation ($50m - $20m) ×20%	-	6,000
	50,000	26,000

Carrying value $24m

The surplus asset is removed from non-current assets and shown as a current asset at the lower of its carrying value and net realisable value. The loss on reclassification is charged to the income statement, but the asset will no longer be depreciated.

3 Non-current asset held for sale

	$'000
Cost transferred from non-current assets	16,000
Less depreciation	(6,000)
Original carrying value	10,000
New carrying value ($7.5m × 92%)	6,900
Loss recognised	3,100

4 Development expenditure

	$'000
Cost	40,000
Less amortisation	(8,000)
Opening carrying value	32,000
Impairment charge (balancing figure)	(14,000)
Impaired closing carrying value	18,000

5 Taxation

	$'000
Tax on current year's profits	4,000
Under provision in prior year	1,000
Increase in deferred tax ($17.6m - $15m)	2,600
	7,600

(c) Earnings per share

Basic

Earnings	$13,1000,000	= 8.2 cents
Number of shares in issue ($40m ÷ $0.25)	160,000,000	

Fully diluted

Earnings	$130,000,000	= 7.4 cents
Number of shares in issue (see below)	176,000,000	

Working

Existing shares		160,000,000
Dilutive shares		
Number of shares to be issued		24,000,000
Proceeds of share option	$7,200,000	
Number of shares this would buy	$7.2m ÷ $0.90 =	(8,000,000)
Dilutive shares issued for free		16,000,000
Total shares for diluted EPS calculation		176,000,000

7 Allgone

Text reference. Chapter 3.

Top tips. As well as examining you on the format and content of the financial statements, this question also tests your knowledge of six specific situations.

As always, be methodical and don't get bogged down in the detail.

Easy marks. Provided you are methodical, you should obtain at least 13 marks quite easily just by using the proformas and slotting in the figures that are straightforward.

Examiner's comments. Many candidates showed weakness in areas already examined in Paper 1.1 e.g. calculation and accrual of interest and depreciation on revalued assets. Also too many candidates did not produce a statement of changes in equity.

Marking scheme

		Marks
(a)	Income statement	
	Sales revenue	1
	Cost of sales	3
	Operating costs	1
	Finance costs	2
	Taxation	2
	Available	**9**
	Maximum	**7**
(b)	Changes in equity	
	Unrealised gains and losses 1 each	2
	Prior year adjustment	1
	Depreciation adjustment	2
	Maximum	**5**
(c)	Balance sheet	
	Software	1
	Property, plant and equipment	3
	Investments	1
	Inventory	1
	Trade receivables and payables	1
	In substance loan	1
	Share capital	1
	Revaluation reserve	2
	Retained earnings	1
	Non-current liabilities	1
	Accrued finance costs	2
	Income tax provision	2
	Available	**17**
	Maximum	**13**
	Maximum for question	**25**

(a)   ALLGONE: INCOME STATEMENT FOR THE YEAR ENDED 31 MARCH 20X6

	$'000
Sales revenue (236,200 – 8,000 (W1))	228,200
Cost of sales (W2)	(147,000)
Gross profit	81,200
Operating expenses (W3)	(15,400)
Finance costs (W4)	(5,850)
Profit before tax	59,950
Income tax expense (W5)	(13,100)
Profit for the year	46,850

(b)   ALLGONE: STATEMENT OF CHANGES IN EQUITY FOR THE YEAR TO 31 MARCH 20X6

	Share Capital $'000	Revaluation Reserve $'000	Retained Earnings $'000	Total $'000
Opening balance as previously stated	60,000	5,000	4,350	69,350
Correction of prior period error	–	–	(32,000)	(32,000)
Opening balance as restated	60,000	5,000	(27,650)	37,350
Revaluation surplus: Land & buildings (W6)	–	40,000	–	40,000
Investments (W9)	–	(1,200)	–	(1,200)
Transfer of depreciation on revaluation (W7)	–	(1,000)	1,000	–
Profit for the year	–	–	46,850	46,850
Closing	60,000	42,800	20,200	123,000

(c)   ALLGONE: BALANCE SHEET AS AT 31 MARCH 20X6

	$'000
Assets	
Non-current assets	
Property, plant and equipment (W6)	177,000
Investments (W9)	10,800
	187,800
Current assets	
Inventories (W2)	14,300
Trade receivables	23,000
	37,300
Total assets	225,100
Equity and liabilities	
Equity	
Share capital	60,000
Revaluation reserve	42,800
Retained earnings	20,200
	123,000
Non-current liabilities	
Preference shares	20,000
Loan note	40,000
Deferred tax (W5)	4,800
	64,800
Current liabilities	
Trade payables	15,200
Bank overdraft	350
Accruals (W10)	2,450
Funders Bank (W1)	8,000
Income tax	11,300
	37,300
Total equity and liabilities	225,100

Prior period error

The fraud took place before the employee left in January 20X5, but was not discovered until the current accounting period. This means that the prior period financial statements were misstated. To correct prior period errors, IAS 8 requires all prior period financial statements to be restated correctly. The correction must not be included in the current year's income statement. IAS 1 also requires the cumulative correction to be reported as a restatement of the opening balance on retained earnings in the statement of changes in equity.

Workings

1   *Sale to Funders Bank*

The substance of this transaction is a short-term loan. This is shown by the Bank's option to demand repurchase within one month of the year-end at cost plus $250,000, which means that Allgone still bears the risks and benefits of these items. Therefore, the revenue ($8m) and related cost of sales ($6m) will be removed from the income statement. The balance sheet will show a loan of $8m, and the inventories will be shown at their original cost of $6m. The $250,000 is a finance cost which will be charged to the income statement. In the absence of detailed information about the timing of the initial transaction, this answer assumes that the full $250,000 should be charged in this year's income statement.

2   *Cost of sales and closing inventories*

	$'000	$'000
Purchases		127,850
Opening inventories		19,450
Closing inventories:		
From Note (i)	8,500	
Less NRV allowance (500 – 300)	(200)	
Add cost of inventories "sold" to Funders Bank	6,000	
Value of closing inventory		(14,300)
		133,000
Depreciation (W8)		14,000
		147,000

3   *Operating expenses*

	$'000
Operating expenses from the trial balance	12,400
Depreciation of land and buildings (W6)	3,000
	15,400

4   *Finance costs*

	$'000
Loans: $40m \times {}^9/_{12} \times 12\%$	3,600
Preference shares: $1m paid + $1m accrued	2,000
Accrued finance charge to Funders Bank	250
	5,850

5   *Income tax expense*

	$'000	$'000
Income tax expense from the question		11,300
Deferred tax: brought forward	3,000	
carried down ($16m \times 30\%$)	4,800	
increase		1,800
Tax charge in the income statement		13,100

6   Property, plant and equipment

	Land $'000	Buildings $'000	Plant & Eqmt $'000	Software $'000	Total $'000
Cost or valuation					
Opening cost	20,000	80,000	84,300	10,000	194,300
Revaluation	5,000	25,000	-	-	30,000
Closing	25,000	105,000	84,300	10,000	224,300
Depreciation					
Opening	-	10,000	24,300	6,000	40,300
Revaluation (W7)	-	(10,000)	-	-	(10,000)
Charge for the year (W7 & W8)	-	3,000	12,000	2,000	17,000
Closing	-	3,000	36,300	8,000	47,300
Carrying value	25,000	102,000	48,000	2,000	177,000

Total revaluation surplus: $5m + $25m + $10m = $40m.

7   Depreciation and revaluation of the buildings

At revaluation the property had been owned for 5 years out of an expected useful life of 40 years. The accumulated depreciation on the buildings was $80m × $5/40 = $10m. This will be eliminated on revaluation.

The new valuation of $105m will be depreciated over the remaining 35 year useful life of the asset, giving an annual charge of $3m. This is charged to operating expenses.

The $1m difference between the revalued charge and the historic cost charge is adjusted for by a transfer of $1m per annum from the revaluation reserve to retained earnings. This is reported in the **statement of changes in equity.**

8   Depreciation included in cost of sales

	$'000
Plant & equipment [(20% reducing balance) (84,300 − 24,300) × 20%]	12,000
Software (sum of the digits over 5 years) ($3/15 × $10m)	2,000
	14,000

9   Investments

	Asset $'000	Revaluation $'000
Opening valuation and related revaluation reserve @ $2.50	12,000	5,000
Change (balancing figure)	(1,200)	(1,200)
Closing valuation and related revaluation reserve @ $2.25	10,800	3,800

IAS 39 paragraph 55 (b) states that gains and losses on fair valuing available-for-sale financial assets shall be recognised directly in equity and reported in the statement of changes in equity.

10   Accruals

	$'000
Interest on loan notes (W4)	1,200
Preference share dividend (W4)	1,000
Accrued finance charge to Funders Bank	250
	2,450

8 Tadeon

Top tips. Start by working through (i) to (v). Read each requirement twice and then do neat workings which the marker can read. If you cannot do one of these, leave it.

Easy marks. The actual financial statements were easy once you had worked through the issues which needed to be brought in. You may have had trouble with the deferred tax but the depreciation and suspense account workings were easy. Don't spend time on any issues which you don't understand or can't do, just move on.

		Marks
(a)	Income statement	
	revenue	1
	cost of sales	1
	operating expenses	1
	investment income	1
	finance costs	3
	income tax expense	3
	available	10
	maximum	**8**
(b)	Balance sheet	
	property, plant and equipment	3
	investment	1
	inventory and trade receivables	1
	share capital and premium	3
	revaluation reserve	2
	retained earnings (including 1 mark for the dividend)	2
	loan note	2
	deferred tax	1
	lease obligation (1 for current, 1 for long-term)	2
	trade payables and overdraft	1
	accrued lease finance costs	1
	income tax payable	1
	available	20
	maximum	**17**
	Maximum for question	**25**

(a) TADEON
INCOME STATEMENT FOR THE YEAR ENDED 30 SEPTEMBER 2006

	$'000
Revenue	277,800
Cost of sales (118,000 + 26,000 (W1))	(144,000)
Gross profit	133,800
Investment income	2,000
Operating expenses (40,000 + 1,200 (W3))	(41,200)
Finance cost (2,750 (W2) + 1,500 (W3))	(4,250)
Profit before tax	90,350
Income tax expense (W5)	(36,800)
Profit for the period	53,550

(b) TADEON
BALANCE SHEET AS AT 30 SEPTEMBER 2006

	$'000	$'000
Non-current assets		
Property, plant and equipment (W1)		299,000
Investments		42,000
		341,000
Current assets		
Inventories	33,300	
Trade receivables	53,500	
		86,800
Total assets		427,800
Equity and liabilities		
Equity		
Equity shares (150,000 + 50,000 (W6))		200,000
Share premium (W6)		28,000
Revaluation reserve (20,000 (W1) – 4,000 (W5))		16,000
Retained earnings (18,600 + 53,550 – 30,000 (W6))		42,150
		286,150
Non-current liabilities		
Amount due under finance lease (W3)	10,500	
Loan note (W2)	51,750	
Deferred tax (W5)	14,800	
		77,050
Current liabilities		
Amount due under finance lease (W3)	6,000	
Trade payables	18,700	
Income tax payable	38,000	
Overdraft	1,900	
		64,600
Total equity and liabilities		427,800

Workings

1 Property, plant and equipment

	Property $'000	Plant & equipment $'000	Vehicle $'000	Total $'000
Cost	225,000	181,000		406,000
Accumulated depreciation	(36,000)	(85,000)		(121,000)
Addition			20,000	20,000
Current year depreciation	(9,000)	(12,000)	(5,000)	(26,000)
Revaluation (W4)	20,000	-	-	20,000
	200,000	84,000	15,000	299,000

2 Loan note

	$'000
Proceeds	50,000
Interest @ 5.5%	2,750
Interest paid	(1,000)
Carrying value	51,750

3 *Finance lease*

	$'000
Fair value of asset	20,000
Deposit paid	(5,000)
	15,000
Interest to 30 September 2006	1,500
Balance at 1 October 2006	16,500
Amount due within one year	(6,000)
Amount due after one year	10,500

Therefore $1.2m is charged to operating lease rentals and $1.5m to finance costs on the finance lease.

4 *Revaluation*

	$'000
Carrying value of leasehold at 1 October 2005	189,000
Depreciation to 30 September 2006 (225,000/25)	(9,000)
	180,000
Revaluation	20,000
Carrying value at 30 September 2006	200,000
Revaluation reserve balance (20,000 − 4,000 (W5))	16,000

5 *Income tax expense*

	$'000
Current year tax charge	38,000
Transfer from deferred tax ((54,000 × 20%) − 12,000)	(1,200)
Income statement charge	36,800
Deferred tax balance (74,000 × 20%)	14,800

Note

Deferred tax on revaluation (20,000 × 20%) charged to revaluation reserve	4,000

6 *Suspense account*

	$'000
Dividend paid (750m shares @ 80c × 5%)	(30,000)
Rights issue – shares (250m × 20c)	50,000
Rights issue – premium (250m ×12c)	30,000
Issue costs – to share premium account	(2,000)
Balance on suspense account	48,000
Net amount to share premium (30,000 − 2,000)	28,000

9 Derringdo

Grant

(a)   *Liability*

There are two issues here:

1   Should a capital grant be treated as deferred income in the financial statements, and
2   Should a liability be recognised for the potential repayment of the grant.

Derringdo has credited the $240,000 grant to a deferred income account which is shown as a liability in the balance sheet. It is then released to the income statement over the ten year life of the related asset. However, the framework states that a liability should only be recognised if there is a probable outflow of economic benefits. This is not true for a grant; under normal circumstances the grant will not have to be repaid and so a liability does not exist.

This example is complicated by the possibility of having to repay the grant if the asset is sold. At the balance sheet date the asset has not been sold, and so there is no past event to give rise to a liability. Derringdo intends to keep the asset for its ten year useful life. Nor can it be classified as a contingent liability. Under IAS 37 the "uncertain future event" that creates a contingent liability must be "not wholly within the control of the entity". In this case Derringdo will make the decision to keep or sell the asset.

Following on from the above, the framework would not permit the grant to be shown as a liability. Instead the grant would be claimed as income in the year that it was received (provided that there was no intention to sell the asset within the four year claw-back period). However, the treatment of the grant as deferred income is in accordance with IAS 20 *Accounting for Government Grants*.

(b)   *Extracts*

Company policy. This complies with one of the two alternatives in IAS 20

INCOME STATEMENT	$
Operating expenses	
Depreciation charge (W1)	34,000
Release of grant (W2)	(12,000)
	22,000

BALANCE SHEET	$'000
Non-current assets	
Property, plant and equipment (W1)	766,000
Non-current liabilities	
Deferred income (W2)	24,000
Current liabilities	
Deferred income (W2)	204,000
	228,000

Workings

1	Property, plant, equipment	$'000
	Cost (gross, excluding grant)	800,000
	Depreciation (10 years straight line, 15% residual value for 6 months	
	$800,000 \times 85\% \times 10\% \times {}^{6}/_{12}$)	(34,000)
	Carrying value	766,000

2	Deferred income	$
	Grant received ($800,000 × 30%)	240,000
	Release for this year ($240,000 $\times$ 10% $\times$ ${}^{6}/_{12}$)	(12,000)
	Total balance at year-end	228,000
	Presentation	
	Current liability ($240,000 × 10%)	24,000
	on-current liability (balance)	204,000
		228,000

Theoretical approach under the Framework

Because the "deferred" element of the grant cannot be recognised as a liability, the grant will be claimed in full in the year that it is received. The repayment clause will not affect this policy because, at the balance sheet date, Derringdo has not sold the asset and so no liability exists.

INCOME STATEMENT

	$
Operating expenses	
Depreciation charge (as before)	34,000
Grant received and claimed	(240,000)
	(206,000)

BALANCE SHEET

	$'000
Non-current assets	
Property, plant and equipment	766,000

10 Broadoak

Text reference. Chapter 4.

Top tips. The question was on a recent accounting standard dealing with non-current assets. Parts (a) and (b) were written sections covering the principles of identifying the cost of assets, the capitalisation of subsequent expenditure, and the requirements with regard to the revaluation of non-current assets including the treatment of gains and losses. Part (c) contained two small numerical examples to test the principles in (a) and (b).

Examiner's comment. Answers to this question were rather polarised. Good candidates did very well whereas weaker students gave poor answers – there did not seem too much in the middle ground. In general answers to Parts (a) and (b) were above average, particularly with regard to subsequent expenditures. Most candidates had a grasp of the basis principles. However, for the cost of fixed assets, many students gave the rules relating to determining whether an asset was impaired. Other incorrect answers discussed the fair values of assets. Most candidates scored well on Parts (c)(i) and (ii), but there were some common errors, for example incorrect capitalisation of maintenance costs.

Answer plan

It always pays to answer the discussion parts first, as these will often highlight the particular difficulties to be found in the calculations.

Part (a)

(i) IAS 16: cost = purchase price + import duties + directly attributable costs.

Deal with each item separately. Mention costs that must be dealt with as expenses e.g. admin costs. Consider IAS 20 and IAS 23.

Bonus points: mention the treatment of self-constructed assets and abnormal costs.

(ii) Subsequent expenditure – give treatment per IAS 16. For three marks, give three examples of subsequent expenditure.

Part (b)

Revaluation – measured reliably
  – consistency
  – whole class of asset
  – regular revaluations
  – up to date
  – treatment of surplus
  – treatment of deficit

Disposal – treatment of gains
  – treatment of losses

Part (c)

(i)   Use information given to calculate the initial capitalisation. Remember that you need to consider all the items in part (a)(i).

(ii)   If you follow the points on revaluation in part (b), you will need the following extracts:

INCOME STATEMENT

	20X1	20X2
	$	$
Amortisation	X	X
Revaluation loss		X
BALANCE SHEET		
Leasehold	X	X
Revaluation surplus	X	

(a)   (i)   IAS 16 states that an item of property which qualifies for recognition as an asset must initially be measured at **cost.** Cost comprises the following components.

(1)   **Purchase price**, less any trade discounts or rebates, but not settlement discounts

(2)   **Import duties** and non-refundable purchase taxes

(3)   **Directly attributable costs** of bringing the asset to working condition for its intended use. These include the cost of site preparation, initial delivery and handling costs, installation costs and professional fees. Also included is the estimated cost of removing the asset and restoring the site, to the extent that it is recognised as a provision under IAS 37 *Provisions, contingent liabilities and contingent assets*.

Certain costs **will not normally be part of the cost** of property, plant and equipment, and must instead be expensed. These are administration costs, start-up costs and initial operating losses.

In the case of **self-constructed assets, the principles are the same** as for acquired assets. This may include labour costs of the entity's own employees. **Abnormal costs** such as wastage and errors are **excluded.**

In addition to IAS 16 and IAS 37, two other standards affect the cost of an asset as shown in the financial statements. IAS 20 on government grants states that the **cost of an asset may be reduced by any such grants.** In addition, **directly attributable borrowing costs may be capitalised** under IAS 23 *Borrowing costs*.

(ii)   There may be **subsequent expenditure** on an item of property, plant or equipment, after its purchase and recognition. Such expenditure may be **added to the carrying amount of the asset,** but only when the **original criteria** are met. **All other subsequent expenditure is recognised as an expense as it is incurred.**

The standard gives **examples** of the kind of improvements that would allow subsequent expenditure to be capitalised.

(1)   **Modification** of an item of plant to extend its useful life

(2)   **Upgrade** of machine parts to improve the quality of output

(3)   Adoption of a **new production process,** leading to large reductions in operating costs

(b) IAS 16 allows property, plant and equipment (most commonly property) to be shown at a revalued amount. Such **revaluations are permitted** under the allowed alternative treatment rules providing that the **fair value of the asset can be measured reliably.** However, revaluation, particularly of property has been open to abuse, with companies **'cherry picking'** those properties whose valuation is favourable to show at valuation. Accordingly, IAS 16 tries to bring some **consistency** to the practice of revaluation.

When an item of property, plant and equipment is revalued, **the whole class of assets to which it belongs should be revalued.** All the items within a class should be **revalued at the same time** to prevent selective revaluation of certain assets and to avoid disclosing a mixture of costs and values from different dates in the financial statements. Revaluations must be **sufficiently regular**, so that the carrying value of an asset does not differ significantly from its market value. In addition, **revaluations must be kept up to date.**

Surpluses and deficits

In the case of a **surplus**, IAS 16 requires the increase to be credited to a **revaluation surplus** (part of owners' equity). This is generally the statement of recognised income and expense. The **exception** is when the increase is **reversing a previous decrease which was recognised as an expense.** Then it is treated as **income.**

The treatment is similar for a **decrease in value** on revaluation. Any decrease should be **recognised as an expense, except where it offsets a previous increase** taken as a revaluation surplus. Any **decrease greater** than the previous upwards increase in value must be taken as an expense in the income statement.

Gains and losses on disposal

Gains or losses are the difference between the estimated net disposal proceeds and the carrying amount of the asset. They should be **recognised as income or expense in the income statement**. Any **revaluation surplus** standing to the credit of a disposed asset should be **transferred to retained earnings** as a reserve movement.

(c) (i) Following IAS 16, not all the components of the cost of the item of plant may be capitalised. While trade discounts may be capitalised, **settlement discounts** may not. Such discounts are a **revenue item** and will probably be deducted from administration costs in the income statement. Likewise, **maintenance** is a **revenue item**. There will be a prepayment in the balance sheet for maintenance costs relating to subsequent years. The cost of the **error** in specifying the power loading is an **abnormal cost** and must be charged to the income statement. The costs to be capitalised may now be calculated as follows.

	$'000	$'000
Basic list price of plant		240,000
Less trade discount at 12.5% on list price		(30,000)
		210,000
Shipping and handling costs		2,750
Estimated pre-production testing		12,500
Site preparation costs		
Electrical cable installation (14,000 – 6,000)	8,000	
Concrete re-inforcement	4,500	
Own labour costs	7,500	
		20,000
Dismantling and restoration costs (15,000 + 3,000)		18,000
Initial cost of plant		263,250

(ii) BROADOAK

INCOME STATEMENT (EXTRACT) FOR THE YEAR TO 30 SEPTEMBER

	20X1	20X2
	$	$
Amortisation	(20,000)	(21,000)
Revaluation loss		(25,000)

BROADOAK

BALANCE SHEET (EXTRACT) AS AT 30 SEPTEMBER

	20X1	20X2
	$	$
Leasehold	231,000	175,000
Revaluation surplus		
Balance at 1 October 20X0	50,000	
Revaluation gain (see working)	11,000	
	61,000	
Transfer to retained earnings (11,000 × 1/11)	(1,000)	
Portion of revaluation loss (W)	(10,000)	
	50,000	

Working

	$
Cost at 1 October 20X0	240,000
Amortisation for year to 30 September 20X1: $\dfrac{240,000}{12 \text{ years}}$	(20,000)
	220,000
Revaluation gain	11,000
Carrying value at 30 September 20X1	231,000
Amortisation to 30 September 20X2 $\dfrac{231,000}{11 \text{ years}}$	(21,000)
	210,000
Revaluation loss to revaluation surplus	(10,000)
Revaluation loss to income statement	(25,000)
Carrying value 30 September 20X2	175,000

11 Elite Leisure

Elite Leisure's cruise ship

Although there is only one ship, the ship is a complex asset made up from a number of smaller assets with different costs and useful lives. Each of the component assets of the ship will be accounted for separately with its own cost, depreciation and profit or loss on disposal.

At 30 September 20X4 the ship is eight years old and its cost and carrying value is as follows:

	Cost	Depreciation period	Accumulated Depreciation	Carrying value
	$m		$m	$m
Ship's fabric	300	8 years / 25 years	96	204
Cabins and entertainment areas	150	8 years / 12 years	100	50
Propulsion system	100	30,000 hours / 40,000 hours	75	25
	550		271	279

Changes during Y/E 30 September 20X5

Replacing the propulsion system $140m

The old engines will be scrapped giving rise to a $25m loss on disposal.

The new engines will be capitalised and depreciated over their 50,000 hour working life. The charge for this year will be $140m $\times \dfrac{5,000 \text{ hours}}{50,000 \text{ hours}} = $14m$.

Upgrading cabins and entertainment areas $60m

These costs can be capitalised because they are improvements and because they extend the useful life of the assets. The revised carrying value at 1 October 20X4 is $110m ($50m + $60m).

The depreciation charge for the year is $22m ($110 ÷ 5 years).

Repainting the ship's fabric $20m

This is a maintenance cost. It will be charged to the income statement for the year. The depreciation for the ship itself will be $12m, based on its $300m cost and 25 year life.

Summary

Balance Sheet	Ship's Fabric	Cabins etc	Propulsion	Total
	$m	$m	$m	$m
Opening carrying value	204	50	25	279
Disposals	-	-	(25)	(25)
Additions	-	60	140	200
Depreciation	(12)	(22)	(14)	(48)
Closing carrying value	192	88	126	406

INCOME STATEMENT	$m
Depreciation	48
Loss on disposal	25
Repainting	20
Total charge	93

12 Myriad

(a) An entity may own land or a building **as an investment** rather than for use in the business, in other words, **to earn rentals or capital appreciation or both.** Such properties are not used in the production or supply of goods and services, or for administrative purposes, nor are they held for sale in the ordinary course of business. As they are held for investment for eventual disposal, it is often considered that the **current values** of the investments and the changes in them are **more important than their original costs**.

IAS 40 *Investment property* governs their accounting treatment. With regard to measurement subsequent to initial recognition, it requires an entity to choose between two models, **the cost model and the fair value model.** Whatever **policy** it chooses should be applied to **all of its investment property.**

Cost model

Under the cost model in IAS 16 investment property should be measured at depreciated cost, less any accumulated impairment losses. An entity that chooses the cost model should disclose the fair value of its investment property.

Fair value model

After initial recognition, an entity that chooses the fair value model should measure all of its investment property at fair value, except in the extremely rare cases where this cannot be **measured reliably**. In such cases it should apply the IAS 16 cost model.

A **gain or loss** arising from a change in the fair value of an investment property should be included in **net profit or loss** for the period in which it arises. The fair value of investment property should reflect the actual market state and circumstances as at the balance sheet date, not at either a past or future date.

(b) MYRIAD CONSOLIDATED BALANCE SHEET (EXTRACTS)
AS AT 30 SEPTEMBER 20X2

	Cost/ valuation $'000	Accumulated depreciation $'000	Carrying value $'000
Non-current assets			
Property, plant and equipment: A	150	6	144
(2 years accum. depn.)			
Investment properties: B	145	-	145
C	150	-	150

MYRIAD
CONSOLIDATED INCOME STATEMENT (EXTRACT)
FOR THE YEAR TO 30 SEPTEMBER 20X2

	$'000
Depreciation: Property A (150/5 years)	3
Deficit in fair value of Investment Property B (180 – 145)	(35)
Surplus in fair value of Investment Property C (140 – 150)	10

The question asks for the **consolidated** financial statements of Myriad. Property A is let to a subsidiary of Myriad, so in the consolidated financial statements it would be treated as an owner- occupied property. Its fair value ($200,000) would be shown in the entity financial statements, where it would be treated as an investment property.

13 Merryview

Revaluation

Extracts from Merryview's financial statements for the year to 31 March 20X3

INCOME STATEMENT

		$'000
Depreciation (W1)	(24 + 30 + 18 + 30)	102
Revaluation deficit (W1)	(300 – 90)	210
		312

BALANCE SHEET

Non-current assets (W1)	(2,020 + 920)	2,940
Revaluation surplus (W2)		514

Workings

1   *Land buildings*

		Head office			Training premises		
		Land	Building	Total	Land	Building	Total
		$'000	$'000	$'000	$'000	$'000	$'000
Cost/valuation							
	Opening	500	1,200	1,700	300	900	1,200
	Revaluation	200[a]	150[a]	350	50[f]	(300)[f]	(250)
	Closing	700	1,350	2,050	350	600	950
Depreciation							
	Opening	-	96[b]	96	-	72[g]	72
	Charge	-	24[c]	24	-	18[h]	18
		-	120[d]	120	-	90[i]	90
	Revaluation	-	(120)[d]	(120)	-	(90)[i]	(90)
	Charge	-	30[e]	30	-	30[j]	30
	Closing	-	30	30	-	30	30
NBV		700	1,320	2,020	350	570	920

Head office

(i)   The increase in the value of the land and the buildings is credited to the revaluation surplus.

(ii)   Opening depreciation: $1,200,000 × 2 years/25 years = $96,000.

(iii)   Charge for the six months up to the revaluation: $1.2m × 6 months/25 years = $24,000.

(iv)   The cumulative depreciation at the date of revaluation is credited to the revaluation surplus.

(v)   The charge for the six months after revaluation is based on the revalued amount and the remaining life of the asset: $1,350,000 × 6 months/22.5 years = $30,000.

Training premises

(vi)   The increase in the value of the land is credited to the revaluation surplus. The fall in the value of the buildings will be charged to the income statement. This is because there is no prior revaluation surplus to set the deficit against. Also, because the land and the buildings are treated as separate items the deficit on the buildings cannot be set off against the surplus on the land.

(vii)   Opening depreciation: $900,000 × 2 years/25 years = $72,000.

(viii) Charge up to the revaluation: $900,000 × 6 months/25 years = $18,000.

(ix)   The cumulative depreciation at the date of revaluation is set off against the revaluation deficit. The net amount is charged to the income statement. $300,000 − $90,000 = $210,000.

(x)   The charge for the six months after revaluation is based on the revalued amount and the remaining life of the asset: $600,000 × 6 months/10 years = $30,000.

2   *Revaluation surplus*

			$'000	$'000
Opening				-
Revaluation: office	– building		150	
	– depreciation		120	
			270	
	– land		200	
				470
training	– land			50
				520
Transfer*				(6)
Closing				514

* Transfer of excess depreciation on the revalued office building to retained earnings.

$270,000 × 6 months/22.5 years = $6,000.

14 Myriad II

(a)   **Accounting policies** are defined in IAS 8 as the 'specific principles, bases, conventions, rules and practices applied by an entity in preparing and presenting financial statements'. To maintain consistency, a fundamental assumption, the same accounting policies are usually adopted from one period to the next. This allows users to analyse trends over time in profit, cash flow and financial position.

An entity may change an accounting policy only if the change:

(i)   Is required by a Standard or an Interpretation; or

(ii)   Results in the financial statements providing reliable and more relevant information about the effects of transactions, other events or conditions on the entity's financial position, financial performance or cash flows.

The adoption of an accounting policy for the first time, or when a company applies a policy to transactions that differ substantially from any of its previous transactions, does not constitute a change of accounting policy. As Myriad is correcting a previous incorrect treatment, this is not a change of accounting policy but is correction of an error and so should be accounted for as a prior period adjustment.

(b)   MYRIAD
INCOME STATEMENT (EXTRACT) AS AT 30 SEPTEMBER

	20X2	20X1
	$'000	$'000
Amortisation: 1,060 × 25%/(1,060 − 400) × 25%	265	165

MYRIAD BALANCE SHEET (EXTRACT) AS AT 30 SEPTEMBER

	20X2	20X1
	$'000	$'000
Intangible non-current assets		
Development expenditure: cost (W1)	1,230	670
amortisation (W2)	(505)	(240)
NBV	725	430
Retained earnings		
1 October 20X0 (say)		2,000
Prior period adjustment (W3)		345
		2,345

Workings

1 *Cost as at 30 September 20X1*

	$'000
Cost at 30 September 20X2	1,230
Less amount recognised as an asset in 20X2	560
Cost at 30 September 20X1	670

2 *Amortisation*

	$'000
At 30 September 20X1	
Qualifying in 20X0: 300 × 25% × 2 years	150
Qualifying in 20X1: 360 ×25% × 1 year	90
	240

	$'000
At 30 September 20X2	
Qualifying in 20X0: 300 × 25% × 3 years	225
Qualifying in 20X1: 360 ×25% × 2 years	180
Qualifying in 20X2: 400 × 25% × 1 year	100
	505

3 *Prior period adjustment*

The prior period adjustment is the development expenditure that would have been included in the balance sheet at 30 September 20X0 had the accounting policy then been capitalisation and amortisation. This would have been the net book value, ie cost less amortisation.

	$'000
Amount recognised as an asset as at 30 September 20X0	420
Amortisation (1 year): 300 × 25%	(75)
	345

Note that only $300,000 qualifies for amortisation.

15 Dexterity

Text reference. Chapter 5.

Top tips. Part (a) is a test of memory. Follow the structure given to you in the question; discuss three situations (purchase, business combination, internal generation) for two assets (goodwill and other intangibles). This gives you a minimum of six marks out of ten.

Part (b) requires you to apply theory. Explain both the correct treatment and why alternative treatments have been rejected. For example in (b)(ii) explain why $12m can be capitalised and why $20m can't be.

Easy marks. If you know the standards, then part (a) should be 10 easy marks,

Examiner's comments. Part 9 (a) dealt with the treatment of goodwill and intangible assets. Part (b) included five scenarios to test the application of knowledge.

Candidates usually did very well in part (a) but performed really badly when it came to practical applications in part (b).

Marking scheme

				Marks
(a)		Discussion of goodwill		3
		Other intangibles – separate transactions		2
		– part of an acquisition		3
		– internally developed		3
		Available		**11**
		Maximum		**10**
(b)	(i)	One mark for each item in balance sheet		4
	(ii)	Does it qualify as development expenditure		1
		The need for an active market		1
		Drugs are unique, not homogeneous		1
	(iii)	Neither an acquired asset nor internally generated		1
		Really recognition of goodwill		1
		Can recognise both the asset and the grant at fair value		1
		Or at cost – granted asset has zero cost		1
	(iv)	In reality a valuable asset, in accounting a pseudo-asset		1
		Cannot control workforce		1
		Does not meet recognition criteria		1
	(v)	Effective advertising really part of goodwill		1
		Cannot be recognised as a non-current asset		1
		Prepayment of $2.5 million		1
		Cannot spread over two years		1
		Available		**18**
		Maximum		**15**
		Maximum for question		**25**

(a)   **Recognition and amortisation**

Goodwill

Only goodwill arising from a business combination is recognised. Under IFRS 3 goodwill is the excess of the cost of a business combination over the acquirer's interest in the net fair value of the assets, liabilities and contingent liabilities of the business acquired. Once recognised goodwill is held indefinitely, without amortisation but subject to impairment reviews.

One of the key aspects of goodwill is that it cannot be separated from the business that it belongs to. Therefore goodwill cannot be purchased separately from other assets. In addition, IAS 38 states that internally generated goodwill must not be capitalised.

Other intangible assets

Other intangibles can be recognised if they can be distinguished from goodwill; typically this means that they can be separated from the rest of the business, or that they arise from a legal or contractual right. IAS 38 also requires that:

- The expected future economic benefits will flow to the entity, and
- The cost can be measured reliably.

If an intangible is purchased separately then it will be recognised at cost. If the asset is not purchased for cash then its cost equals the fair value of the consideration.

Intangibles acquired as part of a business combination are recognised provided that they can be valued separately from goodwill. The acquirer will recognise an intangible even if the asset had not been recognised previously. If an intangible cannot be valued, then it will be subsumed into goodwill. Intangibles cannot be recognised if they create negative goodwill.

Internally generated intangibles can only be recognised if they are distinct from goodwill and if the expenditure is separate from the general cost of developing a business. For example, a brand name acquired in a business combination is capitalised whereas an internally generated brand isn't. There are also specific rules for capitalising development expenditure.

Goodwill and intangibles with an indefinite useful life are not amortised but tested annually for impairment.

(b)   **Dexterity**

(i)   *Temerity*

The following assets will be recognised on acquisition:

	$m
Fair value of sundry net assets	15
Patent at fair value	10
Research carried out for customer	2
Goodwill (balancing figure)	8
Total consideration	35

The patent is recognised at its fair value at the date of acquisition, even if it hadn't previously been recognised by Temerity. It will be amortised over the remaining 8 years of its useful life with an assumed nil residual value.

The higher value of $15m can't be used because it depends on the successful outcome of the clinical trials. The extra $5m is a contingent asset, and contingent assets are not recognised in a business combination. (Only assets, liabilities and contingent liabilities are recognised.)

Although research is not capitalised, this research has been carried out for a customer and should be recognised as work-in-progress in current assets. It will be valued at the lower of cost and net realisable value unless it meets the definition of a construction contract.

The goodwill is capitalised at cost. It is not amortised but it will be tested for impairment annually.

(ii)   *New drug*

Under IAS 38 the $12m costs of *developing* this new drug are capitalised and then amortised over its commercial life. (The costs of *researching* a new drug are never capitalised.)

Although IAS 38 permits some intangibles to be held at valuation it specifically forbids revaluing patents, therefore the $20m valuation is irrelevant.

(iii)   *Government licence*

The general rule for intangibles are that they are initially measured at cost (in this case $Nil) and then only revalued if an active market exists (which is not the case for this exclusive licence).

However, *IAS 38 Para 44* states that assets acquired as a result of a government grant may be capitalised at fair value, along with a corresponding credit for the value of the grant.

Therefore Dexterity may recognise an asset and grant of $10m which are then amortised/released over the five year life of the license. The net effect on profits and on shareholders funds will be nil. The general rule for intangibles are that they are initially measured at cost (in this case $Nil) and then only revalued if an active market exists (which is not the case for this exclusive licence).

However, *IAS 38 Para 44* states that assets acquired as a result of a government grant may be capitalised at fair value, along with a corresponding credit for the value of the grant.

Therefore Dexterity may recognise an asset and grant of $10m which are then amortised/released over the five year life of the license. The net effect on profits and on shareholders funds will be nil.

(iv)   *Training costs*

Although well trained staff add value to a business IAS 38 prohibits the capitalisation of training costs. This is because an entity has "insufficient control over the expected future economic benefits" arising from staff training; in other words trained staff are free to leave and work for someone else. Training is part of the general cost of developing a business as a whole.

(v)   *Advertising costs*

IAS 38 Para 69 states that advertising and promotional costs should be recognised as an expense when incurred. This is because the expected future economic benefits are uncertain and they are beyond the control of the entity.

However, because the year-end is half way through the campaign there is a $2.5m prepayment to be recognised as a current asset.

16 Derwent

Advent

(a)   *Balance sheet extracts 30 September 20X9*

Assets	$m
Non-current assets	
Property, plant and equipment (Note 1)	316
Other intangible assets (Note 2)	100
	416

Note 1 *Property, plant and equipment*

	Land and buildings	Plant	Total
	$m	$m	$m
1 October 20X8			
Cost/ valuation	280	150	430
Accumulated depreciation	(40)	(105)	(145)
	240	45	285
30 September 20X9			
Cost/ valuation	265	200	465
Accumulated depreciation	(9)	(140)	(149)
	256	60	316
Carrying value			
1 October 20X8	240	45	285
Additions		50	50
Revaluations	(15)	–	(15)
Depreciation:			
Charge for year	(9)	(35)	(44)
On revaluation	40	–	40
	256	60	316

Buildings are depreciated over 25 years and plant over 5 years.

On 1st October 20X8 the land and buildings were valued by XYZ, Chartered Surveyors, on an open market existing use basis.

Workings

1   *Plant*

Installation and commissioning costs are included in the cost of the asset.

Depreciation	$m
Opening cost of $150m (full year at 20%)	30
Additions of $50m (half year at 20%)	5
	35

2   *Property*

	Land	Buildings: Value	Total Value	Building Dep'n	Carrying Value
	$m	$m	$m	$m	$m
Opening	80	200	280	(40)	240
Revaluation	5	(20)	(15)	40	25
	85	180	265	-	265
Depreciation (20 years)	-	-	-	(9)	(9)
Closing	85	180	265	(9)	256

Note 2 *Intangible assets: Telecommunications license*

	$m
Cost	
Opening and closing	300
Depreciation	
Opening	30
Charge	30
Impairment loss	140
Closing	200

BPP
LEARNING MEDIA

$m

Carrying value
30 September 20X9   100
30 September 20X8   270

The closing carrying value must not exceed the impaired value of $100m; therefore the accumulated depreciation must be fixed at $200m. This in turn gives the impairment charge as a balancing figure of $140m.

The new carrying value of $100m will be depreciated over the remaining 8 year life of the license.

(b)   *Usefulness of the disclosures*

The disclosures give the reader more information about the nature and value of the non-current assets.

Firstly, there is the split between tangible assets (property, plant and equipment) and intangible assets. Lenders are less willing to use intangibles as security for loans than tangibles, and in the event of a winding up intangibles are often worthless without the business to support them.

Within property, plant and equipment there is the split between land and buildings and the rest. Land and buildings are often seen as the best source of security by lenders.

Land and buildings can go up in value as well as down, and so the note indicates the effect of revaluations during the year. The revaluation reserve note elsewhere in the financial statements will show the total revaluation compared with original cost. Because valuations are subjective the identity and qualifications of the valuer are disclosed.

The rates of depreciation indicate how prudent (or otherwise) the depreciation policies are, and whether the reported profits are fairly stated. The ratio between carrying value and cost gives a rough idea of the age of the assets, and of how soon they will need replacing.

The disclosure of the impairment loss flags a bad investment; the shareholders will want more information about this at their annual general meeting.

17 Wilderness

Text reference. Chapters 5 and 6.

Top tips. Part (a) is a straight forward description of impairment and how it is accounted for.

Part (b) applies the theory. In (b) (ii) remember that the impairment of the brand name should have been accounted for when it happened in April 20X5. This is before the impairment review of the whole cash generating unit in September.

Easy marks. Part (a) was 2 easy marks for very basic knowledge. In part (b) you must set out all your assumptions clearly.

Examiners comments. This question tested the principles of impairment of assets. It was not a popular question and candidates who attempted it scored on average less than half marks.

Answers to part (a) were generally correct but lacked important detail. The numerical examples in (b) were less well answered, showing an inability to apply principles. Part (b) (ii) answers were even worse. Many candidate did not realise that the Phoenix brand name was an internally – generated asset and could not be recognise. In some cases, no attempt was made to apportion the impairment loss over the relevant assets.

				Marks
(a)	(i)	Impairment where carrying amounts higher than recoverable amounts		1
		Discussion of fair value		2
		Discussion of value in use		2
		Discussion of CGU		1
		Goodwill/ intangibles with in definite life tested annually		1
		Review for indicators of impairment each balance sheet date		1
		Only test if there is an indication of impairment		1
			Available	9
			Maximum	6
	(ii)	Impairment loss – individual asset:		
		Impairment loss applied to carrying value of asset		1
		And changed to any previous revaluation surplus then income		2
		CGU:		
		Applied to goodwill		1
		Then pro rata to other assets		1
		Other assets not reduced below fair value/ value in use		1
			Available	6
			Maximum	5
(b)	(i)	Depreciation/ carrying value 1 April 2004		2
		Fair value less costs to sell is disposal value of $20,000, not trade-in value		2
		Recoverable is therefore $150,000		1
		Impairment loss is $50,000		1
		Depreciation six months to 30 September 2004		1
		Carrying value $112,500		1
			Available	8
			Maximum	7
	(ii)	Old brand written off, cannot recognise new brand		2
		Inventories correct at cost		2
		Improvement to plant not relevant		1
		Impairment loss is $5 million		1
		Land reduced to $9 million		1
		Plant reduced to $6 million		1
			Available	8
			Maximum	7
			Maximum for question	25

(a)   (i)   **Define an impairment loss**

An impairment occurs when the carrying value of an asset exceeds its recoverable amount. Recoverable amount represents the amount of cash that an asset will generate either through use (value in use) or through disposal (fair value less costs to sell).

The value in use is the present value of all future cash flows derived from an asset, including any disposal proceeds at the end of the asset's life. The present value of future cash flows will be affected by the timing, volatility and uncertainty of the cash flows. This can be reflected in the forecasted cash flows or the discount rate used.

Very few business assets generate their own cash flows, and so assets are often grouped together into cash generating units for impairment purposes. A cash generating is the smallest group of assets generating independent cash flows

Fair value less costs to sell is the amount obtainable for an asset in an arm's length transaction between knowledgeable, willing parties, less the cost of disposal. The fair value of used assets with no active market will have to be estimated. Valuations are based on willing parties, and so a "forced sale" value would not normally be used.

Impairment reviews

- At each reporting date an entity shall assess whether there are any indications that an impairment has occurred; if there are such indications then the recoverable amount of the asset must be estimated.

- Intangible assets with indefinite lives (and those not ready for use) should be reviewed for impairment annually. The review should take place at the same time each year.

- Cash generating units that include goodwill should be reviewed for impairment annually.

(ii) **Accounting for an impairment loss**

Impairment losses should be recognised immediately. They will normally be charged to the income statement alongside depreciation, but the impairment of a revalued asset should be taken directly to the revaluation reserve (unless the impairment is below depreciated historic cost). In the balance sheet the impairment will normally be included within accumulated depreciation, although it could be disclosed separately if material. Future depreciation charges will be based on the impaired value and the remaining useful life at the date of the impairment.

Impairments of cash generating units must be apportioned to the individual assets within that unit. The impairment is firstly allocated to goodwill, and then it is apportioned to all other assets (both tangible and intangible) on a pro rata basis. However, individual assets are not impaired below their own realisable value; any unused impairment being re-apportioned to the other assets.

(b) (i) **Wilderness**

Summary

INCOME STATEMENT

		$
Depreciation	First six months	40,000
	Second six months	37,500
Impairment		50,000
		127,500

BALANCE SHEET 30 SEPTEMBER 20X5

	$
Cost	640,000
Accumulated depreciation and impairment	
($400,000 + $40,000 + $50,000 + $37,500)	(527,500)
Carrying value	112,500

At 1 April 20X5 the asset should be restated at the lower of carrying value and recoverable amount. Recoverable amount is the higher of *value in use* and *fair value less costs to sell*.

Carrying value 1 April 20X5	$
Cost	640,000
Opening depreciation	(400,000)
Depreciation for 6 months ($640,000 $\times$ 12^1/$_2$% $\times$ ^{6}/$_{12}$)	(40,000)
Carrying value 1 April 20X5	200,000

	$
Recoverable amount	
Value in use and recoverable amount	150,000
Fair value less costs to sell*	20,000

* Wilderness does not intend to replace the machine and so the trade-in value of $180,000 is irrelevant.

The asset is impaired and should be written down to the recoverable amount of $150,000, giving an impairment loss of $50,000. This new valuation will then be depreciated over the remaining useful life of the asset, which is two years from the date of the accident.

Carrying value 30 September 20X5		$
Impaired value 1 April 20X5		150,000
Depreciation for 6 months	$150,000 × $^6/_{24}$	(37,500)
Carrying value 1 April 20X5		112,500

(b)   (ii)   **Mossel**

The question raises four issues:

- The value of the Quencher brand name,
- The $1.5m upgrade costs,
- The old bottles in inventories, and
- The overall impairment of the whole operation.

(1)   *The value of the Quencher brand name*

The $7m Quencher brand name should have been written off in April as it is no longer used. The Phoenix brand name is internally generated and so it cannot be capitalised. This will reduce the carrying value of the net assets at 30 September to $25m.

(2)   *The $1.5m upgrade costs*

These costs reflect the directors' intentions for the coming year. There is no obligation to incur these costs and so they cannot be recognised in the current year. However they may be disclosed in the notes.

(3)   *The old bottles in inventories*

These should be stated at the lower of normal cost ($2m) and net realisable value ($2.75m), therefore they remain at their cost of $2m. The NRV is the normal sales price of $3m (normal cost of $2m plus 50%) less the $250,000 re-labelling costs.

(4)   *The overall impairment of the whole operation at September 20X5*

The value in use and recoverable amount of the whole operation has been reduced to $20m. This is less than the carrying value of $25m and so an impairment has to be accounted for and apportioned to the assets within the cash generating unit. This is done as follows:

	Carrying value	*Impairment*	*Impaired values*
	$'000	$'000	$'000
Brand (already impaired)	-	-	-
Land	12,000	(3,000)	9,000
Plant	8,000	(2,000)	6,000
	20,000	(5,000)	15,000

Note: Inventory of $5m is not subject to impairment.

18 Multiplex

The impairment losses are allocated as required by IAS 36 *Impairment of assets.*

	Asset @ 1.1.20X2 $'000	1st provision (W1) $'000	Assets @ 1.2.20X2 $'000	2nd provision (W2) $'000	Revised asset $'000
Goodwill	200	(200)	-	-	-
Operating licence	1,200	(200)	1,000	(100)	900
Property: stations/land	300	(50)	250	(50)	200
Rail track/coaches	300	(50)	250	(50)	200
Steam engines	1,000	(500)	500	-	500
	3,000	(1,000)	2,000	(200)	1,800

Workings

1 *First provision*

$500,000 relates directly to an engine and its recoverable amount can be assessed directly (ie zero) and it is no longer part of the cash generating unit

IAS 36 then requires goodwill to be written off. Any further impairment must be written off the remaining assets pro rata, except the engine which must not be reduced below its fair value less costs to sell of $500,000

2 *Second provision*

The first $100,000 of the impairment loss is applied to the operating licence to write it down to fair value less costs to sell.

The remainder is applied pro rata to assets carried at other than their fair values less costs to sell, ie $50,000 to both the property and the rail track and coaches.

19 Preparation question: Research Co

Research Co balance sheet extracts

	20X1 $'000	20X0 restated $'000
Other assets	3,300	2,240
Share capital	550	500
Revaluation surplus	120	–
Retained earnings	1,600	1,100
	2,270	1,600
Liabilities	1,030	640
	3,300	2,240

Statement of recognised income and expense

	20X1	20X0 restated
	$'000	$'000
Gain on revaluation of properties	120	–
Net income recognised directly in equity	120	–
Profit for the period (2,130 – 1,460 – 220 + 50)	500	
(410 + 50 –180)		280
Total recognised income and expense for the period	620	280
Effect of prior period error*		(230)

*   affecting income of periods prior to those shown/restated in the statement of recognised income and expense

Statement of changes in equity

	$'000 Share capital	$'000 Revaluation surplus	$'000 Retained earnings	$'000 Total
Balance at 31 December 20W9 (1,460 – 410)	500	-	1,050	1,550
Prior period error (360 – 180 + 50)			(230)	(230)
Restated balance	500	-	820	1,320
Profit for the period (restated) (410 + 50 –180)			280	280
Total recognised income and expense for the period			280	280
Dividends			-	-
Balance at 31 December 20X0	500	-	1,100	1,600
Balance at 31 December 20X0 (as previously reported)	500	-	1,460	1,960
Prior period error			(360)	(360)
Restated balance	500		1,100	1,600
Gain on property revaluation		120		120
Net income recognised directly in equity		120		120
Profit for the period (2,130 – 1,460 – 220 + 50)			500	500
Total recognised income and expense for the period		120	500	620
Dividends			-	-
Issue of share capital	50			50
Balance at 31 December 20X1	550	120	1,600	2,270

20 Derringdo

Carpets

A change of accounting policy is when a new policy is used to report the same situations. In this case there is a new situation, Derringdo's terms of trade have changed, and so a new policy has been applied to report it. This is not a change of policy. The old trade will still be reported under the old method and the new trade will be reported under the new method.

INCOME STATEMENT

	$'000
Carpets fitted under the old terms of trade	1,200
(these will not have been claimed in the previous year)	
Carpets sold under the new terms of trade	23,000
Total revenue for this year	24,200

21 Telenorth

Text reference. Chapters 7 and 18.

Top tips. This was a 'typical' published financial statements type question with an earnings per share calculation. Candidates had to prepare the financial statements from a trial balance and include several adjustments which were used to cover many areas of the syllabus.

Examiner's comment. This was the one question where some less methodical candidates appeared to run out of time. On the whole this was well answered and remarkably some candidates scored full marks on Part (a). Again the 'trickier' adjustments proved to be stumbling blocks. Two of the worst errors were:

(a)   Not providing for the second half of the debenture (loan) interest and preference dividend.

(b)   Incorrect calculation of basic depreciation charges and inclusion of them in the wrong category. (The question was specific as to where depreciation should be charged.)

Answers to Part (b), the calculation of the earnings per share figure, were surprisingly disappointing. A significant proportion of candidates did not even attempt this section, of those that did very few correctly handled the rights issue and several candidates thought that the question involved a dilution calculation.

(a)   (i)   TELENORTH
                INCOME STATEMENT FOR THE YEAR ENDED 30 SEPTEMBER 20X1

	$'000
Revenue	283,460
Cost of sales (W1)	(155,170)
Gross profit	128,290
Other income	1,500
Distribution costs	(22,300)
Administrative expenses (W2)	(42,200)
Finance cost: (W11)	(1,656)
Profit before tax	63,634
Income tax expense (W10)	(24,600)
Profit for the period	39,034

(ii)   TELENORTH
         BALANCE SHEET AS AT 30 SEPTEMBER 20X1

	$'000	$'000
Assets		
Non-current assets		
Property, plant and equipment (W3)		83,440
Investments		34,500
		117,940
Current assets		
Inventory (W4)	16,680	
Trade accounts receivable: 35,700 + 12,000 (W5)	47,700	
		64,380
Total assets		182,320
Equity and liabilities		
Equity		
Ordinary shares of $1 each (W8)		30,000
Revaluation surplus 3,400 – 1,000		2,400
Share premium (W8)		16,000
Retained earnings (W9)		51,194
		99,594
Non-current liabilities		
8% preference shares	12,000	
6% loan notes	10,000	
Deferred tax: 5,200 + 2,200	7,400	
		29,400
Current liabilities		
Trade and other accounts payable (W6)	18,070	
Loan from factor: 9,600 + 96 (W5)	9,696	
Current tax payable	23,400	
Preference dividend payable (W7)	480	
Bank overdraft	1,680	
		53,326
Total equity and liabilities		182,320

Workings

1   Cost of sales

	$'000
Opening inventory	12,400
Purchases	147,200
	159,600
Closing inventory (W4)	(16,680)
	142,920
Depreciation of leasehold and plant (W3)	12,250
	155,170

2   Administration expenses

	$'000
Per question	34,440
Depreciation of computer system (W3)	10,160
Incorrect factoring charge (W5)	(2,400)
	42,200

3 *Property, plant and equipment*

	Cost	Depn	NBV
	$'000	$'000	$'000
Leasehold	56,250	20,250*	36,000
Plant and equipment	55,000	22,800*	32,200
Computer system	35,000	19,760*	15,240
			83,440

	$'000
*Depreciation charge:	
Leasehold: 56,250/25 years	2,250
Plant: (55,000 − 5,000)/5 years	10,000
Charge cost of sales	12,250
Computer equipment: charged to administration (35m − 9.6m) × 40%	10,160

4 *Closing inventory*

No inventory count took place at the year end. To arrive at the figure for closing inventory, the count needs to be adjusted for the movements between 30 September and 4 October, making appropriate adjustments for mark ups.

	$'000
Balance as at 4 October 20X1	16,000
Normal sales at cost: $1.4m × 100/140	1,000
Sale or return at cost: 650,000 × 100/130	500
Less goods received at cost	(820)
Adjusted inventory value	16,680

5 *Accounts receivable and factoring*

In the case of factoring of receivables, the **substance of a transaction** rather than its legal form needs to be considered. It may be that it is not appropriate to remove a receivable from the balance sheet. In this case, Telenorth bears the risk of slow payment and bad debts. This means that the substance of the transaction is a loan, which in turn will incur finance charges. It was therefore incorrect to derecognise the amount receivable. Also, the difference between the amount due from the customer ($12m) and the amount received from the factor ($12m × 80% = $9.6m) should not have been charged to administration costs. Adjustments need to be made to reinstate the amount receivable, accrue one month's finance charge and add back the incorrect charge to administration expenses, as follows.

	Dr	Cr
	$'000	$'000
Accounts receivable	12,000	
Loan from factor		9,600
Administration: $12m − $9.6m		2,400
Finance costs: accrued interest $9.6m × 1%	96	
Accruals		96
	12,096	12,096

There will also be loan note interest of $600,000, $300,000 paid and $300,000 accrued.

6 *Current liabilities*

	$'000
Trade and other payables	
Per question	17,770
Interest on loan note	300
	18,070

7 *Dividend payable*

	$'000
Preference: ($12m × 8%) – 480	480

8 *Share capital and suspense account*

Elimination of suspense account:

	Dr	Cr
	$'000	$'000
Suspense account (per trial balance)	26,000	
Directors' options: share capital (4m at $1)		4,000
share premium (4m at $1)		4,000
Rights issue: $\frac{20m + 4m}{4}$		6,000
Share premium 6m × (3 – 1)		12,000
	26,000	26,000

Share capital: $20m + $4m + $6m = $30m

Share premium: $4m + $12m = $16m

9 *Retained earnings*

	$'000	$'000
As at 1 October 20X0		14,160
Net profit for the year (Part (a))		39,034
Dividend: ordinary		(2,000)
		51,194

10 *Income tax*

	$'000	$'000
Provision for year		23,400
Increase in deferred tax provision	2,200	
Less charged to revaluation surplus	(1,000)	
		1,200
		24,600

11 *Finance costs*

	$'000
8% Preference shares	960
6% Loan notes	600
Factoring finance cost (W5)	96
	1,656

(b) TELENORTH

EARNINGS PER SHARE FOR THE YEAR TO 30 SEPTEMBER 20X1

	'000
Number of shares at 1 October b/forward	20,000
Exercise of options on 1 October 20X0	4,000
	24,000
Rights issue 1 for 4 on 1 July 20X1 24,000/4	6,000
Number of shares in issue at year end	30,000

Bonus fraction:

	$
4 shares @ $4.00	16
1 share @ $3.00	3
5	19

$\therefore$ Theoretical ex-rights price = $\dfrac{19}{5}$ = \$3.80

$\therefore$ Bonus fraction = $\dfrac{4.00}{3.80}$

Weighted average number of shares:

	'000
$24{,}000 \times 9/12 \times \dfrac{4}{3.80}$	18,947
$30{,}000 \times 3/12$	7,500
	26,447

	\$'000
Earnings attributable to ordinary shares	39,034

$\therefore$ EPS = $\dfrac{39{,}034}{26{,}447}$ = 148c

22 Tourmalet

Text reference. Chapters 7 and 15.

Top tips. As well as examining you on the format and content of the income statement and statement of changes in equity, this question also tests your knowledge of seven specific situations.

One key point is to separate out the discontinued activities. Under IFRS 5 the profit or loss on these activities is reported after the profit after tax for continuing activities.

As always, be methodical and don't get bogged down in the detail.

Easy marks. Parts (a) and (c) are 8 easy marks. You should be able to answer these even if you get bogged down in the income statement.

Examiner's comments. Part (a) covered the sale and leaseback of plant. Most candidates realised that this should be treated as a secured loan. However, some failed to recognise the correct treatment.

In part (b), candidates had to prepare an income statement and this was generally well-answered. However some problems arose: discontinued operation, provision for slow moving inventory, and the treatment of interest on the loan from part (a).

Part (c) was generally ignored. Those who did attempt the statement of changes in equity failed to realise that the preference shares should be treated as debt and so the preference dividend should be treated as a finance cost.

			Marks
(a)	Should not be treated as sales/cost of sales		1
	Normally only the profit in income (may require disclosure)		1
	The substance of the transaction is a secured loan		1
	Plant should be left on balance sheet		1
	'Sale' proceeds of $50 million shown as loan		1
	Rentals are partly interest and partly capital repayments		1
		Available	**6**
		Maximum	**5**
(b)	Income statement		
	Discontinuing operations figures		3
	Sales		2
	Cost of sales		5
	Distribution expenses		1
	Administration expenses		2
	Finance costs (including 1 for preference dividends)		2
	Loss on investment properties		1
	Investment income		1
	Taxation		2
		Available	**19**
		Maximum	**17**
(c)	Changes in equity		
	Profit for period		1
	Dividends		1
	Transfer to realised profits		1
		Maximum	**3**
		Maximum for question	**25**

(a) **Sale of plant**

The substance of this transaction is a financing arrangement, not a sale.

- Tourmalet will continue to enjoy the risks and benefits of ownership for the remainder of the asset's life because of the leaseback deal.

- The lease appears to be a finance lease, so Tourmalet will continue to recognise the asset.

- Over the period of the lease Tourmalet will repay the sale proceeds in full, plus interest at 12%, indicating that this is a loan and not a sale.

Tourmalet should continue to recognise the asset at its original cost, and depreciate it as before. The sale proceeds will be treated as a loan, and the lease payments will be split between repayment of this loan and a finance charge.

Even if the sale was a genuine sale, it should not have been included with the normal trading revenues and cost of sales.

(b) TOURMALET
INCOME STATEMENT FOR THE YEAR ENDED 30 SEPTEMBER 20X4

Continuing operations		$'000
Sales revenues (W1)		247,800
Cost of sales (W2)		(128,800)
Gross profit		119,000
Other income (W3)		1,200
Distribution costs (W4)		(26,400)
Administrative expenses (W5)		(20,000)
Other expenses (W6)		(200)
Finance costs (W7)		(3,800)
Profit before tax		69,800
Income tax expense (W8)		(7,100)
Profit for the year from continuing activities		62,700

Discontinued operations		
Loss for the year from discontinued operations (W9)		(5,500)
Profit for the year		57,200

Workings

Continuing operations		$'000	$'000
1	Sales revenues		
	From TB		313,000
	Disposal of plant		(50,000)
	Discontinued activities		(15,200)
			247,800
2	Cost of sales		
	Opening inventory		26,550
	Purchases		158,450
	Disposal of plant		(40,000)
	Closing inventory: Cost	28,500	
	NRV allowance (4,500 – 2,000)	(2,500)	
			(26,000)
	Depreciation		
	Leased item $40m / 5 years		8,000
	Others ($98.6m - $24.6m) × 20%		14,800
	Buildings ($120m / 40 years)		3,000
	Discontinued activities		(16,000)
			128,800
3	Other income		
	From the TB		1,200
4	Distribution costs		
	From the TB		26,400
5	Administrative expenses		
	From the TB		23,200
	Discontinued activities		(3,200)
			20,000
6	Other expenses		
	Fall in value of investment property (10m – 9.8m)		200

7   *Finance costs*
Interim preference dividend from the TB	900
Accrued final preference dividend ($30m × 6% × 6/12)	900
Finance cost of lease back ($50m × 12% × 4/12)	2,000
	3,800

8   *Income tax expense*
Over-provision from the trial balance	(2,100)
Charge for the year	9,200
	7,100

9   *Discontinued operations*
Revenue	15,200
Operating expenses (16,000 + 3,200 + 1,500 termination penalty)	(20,700)
Loss	(5,500)

(c)   TOURMALET
STATEMENT OF CHANGES IN EQUITY FOR THE YEAR TO 30 SEPTEMBER 20X4

	Share Capital	Revaluation Reserve	Retained Earnings	Total
	$'000	$'000	$'000	$'000
Opening	50,000	18,500	47,800	116,300
Transfer of depreciation on revaluation	-	(500)	500	-
Profit for the year	-	-	57,200	57,200
Equity dividend paid	-	-	(2,500)	(2,500)
Closing	50,000	18,000	103,000	171,000

23 Partway

Text reference. Chapter 7.

Top tips. This question covers discontinued operations and changes of accounting policy. Not to be attempted unless you knew something about both of these. There are 5 separate parts to this question. Do something on each of them, do not get carried away with the income statement.

Easy marks. (a) (i) and (ii) and (b) (i) were quite easy and you should have been able to do well on them. (a) (iii) was not difficult but you may have ended up spending too long on it and (b) (ii) was a bit tricky. However you were asked to comment, so a sensible comment supported by the evidence would have secured you a mark or two.

				Marks
(a)	(i)	definitions		2
		usefulness of information		2
			maximum	4
	(ii)	discussion of whether a discontinued operation		3
		conclusion		1
			maximum	4
	(iii)	figures for revenue from continuing operations (2005 and 2006)		1
		figures for revenue from discontinued operations (2005 and 2006)		1
		figures for cost of sales from continuing operations (2005 and 2006)		1
		figures for cost of sales from discontinued operations (2005 and 2006)		1
		figures for profit from continuing operations (2005 and 2006)		1
		figures for profit from discontinued operations (2005 and 2006)		1
			maximum	6
(b)	(i)	1 mark per relevant point	maximum	5
	(ii)	1 mark per relevant point	maximum	6
			Maximum for question	25

(a) (i) IFRS 5 defines 'non-current assets held for sale' to be those non-current assets whose carrying amount will be recovered principally through a sale transaction rather than through continuing use.

A discontinued operation is described in IFRS 5 as:

'a component of an entity that either has been disposed of, or is classified as held for sale, and:

(a) represents a separate major line of business or geographical area of operations

(b) is part of a single co-ordinated plan to dispose of a separate major line of business or geographical area of operations or

(c) is a subsidiary acquired exclusively with a view to resale.'

IFRS 5 states that *a component of an entity* comprises operations and cash flows that can be clearly distinguished, operationally and for financial reporting purposes, from the rest of the entity.

This very precise definition is needed to ensure that only operations which can properly be regarded as discontinued are classified as such. Users of accounts, particularly financial analysts, will be more interested in the results of continuing operations as a guide to the company's future profitability and it is not unacceptable for discontinued operations to show a loss. Companies could therefore be tempted to hide loss-making activities under the umbrella of discontinued operations, hence the requirement for the operations and cash flows of the discontinued operation to be clearly distinguishable from those of continuing operations. It is also conceivable that a company could seek to include the results of a profitable operation which has been sold under continuing operations.

IFRS 5 requires an entity to disclose a single amount on the face of the income statement comprising the total of:

(i) the post tax profit or loss of discontinued operations and

(ii) the post-tax gain or loss recognised on the measurement to fair value less costs to sell or on the disposal of the assets constituting the discontinued operation

The separation of the results of continuing and discontinued operations on the face of the income statement makes possible more meaningful year on year comparison. The inclusion of prior year information for discontinued operations means that it can be seen exactly how the continuing operations have performed, and it is possible to forecast more accurately how they can be expected to perform in the future.

(ii)   This can be correctly classified as a discontinued operation. The termination was completed before the end of the financial year. The interested parties were notified at that time and an announcement was made in the press, making the decision official. Although the company will continue to sell holidays over the internet, the travel agency business represents a separate major line of business. The internet business will have quite different property and staffing requirements and a different customer base. The results of the travel agency business are clearly distinguished.

(iii) PARTWAY
       INCOME STATEMENT FOR THE YEAR ENDED

	31 October 2006	31 October 2005
Continuing operations	$'000	$'000
Revenue	25,000	22,000
Cost of sales	(19,500)	(17,000)
Gross profit	5,500	5,000
Operating expenses	(1,100)	(500)
Profit from continuing operations	4,400	4,500
Profit(loss) from discontinued operations	(4,000)	1,500
Profit for the period	400	6,000
Discontinued operations		
Revenue	14,000	18,000
Cost of sales	(16,500)	(15,000)
Gross profit (loss)	(2,500)	3,000
Operating expenses	(1,500)	(1,500)
Profit(loss) from discontinued operations	(4,000)	1,500

(b)   (i)   Accounting policies can be described as the principles, conventions, rules and practices applied by an entity that prescribe how transactions and other events are to be reflected in its financial statements. This includes the recognition, presentation and measurement basis to be applied to assets, liabilities, gains, losses and changes to shareholders funds. Once these policies have been adopted, they are not expected to change frequently and comparability requires that ideally they do not change from year to year. However, IAS 8 does envisage situations where a change of accounting policy is required in the interests of fair presentation.

An entity may have to change an accounting policy in response to changes in a Standard or in applicable legislation. Or it may be an internal decision which can be justified on the basis of presenting a more reliable picture. An accounting policy adopted to deal with transactions or events which did not arise previously is not treated as a change of accounting policy.

Where a change of accounting policy has taken place it must be accounted for by retrospective restatement. This means that the comparative financial statements must be restated in the light of the new accounting policy. This makes it possible to compare results for these years as if the new accounting policy had always been in place. The financial statements must disclose the reason for the change of accounting policy and the effects of the change on the results for the previous year.

(ii)   The directors' proposal here is that revenue recognition can be accelerated based on the imposition of compulsory holiday insurance. This is based on the presumption that the risk of not receiving the balance of the payment has now been covered. However, at the point when the deposit is received, Partway has not yet done anything to earn the revenue. Under IAS 18 *Revenue,* revenue from a service contract should be recognised by reference to the stage of completion of the transaction. Under this method, revenue is recognised in the accounting periods in which the services are

BPP
LEARNING MEDIA

rendered. In this case the service is rendered at the time when the holiday is taken. The existing policy is therefore correct and should not be changed.

If this change were to be made it would not be a change in accounting policy as it is a change in timing, rather than recognition, presentation or measurement basis. The directors would of course prefer it not to be recognised as a change of accounting policy, as the restatement of comparatives would defeat the purpose of the change.

24 Preparation question: Simple consolidation

BOO GROUP
CONSOLIDATED INCOME STATEMENT
FOR THE YEAR ENDED 31 DECEMBER 20X8

	$'000
Revenue (5,000 + 1,000 – 100)	5,900
Cost of sales (2,900 + 600 – 80)	(3,420)
Gross profit	2,480
Other expenses (1,700 + 320)	(2,020)
Profit before tax	460
Tax (130 + 25)	(155)
Profit for the year	305
Attributable to	
Parent	294
Minority interest (20% × 55)	11
	305

CONSOLIDATED STATEMENT OF CHANGES IN EQUITY (retained earnings only)

	$'000
Opening retained earnings (230 + (185 × 80%))	378
Profit for the year	294
Closing retained earnings	672

CONSOLIDATED BALANCE SHEET AS AT 31 DECEMBER 20X8

	$'000	$'000
Assets		
Non-current assets (2,000 + 200 – 80)		2,120
Current assets		
Inventory (500 + 120 + 80)	700	
Trade receivables (650 – 100 + 40)	590	
Bank and cash (390 + 35)	425	
		1,715
Total assets		3,835
Equity and liabilities		
Equity attributable to the equity holders of the parent		
Share capital (Boo only)		2,000
Retained earnings (W3)		672
		2,672
Minority interest (W2)		68
Total equity		2,740
Current liabilities		
Trade payables (910 + 30)	940	
Tax (130 + 25)	155	
		1,095
Total equity and liabilities		3,835

Workings

1   *Inter company issues*

Step 1: Record Goose's purchase

DEBIT Purchases	$100,000	
CREDIT Payables		$100,000
DEBIT Closing inventory (B/S)	$100,000	
CREDIT Closing inventory I/S (COS)		$100,000

Step 2: Cancel unrealised profit

DEBIT COS (and retained earnings) in BOO	$20,000	
CREDIT Inventory (B/S)		$20,000

Step 3: Cancel intragroup transaction

DEBIT Revenue	$100,000	
CREDIT Cost of sales		$100,000

Step 4: Cancel intragroup balances

DEBIT Receivables	$100,000	
CREDIT Payables		$100,000

2   *Minority interest*

	$'000
Share capital (20% × 100)	20
Retained earnings (20% × 240)	48
	68

3   *Retained earnings*

	Boo	Goose
	$'000	$'000
Per question	500	240
Unrealised profit (W1)	(20)	
	480	
Less pre acquisition		-
		240
Goose: 80% × 240	192	
Total, as per Statement of Changes in Equity	672	

20 Hideaway

IAS 24 Related Parties

(a)   *Circumstances giving rise to related parties*

A party is related to an entity if:

- It directly or indirectly controls, is controlled by or is under common control of the entity,
- It has significant influence over the entity, or is an associate of the entity,
- It has joint control over the entity, or is itself jointly controlled by the entity,
- They are a member of the entity's management team,
- They are a close family member of a related party,
- They are a post-employment benefit plan for the entity (or for a related party of the entity).

(b)   *Importance of related party disclosures*

Investors invest in a business on the assumption that it aims to maximise its own profits for the benefit of its own shareholders. This means that all transactions have been negotiated at arm's length between willing and informed parties. The existence of related parties may encourage directors to make decisions for the benefit of another entity at the expense of their own shareholders. This can be done actively by selling goods and services cheaply to related parties, or by buying in goods and services at an above market price. It can also happen when directors chose not to compete with a related party, or offer guarantees or collateral for other party's loans.

Disclosure is particularly important when a business is being sold. It may receive a lot of custom, supplies, services or general help and advice from family or group companies. When the company is sold these benefits may be withdrawn.

Related party transactions are not illegal, nor are they necessarily a bad thing. However shareholders and potential investors need to be informed of material related party transactions in order to make informed investment and stewardship decisions.

(c)   *Hideaway, Benedict and Depret*

The directors and shareholders of Hideaway, the parent, will maximise their wealth by diverting profitable trade into wholly owned subsidiaries. They have done this by instructing Depret (a 55% subsidiary) to sell goods to Benedict (a 100% subsidiary) at $5m below fair value. As a result the minority shareholders of Depret have been deprived of their 45% interest in those lost profits, amounting to $2.25m. The non-group directors of Depret will also lose out if their pay is linked to Depret's profits.

Because Depret's profits have been reduced, the minority shareholders might be persuaded to sell their shares to Hideaway for less than their true value. Certainly potential shareholders will not be willing to pay as much for Depret's shares as they would have if Depret's profits had been maximised.

The opposite possibility is that the Directors of Hideaway are boosting Benedict's reported performance with the intention of selling it off for an inflated price.

Depret's minority shareholders might be able to get legal redress because the majority shareholders appear to be using their power to oppress the minority. This, however, will depend on local law. The tax authorities might also suspect Depret of trying to avoid tax, especially if Benedict is in a different tax jurisdiction.

26 Highveldt

Text reference. Chapter 9.

Top tips. Don't forget **Part (b).** There are five marks here for explaining the purpose of consolidated financial statements. Do it first, before getting tied up with Part (a).

Part (a) Make sure that you read the question before doing anything. You are not asked to prepare a balance sheet; just the goodwill and reserves. This makes the question easier to manage as effectively you are just doing the workings without having to tie it all together in a set of financial statements.

There are quite a few complications to consider. For each calculation go through each of the six additional pieces of information and make appropriate adjustments when relevant.

Easy marks. Part (b) is 5 easy marks.

Examiner's comments. Part (a) was unusual in asking for extracts of the balance sheet. Many candidates were confused by this and wasted time preparing a full balance sheet. Other common errors were: fair value adjustments; consolidated reserves; revaluation and share premium reserves; and the cost of the investment.

Part (b) was disappointing as many candidates did not answer the question set, i.e. **why** consolidated accounts are prepared.

Marking scheme

				Marks
(a)	(i)	*Goodwill*		
		– Consideration given		2
		– Share capital and premium		1
		– Pre-acquisition profit		2
		– Fair value adjustments		2
		– Goodwill impairment		$\frac{1}{8}$
			Maximum	8
	(ii)	*Minority interest*		
		– Share capital and premium		1
		– Retained earnings		2
		– Fair value adjustment		$\frac{1}{4}$
			Maximum	4
	(iii)	*Consolidated reserves*		
		– Share premium		1
		– Revaluation reserve		2
		Retained earnings		
		– Post acquisition profit		2
		– Interest receivable		1
		– Finance cost		1
		– Goodwill impairment		$\frac{1}{8}$
			Maximum	8
(b)		1 mark per relevant point to	**Maximum**	5
			Maximum for question	25

(a)   *Group Structure as at 31 March 20X5*

Highveldt
parent

75% | Since 1-4-04

Samson
subsidiary

BPP
LEARNING MEDIA

(i) *Goodwill in Samson*

	$m	$m
Cost of business combination		
80m shares × 75% × $3.50		210
Deferred consideration; $108m × $1/_{1.08}$		100
		310
Share of the net assets acquired at fair value		
Carrying value of net assets at 1-4-20X4:		
Ordinary shares	80	
Share premium	40	
Retained earnings	134	
	254	
Fair valuation adjustments		
Revaluation of land at the date of acquisition	20	
Recognition of the fair value of brands acquired	40	
Derecognition of capitalised development expenditure	(18)	
Fair value of the net assets at acquisition	296	
75% Group share		(222)
Cost of Goodwill		88
Impairment charge given in question		(22)
Carrying value at 31 March 20X5		66

Notes (not required in the exam)

Goodwill is based on the present value of the deferred consideration. During the year the $8m discount will be charged to Highveldt's income statement as a finance cost. (In (a)(iii) retained earnings will be adjusted for this accrued interest.)

Only the $20m fair valuation is relevant at the date of acquisition. The $4m arising post acquisition will be treated as a normal revaluation and credited to the revaluation reserve. (See (a)(iii) below.)

Samson was right not to capitalise an internally developed brand name because, without an active market, its value cannot be measured reliably. However the fair value of a brand name can be measured as part of a business combination. Therefore the $40m fair value will be recognised at acquisition and an additional $4m amortisation will be charged in the consolidated income statement.

At acquisition Samson had capitalised $18m of development expenditure. Highveldt does not recognise this as an asset, so the net assets at acquisition are reduced by $18m. A further $32m is capitalised by Samson post acquisition; this will be written off in the consolidated income statement (net of the $10m amortisation already charged).

(ii) *Minority interest in Samson's net assets*

	$m
Samson's net assets from the question	330
Fair valuation of land at acquisition	20
Revaluation of land post acquisition	4
Carrying value of capitalised brand ($40m - $4m amortisation)	36
Less: carrying value of the capitalised development expenditure	
($50m - $10m amortisation)	(40)
Less: allowance for unrealised profit ($1/_3$ $6m)	(2)
Consolidated value of Samson's net assets	348
Minority 25% interest	87

(iii) *Consolidated Reserves*

Share premium

The share premium of a group, like the share capital, is the share premium of the parent only ($80m)

Revaluation reserve

	$m
Parent's own revaluation reserve	45
Group share of Samson's post acquisition revaluation; $4m × 75%	3
	48

Retained earnings

Retained earnings attributable to the equity holders of the parent

	Highveldt $m	Samson $m
Per question	350	76
Accrued interest from Samson ($60m × 10%)	6	–
Unwinding of discount on deferred consideration	(8)	–
Amortisation of brand ($40m/10 years)	–	(4)
Write off development expenditure as incurred ($50m – $18m)	–	(32)
Write back amortisation of development expenditure	–	10
Allowance for unrealised profit	–	(2)
	348	48
Group share (75%)	36	
Impairment of goodwill in Samson	(22)	
	362	

(b)   *Usefulness of consolidated financial statements*

The main reason for preparing consolidated accounts is that groups operate as a single economic unit, and it is not possible to understand the affairs of the parent company without taking into account the financial position and performance of all the companies that it controls. The directors of the parent company should be held fully accountable for all the money they have invested on their shareholders behalf, whether that has been done directly by the parent or via a subsidiary.

There are also practical reasons why parent company accounts cannot show the full picture. The parent company's own financial statements only show the original cost of the investment and the dividends received from the subsidiary. As explained below, this hides the true value and nature of the investment in the subsidiary, and, without consolidation, could be used to manipulate the reported results of the parent.

- The cost of the investment will include a premium for goodwill, but this is only quantified and reported if consolidated accounts are prepared.

- A controlling interest in a subsidiary can be achieved with a 51% interest. The full value of the assets controlled by the group is only shown through consolidation when the minority's interest is taken into account.

- Without consolidation, the assets and liabilities of the subsidiary are disguised.

  - A subsidiary could be very highly geared, making its liquidity and profitability volatile.

  - A subsidiary's assets might consist of intangible assets, or other assets with highly subjective values.

- The parent company controls the dividend policy of the subsidiary, enabling it to smooth out profit fluctuations with a steady dividend. Consolidation reveals the underlying profits of the group.

- Over time the net assets of the subsidiary should increase, but the cost of the investment will stay fixed and will soon bear no relation to the true value of the subsidiary.

27 Hample

> **Top tips.** The main difficulties in this question relate to the fair value adjustments on the non-current assets. There are lots of easy marks to be gained for straightforward adjustments, such as those for intragroup transactions.

CONSOLIDATED BALANCE SHEET AS AT 31 MARCH 20X9

	$'000	$'000
Assets		
Non-current assets		
Property, plant and equipment (W1)	4,020	
Goodwill (W2)	480	
Software (W3)	1,440	
Investments (65 + 210)	275	
		6,215
Current assets		
Inventory (W4)	1,274	
Trade receivables (524 + 328)	852	
Cash and bank (20 + 55 cash in transit)	75	
		2,201
Total assets		8,416
Equity and liabilities		
Equity attributable to the equity holders of the parent		
Share capital	2,000	
Share premium	2,000	
Retained earnings (W7)	2,420	
		6,420
Minority interest (W6)		350
Non current liabilities		
Government grants (230 + 40)		270
Current liabilities		
Trade payables (475 + 472)	947	
Overdraft	27	
Provisions for tax (228 + 174)	402	
		1,376
Total equity and liabilities		8,416

Workings

1   *Property, plant and equipment*

	$'000
Hample	2,120
Sopel	1,990
Fair value adjustment (Note (i))	(120)
Reduced depreciation arising from fair value (Note (ii))	30
	4,020

Notes

(i) The leasehold carrying value would be based upon present value of future rentals (receivable in advance):

	$'000
80 + (80 × 2.5*)	280
Book value	400
Reduction	120

*2.5 is the annuity factor for years 1-3 at 10%.

(ii) Depreciation is based upon $\frac{280}{4} = 70$

Depreciation in Sopel books = 100
Reduction: 100 − 70 = 30

2 *Goodwill*

	$'000	$'000
Cost of investment		4,110
Less share of net assets acquired		
Equity shares	1,500	
Share premium	500	
Retained earnings at 1 April X8 (2,200 − 300 (W5))	1,900	
	3,900 × 90%	(3,510)
		600
Impairment		(120)
Carrying value		480

3 *Software*

	Sopel accounts	Consolidated
	$'000	$'000
Capitalised	2,400	2,400
Depreciation to 31 March 20X8 (8 yrs/5 yrs)	(300)	(480)
NBV at acquisition	2,100	1,920
Depreciation to 31 March 20X9	(300)	(480)
NBV 31 March 20X9	1,800	1,440

Note. There is a fair value adjustment of 180 plus extra depreciation of 180.

4 *Inventories*

	$'000
Hample	719
Sopel	560
	1,279
Unrealised profit (25 × 25/125)	(5)
	1,274

5 *Fair value adjustments*

	1.4.X8	In year	31.3.X9
	$'000	$'000	$'000
Leasehold (4 yr life)	(120)	30	(90)
Software (W3)	(180)	(180)	(360)
	(300)	(150)	(450)

6	Minority interest		$'000
	Net assets per question		3,955
	Less unrealised profit (W4)		(5)
	Fair value adj (W5)		(450)
			3,500
			× 10%
			350

Minority interest: $3,500,000 × 10% = $350,000

7	Retained earnings	Hample	Sopel
		$'000	$'000
	Per question	2,900	1,955
	Fair value adj (180 – 30)		(150)
	Unrealised		(5)
	Pre-acquisition		(2,200)
			(400)
	Share of post acquisition		
	Sopel: (400) × 90%	(360)	
	Less goodwill impairment (W2)	(120)	
		2,420	

8	Elimination of current account		
			$'000
	Sopel in Hample accounts		75
	Less cash in transit		(15)
	Hample in Sopel accounts		60

9	Intragroup loan		
			$'000
	Investment in Hample accounts		200
	Repayment in transit		(40)
	Liability in Sopel accounts		160

28 Preparation question: Acquisition during the year

(a) PORT GROUP: CONSOLIDATED INCOME STATEMENT FOR THE YEAR ENDING 31 DECEMBER 20X4

	Port	Alfred 2/12	Adjustment	Group
	$'000	$'000		$'000
Revenue	100	166		266
Cost of sales	(36)	(43)		(79)
Gross profit				187
Interest on loan to Alfred	276	-	(46)	230
Other investment income	158	-		158
Operating expenses	(56)	(55)		(111)
Finance costs	-	(46)	46	-
Profit before tax				464
Taxation	(112)	(6)		(118)
Profit after tax				346
Attributable to				
Equity holders of the parent				342
Minority interests (W4)				4
				346

PORT GROUP BALANCE SHEET AS AT 31 DECEMBER 20X4

		Adjustments	Group $'000
Assets			
Non-current assets			
Goodwill		(W2)	275
Property, plant and equipment	100 + 3,000		3,100
Investments			
Loan to Alfred	2,300 + 0	(2,300)	-
Other investments	600 + 0		600
			3,975
Current assets	800 + 139		939
Total assets			4,914
Equity and liabilities			
Equity attributable to the equity holders of the parent			
$1 equity shares		(W3)	235
Share premium		(W3)	1,115
Retained earnings		(W5)	2,912
			4,262
Minority interest		(W4)	129
Total equity			4,391
Non-current liabilities			
Loan from Port	0 + 2,300	(2,300)	-
Current liabilities			
Sundry	200 + 323		523
Total equity and liabilities			4,914

(b) PORT GROUP
CONSOLIDATED STATEMENT OF CHANGES IN EQUITY
FOR THE YEAR ENDING 31 DECEMBER 20X4

		Share capital $'000		Share premium $'000	Retained earnings $'000		Minority interests $'000		Total $'000
Opening		200		500	2,640		-		3,340
Share issue	(W3)	35	(W3)	615	-		-	(W3)	650
New subsidiary		-		-	-	(W4)	125		125
Profit for the year		-		-	342	(W4)	4		346
Dividends for the year		-		-	(70)				(70)
Closing		235		1,115	2,912		129		4,391

Workings

1   *Group structure*

Port
75% Subsidiary Two months only
Alfred

2 *Calculation of the cost of investment and goodwill*

	$'000	$'000	$'000
Fair value of shares issued			650
Net assets at date of acquisition (Note)			
Shares		100	
Share Premium		85	
Retained earnings			
Opening	235		
Add: accrued profit for the year: $96,000 × 10/12	80		
Pre-acquisition retained earnings		315	
Net assets		500	
Group share: 75%			(375)
Goodwill capitalised at cost			275

Note. The net assets at the date of acquisition are also calculated by time-apportioning profits. The share capital and retained earnings brought forward obviously all arose before acquisition. The profit for the year is assumed to have arisen evenly over time.

3 *Issue of shares*

	Draft $'000	New issue $'000	Revised $'000
Share Capital	200	35	235
Share Premium	500	615	1,115
Fair value of proceeds		650	

4 *Minority interests*

Income statement and statement of changes in equity

The rule here is to time apportion the minority interest in the subsidiary acquired during the year. After all, you can only take out in respect of the minorities what was put in in the first place. So, if two months were consolidated then two months of minority interest will be deducted. (The same rule applies when a subsidiary is disposed of.)

$96,000 × 2/12 × 25% = $4,000.

At acquisition in the statement of changes in equity

The net assets at acquisition were $500,000, so the minority interest will be 25% of that = $125,000.

Balance sheet

Alfred's equity is $516,000. The minority interest is 25% of that = $129,000.

5 *Group retained earnings*

	Port $'000	Alfred $'000
Per question	2,900	331
Less pre acquisition (W2)		(315)
		16
Share of Alfred: (16 × 75%)	12	
	2,912	

29 Hillusion

Text reference. Chapters 9 and 10.

Top tips. Don't forget **Part (b)** There are five quick and easy marks here, but to score them all you must use numbers from your answer to Part (a). So, do Part (b) as soon as you have calculated the unrealised profit.

Part (a) This is a straight forward consolidation. Although there is a lot of time pressure on you to prepare the income statement and the balance sheet, this is balanced by the absence of any serious complications in the question. A methodical approach will earn high marks.

(Although Hillusion intends to sell Skeptik within two to three years, Skeptik must still be consolidated. IAS 27 only allows non-consolidation if the subsidiary was acquired with the intention of selling it within twelve months.)

1   Sketch out the group structure, noting percentage holdings and the date of acquisition.

2   Prepare a pro-forma income statement and balance sheet for your answer.

3   Note the adjustments for fair valuations, inter-company balances, inter-company trade and unrealised profit.

4   Calculate the carrying value of the goodwill in the subsidiary, and the impairment charge in the income statement.

5   Calculate the profit attributable to the parent and to the minority.

6   Calculate the minority interest in the subsidiary's net assets.

7   Calculate the Group retained earnings.

Easy marks. Part (b) is 5 easy marks.

Examiner's comments. This was a fairly straightforward consolidated income statement and balance sheet. The adjustments involved were simpler than if just one statement had been required. The main concern was that a number of candidates used proportional consolidation to account for the subsidiary.

Part (b) was generally well understood and answered. However some candidates chose to answer how such profits arrive and how they are eliminated. The question asks **why** they are eliminated. Many candidates either did not answer this question or based their answer on the group statement instead of the entity's statements.

		Marks
(a)	*Income statement*	2
	Sales revenue	3
	Cost of sales	2
	Operating expenses including goodwill	1
	Loan interest	1
	Tax	1
	Minority interest	1
	Accumulated profit b/f	1
	Balance Sheet:	
	Goodwill	3
	Tangible non-current assets	2
	Current assets	2
	Accumulated profits	1
	Minority interest	2
	10% loan notes	1
	Current liabilities	2
		Available 24
		Maximum 20
(b)	1 mark per relevant point to	**Maximum** 5
		Maximum for
		question 25

(a) THE HILLUSION GROUP
CONSOLIDATED INCOME STATEMENT FOR THE YEAR ENDED 31 MARCH 20X3

	$'000
Sales revenues $(60,000 + {}^9/_{12} \, 24,000 - 12,000)$	66,000
Cost of sales $(42,000 + {}^9/_{12} \, 20,000 - 12,000 + 500 \, (W4) + 600 \, (W3))$	(46,100)
Gross profit	19,900
Impairment of goodwill (W2)	(300)
Operating expenses $(6,000 + 150)$	(6,150)
Finance costs $(200 \times {}^9/_{12} \text{ less } 75 \text{ income})$	(75)
Profit before tax	13,375
Income tax expense $(3,000 + 600 \times {}^9/_{12})$	(3,450)
Profit for the year	9,925
Attributable to:	
Equity holders of the parent (W5)	9,595
Minority interest (W5)	330
	9,925

CONSOLIDATED BALANCE SHEET AS AT 31 MARCH 20X3

	$'000
Assets	
Non-current assets	
Property, plant and equipment $(19,320 + 8,000 + 2,600 \text{ fair valuation (W3)})$	29,920
Goodwill *(W2)*	900
Investments $(11,280 - 10,280 \, (W2) - 1,000 \text{ loan notes})$	-
	30,820
Current assets $(15,000 + 8,000 - 500 \text{ unrealised profit (W4)} - 750 \text{ inter-company})$	21,750
Total assets	52,570

183

$'000

Equity and liabilities
Equity attributable to equity holders of the parent

Share capital (Parent only)	10,000
Retained earnings (W6)	26,120
	36,120
Minority interest (10,400 + 2,600 (W3)) × 20%	2,600
Non-current liabilities (0 + 2,000 – 1,000 loan notes)	1,000
Current liabilities (10,000 + 3,600 – 750 inter-company)	12,850
	52,570

Workings

1   *Group Structure as at 31 March 20X3*

Hillusion

80% purchased for $10.28m on 1 July 2002.

Skeptik is Hillusion's subsidiary for $^9/_{12}$ of the year.

Skeptik

2   *Goodwill in Skeptik*

	$'000	$'000
Cost of business combination		10,280
Share of the net assets acquired at fair value		
Share Capital	2,000	
Opening retained earnings	5,400	
Time apportioned profits for the year; $3m × $^3/_{12}$	750	
Fair value increase for the plant	3,200	
Fair value of the net assets at acquisition	11,350	
80% Group share		(9,080)
Cost and carrying value of goodwill		1,200

Impaired value of the goodwill at the year-end: (1,200 – 300)	B/S		900
Charge to income statement for impairment	I/S		300
			1,200
Minority share of net assets at acquisition: $11,350,000 × 20%			2,270

3   *Fair valued plant*

		$'000
Fair value at acquisition		3,200
Depreciation over four years for four months; $3.2m × ¼ × $^9/_{12}$	I/S	(600)
Carrying value of licence 31 March 20X2	B/S	2,600

The extra $600,000 depreciation is taken into account when apportioning the profit for the year between the parent and the minority interest. It also affects the group's retained earnings in the balance sheet.

The minority interest in the balance sheet is adjusted for the $2,600 closing carrying value.

4   *Intra group trade and the provision for unrealised profit*

Group revenues and cost of sales are reduced by the $12m of intra-group sales at invoiced value. This adjustment does not affect profits.

An adjustment is made for the unrealised profit on goods sold by Hillusion to Skeptik but still unsold at the year-end. This increases the cost of sales in the income statement and reduces the balance sheet value of the inventories. The gross profit margin was 25% ($3m/$12m).

	$'000
Goods unsold at the year-end; $12m - $10m	2,000
Unrealised profit: $2m × 25%	500

5   *Attributable profit in the income statement*

Attributable to the parent	$'000
Hillusion's company profit	9,075
Add: Time apportioned share of Skeptik's profits for the year ($3m × $^9/_{12}$ × 80%)	1,800
Less: Impairment of goodwill (W2)	(300)
Depreciation on fair valuation (W3) ($600,000 × 80%)	(480)
Provision for unrealised profit (W4)	(500)
	9,595

Attributable to the minority interest	
Time apportioned share of Skeptik's profits for the year ($3m × $^9/_{12}$ × 20%)	450
Less: depreciation on fair valuation (W3) ($600,000 × 20%)	(120)
	330

6   *Retained earnings attributable to the equity holders of the parent*

	Illusion	*Skeptik*
	$'000	$'000
Per question	25,600	8,400
Pre-acquisition reserves	–	(6,150)
Provision for unrealised profit (W4)	(500)	–
Depreciation on fair valuation (W3)	–	(600)
	25,100	1,650
Group share (80%)	1,320	
Impairment of goodwill (W2)	(300)	
	26,120	

(b) **Unrealised profits**

Unrealised profits arise when group companies trade with each other. In their own individual company accounts profits and losses will be claimed on these transactions, and goods bought from a fellow group company will be recorded at their invoiced cost by the purchaser.

However, consolidated accounts are drawn up on the principle that a group is a single economic entity. From a group point of view, no transaction occurs when goods are traded between group companies, and no profits or losses arise. Revenue and profits will only be claimed when the goods are sold onto a third party from outside of the group.

In this example, Hillusion sold $12m of goods to Skeptik making a profit of $3m. The sale by Hillusion and the purchase by Skeptik must be eliminated from the group income statement. This adjustment will not affect profits because both the sales and the purchases have been reduced by the same amount.

By the year-end Skeptik had sold $10m of these items making a profit of $5m. From a group point of view, the profit on these items, including their share of the profit claimed by Hillusion, has now been realised. However, Skeptik still has $2m of goods bought from Hillusion. This valuation includes an element of profit ($500,000) that has not yet been realised and needs to be eliminated. This will reduce the carrying value of the inventory to the amount originally paid for them by Hillusion. If unrealised profits were not eliminated, then groups could boost their profits and asset values by selling goods to each other at inflated prices.

A future purchaser of Skeptik would obviously review Skeptik's own financial statements. These show a $3.6m profit before tax, which gives a very healthy 15% net profit on revenues. However, over 60% of Skeptik's revenue comes from selling goods supplied by Hillusion. The gross profit earned on these items is $5m, which is more than the $4m gross profit for the company as a whole. A new owner might not get such favourable terms from Hillusion, leaving them with the loss making products. Nobody would be interested in buying such a business, but this information cannot be gleaned from the entity's own financial statements.

30 Hydan

Text reference. Chapters 9 and 10.

Top Tips. Note that Systan made a loss in the post-acquisition period – therefore the retained earnings at acquisition were higher than the retained earnings at the year end. This means that, in the income statement, the minority will be allocated their share of a loss. This is unusual – do not be put off by it.

Easy marks. In general this was an easier consolidation question than many we have seen. You were told what the additional depreciation was on the fair value adjustment, and the unrealised profit calculation was simple. The rest was straightforward consolidation procedure, with easy marks for issues such as cancelling out the intercompany loan.

The information in the question and your answer will have told you all you needed to know to answer (b), and there were five easy marks available there

Examiner's comments. The most common errors in this question were:

- Incorrect cost of investment. Some candidates included the loan and some were unable to calculate the value of the shares
- Post-acquisition results of subsidiary treated as profits
- Fair value adjustments omitted
- Problems with minority interest
- Errors dealing with intra group transactions, tax relief and unrealised profit

Marking scheme

			Marks
(a)	**Income statement**		
	Revenue	2	
	Cost of sales	3	
	Operating expenses including 1 mark for goodwill	2	
	Interest receivable/payable	1	
	Income tax	1	
	Minority interest	2	
	Balance sheet		
	Goodwill	3	
	Tangible non-current assets	2	
	Investments	1	
	Current assets/current liabilities	2	
	7% bank loan	1	
	Elimination of 10% intra-group loan	1	
	Minority interest	2	
	Share capital and share premium	1	
	Retained earnings	1	
		Available 25	
		Maximum	20
(b)	1 mark per relevant point to	Maximum	5
		Maximum for question	25

(a)   HYDAN CONSOLIDATED INCOME STATEMENT YEAR ENDED 31 MARCH 20X6

	$'000
Revenue (98,000 + 35,200 – 30,000 intra-group)	103,200
Cost of sales (W2)	(77,500)
Gross profit	25,700
Operating expenses (11,800 + 8,000 + 375 (W1))	(20,175)
Interest receivable (W3)	150
Finance costs	(420)
Profit before tax	5,255
Income tax expense (4,200 – 1,000)	(3,200)
Profit for the period	2,055

Attributable to:

Equity holders of the parent	3,455
Minority interest (W4)	(1,400)
	2,055

HYDAN CONSOLIDATED BALANCE SHEET AT 31 MARCH 20X6

	$'000
Non-current assets	
Property, plant and equipment (18,400 + 9,500 + 1,200 – 300 (W2))	28,800
Goodwill (W1)	2,625
Investments (16,000 – 10,800 (W1) – 4,000)	1,200
Current assets (W5)	24,000
Total assets	56,625
Equity and liabilities	
Equity attributable to equity holders of the parent	
Ordinary shares of $1 each	10,000
Share premium	5,000
Retained earnings (W7)	17,525
	32,525
Minority interest (W8)	3,800
	36,325
Non-current liabilities	
7% bank loan	6,000
Current liabilities (W6)	14,300
Total equity and liabilities	56,625

1   *Goodwill in Systan*

	$'000	$'000
Cost of acquisition (1,200 × $9)		10,800
Share of net assets acquired:		
Ordinary shares	2,000	
Share premium	500	
Pre-acquisition reserves (6,300 + 3,000)	9,300	
Fair value adjustment	1,200	
	13,000	
Group share 60%		(7,800)
Goodwill		3,000
Impairment		375

2   *Cost of sales*

	$'000
Hydan	76,000
Systan	31,000
Intra-group purchases	(30,000)
Unrealised profit in inventory (4,000 × 5%)	200
Fair value adjustment – additional depreciation	300
	77,500

3   *Interest receivable*

	$'000
Per Hydan income statement	350
Intra-company (4,000 × 10% × 6/12)	(200)
	150

4   *Minority interest: income statement*

	$'000
Post-acquisition loss	3,000
Unrealised profit in inventory (W2)	200
Additional depreciation (W2)	300
Adjusted loss	3,500
Minority share 40%	1,400

5   *Current assets*

	$'000
Hydan	18,000
Systan	7,200
Unrealised profit in inventory	(200)
Intra-group debt	(1,000)
	24,000

6   *Current liabilities*

	$'000
Hydan	11,400
Systan	3,900
Intra-group debt	(1,000)
	14,300

7   *Group reserves*

	Hydan	Systan
	$'000	$'000
Per question	20,000	6,300
Pre-acquisition		(9,300)
Unrealised profit in inventory		(200)
Additional depreciation		(300)
Goodwill impairment	(375)	
	19,625	(3,500)
Group share of Systan ((3,500) × 60%)	(2,100)	
	17,525	

8   *Minority interest: balance sheet*

	$'000
Ordinary shares	2,000
Share premium	500
Retained earnings	6,300
Unrealised profit in inventory	(200)
Additional depreciation	(300)
Fair value adjustment	1,200
	9,500
Minority share 40%	3,800

(b) If we look at Systan's pre-acquisition operating performance, we can see a gross profit margin of 25% and a net profit margin of 15%. During the post-acquisition 6-month period revenue is up by 46% but the gross profit margin is only 12% and the company has made a net loss of 8.5%. Clearly this requires some explanation.

Hydan obtained a controlling interest in Systan in order to secure its supplies of components. In the post-acquisition period $30m of Systan's $35m sales were to Hydan and realised 5% gross profit. In order to compensate for this, Systan has substantially increased the price charged to its other customers to give a 50% gross profit margin on those sales. The eventual result of this may be that it will no longer have any other customers.

Systan's results for the second half-year have also suffered from a large rise in operating expenses – from $1.2m in the pre-acquisition half year to $8m in the post-acquisition half year. It looks as though Systan has been charged a large share of group operating expenses. Hydan itself has operating expenses for the year of $11.8m on a revenue of $98m, while Systan has expenses of $8m on 6 months revenue of $35m. As there are no current account balances outstanding, Systan has obviously had to pay the intra-group portion of this $8m, facilitated by a loan from Hydan at 10%. At the same time, Hydan owes Systan $1m on which no interest is being paid.

The overall conclusion must be that Systan's position has been adversely affected by the acquisition and by the resulting related party transactions. Hydan has used transfer pricing and inter-company charges to transfer profits from the subsidiary to the parent company, thus benefiting its own shareholders at the expense of the minority.

31 Hydrate

Text reference. Chapters 9 and 10.

Top tips. Start with **Parts (b)** and **(c).** There are seven easy marks here.

Part (a) Although there are quite a few parts to this question, each part is in itself quite straightforward. If you take a methodical approach then you should earn high marks.

(1)   Sketch out the group structure, noting percentage holdings and the date of acquisition.

(2)   Prepare a pro-forma income statement and balance sheet for your answer, including the assets and liabilities of the parent and its subsidiary.

(3)   Adjust for the fair valuation.

(4)   Calculate the carrying value of the goodwill in the subsidiary.

(5)   Calculate the balance on the consolidated retained earnings.

(6)   Draft the statement of changes in equity.

Easy marks. A straightforward question and you should easily gain 13 marks just by being methodical.

Examiner's comments. This was a fairly straightforward question and was generally well answered. In the balance sheet, the calculations of goodwill, share capital and reserves caused problems. Some poorly prepared candidates calculated minority interest when the question stated that the parent had acquired 100% of the subsidiary.

(a) THE HYDRATE GROUP
     CONSOLIDATED INCOME STATEMENT FOR THE YEAR ENDED 30 SEPTEMBER 20X2

	$'000
Sales revenue (24,000 + 6/12 × 20,000)	34,000
Cost of sales (16,600 + 6/12 × 11,800)	(22,500)
Gross profit	11,500
Operating expenses (1,600 + (6/12 × 1,000) + 3,000 impairment)	(5,100)
Profit before tax	6,400
Income tax expense (2,000 + 2,000 + (6/12 × 3,000))	(3,500)
Profit for the year	2,900

CONSOLIDATED BALANCE SHEET AS AT 30 SEPTEMBER 20X2

	$'000	$'000
Assets		
Non-current assets		
Property, plant and equipment (64,000 + 35,000)		99,000
Goodwill (W2)		27,000
Available for sale investments (0 + 12,800 + 5,000 fair valuation)		17,800
		143,800
Current assets		
Inventory (22,800 + 23,600)	46,400	
Trade receivables (16,400 + 24,200)	40,600	
Bank and cash (500 + 200)	700	
		87,700
Total assets		231,500
EQUITY AND LIABILITIES		
Equity attributable to the equity holders of the parent		
Share capital (Parent only) SOCIE		35,000
Share premium (Parent only) SOCIE		79,000
Retained earnings (W3)		56,300
		170,300
Non-current liabilities		
8% Loan Notes (5,000 + 18,000)		23,000
Current liabilities		
Trade payables (15,300 + 17,700)	33,000	
Income tax (2,200 + 3,000)	5,200	
		38,200
Total equity and liabilities		231,500

CONSOLIDATED STATEMENT OF CHANGES IN EQUITY FOR THE YEAR

	Share Capital	Share premium	Retained Earnings	Total
	$'000	$'000	$'000	$'000
Opening	20,000	4,000	53,400	77,400
Share issue (W2)	15,000	75,000	-	90,000
Profit for the year	-	-	2,900	2,900
	35,000	79,000	56,300	170,300

Workings

1   *Group Structure as at 30 September 20X2*

```
┌─────────────────────────────┐
│          Hydrate            │
│         The Parent          │
└─────────────────────────────┘
              │
    100%      │
    1 April 20X2
              │
┌─────────────────────────────┐
│          Sulphate           │
│        The Subsidiary       │
└─────────────────────────────┘
```

Consolidate in full for six months

2   *Cost of business combination and goodwill in Sulphate*

Number of shares issued: 12m × 5/4 = 15 million

		$'000
Nominal value	$1	15,000
Share premium (balancing figure)	$5	75,000
Fair value of shares and cost of the business combination	$6	90,000

Fair value of the net assets acquired		
Share Capital		12,000
Share premium		2,400
Retained earnings at 30 September 2002	42,700	
Less post acquisition profits (6/12 × $4.2m)	(2,100)	
		40,600
Fair value increase in the value of the investments		5,000
Fair value of the net assets at acquisition		60,000

Goodwill at cost		30,000
Impairment		(3,000)
Carrying value		27,000

3   *Group retained earnings*

	$'000	$'000
Parent's retained earnings		57,200
100% share of subsidiary's post acquisition profits ((\$4.2m × 6/12)		2,100
Impairment of goodwill		(3,000)
		56,300

32 Preparation question: Laurel Co

Consolidated balance sheet as at 31 December 20X9

	$'000
Non-current assets	
Property, plant and equipment (220 + 160 + (W3) 3)	383
Goodwill (W4)	5
Investment in associate (W5)	96.8
	484.8
Current assets	
Inventories (384 + 234 − (W2) 10)	608
Trade receivables (275 + 166)	441
Cash (42 + 10)	52
	1,101
	1,585.8
Equity attributable to equity holders of the parent	
Share capital – $1 ordinary shares	400
Share premium	16
Retained earnings (W7)	323.8
	739.8
Minority interest (W6)	46
	785.8
Current liabilities	
Trade payables (457 + 343)	800.0
	1,585.8

Workings

1   *Group structure*

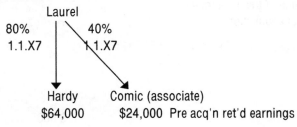

Laurel

80%   1.1.X7   40%   1.1.X7

Hardy   Comic (associate)
$64,000 $24,000   Pre acq'n ret'd earnings

2   *Unrealised profit*

Laurel's sales to Hardy: $32,000 − $22,000 = $10,000

| Dr retained earnings (Laurel) | $10,000 |
| Cr group inventories | $10,000 |

Laurel's sales to Comic (associate) ($22,000 − $10,000) × ½ × 40% share = $2,400.

| Dr retained earnings (Laurel) | $2,400 |
| Cr Investment in associate | $2,400 |

3   *Fair value adjustments*

	At acquisition date $'000	*Movement* $'000	*At B/S date* $'000
PPE (57 − 45)	+12	(9)*	+3
	↓	↓	↓
	Goodwill	Ret'd earnings	PPE/MI

*Extra depreciation $12,000 × ¾

BPP
LEARNING MEDIA

4   *Goodwill*

	Hardy Co	
	$'000	$'000
Cost of combination		160
Share of net assets acquired:		
Share capital	96	
Share premium	3	
Retained earnings	64	
Fair value adjustment (W3)	12	
	175 × 80%	(140)
Goodwill		20
Impairment losses		(15)
		5

5   *Investment in associate*

	$'000
Cost of associate	70
Share of post acquisition retained reserves ((97,000 − 24,000) × 40%)	29.2
Unrealised profit (W2)	(2.4)
Impairment losses	(0)
	96.8

6   *Minority interest*

	$'000	$'000
Net assets per question	227	
Fair value adjustment (W3)	3	
	230 × 20%	46

7   *Consolidated retained earnings*

	Laurel	*Hardy*	*Comic*
	$'000	$'000	$'000
Ret'd earnings per question	278	128	97
Less: PUP re Hardy (W2)	(10)		
PUP re Comic (W2)	(2.4)		
Fair value adjustment movement (W3)		(9)	
	265.6	119	97
Less: pre-acquisition ret'd earnings		(64)	(24)
		55	73
Hardy (55 × 80%)	44		
Comic (73 × 40%)	29.2		
Less: impairment losses	(15.0)		
	323.8		

33 Preparation question: Tyson Co

Consolidated profit and loss account for the year ended 31 December 20X9

	$'000
Revenue (500 + 150 – 66)	584
Cost of sales (270 + 80 – 66 + (W2) 18)	(302)
Gross profit	282
Other expenses (150 + 20 + (W3) 38))	(208)
Finance income (15 + 10)	25
Finance costs	(20)
Share of profit of associate [(10 × 40%) – 2.4*]	1.6
Profit before tax	80.6
Income tax expense (25 + 15)	(40)
Profit for the period	40.6
Attributable to:	
Equity holders of the parent	35.2
Minority interest [(45 – (W2) 18) × 20%]	5.4
	40.6

*   Impairment losses could either be included in expenses or deducted from the share of profit of associates figure. IAS 28 is not prescriptive.

Workings

1   *Group structure*

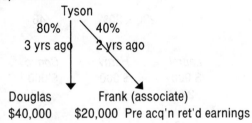

Douglas   Frank (associate)
$40,000 $20,000 Pre acq'n ret'd earnings

2   *Unrealised profit*

	$'000
Selling price	66
Cost	(48)
PUP	18

3   *Goodwill*

		In Douglas Co
		$'000
Cost of combination		188
Net assets acquired:-		
Share capital	100	
Retained earnings	40	
	140	
Group share	× 80%	(112)
		76
Impairment loss (½ per question)		38

34 Hepburn

(a) HEPBURN PLC
CONSOLIDATED INCOME STATEMENT
FOR THE YEAR ENDED 31 MARCH 20X1

	$'000
Sales revenue (W1)	1,600
Cost of sales (W2)	(890)
Gross profit	710
Operating expenses (W3)	(184)
Debenture interest (12 × 6/12)	(6)
Profit before tax	520
Taxation (100 + 40 × 6/12)	(120)
Profit for the period	400
Attributable to:	
Equity holders of the parent	380
Minority interest (200 × 6/12 × 20%)	20
	400

HEPBURN
CONSOLIDATED BALANCE SHEET
AS AT 31 MARCH 20X1

	$'000	$'000
Assets		
Non-current assets		
Intangible: goodwill (W4)		180
Tangible		
Property (400 + 150 + 125)		675
Plant and equipment (220 + 510)		730
Investments (20 + 10)		30
		1,615
Current assets		
Inventories (240 + 280 − 10 (W2))	510	
Accounts receivable (170 + 210 − 56)	324	
Bank (20 + 40 + 20)	80	
		914
Total assets		2,529
Equity and liabilities		
Equity attributable to the equity holders of the parent		
Equity shares $1 each (400 + 300 (W4))		700
Share premium account (900 − 300 (W4))		600
Retained earnings (W5)		500
		1,800
Minority interest (W6)		195
Total equity		1,995
Non-current liabilities		
8% debentures		150
Current liabilities		
Accounts payable (170 + 155 − 36)	289	
Taxation (50 + 45)	95	
		384
Total equity and liabilities		2,529

Workings

		$'000
1	*Sales revenue*	
	Hepburn	1,200
	Salter (1,000 × 6/12)	500
	Less intragroup sales	(100)
		1,600

		$'000
2	*Cost of sales*	
	Hepburn	650
	Salter (660 × 6/12)	330
	Less intragroup sales	(100)
	Unrealised profit in inventory (100 × 50% × 25/125)	10
		890

		$'000
3	*Operating expenses*	
	Hepburn	120
	Salter (88 × 6/12)	44
	Impairment of goodwill (W4)	20
		184

4 *Goodwill*

	$'000	$'000
Cost of investment in Salter 150 × 80% × 5/2 (= 300) × $3		900
Fair value of net assets acquired		
Equity shares	150	
Retained earnings:		
At 1 April 20X0 (700 – 200)	500	
Profit to 1 Oct 20X0 (200 × 6/12)	100	
Fair value adjustment	125	
	875	
Group share (80%)		700
Goodwill at cost		200
Closing impaired value from question		180
Impairment loss (balancing figure)		20

5	*Retained earnings*	Hepburn	Salter
		$'000	$'000
	Per question	450	700
	Unrealised profit in inventory	(10)	
	Pre-acquisition profit		(600)
			100
	Salter: 100 × 80%	80	
	Goodwill impairment charge (W4)	(20)	
		500	

6	*Minority interest*	$'000
	Equity shares: 20% × 150	30
	Retained earnings: 20% × 700	140
	Fair value adjustment of land: 20% × 125	25
		195

(b) In **voting rights**, Hepburn's interest in Woodbridge is **60%;** however it is correct that it is only entitled to 6,000/24,000 = 25% of any dividends paid.

The approach taken by Hepburn to its investment in Woodbridge seems to be based on the view that, with a **25% equity holding**, the investment would normally be treated as an associate and equity accounting applied. However, Hepburn does not exert any significant influence over Woodbridge and hence under IAS 28 *Investments in associates* it can rebut the presumption of associate status.

This overlooks the fact that IAS 27 *Consolidated and separate financial statements* bases the treatment of an investment in another entity on the notion of **control** rather than **ownership**. Hepburn can control Woodbridge by virtue of its holding **the majority of the voting rights** in the company.

Woodbridge is thus a **subsidiary** and should be **consolidated in full** in Hepburn's group accounts, **from the date of acquisition.**

Hepburn's directors may wish to avoid consolidation because of Woodbridge's losses. But these **losses** may indicate that the **value of the investment** in Woodbridge in Hepburn's own individual accounts may be **overstated**. A test for **impairment**, as required by IAS 36 *Impairment of assets*, may reveal that the **recoverable amount** of the investment has fallen below $20,000, thus requiring a write down in Hepburn's own accounts and a write down of Woodbridge's assets in the consolidated accounts.

35 Holdrite

Text reference. Chapters 10 and 11.

Top tips. Part (a) The acquisitions take place in the middle of the year and so the post tax profits have to be time apportioned in order to calculate the net assets at acquisition. Both the consideration and the net assets acquired need to be fair valued.

Part (b) This is a straight forward consolidated income statement.

1   Sketch out the group structure, noting percentage holdings and dates of acquisition.

2   Prepare a pro-forma income statement for your answer. Remember the line for "Share of profit of associate".

3   Time apportion the income and expenses of the subsidiary, the share of the associate's profit, and the minority interest.

4   Note the adjustments for inter-company balances and unrealised profit.

5   The goodwill impairment charge is given in the question.

Part (c) The parent had no subsidiaries at the start of the year.

Easy marks. You should be able to obtain half marks (13 marks) just by being methodical.

Examiner's comments. The main part of this question required a consolidated income statement. In general this question was very well answered. However there were problems with goodwill and minority interest.

		Marks
(a)	*Goodwill of Staybrite:*	
	Value of shares exchanged	1
	8% loan notes issued	1
	Equity shares and share premium	1
	Pre-acquisition reserves	1
	Fair value adjustments	1
	Goodwill of Allbrite:	
	Value of shares exchanged	1
	Cash paid	1
	Equity shares and share premium	1
	Pre-acquisition reserves	1
	Available	**9**
	Maximum	**8**
(b)	*Income statement:*	2
	Revenue	4
	Cost of sales	2
	Operating expenses	1
	Interest expense	2
	Income from associate	2
	Income tax	2
	Minority interest	3
	Available	**16**
	Maximum	**15**
(c)	Dividends	1
	Retained profits b/f and c/f	1
	Maximum	**2**
	Maximum for question	**25**

(a) *Goodwill*

Goodwill in Staybrite

	$'000	$'000
Cost of business combination		
Share exchange: $(2/3 \times 75\% \times 10\text{m shares}) \times \$6$		30,000
Loan Note: $(100/250 \times 75\% \times 10\text{m shares}) \times \$1$		3,000
		33,000
Share of the net assets acquired at fair value		
Share Capital	10,000	
Share premium	4,000	
Opening retained earnings	7,500	
Time apportioned profits for the year; $\$9\text{m} \times {}^{6}/_{12}$	4,500	
Fair value increase for the land $(23 - 20)$	3,000	
Fair value increase for the plant $(30 - 25)$	5,000	
Fair value of the net assets at acquisition	34,000	
75% Group share		(25,500)
Cost of Goodwill		7,500

The fair value of the share exchange is the market price of the shares issued by the acquirer.

The fair value of the loan note is its nominal value.

Goodwill in Allbrite

	$'000	$'000
Cost of business combination		
Share exchange: (3/4 × 40% × 5m shares) × $6		9,000
Cash: ($1 × 40% × 5m shares)		2,000
		11,000
Share of the net assets acquired at fair value		
Share Capital	5,000	
Share premium	2,000	
Opening retained earnings	6,000	
Time apportioned profits for the year; $4m × $^6/_{12}$	2,000	
Fair value of the net assets at acquisition	15,000	
40% Group share		(6,000)
Cost of Goodwill		5,000

(b)   THE HOLDRITE GROUP
CONSOLIDATED INCOME STATEMENT FOR THE YEAR ENDED 30 SEPTEMBER 20X4

	$'000
Sales revenues (W2)	85,350
Cost of sales (W2)	(48,750)
Gross profit	36,600
Operating expenses (W2)	(15,730)
Finance costs	(170)
Share of profit of associate (W3)	800
Profit before tax	21,500
Income tax expense (4,800 + ($^6/_{12}$ × 3,000))	(6,300)
Profit for the year	15,200
Attributable to:	
Equity holders of the parent	14,200
Minority interest (W4)	1,000
	15,200

Workings

1   *Group Structure as at 30 September 20X4*

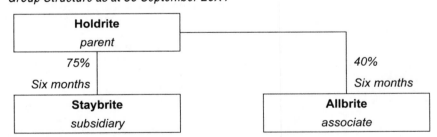

2   *Revenue and expenses*

	Revenue $'000	Cost of sales $'000	Operating Expenses $'000
Parent	75,000	47,400	10,480
Six months time apportioned from subsidiary's own I/S	20,350	9,850	4,500
Inter-company trade	(10,000)	(10,000)	-
Extra depreciation on fair valuation	-	500	-
Unrealised profit *($4m × ¼ in parent's books)*	-	1,000	-
Impairment of goodwill	-	-	750
	85,350	48,750	15,730

3   *Share of profit of associate*

Six months of parent's 40% share of the profit attributable to the equity holders of the associate.

$^6/_{12}$ × 40% × profit after tax of $4m = $800,000

4   *Minority interest*

	$'000
Subsidiary's own profit after tax, time apportioned: $^6/_{12}$ × $9m	4,500
Less: extra depreciation on fair valuation	(500)
	4,000
25% Minority share	1,000

(c)   *Movement on consolidated retained earnings*

	$'000
Opening (Parent only, as there were no subsidiaries or associates.)	18,000
Profit for the year attributable to parent company shareholders	14,200
Equity dividends paid	(5,000)
	27,200

36 Hapsburg

Text reference. Chapters 9 and 11.

Top tips. Don't forget **Part (b).** There are five marks here for rehearsing some of the criticisms of the equity method. Do it first, before getting bogged down in Part (a).

Part (a) This consolidated balance sheet includes an associate accounted for using the equity method. The interest in the associate was acquired during the year and so profits will have to be time apportioned in order to find the net assets acquired.

As always, be methodical.

- Sketch out the group structure, noting percentage holdings and the date of acquisition.
- Prepare a pro-forma balance sheet for your answer.
- Note the adjustments for fair valuations, inter-company balances and unrealised profit.
- Calculate the carrying value of the goodwill in the subsidiary. Don't forget the impairment.
- Calculate the carrying value of the associate. This is the group's share of the associate's net assets plus the goodwill less the impairment.
- Calculate the minority interest in the subsidiary's net assets.
- Calculate the Group retained earnings.

Easy marks. Part (b) is five easy marks.

Examiner's comments. The question asked for a consolidated balance sheet for a group including a subsidiary and an associate.

Part (a) required the consolidated balance sheet and was very well-answered, although there are still some candidates who persist in using proportional consolidation.

Part (b) required a discussion of equity accounting and was either ignored or very badly answered. Even candidates who had used equity accounting correctly to account for the associate in part (a) had very little idea why this was the treatment.

ANSWERS

Marking scheme

		Marks
(a)	Balance sheet	5
	Goodwill (four for total figure, one for depreciation)	1
	Land and buildings	2
	Plant	2
	Investment in associate	3
	Other investments	1
	Inventory	2
	Trade receivables and cash	1
	Current liabilities	1
	10% loan notes	1
	Deferred consolidation	2
	Minority interest	2
	Share capital and share premium	1
	Retained earnings	3
	Available	**25**
	Maximum	**20**
(b)	Reasoning behind equity accounting	3
	Discussion of off balance sheet financing	2
	Maximum	**5**
	Maximum for question	**25**

(a) THE HAPSBURG GROUP
CONSOLIDATED BALANCE SHEET AS AT 31 MARCH 20X4

		$'000
Assets		
Non-current assets		
Property, plant and equipment	(41,000 + 34,800 + 3,750 (W3))	79,550
Goodwill (W2)		12,800
Investments (at fair value)		4,500
Investment in associate (W6)		15,150
		112,000
Current assets		
Inventories (9,900 + 4,800 – 300 W5)		14,400
Trade and other receivables (3,600 + 8,600)		22,200
Cash and cash equivalents (1,200 + 3,800)		5,000
		41,600
Total assets		153,600

	$'000
Equity and liabilities	
Equity attributable to equity holders of the parent	
Share capital (Parent only)	36,000
Share premium (Parent only)	24,000
Retained earnings (W8)	8,050
	68,050
Minority interest (W9)	9,150
Total equity	77,200
Non-current liabilities	
Loans	20,200
Deferred consideration (W4)	19,800
	40,000
Current liabilities	
Trade and other payables (16,500 + 6,900)	23,400
Taxation (9,600 + 3,400)	13,000
	36,400
Total equity and liabilities	153,600

Workings

1 *Group Structure as at 31 March 20X4*

2 *Goodwill in Sundial*

	$'000	$'000
Cost of business combination		
24m shares × 2/3 × $2 (share exchange)		32,000
24m shares × $0.75 × (deferred consideration of $1 in 3 years time)		18,000
		50,000
Share of the net assets acquired at fair value		
Net assets at 31 March 20X4	40,500	
Less retained profit for the year	(4,500)	
Fair value increase for the plant (15,000 – 10,000)	5,000	
Fair value increase for the investments (4,500 – 3,000)	1,500	
Fair value of the net assets at acquisition	42,500	
80% Group share		(34,000)
Cost of Goodwill		16,000
Impairment		(3,200)
Carrying value at 31 March 20X4		12,800

3 *Fair valued plant*

	$'000
Fair value increase at acquisition	5,000
Depreciation over four years remaining life	(1,250)
Carrying value 31 March 20X4	3,750

The subsidiary's retained earnings will be reduced by $1,250,000. This will affect both the group's share of those earnings and the minority interest.

4 *Deferred consideration*

	$'000
Present value of consideration at acquisition	18,000
Finance cost @ 10% (reduces group retained earnings)	1,800
Carrying value 31 March 20X4	19,800

5 *Unrealised profit on associate's sales*

$1.6m profit was made on sales of $4m. Only $2.5m is left on hand, including profit of $1m.

Because the sale was made by the associate, only the group's 30% share will be accounted for, which is $300,000. These items are part of the parent's inventory, and so group inventories will be reduced by $300,000.

6 *Carrying value of associate*

	$'000
Share of net assets ($28m × 30%)	8,400
Carrying value of goodwill (W7)	6,750
	15,150

7 *Goodwill in associate*

	$'000	$'000
Cost of investment		15,000
Share of net assets acquired		
Net assets at 31 March 20X4	28,000	
Less retained profit for six months (6/12 × $6m)	(3,000)	
	25,000	
30% Group share		(7,500)
Cost of Goodwill		7,500
Impairment		(750)
Carrying value at 31 March 20X4		6,750

8 *Retained earnings attributable to the equity holders of the parent*

	Hapsburg	Sundial	Aspen
	$'000	$'000	$'000
Per question	10,600	4,500	6,000
Adjustment for pre-acquisition profits (6/12)	–	–	(3,000)
Unwinding of discount on deferred consideration (W4)	(1,800)	–	–
Provision for unrealised profit (W5)	(300)	–	
Depreciation of fair valuation (W3)	–	(1,250)	–
	8,500	3,250	3,000
Group share of subsidiary (80%)	2,600		
Group share of associate (30%)	900		
Impairment of goodwill in Sundial (W2)	(3,200)		
Impairment of goodwill in Aspen (W7)	(750)		
	8,050		

9 *Minority interest*

	$'000	$'000
Sundial's net assets from the question		40,500
Carrying value of fair value increase for plant W3		3,750
Fair value increase for investments		1,500
		45,750
Minority 20% interest		9,150

(b)   *The Equity Method*

Associates normally arise when an investing company acquires between 20% and 50% of the equity of another, giving it significant influence (but not control) over its investment; in particular it is able to participate in the financial and operating policy decisions of the investee, including its dividend policy. Before IAS 28 *Investments in Associates* such an investment would have been held at cost in the balance sheet even if the underlying net assets had increased, and the income statement would only recognise dividends received. As a result shareholders were unable to tell how well (or badly) these investments were performing. Also, directors could manipulate reported profits by encouraging the associate to pay large dividends (provided the other shareholder's were willing).

Under IAS 28 the carrying value of an associate is its cost plus the investee's share of changes in the associate's net assets since acquisition, with any changes in value being reported in the income statement. As a result it is harder for the investor to manipulate profits, and the underlying performance of the associate is reported by the investor. This method is sometimes called "one-line consolidation" because the income statement only shows the investor's share of the associate's profit after tax, and the balance sheet only shows the investor's share of the associate's net assets. This has the disadvantage that the financial risks affecting the associate are hidden. For example if the net assets are $3m this could represent $4m of assets and $1m of liabilities (which is safe) or it could be $100m of assets and $97m of liabilities (which is high risk). Likewise in the income statement, such key performance indicators as gross profit and interest cover are hidden. Proportional consolidation would solve some of these problems by recognising the investee's share of each item in the income statement and balance sheet. This method is not allowed by IAS 28 because it implies that the investor has control over a part of the associate's trade and net assets, rather than influence over all of it.

37 Hedra

Text reference. Chapters 9 and 11.

Top tips. This is a big question, but as always a methodical approach will ensure a good score.

Look out for the fair value adjustments to Salvador, and remember that increases in fair value *after* acquisition are treated as normal revaluations. The deferred consideration is now payable, which will increase the goodwill and be recognised as a liability. Finally the goodwill in Salvador has been impaired.

Aragon's net assets at acquisition and fair value of consideration must be calculated.

Easy marks. There are no particular easy marks here. Read the question carefully and make your workings very clear.

Examiners comments. A majority of candidates show a good knowledge of the basic principles of consolidation. The main errors were:

- Use of proportional consolidation for the subsidiary. This demonstrates that a candidate has not studied the most important topic in the syllabus and has not attempted past questions.

- Use of full consolidation or proportional consolidation (rather than equity accounting) for the associate.

- Incorrectly calculating cost of the investment in the subsidiary.

- Not including fair value adjustments in the majority interest.

Marking scheme

	Marks
Goodwill	5
Goodwill impairment	1
Property, plant and equipment	3
Investment in associate	3
Other investments	1
Inventories and trade receivables	1
Cash and bank	1
Share capital and premium	1
Revaluation reserve	2
Retained earnings	3
Minority interest	4
Deferred consolidation	1
Deferred tax	1
Elimination of 8% loan note	1
Trade payables and tax	1
Overdraft	1
Available	30
Maximum	25

Group Structure as at 30 September 20X5

Hedra *Parent*	40% 1.4.X5	Aragon *associate*

60%   01-10-04

Salvador *Subsidiary*

CONSOLIDATED BALANCE SHEET AS AT 30 SEPTEMBER 20X5

	$m	$m
Assets		
Non-current assets		
Property, plant and equipment (W3)		650
Investment in associate (W4)		220
Investment in Salvador:Equity (195 taken to cost of control)		-
Loan Notes (50 inter-company)		-
Investments		45
Goodwill (W1)		80
		995
Current assets		
Inventories (130 + 80)	210	
Trade receivables (142 + 97)	239	
Cash at bank	4	
		453
Total assets		1,448

	$m	$m
Equity and liabilities		
Equity attributable to equity holders of parent		
Share capital (Parent only; 400 + 80 (W4))		480
Share premium (Parent only; 40 + 120 (W4))		160
Revaluation reserve (15 + (5 × 60%) + 12)		30
Retained earnings (W5)		261
		931
Minority interest (W6)		112
		1,043
Non-current liabilities		
8% Loan Notes (50 inter-company)	-	
Deferred tax (45 – 10 (tax losses))	35	
		35
Current liabilities		
Trade payables (118 + 141)	259	
Bank overdraft	12	
Current tax payable	50	
Deferred consideration now due (W1)	49	
		370
Total equity and liabilities		1,448

Workings

1   *Goodwill in Salvador*

	$m	$m
Cost of business combination		
Cash		195
Deferred consideration now payable		49
		244
Share of the net assets acquired at fair value		
Carrying value of net assets at 1-4-20X4:		
Ordinary shares	120	
Share premium	50	
Retained earnings	20	
Fair valuation adjustments		
Land	20	
Plant	20	
Deferred tax asset ($40m × 25%)	10	
Fair value of the net assets at acquisition	240	
60% Group share		(144)
Cost of Goodwill		100
Impairment loss given in question		(20)
Carrying value at 30 September 20X5		80

Salvador's profits have exceeded the agreed amount and the $49m deferred consideration is now payable. It will increase the consideration and be accrued for as a current liability.

The $5m increase in the fair value of Salvador's land post acquisition is treated as a revaluation. This will be shared between the parent (60% = $3m) and the minority (40% = $2m).

2 Fair value adjustments

	Acquisition 1.10.04	Movement	B/S date 30.9.05
Land	20	-	20
Plant	20	(5)	15
Deferred tax asset	10		10
	50	(5)	45
	(W1)	(W5)	(W6)

3 Non-current assets

	$m	$m
Hedra		358
Revaluation		12
		370
Salvador	240	
Fair valuation increase of land	20	
Revaluation of land	5	
Fair valuation increase of plant	20	
25% Depreciation on fair valuation	(5)	
		280
		650

4 40% Investment in associate

	$m
Cost of acquisition	
2 shares in Hedra issued for each of 40m shares acquired in Aragon	
Fair value = 80m shares × $2.50	200
Hedra's share of post acquisition profits	
40% × ½ (300 – 200)	20
Carrying value of associate	220

Nominal value and premium of shares issued

	$m
Nominal value of shares issued ($1)	80
Share premium (balancing figure)	120
Fair value ($2.50)	200

5 Retained earnings attributable to the equity holders of the parent

	Hedra $m	Salvador $m	Aragon $m
Per question	240	60	300
Additional depreciation (25% × $20m)	–	(5)	–
Pre-acquisition profits – Salvador	–	(20)	–
– Aragon (200 + ½ (300 – 200))	–	–	(250)
	240	35	50
Group share of subsidiary (60%)	21		
Group share of associate (40%)	20		
Impairment of goodwill in Salvador	(20)		
	261		

6   *Minority interest in Salvador's net assets*

	$m
Salvador's net assets from the question	230
Fair valuation of unrelieved tax losses ($40m × 25%)	10
Fair valuation increase of land at acquisition	20
Revaluation of land post acquisition	5
Fair valuation increase of plant at acquisition	20
Less: depreciation on fair valuation	(5)
Consolidated value of Salvador's net assets	280
Minority 40% interest	112

38 Hosterling

Text reference. Chapters 10 and 11.

Top tips. This is a consolidated income statement including an associate, less common than a consolidated balance sheet but with no serious problems. Start by noting down the shareholdings and the number of months during which the investment in the associate has been held, then do (a) and (b) and get the proforma down for (c).

Easy marks. The only complex part of this question was dealing with the associate. Accounting for the subsidiary was very straightforward and you should have had no trouble with the unrealised profit or the fair value adjustment. So make sure you get these simple parts of the question correct.

Marking scheme

			Marks
(a)	Goodwill of Sunlee:		
	consideration		1
	equity shares		1
	pre acquisition reserves		1
	fair value adjustments		2
		maximum	5
(b)	Carrying amount and impairment of Amber:		
	cash paid		1
	6% loan note		1
	post acquisition		2
		maximum	4
(c)	Income statement:		
	revenue		2
	cost of sales		4
	distribution costs and administrative expenses		1
	finance costs		1
	impairment of goodwill		1
	impairment of associate		1
	share of associate's loss		2
	income tax		1
	minority interests		2
	eliminate dividend from Sunlee		1
		maximum	16
		Maximum for question	**25**

(a) **Goodwill in Sunlee**

	$'000	$'000
Consideration (16,000 × 5 × 3/5)		48,000
Shares	20,000	
Pre-acquisition reserves	18,000	
Fair value adjustment (W)	12,000	
	50,000	
Group share 80%		(40,000)
Goodwill		8,000

Working

Total fair value adjustment = 4,000 + 3,000 + 5,000 = $12m.

(b) **Investment in Amber**

	$'000
Cost of investment (6m × $4) ($3 cash + $1 loan note)	24,000
Share of post-acquisition loss (20m × 3/12 × 40%)	(2,000)
Goodwill impairment (bal fig)	(500)
	21,500

Prior to the impairment test, the investment in Amber had a carrying amount of $22m at 30 September 2006.

Working

Goodwill

	$'000	$'000
Consideration (as above)		24,000
Shares	15,000	
Reserves:		
Prior year	35,000	
Current year ((20m) × 9/12)	(15,000)	
	35,000	
Group share 40%		(14,000)
Goodwill		10,000
Impairment		(500)
		9,500

Alternative calculation

Investment in Amber

	$'000
Share of net assets ((15,000 + 35,000 − 20,000) × 40%)	12,000
Remaining goodwill (10,000 − 500)	9,500
	21,500

(c)   HOSTERLING GROUP
      CONSOLIDATED INCOME STATEMENT FOR THE YEAR ENDED 30 SEPTEMBER 2006

	$'000
Revenue (105,000 + 62,000 – 18,000)	149,000
Cost of sales (W1)	(89,000)
Gross profit	60,000
Distribution costs (4,000 + 2,000)	(6,000)
Administrative expenses (W2)	(16,100)
	37,900
Share of loss of associate (W3)	(2,500)
Finance costs (1,200 + 900)	(2,100)
Profit before tax	33,300
Income tax expense (8,700 + 2,600)	(11,300)
Profit for the period	22,000
Attributable to:	
Equity holders of the parent	19,600
Minority interest ((13,000 – 1,000 (W1) × 20%)	2,400
	22,000

Workings

1   *Cost of sales*

	$'000
Hosterling	68,000
Sunlee	36,500
Intra-group	(18,000)
Unrealised profit in inventory (7,500 × 25/125)	1,500
Depreciation on fair value adjustment (5,000/5)	1,000
	89,000

2   *Administrative expenses*

	$'000
Hosterling	7,500
Sunlee	7,000
Goodwill impairment on Sunlee	1,600
	16,100

3   *Share of loss of associate*

	$'000
Share of loss after tax (20,000 × 3/12 × 40%)	2,000
Goodwill impairment ((b) above)	500
	2,500

39 Preparation question: Contract

	Contract 1 $	Contract 2 $	Contract 3 $	Contract 4 $
Income statement				
	(W1)	(W2)	(W3)	(W4)
Revenue	54,000	8,000	84,000	125,000
Expenses	(43,200)	(8,000)	(92,400)	(105,000)
Expected loss	–	–	(15,600)	–
Recognised profit/(loss)	10,800	–	(24,000)	20,000

	Contract 1 $	Contract 2 $	Contract 3 $	Contract 4 $
Gross amounts due from/to customers				
Contract costs incurred	48,000	8,000	103,200	299,600
Recognised profits less recognised losses	10,800	–	(24,000)	56,000
	58,800	8,000	79,200	355,600
Less: progress billings to date	(50,400)	–	(76,800)	(345,200)
	8,400	8,000	2,400	10,400
Trade receivables				
Progress billings to date	50,400	–	76,800	345,200
Less: cash received	(50,400)	–	(76,800)	(345,200)
	–	–	–	–

Workings

1   *Contract 1*

Revenue 45% ×120,000 =	54,000
Expenses 45% × (48,000 + 48,000) =	43,200

2   *Contract 2*

Expenses All costs to date charged as expense ∴ 8,000
Revenue   Probable that all costs incurred will be recovered ∴ 8,000

3   *Contract 3*

Revenue 35% × 240,000 =	84,000
Expenses 35% × (103,200 + 160,800) =	(92,400)
Loss	(8,400)
∴ Expected loss	(15,600)
Total loss 240,000 – (103,200 + 160,800) =	(24,000)

4   *Contract 4*

Revenue (70% × 500,000) – 225,000 =	125,000
Expenses (70% × 420,000) – 189,000 =	105,000

40 Merryview

Construction contract

In the income statement revenues and profits are claimed in proportion to the cost of work done compared with the total contract costs.

In the balance sheet the amount due from the customer will be the cumulative costs to date *plus* cumulative profits recognised to date *less* billings to date. The costs to date will also include any materials allocated to the contract but not yet used. Billings to date are deducted from the contract balance because they will be recognised elsewhere as an ordinary trade receivable.

(a)   FINANCIAL STATEMENTS FOR THE YEAR TO 31 MARCH 20X2
       INCOME STATEMENT

	$'000
Revenue (W5)	14,000
Cost of sales (W1)	(9,100)
Gross profit (W5)	4,900

BALANCE SHEET

Non-current assets

Plant at cost	3,600
Depreciation	(900)
Net book value	2,700

Current assets

Amount due from customers for contract work

Inventories (unused inventories charged to customer)	300
Costs incurred to date	9,100
Recognised profits to date	4,900
Less progress billings (all received)	(12,800)
Due from customers	1,500

Workings for 20X2

1 *Total costs to date*

	$'000	$'000
Professional fees		500
Materials: delivered to the site	3,100	
less unused at the year-end	(300)	
materials consumed		2,800
Direct labour costs		3,500
Overheads ($3,500 × 40%)		1,400
Depreciation ($3,600 – 600) × 9 months/30 months		900
		9,100

2 *Costs to complete*

	$'000
Given in question	14,800
Depreciation ($3,600 – $900 charges – $600 residual value)	2,100
	16,900

3	Total cost ($9.1m + $16.9m)	$26,000
4	Expected profit ($40m revenue less $26m costs)	$14,000

5 *Proportion of revenues and profit earned to date*

	$'000
$40m (total revenue) × $9.1m (costs to date)/$26m (total costs)	14,000
$14m (expected profit) × $9.1m (costs to date)/$26m (total costs)	4,900

(b) FINANCIAL STATEMENTS FOR THE YEAR TO 31 MARCH 20X3
INCOME STATEMENT

	$'000
Revenue (W5)	16,000
Cost of sales (W6)	(13,400)
Gross profit (W7)	2,600

213

BALANCE SHEET

	$'000
Non-current assets: plant ($3,600 – $2,100)	1,500

Current assets
Amount due from customers for contract work

	$'000
Costs incurred to date (WI)	22,500
Recognised profits to date (W7)	7,500
Less progress billings ($12.8m + $16.2m)	(29,000)
Due from customers	1,000

Workings for 20X3

1   Total costs to date

	$'000
Cumulative costs to date given in the question	20,400
Cumulative depreciation on plant (12 + 9 months)	2,100
	22,500

2   Costs to complete

	$'000
Given in question	6,600
Depreciation ($3,600 – $2,100 charged – $600 residual value)	900
	7,500

3   Total cost ($22.5m + $7.5m) $30,000

4   Expected profit ($40m revenue less $30m costs) $10,000

Changes to expected profit are recognised in the year that they arise. They do not give rise to prior period adjustments.

5   Proportion of revenue recognised in 20X3

	$'000
$40m (total revenue) × $22.5m (costs to date)/$30m (total costs)	30,000
Less revenue recognised in previous years	(14,000)
	16,000

6   Costs recognised in 20X3 ($22.5m – $9.1m charged in 20X2)   13,400

7   Profit recognised in 20X3

	$'000
$10m (expected profit) × $22.5m (costs to date)/$30m (total costs)	7,500
Less profit recognised in 20X2	(4,900)
	2,600

41 Linnet

(a)   *Two methods of accounting for contracts*

When the outcome of a contract can be estimated reliably, then revenue is recognised by reference to the stage of completion of contract activity. As a result revenue reflects the value of work done and profit is claimed in proportion to the work done. This is an application of the accruals principle.

If the outcome of a contract cannot be estimated reliably (for example if the contract has only just begun) then the amount of revenue claimed will not exceed the costs incurred. This means that revenue reflects the cost of work done rather than its value and no profit is claimed. The conforms with the prudence concept. As soon as the outcome of the contract is known revenue should be based on the stage of completion. This means that profits might be artificially low in the early stages of a contract and then unrealistically high in the period when the change to the stage of completion method occurs.

Losses are always provided for in full as soon as they are foreseen, regardless of how revenues are being calculated.

(b)   *Football stadium*

Income Statement (extracts)

	$m
Revenue	70
Cost of sales	(81)
Gross loss	(11)

Balance sheet (extracts)

	$m
Current assets	
Amounts recoverable on construction contracts	59

Workings

This year's revenues, cost of sales and profit is the difference between the cumulative amounts at the beginning and end of the year. The rectification costs will be charged in full as they are incurred. As they cannot be recovered from the customer they will be excluded from the calculation of attributable revenue and profit.

Income Statement

	(a)	Revenue	(b)	Cost of sales	(c)	Profit
Cumulative to 31 March 20X4		220		176		44
Cumulative to 31 March 20X3 (from q)		(150)		(112)		(38)
Recognised this year		70		64		6
Rectification costs				17		(17)
				81		(11)

(i)   *Revenue*

$180m of progress payments received for work done to 29 February = 90% of value of work done.

100% value of work done to 29 February	200
Value of further work done to 31 March	20
Total work done to 31 March 20X4	220

(ii)   *Cost of sales*

Balancing figure; 220 (revenue) – 44 (profit) = 176 (cost of sales).

(iii) *Profit*

Contract price	300
Costs to date	(195)
Costs to complete	(45)
Expected contract profit	60

Recognised to date:					
Value of work done to date:	220	×	60	=	44
Total contract price	300				

Balance Sheet

	$m
Costs to date	212
Profit recognised to date	44
Less rectification costs	(17)
Less progress billings	(180)
Gross amount due from customers	59

42 Torrent

Alfa

INCOME STATEMENT

	$m
Revenue ((12.6 − 5.4) × 100/90)	8
Cost of sales (balancing figure)	(7)
Profit (W1)	1

BALANCE SHEET

Gross amount due from customers (W2)	1.0

Workings

1   *Profit*

	$m	$m
At 31 March 20X5		
Total expected profit	5	
Invoiced to date (5.4 × 100/90)	6	
Profit recognised (5 × 6/20)		1.5
At 31 March 20X6		
Total expected profit	5	
Invoiced to date (12.6 × 100/90)	14	
Profit recognised (5 × 14/20)		3.5
Less recognised in 20X5		(1.5)
Less rectification costs		(1.0)
Profit 20X6		1.0

2   *Gross amount due from customers*

	$m
Costs to date	12.5
Recognised profit (1.5 + 1)	2.5
Progress billings (12.6 × 100/90)	(14.0)
Due from customers	1.0

Beta

INCOME STATEMENT

	$m
Revenue (1.8 × 100/90)	2.0
Cost of sales (balancing figure)	(3.5)
Loss for the year (total loss on contract now recognised)	(1.5)

BALANCE SHEET

Gross amount due to customers (W)	(1.5)

Working

Costs to date	2.0
Recognised loss	(1.5)
Progress billings (1.8 × 100/90)	(2.0)
Gross amount due to customers	(1.5)

Ceta

INCOME STATEMENT

	$m
Revenue (balancing figure)	4.8
Cost of sales	(4.0)
Profit (2 × 4/10)	0.8

BALANCE SHEET

Gross amount due from customers (W)	4.8

Working

Costs to date	4.0
Recognised profit	0.8
Gross amount due from customers	4.8

Total

INCOME STATEMENT

	$m
Revenue (8 + 2 + 4.8)	14.8
Cost of sales (7 + 3.5 + 4)	(14.5)
Profit/(Loss) (1 + (1.5) + 0.8)	0.3

BALANCE SHEET

Amounts due from customers (1.0 + 4.8)	5.8
Amount due to customers	(1.5)
Receivables ((14 + 2) × 10%)	1.6

43 Multiplex II

Income statement	$m
Contract revenue (W2)	18.0
Cost of sales (balancing figure)	(14.1)
Profit (W3)	3.9

Balance sheet $m

Current assets

Gross amount due from customers (W5)	11.0

Workings

1   *Percentage completion*

Percentage completion = $\dfrac{\text{Work certified}}{\text{Contract price}}$

20X1   *20X2(including variation)*

$\dfrac{\$12m}{\$40m} = 30\%$ $\dfrac{\$30m}{\$45m} = 66.7\%$ (ie $^2/_3$)

2   *Contract revenue*

Accumulated revenue to 31 March 20X2 = $\$45m \times {}^2/_3 = \$30m$

In 20X2 revenue = $30m − $12m (20X1) = $18m

3   *Profit*

Revised estimated total profit = $45m − $30m = $15m

Accumulated to 31 March 20X2 = $\$15m \times {}^2/_3 = \$10m$

Total profit for year ended 31 March 20X2:

	$m
Accumulated to date	10.0
Less 20X1 profit taken (W4)	(3.6)
Less rectification costs	(2.5)
	3.9

4   *Profit for 20X1*

	$m
Revenue	12.0
Cost of sales (bal fig)	(8.4)
Profit = ($40m − $28m) × 30%	3.6

5   *Amount due from customers*

	$m
Costs incurred to date	28.5
Add recognised profits (3.6 + 3.9)	7.5
Less progress billings	(25.0)
	11.0

44 Bodyline

Text reference. Chapter 13.

Top tips. Parts (a) and (b) require you to rehearse the standard discussion about the nature of provisions and the need for IAS 37. The well-prepared candidate should score highly.

The calculations in Part (c) can be tricky, but if you lay out your workings in a methodical manner then you should score good marks even if you don't get the answer perfectly right.

Part (d) requires you to criticise the directors' proposed treatment and then to outline and explain the correct accounting treatment.

Easy marks. The discussion parts (a) and (b) represent 12 easy marks.

Examiner's comments. This question dealt with the nature and treatment of provisions. Parts (a) and (b) were discursive; while (c) and (d) were practical examples of the application.

Generally candidates answered parts (a) and (b) well, but failed to deal with the practical applications in part (c) and (d).

Marking scheme

		Marks
(a)	One mark per valid point to max	6
(b)	The need for the Standard and examples to a max of 2 each	6
(c)	28 day refund policy – constructive obligation	1
	Calculation of provision for unrealised profits where goods resold at full price	1
	Calculation of provision for loss on goods sold at half normal price	1
	The product warranties are treated collectively	1
	Warranty cost can be estimated reliably therefore a liability, not a contingency	1
	Faulty goods other than from Header – not a loss, but	1
	Must remove profit made on them – quantified	1
	Return of faulty goods manufactured by Header creates a loss	1
	Quantification of loss	1
	Available	**9**
	Maximum	**8**
(b)	Director's treatment is incorrect	1
	This is an example of a complex asset	1
	Depreciation is $1.65m per annum plus $1,500 per machine hour	2
	Replacement does not meet the definition of a liability **Maximum**	**5**
	Maximum for	
	question	**25**

(a) Provisions and IAS 37

Provisions are liabilities of uncertain timing or amount. Because they are liabilities they must meet the recognition criteria for liabilities - that is there must be:

- a *present* obligation arising from *past* transactions or events,
- the *transfer* of economic benefits to settle the obligation must be *probable*,
- a *reliable estimate* can be made of the amount of the obligation.

The obligation giving rise to a provision can be legal or constructive. A constructive obligation can arise when the actions or statements made by an entity create an expectation that they will meet certain obligations, even if there is no legal requirement for them to do so; for example they may have a well- known policy of replacing goods beyond the normal warranty period.

Provisions are recognised in full as soon as an entity is aware of them, but long term provisions are recognised at present value. As time goes by the discount unwinds, increasing the provision. The increase in the provision is charged to the income statement as a finance cost.

If an obligation depends upon a future event, then it is a contingent liability, not a provision. Also, if the amount of an obligation cannot be measured reliably, then it is a contingent liability. Contingent liabilities are not recognised in the financial statements, although they need to be disclosed unless the possibility of an outflow of economic benefits is remote.

(In the past the term provision has been used to describe the reduction in the carrying value of an asset; for example the provision for depreciation. This use of the word provision does not meet the criteria of IAS 37, and so the term allowance is used instead; for example the allowance for receivables.)

(b)   **The need for a standard**

Although provisions have been a key area of financial reporting for many years, IAS 37 was the first standard to address this issue. Before IAS 37 there were no rules governing the

- definition,
- recognition,
- measurement,
- use, and
- presentation

of provisions.

IAS 37 definition of a provision as a liability of uncertain timing or amount means that provisions must meet the recognition for liabilities. This means that provisions cannot be created to suit management needs. In the past provisions were often created and released in order to smooth profits, rather than to provide for a specific liability. These were sometimes called "big bath provisions" because they could be used for any and every purpose.

A specific example of this was the creation of provisions for reorganisation or restructuring. The charge to set these provisions up could be explained away by management to their investors as one-off exceptional items, but the release of the provision in the future would boost profits. Under IAS 37 provisions for restructuring can only be recognised if the restructuring has begun or if the restructuring has been announced publicly.

The measurement rules have standardised practice in an area where there were genuine differences of opinion. For example there are at least three ways in which the cost of cleaning up an industrial site after it is closed down (restoration costs) can be accounted for:

- ignore the costs until the site is abandoned,
- accrue the costs evenly over the productive life of the site, or
- provide for the costs in full immediately.

IAS 37 states that these costs should be provided for in full immediately, but at their present value.

Under IAS 37 provisions can only be used for the purpose that they were created for; if a provision is no longer needed it must be released. In the past provisions were sometimes created for one purpose and then used to cover the costs of another.

IAS 37 includes detailed disclosure requirements, including the movement on provisions during the year and an explanation of what each provision has been created for. This ensures that the rules set out above have been complied with.

(c)   **Bodyline**

This provision can be reliably measured on the basis of past experience. Although Bodyline does not know which items will be returned or develop faults, it can make an estimate of the total value of returns and faults that there will probably be.

The question does not make it clear whether the 28 day refund is part of the sales contract (in which case it is a legal obligation) or whether it is just a well-known and established part of Bodyline's trading practices (in which case it is a constructive obligation). Either way, an obligation exists that needs to be provided for.

The provision itself can be reliably measured on the basis of past experience. Although Bodyline does not know which items will be returned or develop faults, it can make an estimate of the total value of returns and faults that there will probably be.

The returns provision is $52,850, calculated as follows:

- Of the 10% of sales that are returned under this policy, 70% are resold at the full price. Therefore only the profit element is provided against on these items.

- A further 30% are sold at half the normal sales price, so the provision required will be half of the sale proceeds.

		$
70% resold at full price		
Goods from Header	$1.75m × 20% × 10% × 70% × 40/140	7,000
Other goods	$1.75m × 80% × 10% × 70% × 25/125	19,600
		26,600
30% resold at half price	$1.75m × 10% × 30% × ½	26,250
		52,850

The faulty goods provision is $57,600, calculated as follows:

- 20% of the goods returned will have been supplied by Header; Bodyline will suffer the loss in full on these items.

- Bodyline reclaims the cost of the other 80% returned. Only the profit element is provided for.

		$
Goods from Header	$160,000 × 20%	32,000
Other goods	$160,000 × 80% × 25/125	25,600
		57,600

(d)   **Rockbuster**

No obligation exists to replace the engine and so it is wrong to create a provision for its replacement. Rockbuster may decide to trade in the earthmover rather than replace the engine. Also, the $2.4m depreciation charge includes an element in respect of the engine, so to make a provision as well is double-counting.

Instead IAS 16 states that the earth-mover should be treated as an asset with two separate components (the engine and the rest) with different useful lives. The engine (cost $7.5m) will be depreciated on a machine hours basis over 5,000 hours, while the rest of the machine (cost $16.5m) will be depreciated over ten years.

	Cost	Depreciation charge
	$'000	
Engine	7,500	Depreciated on a machine hours basis over 5,000 hours. The charge is $1,500 per hour
The rest	16,500	Depreciated on a straight line basis over its ten year useful life. The charge is $1,650,000 per annum.
Total	24,000	

When the engine is replaced the cost and accumulated depreciation on the existing engine will be retired and the cost of the new engine will be capitalised and depreciated over its working life.

45 Myriad III

There are a number of issues that need to be considered with regard to the inventory.

IAS 2 requires inventories to be stated at the **lower of cost and net realisable value.** Net realisable value may here be calculated as selling price per pack ($45) less the cost of getting the goods into a saleable condition ($4). This comes to $41 per pack. The write-down to NRV is $48 (cost) less $41 (NRV), which is an apparent loss of $7 per pack.

The question then arises as to how to treat this loss. It is an event occurring after the balance sheet date per IAS 10 *Events after the balance sheet date*, but is it **adjusting or non-adjusting?** This question is important, because the treatment of adjusting and non-adjusting post balance sheet events is different.

Adjusting events are those that provide evidence of conditions at the balance sheet date. Such events require **assets and liabilities** as at 30 September 20X2 to be **adjusted. Non adjusting events** are indicative of conditions that arose subsequent to the balance sheet date. Such events must, if material, be **disclosed** in the notes to the financial statements for the year to 30 September 20X2.

The loss of $7 per pack may be split into **two components**: the loss attributable to the water leak and the loss caused by the price reduction in response to competitive pressure in the post balance sheet period. The **loss attributable to the water leak** is cost ($48) less what the year end NRV would have been had it not been for the price reduction, ie $50, less $4 remedial costs, that is $46. This loss, $2, is an **adjusting event,** requiring a write down of $2 per pack.

The remainder of the loss ($5) is attributable to the **price reduction**. The question states that Myriad reduced its price after the year-end which implies that it is a **non-adjusting event** requiring disclosure. However, it also states that it was in response to price cuts by its competitors. If the market price for these items had already fallen by the year-end then the price cut should be reflected in the NRV calculation as an **adjusting event**.

Regarding the sale to Securiprint, if the marks are indeed caused by a manufacturing flaw on the part of Myriad, the entity will be liable to pay **compensation**, comprising a refund of the goods sold and compensation for any consequential losses. Assuming the amount can be measured reliably, as is almost certainly the case, Myriad will have to make a **provision** in the current year for this amount.

It is possible that the marks are not the fault of Myriad, but until this is determined, the entity has a **contingent liability** (IAS 37), which must be disclosed in the notes to the financial statements. The directors need to consider, in addition, whether any of the rest of its inventory is impaired, and whether a further provision needs to be made.

46 Peterlee II

(a)   The goodwill in Trantor is purchased goodwill and can be capitalised and shown as an asset in the consolidated balance sheet at the value calculated. However, the goodwill in Peterlee itself is internally generated goodwill, and per IAS 38 it cannot be capitalised because it cannot be reliably measured. So the directors will be allowed to include the goodwill in Trantor of $2.5 million in the financial statements, but the goodwill estimated to exist in Peterlee cannot be recognised.

(b)   Per IAS 37 this treatment is not correct. The $2 million present value of the landscaping cost should be recognised as a provision at 31 March 2006. The debit will be to the asset account, giving an asset value for the mine of $8 million. This total value will be depreciated over 10 years. In this way the landscaping cost will be charged to the income statement over the life of the mine. At the same time, the discount to present value will 'unwind' over the 10 year period. This will be credited to the provision and charged as a finance cost. At the end of 10 years, the amount in the provision account should equal the amount due to be paid.

(c)   As this is a convertible loan, it must be apportioned between debt and equity. Per IAS 32 and IAS 39 this is
        calculated as follows:

	$'000
Present value of the principal to be repaid: $5 million × 0.75	3,750
Present value of interest: $0.4 million × 2.49 (0.91 + 0.83 + 0.75)	996
Debt element	4,746
Equity element	254
Proceeds of issue	5,000

The income statement and balance sheet amounts will be as follows:

	$'000	$'000
Debt element of loan		4,746
Interest at 10% (income statement)	475	
Interest paid	(400)	
Balance due		75
Balance of loan at 31 March 2006 (balance sheet)		4,821

47 Jedders

Top tips. This is a type of question which is likely to arise in this paper, covering various standards. In this case,
you need to know about IASs 16 and 32.

(a)   (i)   IAS 16 *Property, plant and equipment* does not allow **selective revaluations** of non-current tangible
                assets: if one asset is revalued, all in that class must be revalued, thus avoiding 'cherry picking' of
                asset gains where others in the class may have fallen in value. In addition, non-recording of a fall in
                value of an asset cannot be justified on the basis that a recovery in market prices is expected in the
                future.

        (ii)   INCOME STATEMENT (EXTRACTS)

	$'000
Depreciation charge	
North (($1.2m × 80%)/20 years)	48
Central (($4.8m × 140%)/40 years)	168
South ($2.25m/30 years)	75
	291
Loss on revaluation	
(20% × $1.2m)	240

                BALANCE SHEET (EXTRACTS)

	Cost/revaluation	Depreciation	NBV
	$'000	$'000	$'000
North	960	48	912
Central	6,720	168	6,552
South	2,250	75	2,175
	9,930	291	9,639

        At 1 January 20X0 the accumulated depreciation of the Central property is $1.2m, which represents
        10 years' worth of depreciation, leaving 40 years remaining life. For the South and North properties,
        the respective lives on these calculations are 30 and 20 years. If there is no previous revaluation
        surplus on the North property, then the loss in the current year is classed as an impairment and must
        be taken to the income statement.

(b)   A statement of how the trade receivables should be treated:

        Group A. These are normal non-factor receivables and the allowance should be calculated as usual.

Group B. Although these receivables have been factored, the risks of late collection and irrecoverable debts remain with Jedders. Thus, the outstanding balance less the receivables allowance should still appear in Jedders' balance sheet, with a liability recorded for the amount received from Fab Factors. In addition, an interest charge would be made for the 1% charge for the monies advanced.

Group C. In a non-recourse situation such as this, Jedders has effectively sold its receivables for 95% of their value. The receivables would therefore be taken off Jedders' balance sheet, leaving cash and a residual finance charge.

Applying these treatments to the figures given:

INCOME STATEMENT

	$
Receivables allowance	
Group A (20% × (1,250 × 20%))	50,000
Group B (20% × (1,500 × 10%))	30,000
Group C	nil
	80,000
Finance charge	
Group A	nil
Group B (1% × 1,500) + (1% × 900) + (1% × 450)	28,500
Group C (5% × 2,000)	160,000
	128,500

BALANCE SHEET (EXTRACTS)

Trade receivables		Less allowance	Net balance
			$
Group A	(1,250 × 20%)	20%	200,000
Group B	(1,500 × 10%)	20%	120,000
Group C		nil	nil
			320,000

(c) IAS 32 *Financial instruments: Presentation* requires the issuer of a **hybrid or compound instrument** of this nature – containing elements that are characteristic of both debt and equity – to separate out the components of the instrument and classify them separately. Fab Factors are thus wrong in their advice that such instruments should be recorded and shown as debt.

The proceeds of issue should be split between the amounts attributable to the conversion rights, which are classed as **equity**, and the remainder which must be classed as a **liability**. Although there are several methods that might be used, the question only gives sufficient information to allow the amounts of debt liability to be calculated, leaving the equity element as the residual.

Year	Cash flows	Factor at 10%	Present value
	$'000		$'000
1 Interest ($15m × 7%)	1,050	0.91	955.5
2	1,050	0.83	871.5
3	1,050	0.75	787.5
4	1,050	0.68	714.0
5 Interest + capital	16,050	0.62	9,951.0
Total debt component			13,279.5
Proceeds of issue			15,000.0
Equity component (residual)			1,720.5

INCOME STATEMENT (EXTRACTS)

	$'000
Interest paid (7% × $15m)	1,050
Provision for additional finance costs	
((10% × $13.2795m) – $1.05m) (rounded)	278
	1,328

BALANCE SHEET (EXTRACTS)

	$'000
Non-current liabilities	
7% convertible loan notes	13,279.5
Provision for additional finance costs	278.0
	13,557.5
Equity	
Option to convert to equity	1,720.5

48 Triangle

Text reference. Chapters 13 and 15.

Top tips. This question had four short sections dealing with various matters: environmental costs, event after the balance sheet date, contingent asset and substance over form.

The way to deal with such questions is to identify the issue and so the accounting standard needed. After that, it is simply a matter of applying the provision of the relevant standard.

Easy marks. If you know how to apply the standards, this is 25 very easy marks.

Examiner's comments. This question was not popular and very poorly answered. Candidates still show a lack of understanding in applying standards to practical situations. Even those who understood the areas examined did not go into sufficient depth in their answers.

Marking scheme

			Marks
(i)	Explanation of treatment of provision		2
	Cost of plant at $20 million		1
	Revised depreciation		1
	Provision initially at $5 million		1
	Increase by finance cost		1
	Income statement charges 1 each		2
		Maximum	**8**
(ii)	An example of an adjusting event		1
	No overall effect on profit, but presentation incorrect		1
	Remove from cost of sales and show as an expense		1
	$30,000 is a non-adjusting event if material		1
	Disclose as a note to the financial statements		1
		Maximum	**5**
(iii)	Due to the dispute this is an example of a contingent asset		1
	Describe the treatment of contingent assets		1
	Not probable therefore ignore, financial statements unchanged		2
		Maximum	**4**

(iv) Identify it as a sale and repurchase agreement (or financing arrangement) 1
      Substance is not likely to be a sale 1
      Will repurchase if value is more than $7,320,500 plus storage costs 2
      Business of Factorall is financing therefore terms likely to favour repurchase 1
      Adjustments to – sales/loan; cost of sales/inventory; 2
           – trade receivables/inventory (re storage costs); accrued finance costs/loan 2

Available	**9**
Maximum	**8**
Maximum for question	**25**

(i)   *Contamination*

There are two errors in the current accounting treatment.

Firstly, the obligation to clean up the contamination existed in full from the day that the plant was brought into use. Therefore the provision should be recognised in full immediately at present value; it should not be accrued incrementally over the life of the plant. Over the next ten years the present value will increase as the discount unwinds. This will be reported by increasing the provision and charging the increase to the income statement as a finance cost.

Secondly, on initial recognition, the cost of the plant should include the present value of the decontamination.

The plant and the provision should be reported as follows:

	$'000
Plant (a non-current asset)	
1 April 20X4: cost ($15m + $5m)	20,000
Depreciation ($20m/10 years)	(2,000)
31 March 20X5: carrying value	18,000
Provision (a non-current liability)	
1 April 20X4	5,000
Finance cost @ 8%	400
31 March 20X5	5,400

(ii) *Fraud*

The fraud means that the draft financial statements for the year-ended 31 March 2005 are incorrect. This probably won't affect the net profit for the year, but it will affect the amounts shown for cost of sales and gross profit.

The discovery of this fraud provides new evidence about conditions existing at the balance sheet date, and so it is classified as an adjusting event. The $210,000 fraud that occurred during the year will be charged to the income statement as an operating expense and disclosed.

The $30,000 fraud occurring after the year-end does not affect conditions existing at the balance sheet date and so it will not be adjusted for. However it will be disclosed if it is considered to be material in its own right.

(iii) *Insurance claim*

The insurance claim gives rise to a contingent asset for $240,000. However, under IAS 37 contingent assets are not recognised unless the realisation of income is virtually certain, and this is not the case here because the insurers are disputing the claim.

A contingent asset is disclosed when an inflow of economic benefits is probable, but without legal opinion it is not possible to regard the success of the claim as probable.

Following on from the above, the insurance claim should be ignored altogether in the financial statements for the year-ending 31 March 20X5.

(iv)   *Factorall*

The $5m proceeds from Factorall cannot be claimed as income because the substance of the transaction appears to be a $5m loan secured on the maturing inventory.

This is because Triangle still retains the cost and benefits of ownership through its option to repurchase the inventory before 31 March 2008. Although legally Triangle could refuse to repurchase the inventory, there is evidence of a constructive obligation to do so as noted below:

- The initial sale was below market price, and so there is an opportunity cost arising from not repurchasing.

- The repurchase price is based on the sales price plus interest rather than on its true market value at the date of repurchase. The market price will probably be higher, suggesting an additional opportunity cost from not repurchasing.

- Factorall, as a finance house, will not have the expertise to bring the product to market, and so it will be expecting Triangle to repurchase. If Triangle refuses to repurchase then it is unlikely that Factorall (or any similar company) will be willing to enter into such an agreement with Triangle again.

Because there is a constructive obligation to repurchase the inventory Triangle should recognise this as a liability (at present value) and continue to recognise the inventory at cost (including the storage costs).

For Factorall the benefit of this arrangement is the 10% compound interest receivable, not the purchase of the product.

The correct accounting treatment for this transaction in Triangle's books is as follows:

INCOME STATEMENT

Finance costs ($5m @ 10%)	$500,000

BALANCE SHEET
Current assets

Inventory ($3m + $300,000 holding costs)	$3,300,000

Non-current liabilities

Secured loan ($5m + 10%)	$5,500,000

The journal to correct the old treatment is as follows:

			Debit $'000	Credit $'000
Debit	I/S	Sales (Proceeds)	5,000	
Credit	B/S	Secured loan (Proceeds)		5,000
Debit	B/S	Inventory (Cost of inventory)	3,000	
Credit	I/S	Cost of sales (Cost of inventory)		3,000
Debit	B/S	Inventory (Holding costs)	300	
Credit	B/S	Receivables (Holding costs)		300
Debit	I/S	Finance costs (10% interest)	500	
Credit	B/S	Secured loan (10% interest)		500

49 Forest

Text reference. Chapter 15.

Top tips. Examples other than the ones we discuss might have gained marks. This is not an easy question; although you should have the arguments in (a) to hand, (b) requires more thought. Also, be careful to follow the time allocations.

(a)   The general aim of accounting is to reflect the **economic reality** of transactions undertaken by entities. this can be undermined by structuring transactions so that, if treated according to the letter of the law, the accounts would show a very different effect. The main aim in most cases where legal form does not accord with economic reality is to **take liabilities off balance sheet**. Entities have used various methods for this, the most prevalent of which was the use of '**quasi-subsidiary**' vehicles, into which debt could be loaded, but which was not consolidated into the group accounts.

Showing legal form rather than economic substance therefore **undermines** the relevance of financial reports and produces information that is of little use to users of accounts. Other types of manipulation include **profit-smoothing** over time, often using provisions and accruals, and undertaking **window dressing** transactions around the year end, often to improve specific performance measures.

(b)   In any transaction, there will be a **variety of features** that will indicate its underlying substance. Similarly, there are certain features that frequently indicate where legal form and substance are likely to be different. Each of these features would need to be investigated thoroughly to determine the substance of a transaction.

   (i)   Transactions may be set up where it appears that an asset has been sold, and legal title has passed to another party, whereas in fact the '**vendor**' **still enjoys** substantially all the **benefits** of ownership (and similarly is exposed to substantially all the risks of ownership). If legal form was followed, an asset could be removed from the vendor's balance sheet, along with the ability to pay for it. The principle of ascribing ownership to the beneficial user underpins IAS 17 *Leases*, which requires finance leases to be accounted for by the lessee as if the lessee owned the asset. Although legal title is held by the lessor, it is the lessee that has the risks and rewards of ownership.

   Applying the **substance over form rule** to some transactions where ownership is separated form beneficial use can have **significant results**. For example, in sale and leaseback situations where full use of an asset is retained by the 'vendor', the transaction would be treated as a **borrowing against the security of the asset** not a sale.

   (ii)   Where a transaction appears not to make sense economically, eg it has been transacted at a substantial over or under value, it may be that it is linked to other transactions. **Only when looked at as a whole will the series of transactions make economic sense**. A good example is where an asset, say inventories of maturing whisky, are 'sold' to another party. However, at the same time the 'vendor' is given an option to repurchase the inventory at a future date, often at a pre-determined amount. When both transactions are viewed together, it becomes clear (where it is the case) that the deal has been set up to give the 'purchaser' of the inventory a lender's return, ie the transactions when viewed together are in substance a borrowing against the security of the inventories.

   In these situations is it important to assess the **true economic effect** of the option. Options are used frequently by entities, quite legitimately, to reduce risks. However, in a linked transactions situation it will often by the case that it is almost certain that the option will (or in come cases, will not) be exercised. In other words, it is not a true option.

   (iii)   As noted in (ii) above, transactions undertaken at an **over- or under-value** are likely to be **linked to another transaction**, such that both together create in substance a very different transaction from when each is considered separately For example, an entity may sell an asset to another party for an amount less than its fair value. The asset is then leased back over future years at a rental below normal commercial rates. As the profit foregone on the sale is compensated for by the reduced rental levels, the profit on sale is effectively '**smoothed**' over future years.

(c) (i) **Legal form basis**

Year ended 31 March	20X2 $'000	20X3 $'000	20X4 $'000	Total $'000
Income statement				
Sales	15,000	nil	25,000	40,000
Cost of sales	(12,000)	nil	(19,965)	(31,965)
Gross profit	3,000	nil	5,035	8,035
Balance sheet				
Inventory	nil	nil	nil	
Loan	nil	nil	nil	

(ii) **Substance of the transaction**

Year ended 31 March	20X2 $'000	20X3 $'000	20X4 $'000	Total $'000
Income statement				
Sales	nil	nil	25,000	25,000
Cost of sales	nil	nil	(12,000)	(12,000)
Gross profit	nil	nil	13,000	13,000
Interest @ 10%	(1,500)	(1,650)	(1,815)	(4,965)
Net profit/loss	(1,500)	(1,650)	11,185	8,035
Balance sheet				
Inventory	12,000	12,000	Nil	
Loan: principle	15,000	15,000	15,000	
interest	1,500	3,150	4,965	
			19,965	
Repaid 31 March 20X4			(19,965)	
			-	

Using **legal form** only, **profits have been spread over two years** (20X2 and 20X4), whereas the **substance of the transaction** is that a **loss is made in the first two years** as interest accrues to the lender. Also, using the legal form only allows sales to be inflated, by showing two sales and purchases, rather then the one 'true' sales, as shown in (ii). The substance of the transaction approach shows the interest charge, which is otherwise completely lost under the legal form approach.

Both methods report the same profit in the end, but the substance of the transaction as shown in the accounts will indicate that this is in fact a **borrowing against inventory assets**; it is not a sale and repurchase with normal commercial features.

50 Atkins

(i) This problem arises whenever goods are delivered on a consignment stock basis, with deferred payment and the option to return unsold goods. The question is, who should recognise the goods as an asset between the date of delivery and the date of payment?

The party that bears the risks and benefits of the cars recognises them as assets in their balance sheet. Even though the cars are held at one of Atkins' show rooms does not mean to say that Atkins recognises them as assets. If the benefits are shared between the two parties, then the party that bears most of the risks will recognise the asset.

If the manufacturer still bears the risks and benefits then the manufacturer recognises the cars in its own balance sheet as inventory at production cost. No revenue or profit is claimed by the manufacturer, and no purchase or inventory item is recognised by Atkins.

If Atkins bears the risks and benefits of the cars then Atkins will recognise them as assets at their purchase price, along with the related liability to pay for them. The manufacturer will no longer recognise the cars; instead it will claim a sale and recognise a trade receivable.

In this situation the risks and benefits are borne as follows:

- The price paid by Atkins is fixed at the date of delivery. This means that Atkins bears any risk (or benefit) of price changes arising after that date. (If the retail price falls, then Atkins will lose out because its own purchase price is based on 80% of the retail price on delivery. Likewise if the retail price rises Atkins gets extra profit because its own purchase price is fixed.)

- The 1.5% per month "display charge" represents interest on the money owed by Atkins to the manufacturer from the date of delivery. This means that Atkins bears the risk of slow moving cars, because Atkins will be charged interest for as long as a car remains unsold (or until six months has passed and Atkins pays for the car in full).

- Atkins right to return unsold cars could, in theory, offset the risk of price cuts and slow moving items. However, in practice Atkins has never taken advantage of this right and so it suggests that for commercial reasons it cannot be exercised (for example the manufacturer may stop supplying cars to Atkins if the right is exercised frequently).

- The one area where the manufacturer still appears to have some rights of ownership is in its right to recall or transfer cars held at Atkins' showrooms.

It is clear from this that Atkins bears all the risks attached to these assets from the date of delivery. Therefore Atkins will recognise them as assets from the date of delivery, along with the related trade payable. The "display charge" will be accrued as it is incurred over time.

The manufacturer will recognise a sale as soon as the cars are delivered, and claim the display charge over time. The manufacturer's experience of trading with Atkins will decide the level of provision needed in respect of returns.

(ii) The legal form of this transaction is that Atkins has sold three plots of land costing $1.2m for $2.4m making a profit of $1.2m. However, there are a number of points that suggest that this is a financing arrangement rather than a true sale:

The sale is for below the market price. Why would Atkins make a genuine sale for $800,000 less than its open market value?

On 30 September 20X5 Atkins has the option to repurchase at $3.2m. On that day the open market value may be higher, in which case Atkins can repurchase and resell again. Atkins will then benefit from any price rises occurring after the original sale in 20X2.

If on 30 September 20X5 the price has fallen below $3.2m, and Atkins does not want to exercise its right to repurchase, then Atkins can be forced to repurchase the following day. Atkins will therefore bear any fall in value arising after 20X2.

The difference between the $2.4m sales price in 20X2 and the $3.2m repurchase price in 20X5 represents interest at the market rate of 10% per annum.

The probability that Atkins will benefit from any future price rises and suffer from any price falls, along with the finance charge implicit in the sale and repurchase prices, suggests that this is a secured loan rather than a true sale.

Extracts from the financial statements for the year to 30 September 20X3

(1) Legal form (the land is considered to be sold by Atkins)

INCOME STATEMENT	$'000
Revenue	2,400
Cost of sales	(1,200)
Gross profit	1,200

BALANCE SHEET	$'000
Non-current assets	

Land at cost ($2m - $1.2m)	800

(2) Commercial substance (the transaction is a $2.4m loan secured on the land)

INCOME STATEMENT	$'000
Gross profit	-
Finance cost ($2.4m @ 10%)	(240)

BALANCE SHEET	$'000
Non-current assets	
Land at cost	2,000
Non-current liabilities	
Secured loan due 20X5 (2,400 + 240)	2,640

51 Angelino

Text reference. Chapter 15.

Top tips. This was not a question to attempt unless you knew something about the various issues involved in off balance sheet finance. (a) may look like something you can waffle your way through, but that is not the case. In scenarios like (b) it is always worth taking the time to read the information twice, then you will understand the situation before you try to evaluate it.

Easy marks. (a) may have looked like easy marks, but only if you knew something about the issues. If you did know enough to answer (a), then (b) was easy marks. These were all classic off balance sheet situations and you should have had no trouble dealing with them.

Marking scheme

				Marks
(a)		1 mark per relevant point to a	**maximum**	9
(b)	(i)	1 mark per relevant point to a	**maximum**	5
	(ii)	sale price not at fair value raises substance issues		1
		leaseback is not a finance lease		1
		treat building as sold (derecognise) at a profit of $2.5m		1
		rental treated as: $800,000 rental cost		1
		$200,000 finance cost		1
		$300,000 loan repayment		1
			maximum	6
	(iii)	general discussion of risks and rewards re consignment goods		2
		Issues and accounting treatment relating to supplies from Monza		2
		Issues and accounting treatment relating to supplies from Capri		2
			available	6
			maximum	5
			Maximum for question	25

(a) Off balance sheet finance is a form of creative accounting which seeks to obscure financial transactions. It has been described as 'the funding or refinancing of a company's operations in such a way that, under legal requirements and existing accounting conventions, some or all of the finance may not be shown on its balance sheet.'

In practice, most off balance sheet finance transactions are intended to keep debt off the balance sheet. In order to achieve this, the related asset is also kept off the balance sheet. An example of this is where an asset is actually acquired under a finance lease. Rather than show the asset and the related loan, the acquirer may decide that the asset is not to be capitalised and the lease is accounted for as an operating lease. Or inventory may be purchased on consignment, under a legal agreement which allows the purchaser to not record the current asset or the related trade payable. Potential suppliers doing a credit reference check on the company will not discover the true value of its existing trade payables or be able to accurately assess its payment record. Another example can be where an asset is 'sold' and 'repurchased' under an arrangement which is in substance a loan secured on the asset. The asset disappears from the balance sheet and the loan is represented as sale proceeds.

Obviously, this conflicts with the requirement for 'fair presentation' in financial statements and the IASB has sought to deal with the off balance sheet problem by means of the definitions and recognition criteria for assets and liabilities in the *Framework*. The *Framework* specifically addresses the issue of **substance over form** and refers to a situation such as that above where 'the reporting of a sale would not represent faithfully the transaction entered into'.

Why do companies want to keep debt off the balance sheet? Mainly to improve the appearance of the balance sheet and avoid any impact on gearing. They want to satisfy the expectations of analysts. An increase in borrowing brings an increase in interest payments, which reduces the amount left to distribute to shareholders. An increase in borrowing above a certain limit can therefore be negatively perceived by investors, leading to a possible fall in the share price. A fall in the share price can leave the company vulnerable to takeover.

A company which is short of funds and needs to raise further loans also needs to convince lenders that it is a good risk. If it already has large loans outstanding, lenders will be less willing to make further loans, or will require a higher rate of interest to compensate for the increased risk of default. The company may therefore seek to move some of its borrowing off balance sheet (perhaps by paying off one loan with another disguised as a sale and repurchase) and thereby reduce its gearing to a more acceptable level.

Off balance sheet finance is to some degree a dynamic issue; new forms of it will continue to arise and it will continue to be a problem for standard setters, auditors, lenders and investors. A number of the high-profile collapses of recent years have revealed substantial amounts of borrowing off balance sheet.

(b)   (i)   In this situation the trade receivables have been factored 'with recourse'. Angelino still bears the risks of slow payment (they receive a residual amount depending upon how quickly customers pay) and non-payment (they refund to Omar any balances uncollected after six months). The substance of the transaction is therefore that Omar is providing a loan to Angelino on the security of the trade receivables.

The receivables have therefore not been sold and should not be derecognised. The payment from Omar should be accounted for as a loan. When a customer pays, the amount lent in respect of his balance should be debited to the loan and credited to his account and the amount needed to clear his balance should be charged to loan interest/ debt collection expenses.

(ii)   This is a sale and leaseback transaction in which the sale price has been inflated to include a loan and the lease payments have been inflated to include interest and loan repayments.

Taking the transaction at its face value, Angelino could record the sale at $12m, showing a profit on disposal of $4.5m. The lease payments of $1.3m per annum would be charged to the income statement as rent.

However, representing the substance of the transaction, the sale should be recorded at market value of $10m, giving a profit on disposal of $2.5m and the additional $2m should be recorded as a loan. The $0.5m per annum above market value in the lease payments should be treated as loan repayments.

The loan will be accounted for as follows:

	$'000	$'000
Initial balance 1.10.05	2,000	
Finance cost 10%	200	
Instalment paid	(500)	
Balance 30.9.06	1,700	
Current liabilities (500 – 170)		330
Non-current liabilities (1,700 – 330)		1,370
		1,700

(iii)   Angelino's contract with Monza is a typical consignment agreement. The cars remain the property of Monza and Angelino bears none of the risks of ownership. When Angelino sells a car or decides to keep it at the end of three months, it purchases it at that point from Monza, at the list price in force at that date. This is therefore the point at which the risks and rewards pass to Angelino. Up to that point there is no sale and the cars should not appear in inventory.

The agreement with Capri is of the nature of purchase under a credit agreement. Angelino pays a 10% deposit and obtains ownership of the vehicles at that point. If it fails to pay the balance, it forfeits its deposit and has to return the cars at its own expense, so it has taken on the risks of ownership, principally the risk of not being able to sell the vehicle. In this case Angelino should show the cars in inventory and set up a trade payable for the list price, less the deposit paid. The 1% display charge should be accounted for as interest.

52 Preparation question: Branch Co

INCOME STATEMENT (EXTRACT)

	$
Depreciation (W1)	5,000
Finance costs (W2)	2,074

BALANCE SHEET (EXTRACT)

Property, plant and equipment includes assets held under finance lease with a net book value of $15,000.

Non-current liabilities	$
Finance lease liabilities (W2)	14,786

Current liabilities	$
Finance lease liabilities (W2) (16,924 – 14,786)	2,138

Workings

1   *Depreciation*

$$\frac{20,000}{4} = \$5,000 \text{ pa}$$

2   *Finance leases liabilities*

		$
Year ended 31 December 20X1		
1.1.X1	Liability b/d	20,000
1.1.X1	Deposit	(1,150)
		18,850
1.1.X1 – 31.12.X1	Interest at 11%	2,074
31.12.X1	Instalment	(4,000)
31.12.X1	Liability c/d	16,924

Year ended 31 December 20X2

1.1.X2 – 31.12.X2	Interest at 11%	1,862
31.12.X2	Instalment	(4,000)
31.12.X2	Liability c/d	14,786

53 Evans

INCOME STATEMENT EXTRACT

	20X3
	$
Expenses (note 1)	X
Finance cost (note 2)	1,171

BALANCE SHEET EXTRACT

	20X3
	$
Non-current assets	
Property, plant & equipment (note 3)	X
Finance leases liabilities	X
Current liabilities	
Trade payables	X
Liabilities under finance leases (note 4)	
Due within one year	7,537
Finance charges payable (W2)	1,171
	X
Non-current liabilities	
Debenture loans	X
Liabilities under finance leases (note 4)	51,033
	X

Notes

1   *Expenses*

	20X3
	$
Depreciation of owned assets	X
Depreciation of assets held under finance leases	6,157
Hire of plant and machinery – operating leases	10,000
Other expenses	X
	X

2   *Finance cost*

	$
Finance charges payable - finance leases (W2)	1,171

3 *Non current assets*

Property, plant & equipment	$ Owned	$ Leased
Cost at 1 January 20X3	X	0
Additions	X	61,570
Cost at 31 December 20X3	X	61,570
Accumulated depreciation at 1 January 20X3	X	0
Charge for the year	X	6,157
Accumulated depreciation at 31 December 20X3	X	6,157
Net book value at 31 December 20X3	X	55,413
Net book value at 1 January 20X3	X	0

4 *Finance lease liabilities*

The minimum lease payments to which the company was committed at 31 December 20X3 are as follows.

	$
Under one year	12,000
Two to five years	48,000
Over five years	15,000
	75,000
Less: Interest allocated to future periods	16,430
	58,570
Due within one year (W3)	7,537
Due after more than one year (W3)	51,033
	58,570

Workings

1 *Depreciation charge for the year*

	$
Cost of asset	61,570
Useful life	10 years
Depreciation charge	$6,157

2 *Interest on finance lease*

	$
Cash price	61,570
Instalment 1 October 20X3	(3,000)
	58,570
Interest October - December 20X3 (2%)	1,171
Balance 31 December 20X3	59,741
Instalment 1 January 20X4	(3,000)
	56,741
Interest January - March 20X4 (2%)	1,135
Balance 31 March 20X4	57,876
Instalment 1 April 20X4	(3,000)
	54,876
Interest April - June 20X4 (2%)	1,098
Balance 30 June 20X4	55,974
Instalment 1 July 20X4	(3,000)
	52,974
Interest July - September 20X4 (2%)	1,059
Balance 30 September 20X4	54,033
Instalment 1 October 20X4	(3,000)
	51,033

Total payments 26 × $3,000 =		78,000
Cash price		61,570
Total interest		16,430

3   *Liabilities under finance leases*

	$
Balance at 31 December 20X3 (excluding interest)	58,570
Less: current portion (12,000 − (1,171 + 1,135 + 1,098 + 1,059) interest	
for October 20X3 - September 20X4)	7,537
Deferred portion	51,033

54 Bowtock

Text reference. Chapters 7, 8 and 9.

Top tips. This question covers three unrelated topics. A reasonable knowledge of each topic coupled with strict time control should yield good marks, e.g. 5 marks = 9 minutes maximum.

Easy marks. Part (a) is very straightforward and should earn you 11 easy marks if you understand deferred tax.

Examiner's comments. This question was poorly answered. Part (a) deals with deferred tax, part (b) with finance leases and part (c) with events after the balance sheet date. Candidates showed little understanding of how the standards are applied in practice.

Marking scheme

				Marks
(a)	(i)	One mark per valid point to	**Maximum**	5
	(ii)	Carrying value and tax base at 30 September 20X3		3
		Calculation of deferred tax at 30 September 20X3		2
		Deferred tax credit in income statement		2
			Available	7
			Maximum	6
(b)		Depreciation of lease asset		1
		Lease interest expense		1
		Net book value of leased asset		1
		Current liabilities: accrued lease interest		1
		obligations under finance leases		1
		Non-current liabilities: obligations under finance leases		1
			Available	6
			Maximum	5
(c)	(i)	One mark per valid point to	**Maximum**	4
	(ii)	Discussion of value of inventory to		3
		Discussion of effect on construction contract up to	**Maximum**	5
			Maximum for question	25

Leased asset

The first task is to decide what sort of lease the asset is held under. This is a finance lease because it transfers substantially all the risks and rewards of ownership to the lessee, as shown by the length of the lease and its cost:

- The asset's useful life is five years (as shown by the 20% straight line depreciation policy) and the lease is also for five years. Therefore the asset is being held for the whole of its useful life.

- The minimum lease payments are $60,000 spread over four years. The present value of these payments at an 8% discount rate is $51,745, which is almost the same as the asset's fair value.

The asset is capitalised and depreciated over its five year useful life, and the obligation to make lease payments is recognised as a liability.

Extract's from Bowtock's financial statements for the year-ending 30 September 20X3

	$
Income statement	
Depreciation charge ($52,000 × 20%)	10,400
Finance costs (800 (W3a) + 1,872(W3b))	2,672
Balance sheet	
Non-current assets	
Assets held under finance leases (W1)	33,800
Non-current liabilities	
Finance lease obligations (W2)	21,696
Non-current liabilities	
Finance lease obligations (W2)	11,376

Workings

1 *Carrying value of asset*

	$	$
1 January 20X2: Fair value of lease and asset		52,000
Depreciation to 30 September 20X2 ($52,000 × 20% × 9/12)	7,800	
Depreciation to 30 September 20X3 ($52,000 × 20%)	10,400	
		(18,200)
Carrying value 30 September 20X3		33,800

2 *Presentation of the lease liability*

	$
Total balance 30 September 20X3 (W3c)	33,072
Capital amount due within 12 months	
Payment 1 January 20X4	12,000
Less un-accrued interest on $31,200 at 8% for 3 months	(624)
	11,376
Capital amount due after 12 months	
$33,072 - $11,376	21,696

3   *Movement on the lease liability*

	$
1 January 20X2: Fair value of lease and asset	52,000
First payment 1.1.X2	(12,000)
Balance 1.1 X2	40,000
Interest on $40,000 at 8% for 9 months	2,400
Balance 30 September 20X2	42,400
Interest on $40,000 at 8% for 3 months (W3a)	800
Second payment 1.1.X3	(12,000)
Balance 1.1.X3	31,200
Interest on $31,200 at 8% for 9 months (W3b)	1,872
Balance 30 September 20X3 (W3c)	33,072

55 Preparation question: Julian Co

(a)

	Carrying Value $'000	Tax base $'000	Temporary difference $'000
Property, plant and equipment	460	270	190
Development expenditure	60		60
Interest receivable (55 – 45)	10		10
Provision	(40)		(40)
			220

(b)   **Notes to the balance sheet**

Deferred tax liability (B/S)

	$'000
Accelerated depreciation for tax purposes [(190 – 90) × 30%]	30
Product development costs deducted from taxable profit (60 × 30%)	18
Interest income taxable when received (10 × 30%)	3
Provision for environmental costs deductible when paid (40 × 30%)	(12)
Revaluations (90 × 30%)	27
	66

	$'000
At 1 January 20X4 [(310 – 230) × 30%]	24
Amount charged to income statement (balancing figure)	15
Amount charged to equity (90 × 30%)	27
At 31 December 20X4 (220 × 30%)	66

Note to the income statement

Income tax expense

	$'000
Current tax	45
Deferred tax	15
	60

56 Deferred taxation

> **Top tips**. The explanations and calculations required here are very straightforward.

Answer plan

(a)
- Reasons – permanent differences, timing differences
- Why deferred tax
- Examples – Interest revenue
    - Depreciation
    - Development costs
    - Retirement benefit costs
    - Research costs
    - Fair value / revaluation
- Accounting convention used to apply accruals concept

(b)
- Explain – deferral method
    - liability method
- Record keeping for both methods when tax rates change
- IAS 12 requires liability method.

(c)

	$'000
Timing difference b/f	100
In year (100-90)	10
	110

Deferred tax = 110,000 × 30%
= 33,000

(a) Accounting profits and taxable profits are not necessarily the same. There are several reasons for this but they may conveniently be considered under two headings: permanent differences and timing differences.

(i) **Permanent differences** arise because certain expenditure (such as entertainment of customers in the UK) is not allowed as a deduction for tax purposes although it is quite properly deducted in arriving at accounting profit. Similarly, certain income is not subject to income tax, although it forms part of accounting profit.

(ii) **Timing differences** arise because certain items are included in the accounts of a period different from that in which they are dealt with for taxation purposes.

Deferred taxation is a means of ironing out the tax inequalities arising from timing differences. In years when income tax is saved by timing differences such as accelerated tax depreciation, a charge for deferred taxation is made in the income statement and a provision set up in the balance sheet; in years when timing differences reverse, because the depreciation charge exceeds the capital allowances available, a deferred tax credit is made in the income statement and the balance sheet provision is reduced.

The tax actually payable to the Government is the **current tax liability**. The credit balance on the deferred taxation account represents an estimate of tax saved because of timing differences but expected ultimately to become payable when those differences reverse.

IAS 12 *Income taxes* identifies the main categories in which timing differences can occur, which include the following:

(i) **Interest revenue** is included in accounting profit on a time proportion basis but may, in some jurisdictions, be included in taxable profit when cash is collected. The tax base of any receivable recognised in the balance sheet with respect to such revenues is nil because the revenues do not affect taxable profit until cash is collected;

(ii) **Depreciation** used in determining taxable profit (tax loss) may differ from that used in determining accounting profit. The temporary difference is the difference between the carrying amount of the asset and its tax base which is the original cost of the asset less all deductions in respect of that asset permitted by the taxation authorities in determining taxable profit of the current and prior periods. A taxable temporary difference arises, and results in a deferred tax liability, when tax depreciation is accelerated (if tax depreciation is less rapid than accounting depreciation, a deductible temporary difference arises, and results in a deferred tax asset);

(iii) **Development costs** may be capitalised and amortised over future periods in determining accounting profit but deducted in determining taxable profit in the period in which they are incurred. Such development costs have a tax base of nil as they have already been deducted from taxable profit. The temporary difference is the difference between the carrying amount of the development costs and their tax base of nil.

(iv) **Retirement benefit costs** may be deducted in determining accounting profit as service is provided by the employees, but deducted in determining taxable profit either when contributions are paid to a fund by the entity or when retirement benefits are paid by the entity. A temporary difference exists between the carrying amount of the liability and its tax base; the tax base of the liability is usually nil. Such a deductible temporary difference results in a deferred tax asset as economic benefits will flow to the entity in the form of a deduction from taxable profits when contributions or retirement benefits are paid.

(v) **Research costs** are recognised as an expense in determining accounting profit in the period in which they are incurred but may not be permitted as a deduction in determining taxable profit (tax loss) until a later period. The difference between the tax base of the research costs, being the amount the taxation authorities will permit as a deduction in future periods, and the carrying amount of nil is a deductible temporary difference that results in a deferred tax asset;

(vi) Certain assets may be carried at **fair value**, or may be revalued, without an equivalent adjustment being made for tax purposes. A deductible temporary difference arises if the tax base of the asset exceeds its carrying amount.

Deferred taxation is therefore an accounting convention, which is introduced in order to apply the accruals concept to income reporting where timing differences occur. However, deferred tax *assets* may not be included in financial statements as a rule, because it would not be prudent, given that the recovery of the tax is uncertain.

A comprehensive tax allocation system would be one in which deferred taxation is computed for every instance of timing differences **(full provision)**, which is the method to be used when applying IAS 12.

(b) **G Co**

Timing difference at 31 March 20X3:

	$
Timing differences b/f at 1 April 20X2	100
Arising in year (100 – 90)	10
	110

Deferred tax liability will be 110 × 30% = $33,000

This figure will be included on the balance sheet.

The decrease in the provision of ($35,000 – $33,000) = $2,000 will reduce the tax charge for the year.

57 Bowtock

(a) **Principles of deferred tax**

In many countries different rules are used for calculating accounting profit (as used by investors) and taxable profit. There are two kinds of difference between the two profits; permanent differences and temporary differences.

- Permanent differences arise when either certain items of expenditure are not allowed for tax purposes (such as entertainment) or when some income is not subject to tax (grants, for example). There is no deferred tax on these items.

- Temporary differences arise when income or expenditure is recognised in the financial statements in one year, but is charged or allowed for tax in another. Deferred tax needs to be provided for on these items.

The most important temporary difference is that between depreciation charged in the financial statements and capital allowances in the tax computation. In practice capital allowances tend to be higher than depreciation charges, resulting in accounting profits being higher than taxable profits. This means that the actual tax charge (known as *current tax*) is too low in comparison with accounting profits. However, these differences even out over the life of an asset, and so at some point in the future the accounting profits will be lower than the taxable profits, resulting in a relatively high current tax charge.

These differences are misleading for investors who value companies on the basis of their post tax profits (by using EPS for example). Deferred tax adjusts the reported tax expense for these differences. As a result the reported tax expense (the current tax for the period plus the deferred tax) will be comparable to the reported profits, and in the balance sheet a provision is built up for the expected increase in the tax charge in the future.

There are many ways that deferred tax could be calculated. IAS 12 states that the *balance sheet liability method* should be used. This provides for the tax on the difference between the carrying value of an asset (or liability) and its tax base. The tax base is the value given to an asset (or liability) for tax purposes. The deferred tax charge (or credit) in the income statement is the increase (or decrease) in the provision reported in the balance sheet.

(b) *Bowtock*

The provision for deferred tax in Bowtock's balance sheet at 30 September 2003 will be the potential tax on the difference between the accounting carrying value of $1,400,000 and the tax written down value of $768,000. The difference is $632,000 and the tax on the difference is $158,000.

The charge (or credit) for deferred tax in the income statement is the increase (or decrease) in the provision during the year. The closing provision of $158,000 is less than the opening provision of $160,000, so there is a credit for $2,000 in respect of this year.

Movement in the provision for deferred tax for the year-ending 30 September 20X3

	$
Opening provision	160,000
Credit released to the income statement	(2,000)
Closing provision	158,000

Workings

		Accounting Carrying value		Tax base	Difference	Tax @ 25%
		$		$	$	$
Y/E 09/X1						
Purchase		2,000,000		2,000,000	-	-
Depreciation	W1	(200,000)	W2	(800,000)		
Balance		1,800,000		1,200,000	600,000	150,000
Y/E 09/X2						
Depreciation		(200,000)	W3	(240,000)		
Balance		1,600,000		960,000	640,000	160,000
Y/E 09/X3						
Depreciation		(200,000)	W4	(192,000)		
Balance		1,400,000		768,000	632,000	158,000

(W1) $2,000,000 cost - $400,000 residual value over 8 years.
(W2) $2,000,000 × 40%
(W3) $1,200,000 × 20%
(W3) $960,000 × 20%

58 Preparation question: Fenton Co

(a)

Date	Narrative	Shares	Time	Bonus fraction	Weighted average
1.1.X1	b/d	5,000,000	× $^1/_{12}$	× $^{2.00}/_{1.95}$ × $^{11}/_{10}$	470,085
31.1.X1	Rights issue	+ 1,250,000			
		6,250,000	× $^5/_{12}$	× $^{11}/_{10}$	2,864,583
30.6.X1	FMP	+ 125,000			
		6,375,000	× $^5/_{12}$	× $^{11}/_{10}$	2,921,875
30.11.X1	Bonus issue	+ 637,500			
		7,012,500	× $^1/_{12}$		584,375
					6,840,918

TERP	4 @ 2	=	8.00
	1 @ 1.75	=	1.75
	5		9.75
	∴ 1.95		

EPS for y/e 31.12.X1 = $\dfrac{\$2,900,000}{6,840,918}$ = 42.4c

Restated EPS for y/e 31.12.X0 = 46.4c × $\dfrac{1.95}{2.00}$ × $^{10}/_{11}$ = 41.1c

(b)   **Sinbad Co**

Basic EPS = $\dfrac{\$644,000}{10,000,000}$ = 6.44c

Earnings	
PFP	644,000
Interest saving (1,200,000 @ 5% × 70%)	42,000
	686,000
Number of shares	
Basic	10,000,000
On conversion	4,800,000
	14,800,000

Diluted EPS = $\dfrac{\$686,000}{14,800,000}$ = 4.64c

(c) **Talbot Co**

Basic EPS = $\dfrac{540,000}{5,000,000}$ = 10.8c

Diluted EPS:

Consideration on exercise
400,000 × $1.10 = $440,000

Shares acquired at FV
$440,000/$1.60 = 275,000

∴ shares issued for no consideration
(400,000 − 275,000) = 125,000

EPS = $\dfrac{540,000}{5,000,000\ +\ 125,000}$ = 10.5c

59 Savoir

Shares in issue

	Shares 25c
1 April 20X3	40,000,000
1 July 20X3 FMP	8,000,000
	48,000,000
1 January 20X4 Bonus issue (48/4)	12,000,000
31 March 20X4	60,000,000

(a) *Year ended 31 March 20X4*

	m
Shares	
Existing	40
New issue (8m × 9/12 months)	6
Bonus issue (48/4) (treated as in issue for whole year)	12
	58

Earnings $13.8m, therefore EPS = 13.8/58 = 24c

Comparative

The EPS for 20X3 would be restated to allow for the dilutive effect of the bonus issue as follows:

25c × 48/60* = 20c

*   Existing shares + new issue = 48
Existing shares + new issue + bonus issue = 60

Note that the 8m shares issued at full price are non-dilutive and are therefore added to both sides of the fraction.

Year ended 31 March 20X5

'2 for 5' rights issue takes place halfway through the year and results in 24m additional shares.

Weighted average number of shares calculated as follows:

	m
60 × 6/12 × 2.4 / 2 (market price / theoretical ex-rights price (W))	36
84 × 6/12	42
	78

Earnings $19.5m, therefore EPS = 19.5 / 78 = 25c

Comparative

The EPS for 20X4 is now restated following the rights issue in October 20X4 as follows:

24c × Theoretical ex-rights price (W) / Market price = 24c × 2 / 2.40 = 20c

Working

	$
Theoretical ex-rights price	
5 shares at market price (5 × 2.4)	12
2 shares at $1	2
	14/7 = 2

(b)   Basic EPS = $25.2m/84m = 30c

Diluted EPS:

	Shares	Earnings
	m	$m
Existing	84.0	25.2
Loan stock	10.0	1.2 (W1)
Share options	4.8 (W2)	–
	98.8	26.4

EPS = 26.4 / 98.8 = 26.7c

Workings

1   *Loan stock*

	$m
When conversion takes place there will be a saving of:	
Interest (20m × 8%)	1.6
Less tax (1.6 × 25%)	(0.4)
	1.2

2   *Share options*

Shares issued will be 12m @ $1.50 = $18m.

At market price of $2.50 the value would be $30m.

The shortfall is $12m, which is equivalent to 4.8m shares at market price

60 Niagara

(a)   *Dividend cover*

Dividend cover describes how many times the equity dividend is covered by the profits attributable to the equity holders. A high ratio (say above three) means that the company could maintain its present level of dividend even if profits were to fall in future years; this makes the company attractive to some investors because there is a lower risk of a reduction in investment income. If this ratio is low (say less than 2) then any reduction in profits could easily lead to a forced reduction in the level of equity dividend. This increases the risks of investing in the company, and makes the company less attractive to investors. A ratio below 1 means that the company is using previous year's profits to pay this year's dividend. This is unsustainable in the long run.

Niagara's dividend cover is 2.02. This is not in the danger zone, but it is unspectacular. Although Niagara may not have to reduce its dividend unless profits halve, there is no room for increasing the dividend unless profits rise.

Workings

Niagara's draft accounts show a $2,585,000 profit attributable to the equity holders, but this is before accounting for the preference dividends. The revised profit attributable to the equity shareholders is as follows:

	$
Draft equity shareholders profit	2,585,000
$1m 8% preference shares (full year)	(80,000)
$1m 6% preference shares (half year)	(30,000)
Revised profits attributable to the equity shareholders	2,475,000

Niagara has declared two equity dividends for the year. The interim dividend was paid to its original shareholders, but the final dividend will also be paid to the new shares arising from the one-for-five rights issue:

	Share capital	Nominal Value	Number of shares	Dividend per share	Total dividend $
Interim	$3m	25 cents	12,000,000	3 cents	360,000
Final	$3.6m	25 cents	14,400,000	6 cents	864,000
					1,224,000

Dividend cover = $2,475,000 / $1,224,000 = 2.02

(b) *Basic earnings per share*

This is the profits attributable to the ordinary equity holders of the parent divided by the weighted average number of ordinary shares outstanding during the period. This year's calculation takes into account the rights issue half way through the year. Last year's reported EPS of 24c will have to be adjusted for the bonus element of the rights issue.

Basic EPS

20X3	17.7 cents
20X2 (restated)	22.5 cents

20X3 Basic EPS

$$\frac{\text{Profit attributable to the ordinary equity holders of the parent}}{\text{Weighted average number of ordinary shares outstanding during the period}}$$

$$\frac{\$2,475,000 \text{ (see above)}}{14,000,000 \text{ shares (see below)}} = 17.7 \text{ cents}$$

Weighted average number of ordinary shares

Share holding	Number of shares	Weighting	
Original holding plus "Bonus" element	12,800,000	12/12	12,800,000
"Full market value" element of rights issue	1,600,000	9/12	1,200,000
Closing holding	14,400,000		14,000,000

"Bonus" and "full market" elements of rights issue:

Theoretical ex-rights price

	Number of shares	Price	Market capitalisation $
Original holding	12,000,000	$2.40	28,800,000
Rights issue	2,400,000	$1.50	3,600,000
	14,400,000		32,400,000

Theoretical ex-rights price = $32.4m / 14.4m shares = $2.25 per share

Original shareholding grossed-up for 'bonus' issue

Original holding of 12m shares $\quad \times \quad \dfrac{\$2.40}{\$2.25} \quad = \quad$ 12,800,000 shares

"Full market value" issue

2,400,000 shares less 800,000 bonus issue = 1,600,000 at full market value.

20X2 Restated EPS

Original EPS scaled down for "bonus" issue

24 cents as originally reported $\times \dfrac{\$2.25}{\$2.40} = 22.5$ cents

(c) *Fully diluted earnings per share*

Investors need to be aware of circumstances that might reduce earnings per share in the future. Diluted EPS measures the effect that existing commitments might have on future EPS. The two examples in this question are typical:

- When the convertible loan stock is converted into ordinary shares there will be an increase in the number of shares that the earning must be shared between. However, there will also be an increase in available earnings because the loan interest will no longer be paid.

- When the directors receive their free shares in 2005 there will also be an increase in the number of equity shares, but this time with no compensating increase in profits.'

The net effect of increases in profits and shares can increase or reduce EPS. If the diluted EPS is less than the basic EPS then it must be reported in the financial statements.

Niagara's fully diluted EPS is 16.5 cents, about 7% less than the basic EPS of 17.7 cents. This is not a prediction of what Niagara's EPS will be in 2005, merely an illustration of how this year's profits would have been shared had these events already taken place. It serves to warn investors of the effects of existing obligations to issue shares.

Workings

Revised earnings for the year (W1 below)
Revised number of shares in issue (W2 below) $\quad \dfrac{\$2,573,000}{15,550,000} = 16.5$ cents

1 *Revised earnings*

	$'000
Basic earnings	2,475
Add: Interest saved ($2m × 7%)	140
Less: Tax charge ($140,000 @ 25%)	(42)
Diluted earnings	2,573

2 *Revised number of shares*

Weighted average number of shares in issue this year	14,000,000
Maximum conversion of loan stock: $2m × 40 shares / $100	800,000
Directors' warrants	750,000
Diluted number of shares in issue	15,550,000

61 Preparation question: Analytical review

		20X7	20X6	20X5	20X4	20X3
(a)						
1	Net profit before tax: sales	18.3%	11.1%	14.0%	9.4%	6.9%
2	Net profit before tax: total assets less current liabilities	31.6%	20.8%	28.0%	19.5%	14.7%
3	Working capital ratio	×1.77	×1.68	×1.40	×1.77	×1.65
4	Liquidity ratio	0.60	0.50	0.54	0.68	0.70
5	Sales: non-current assets	×2.65	×3.00	×2.77	×3.54	×3.48
6	Inventory turnover (cost of sales: inventory ratio)	×1.78	×1.50	×2.03	×2.29	×2.53
7	Receivables collection period (average receivables ÷ sales × 365) (Average receivables taken as average value of opening and closing receivables)	51 days	53 days	62 days	62 days	-
8	Age of inventory (average inventory ÷ cost of sales × 365)	199 days	198 days	168 days	143 days	-
9	Sales growth (% pa)	21%	35%	18%	16%	-
10	Cost of sales growth (% pa)	25%	16%	11%	15%	-
11	Net profit growth (% pa)	100%	7%	75%	160%	-
12	Plant/machinery growth (% pa)	60%	67%	50%	33%	-
13	Working capital per $1 sales	20c	20c	14c	20c	18c
14	Gearing ratio (debt including overdraft: equity ratio)	90%	130%	60%	89%	126%
15	Gross profit/sales	46%	47%	39%	35%	33%
16	Payables*/cost of sales × 365	98 days	139 days	174 days	93 days	84 days

*excluding overdraft

(b) (i) **Analysis of the financing proposals**

The company needs some long-term funds, to redeem the debenture inventory in 20X9 and to finance further sales growth.

The amount of **extra long-term capital** required is uncertain; $1.5m is needed to redeem the inventory. The sales growth has been fairly strong for the last four years, and if similar growth rates continue, the company will need funding for extra working capital and for new non-current assets.

It is perhaps significant that the **percentage growth** in **non-current assets** has been well **in excess of sales growth**, indicating perhaps that the company is having to purchase more expensive equipment to remain competitive. Both gross profit/sales and net profit/sales have improved over the years, indicating that in spite of the growth in non-current assets, profitability is improving (due perhaps to greater productivity).

However, **sales as a proportion of non-current assets** was relatively **low** in 20X7, suggesting perhaps that asset utilisation is below capacity and could be improved, thus reducing the requirement for non-current asset purchases.

The source of **additional long-term capital will be debt capital or equity**. The company's net profits are probably insufficient to provide finance from retained earnings, and so extra finance will be needed from debt capital or a new issue of equity.

The company's **financial gearing**, although fluctuating, has been **high**. This raises doubts about whether sufficient debt capital can be raised to meet all the company's finance requirements. Presumably, the existing loan notes are secured; a new issue of loan notes maturing in 20X9 will also need security. The bank borrowing will probably also be secured by a charge, perhaps a floating charge on the company's inventories and receivables. Plant and machinery does not usually provide good security, and so there would be doubts about whether the company could raise sufficient extra loan capital, because of inadequate security (and excessive gearing).

(ii) **Reasonableness of figures**

The **five-year results** show a continuing growth in sales and profits, with a return and profit ratio currently higher than the industry average.

A comparison with the average statistics for the industry indicates that the **control of working capital** by AB Co is not as good as it might be. Although the company has maintained a fairly steady ratio of working capital per $1 of sales at around 20c, its current ratio and liquidity ratio are lower than the industry average.

In spite of this, **turnover of inventory is slower** than the industry average, the average **debt collection period** a little **longer** and the **age of inventory greater**. This suggests that the company is taking longer-than-average credit from suppliers, in spite of the improvement in 20X7. The figures therefore suggest that some attention should be given to working capital and cash flow, with a view to improving inventory turnover, better credit management and improving liquidity. The inventory valuation may not be accurate, which would affect the profit figure.

62 Rytetrend

Text reference. Chapters 19 and 21.

Top tips. **Part (a)** Cash flow questions are a good choice in an exam. The format and content are straight forward and easy to learn. All the information needed for your answer must be given to you in the question. A methodical approach will generate good marks.

Part (b) This question refers to operating performance and financial position, and so the income statement and balance sheet need to be discussed along with the cash flow statement. Note that more marks are available for this analysis than for the cash flow itself, so make sure that you leave yourself enough time for Part (b). Also, with only about 20 to 25 minutes available, you must be economical with the number of ratios you calculate and concentrate on making comments.

Easy marks. Part (a) is 12 easy marks.

Examiner's comments. This question consisted of a cash flow statement and an interpretation of it.

Part (a), the cash flow statement, was relatively straightforward but candidates are still not adjusting for non-cash elements. Also many candidates described inflows as outflows and vice versa.

Part (b), the report analysing performance, was poorly answered. As has happened in the past, candidates calculated ratios but then failed to explain why the ratio had moved. Other candidates calculated too many ratios: the marking scheme gave five marks to calculation and 9 marks to 'appropriate comments'.

Marking scheme

			Marks
(a)	Profit before tax		1
	Depreciation adjustment		1
	Loss on sale of plant		1
	Warranty provision		1
	Working capital changes		2
	Interest paid		1
	Tax paid		1
	Purchase of non-current assets		2
	Share issue; issue/redemption of loan		2
	Ordinary dividends		1
	Decrease in cash		1
		Available	**14**
		Maximum	**12**
(b)	Relevant ratios	**Available**	**5**
	Appropriate comments	**Available**	$\underline{9}$
			14
		Maximum	**13**
		Maximum for question	**25**

(a) RYTETREND
CASH FLOW STATEMENT FOR THE YEAR ENDED 31 MARCH 20X3

	$'000	$'000
Cash flows from operating activities		
Profit before taxation (W1)		3,640
Adjustments for:		
Depreciation (W2)		7,410
Loss on disposal of PPE (W2)		700
Warranty charge		580
Warranty costs paid (150 + 580 – 500)		(230)
Interest expense		460
Operating profit before working capital changes		12,560
(Increase) decrease in trade & other receivables (1,100 – 1,950)		850
(Increase) decrease in inventories (2,650 – 3,270)		620
Increase (decrease) in trade payables (2,850 – 1,980)		870
Cash generated from operations		14,900
Interest paid		(460)
Income taxes paid (630 + 1,000 – 720)		(910)
Net cash from operating activities		13,530
Cash flows from investing activities		
Purchase of property, plant and equipment (W2)	(15,550)	
Net cash used in investing activities		(15,550)
Cash flows from financing activities		
Proceeds from issue of share capital (13,000 – 10,000)	3,000	
Proceeds of 6% Loan Notes	2,000	
Repayment of 10% Loan Notes	(4,000)	
Dividends paid: Ordinary	(430)	
Net cash from financing activities		570
Net decrease in cash and cash equivalents		(1,450)
Opening cash and cash equivalents (Note)		400
Closing cash and cash equivalents (Note)		(1,050)

Note. Cash and cash equivalents

	31.3.X3	31.3.X2
	$'000	$'000
Cash at bank and in hand	-	400
Overdrafts	(1,050)	-
	(1,050)	400

Workings

1   *Construction costs and profit before tax*

The cash flow statement will take into account the changes to assets and profits caused by capitalising $300,000 of construction costs.

	$'000
Profit before tax in the draft income statement	3,400
Add back capitalised installation costs	300
Less 20% depreciation on these costs	(60)
	3,640

2   *Property, plant and equipment*

Movement for the year

	Cost	Depreciation
	$'000	$'000
Opening balance	27,500	10,200
Disposal: Cost	(6,000)	-
Depreciation ($6m × 20% × 4 years)	-	(4,800)
Additions (balancing figure)	15,750	-
Depreciation (balancing figure)	-	7,350
Closing balance (In draft accounts)	37,250	12,750
Capitalised installation costs	300	60
Revised closing balance	37,550	12,810

Depreciation charge

	$'000
Draft (from above)	7,350
Installation costs (from above)	60
Charge for the year	7,410

Loss on disposal

	$'000
Proceeds (trade in allowance)	500
Carrying value of disposals (6,000 – 4,800)	(1,200)
Loss	700

Payments for additions

	$'000
Draft (from above)	15,750
Installation costs (from above)	300
Less trade in allowance	(500)
Loss	15,550

(b)   **Commentary**

Operating performance

Rytetrend has posted a 35% increase in revenues, which is exceptionally good (assuming that inflation is negligible). One way to boost revenues is to cut the selling price in the hope of attracting more customers on the basis of price. This would lead to a steep fall in the gross profit margin. In this case Rytetrend's gross profit margin has fallen from 31.9% to 29.2%, which is only a modest fall. Maybe Rytetrend has attracted new customers owing to the quality of its products as well as because of its prices.

Although operating expenses have increased, they now only account for 17% of revenues rather than 20%. This suggests that Rytetrend has benefited from economies of scale as their business has increased.

Rytetrend's return on capital employed has improved from 14.4% to 18%. This is good, especially considering the $16m of capital expenditure during the year. Next year should be even better as a full year's profits will be earned from these new assets.

Financial position

Although the cash flow statement shows a net decrease in cash of $1.45m, Rytetrend is in a much better financial position now than at the start of the year.

- Rytetrend has generated $14.9m from its operations, which covers its finance costs ($460,000) and dividends ($430,000) sixteen times over.

- The only reason why net cash has decreased is because $15.55m has been invested in new equipment, which should boost profits and cash flows even more next year.

- The burden of Rytetrend's loan finance has been reduced in two ways. Firstly the total amount of debt has been reduced from $4m to $2m. Secondly, the cost of debt has been reduced from 10% to 6%. In the future Rytetrend's finance costs should only be $120,000 instead of $400,000. This reduction was made possible by an extra $3m of share capital raised during the year.

Controls over working capital have also been tightened.

- Inventory days have been reduced from 75 to 43 days. This is good for cash flow and it also reduces the likelihood of obsolescence.

- The cash collection period from trade receivables has been reduced from 30 to 13 days. As well as boosting cash flows this also reduces the chances of debts going bad. This reduction could have been caused by better credit control, or by fewer sales being made on credit.

- The supplier payment period has remained at about 45 days. This is acceptable to most suppliers and also helps Rytetrend's cash flow.

The net effect of these changes is that the working capital cycle has been reduced from 60 days to 10 days, which is good. It also means that the current ratio has reduced from 2.04 to 0.73. In the past this would have been considered worrying, but today's thinking is that this reflects an efficient use of resources, especially by a retail business with strong cash generation.

Overall this business is generating a lot of cash. It will only take 25 working days to pay off the overdraft, and the modest level of dividends compared to profits or investment suggests that the management take a prudent view of their stewardship of the company.

Summary of ratios (based on revised figures)

	20X3	20X2
Increase in revenues	+35%	
Gross profit margin	29.2%	31.9%
Operating expense % $\dfrac{\text{Operating expenses}}{\text{Revenues}}$	17%	20%
Interest cover $\dfrac{\text{Profit before finance costs}}{\text{Finance costs}}$	8.9	5.8
Net profit margin $\dfrac{\text{Profit before tax}}{\text{Revenues}}$	11.4%	10.2%
Return on capital employed $\dfrac{\text{Profit before finance costs}}{\text{Assets - current liabilities}}$	18%	14.6%
Inventory days $\dfrac{\text{Inventory days} \times 365}{\text{Cost of sales}}$	43 days	75 days
Receivables days $\dfrac{\text{Trade receivables} \times 365}{\text{Revenues}}$	13 days	30 days
Payables days $\dfrac{\text{Trade payables} \times 365}{\text{Cost of sales}}$	46 days	45 days

	20X3	20X2
Working capital cycle	10 days	60 days
Current ratio		
$\dfrac{\text{Current assets}}{\text{Current liabilities}}$	0.73	2.04
Finance cover		
$\dfrac{\text{Cash generated from operations}}{\text{Finance costs and dividends}}$	16.7	

63 Harper

Text reference. Chapters 18, 19 and 20.

Top tips. Part (a) There are seven marks here for some quite basic comments and calculations. Remember though that the information on acquisitions is not required by IFRS 5.

Part (b) There are more marks for explanations than for calculations here. If you can remember the reasons for calculating basic and diluted EPS then you should be able to score most of the marks.

Part (c) Basically this question is asking you to explain the calculations and adjustments you make when calculating taxable profits, the tax charge, and tax paid, all of which should be familiar to you.

Easy marks. Part (a) is 7 easy marks.

Examiner's comments. This question was poorly answered with many candidates failing to read the question correctly. A frequent mistake was including discontinued operations when calculating the following year's profit in part (a).

Part (b) was better answered, although some candidates failed to realise that EPS is based on profit.

Part (c) was well answered but some candidates gave only brief outlines and little depth apart from timing differences.

Marking scheme

				Marks
(a)	(i)	1 mark per relevant point to a	**Maximum**	3
	(ii)	$110 for both companies if no information available		1
		Applying the information available – $77 million for Gamma		1
		– $209 million for Toga		2
			Maximum	4
(b)	(i)	1 mark per relevant point to a	**Maximum**	3
	(ii)	Number of shares re loan stock		1
		Interest saved		1
		Dilutive number of share re options		2
		Calculation of diluted EPS		1
			Maximum	5
	(iii)	1 mark per relevant point to a	**Maximum**	4
(c)		1 mark per relevant point to a	**Maximum**	6
			Maximum for question	25

(a)   (i)   Investors use the historic information in financial statements in order to forecast the future performance of a company. If a material part of a business has been discontinued during the year then the results of that business need to be excluded from the forecast, because those profits and losses are not going to recur.

Normally entities will want to sell off poorly performing businesses, so the disposal will hopefully boost future performance. If a profitable business is being sold off then shareholders will want to know why. Is the entity being forced to sell off good businesses in order to pay off debts, or is it a shrewd move, selling a business at its peak when its value is highest?

   (ii)   On the basis of the operating profit alone, both companies are making $100m this year and will be expected to make $110m next year, so there is nothing to choose between them. However, the expected results are very different if the information about discontinued activities and acquisitions is taken into account. With this information, Gamma is expected to make $77m next year and Toga $209m (see below), therefore Mrs Harper should invest in Toga.

Gamma's forecast operating profits	$m
Continuing activities ($70m × 110%)	77
Acquisitions (none disclosed)	
Discontinued activities	-
Total expected operating profits	77

Toga's forecast operating profits	$m
Continuing activities ($90m × 110%)	99
Acquisitions (adjusted for a full year) ($50m × 12/6 × 110%)	110
Discontinued activities	-
Total expected operating profits	209

There are two aspects to the change in the forecast; the exclusion of the discontinued activities and adjusting profits from acquisitions to cover a full twelve months.

However, IFRS 5 *Non-current Assets Held for Sale and Discontinued Activities* only requires information about discontinued activities; it does not require any disclosure of the results of acquisitions during the year. Therefore the fact that Gamma has not disclosed any information about acquisitions does not mean that no acquisitions have taken place.

(b)   (i)   The trend in reported profits shows the overall increase in an entity's profits over time. This increase could have been caused by

(1)   expansion and/or improvement in the entity's own business financed by retained profits or borrowings, or,

(2)   an increase in the size of the business financed by an issue of new shares,

In the first situation all of the increase in profits will belong to the existing shareholders, and so the trend in reported profits and EPS will be the same. In the second situation the increased profits will have to be shared with the new shareholders as well. This means that the increase in EPS will be less than the increase in reported profits. The cake may have got bigger, but it is being shared between more people.

The small investor will be more concerned with the change in profits attributable to their own shareholding, because this will determine the size of their potential dividends in the long run. Therefore Earnings Per Share is a more useful measure of performance for Mrs Harper.

   (ii)

Adjusted earnings	$62m	Earnings per share	=	17.2 cents
Diluted number of shares	360m			

Adjusted earnings		$m	$m
Original earnings			50
Interest saved on conversion	$200m × 8%	16	
Less tax at 25%		(4)	
			12
			62

Diluted number of shares		Number (m)
Original		200
Conversion of loan stock ($200m × 70 shares/$100)		140
Directors options		
Proceeds (50 million shares @ $1.50) = $75m		
$75m buys 30m shares at the market price of $2.50	30	
The directors will receive 50m shares	50	
The dilution is 20m shares		20
Total diluted number of shares		360

(iii) Investors use historic EPS to forecast future EPS. Obviously future EPS will depend on future profitability, but it will also be affected by the entity's existing commitments to issue shares in the future. These may reduce existing shareholders' share of profits even if the reported profits stay the same. Therefore investors need to know what the maximum potential reduction in their share of earnings could be based on the entity's existing obligations.

Two common causes of dilution are the conversion of loan stock (or preference shares), and share options that entitle the option holder to purchase shares at below the market rate.

The conversion of loan stock tends to increase earnings because the entity no longer has to pay interest on the loan. However, if this benefit is outweighed by a large increase in the number of shares in issue then existing shareholders will see their share of profits reduced.

An option to purchase shares at below market price always dilutes profits, because the benefit of the finance raised will be less than the number of shares issued.

In this question the diluted EPS is 17.2 cents. This is not a prediction of future EPS; that will depend on how many shares are issued, and what the future profits of Taylor will be.

(c) The income tax rate of 25% applies to the taxable profits for the year. Not all income is taxable, and some items of expenditure are not allowable for tax. Therefore the taxable profits for the year may be more or less than the accounting profits, giving rise to an effective rate of tax on accounting profits above or below the expected rate.

The tax charge in the accounts also contains other items. In particular there is an adjustment for any over or under provision in previous years. If a material error was made when estimating the income tax in the previous year then the charge for this year will be materially affected by the correction.

The other common item in the tax charge is the increase or decrease in the deferred tax provision. This adjustment tends to bring the charge in the income statement closer to the prevailing rate of tax, as it smoothes out timing differences between when profits are recognised for tax purposes and for accounting purposes.

The difference between the charge for tax in the income statement and the tax paid in the cash flow statement is caused by two things;

(1) Tax tends to be paid in the year following the period in which the tax was charged. So, tax charged in this year's income statement will be paid and reported in next year's cash flow statement.

(2) Deferred tax (mentioned above) provides for tax that may not be payable for many years to come. So, although it is charged in the income statement as it arises, it may be many years before it becomes payable.

64 Comparator

Text reference. Chapters 19 and 20.

Top tips. Part (a) You should be familiar with the standard points in discussing the limitations of ratio analysis. Make sure that you refer to inter-firm comparison services.

Part (b) Only six marks for calculating the ratios. Don't exceed your time allowance here.

Part (c) Do not merely describe the ratio in words, or say that it has gone up or down. Your comments should be on the possible reasons for differences in the accounting ratios, and the possible consequences of those differences. Accounting ratios tend to raise questions rather than provide answers.

Easy marks. Part (b) is 6 easy marks but do not go overboard with your calculations – you have 11 minutes only. See also the examiner's comments.

Examiner's comments. Answers to this question were generally just above average. Once again candidates wasted time calculating too many ratios. Also the answers to part (c) on interpretation of the ratios were very weak and lacked depth. Candidates need to relate the ratios to the business and make suggestions on why the ratios have changed.

Marking scheme

			Marks
(a)	Up to 1 mark for each limitation	**Maximum**	7
	Note: a good answer must refer to interfirm comparison issues		
(b)	½ mark for each relevant ratio	**Maximum**	6
(c)	Format		1
	Discussion of: Profitability		3
	Liquidity (and working capital ratios)		4
	Gearing		2
	Investment ratios		3
	Other issues		2
	Summary		1
		Available	16
		Maximum	12
		Maximum for question	25

(a) **Comparisons**

Accounting ratios can be used to assess the strength and performance of a company. They are mainly used to compare a company's performance over time or to compare one company with another (or to the average for similar companies).

Accounting ratios are calculated from published financial statements, and so they are subject to the same estimates and judgements as the statements. Accounting ratios tend to raise questions rather than answer them; for example a declining gross profit margin might indicate increased input costs or a declining sales price. Because of this, ratio analysis is often used in practice to identify areas that need further investigation.

More problems arise when companies are being compared, as it is difficult to find two companies that really are comparable:

- Big, publicly quoted companies often have diverse business interests located around the globe, unlike their smaller rivals which are more localised and less diversified.

- Different accounting policies can affect key ratios. For example a company that capitalises borrowing costs will have higher profits and net assets than one that doesn't.

- Different business practices may affect reported profits and assets. For example a business operating from rented premises and using rented equipment will have a very low capital employed compared with a similar business that owns its own premises and equipment.

- Balance sheet values may not be typical for the year as a whole. This might be because of seasonal fluctuations (for example a farming business) or because of a deliberate attempt to tidy up the balance sheet for the year-end by collecting in receivables and delaying the payment of suppliers.

- The dividend policy of a publicly quoted company will be very different from that of a small family company.

- Big companies tend to have different economies of scale than smaller companies.

The use of a comparison service will exaggerate these problems:

- Users will not know which firms have been used in the comparison. Because companies themselves are diverse, averages calculated may not be comparable to the user's company. For example, a small brewery may be focused on its core activity of brewing beer, but its competitor companies used by the comparison service may have diversified into hotels, retailing and other leisure activities.

- The year-ends of companies used will affect the ratios calculated.

- Averaged information will not tell you what the typical (modal) ratio is, nor will it tell you what the normal range of ratios is.

Overall, although it is a useful and informative exercise to compare ratios, care must be taken to ensure that like is being compared with like.

(b) **Calculations**

	Comparator	Sector average
Return on capital employed	34.6%	22.1%
$\dfrac{\text{Profit before finance costs}}{\text{Assets - current liabilities}}$	$\dfrac{186 + 34}{1{,}135 - 500}$	
Net asset turnover	3.8	1.8
$\dfrac{\text{Revenues}}{\text{Assets - current liabilities}}$	$\dfrac{2{,}425}{1{,}135 - 500}$	
Gross profit margin	22.9%	30%
$\dfrac{\text{Gross profit}}{\text{Revenues}}$	$\dfrac{555}{2{,}425}$	
Net profit margin	7.7%	12.5%
$\dfrac{\text{Profit before tax}}{\text{Revenues}}$	$\dfrac{186}{2{,}425}$	

	Comparator	Sector average
Net profit margin excluding write-off	12.6%	Not known
$\dfrac{\text{Profit before tax} + \text{write off}}{\text{Revenues}}$	$\dfrac{186 + 120}{2,425}$	
ROCE excluding write off	53.5%	22.1%
$\dfrac{\text{Profit before finance costs} + \text{write off}}{\text{Assets} - \text{current liabilities}}$	$\dfrac{186 + 34 + 120}{635}$	
Current ratio	1.2 : 1	1.6 : 1
$\dfrac{\text{Current assets}}{\text{Current liabilities}}$	$\dfrac{595}{500}$	
Quick ratio	0.6 : 1	0.9 : 1
$\dfrac{\text{Current assets} - \text{inventories}}{\text{Current liabilities}}$	$\dfrac{595 - 275}{500}$	
Inventory holding period	54 days	46 days
$\dfrac{\text{Inventory} \times 365}{\text{Cost of sales}}$	$\dfrac{275 \times 365}{1,870}$	
Accounts receivable collection period	48 days	45 days
$\dfrac{\text{Trade receivables} \times 365}{\text{Revenues}}$	$\dfrac{320 \times 365}{2,425}$	
Accounts payable payment period	68 days	55 days
$\dfrac{\text{Trade payables} \times 365}{\text{Cost of sales}}$	$\dfrac{350 \times 365}{1,870}$	
Working capital cycle	34 days	36 days
	(54 + 48 − 68)	(46 + 45 − 55)
Debt to Equity	90%	40%
$\dfrac{\text{Interest bearing borrowings}}{\text{Equity}}$	$\dfrac{300}{335}$	
Dividend yield	2.5%	6%
$\dfrac{\text{Dividends paid per share}}{\text{Market price per share}}$	$\dfrac{15 \text{ cents}}{\$6}$	
Dividend cover	1.07 times	3 times
$\dfrac{\text{Profit for the year}}{\text{Dividends paid}}$	$\dfrac{96}{90}$	

*Dividend per share

$$\frac{\text{Total dividend}}{\text{Number of shares in issue}} = \frac{\$90,000}{150,000 \times 4} = 15 \text{ cents}$$

(c) **Commentary**

Analysis of the financial performance of Comparator compared with the sector averages

Operating performance

The high ROCE of 34.6% (compared with 22.1% for all companies) shows that Comparator's assets are being used relatively efficiently. This is despite Comparator having a disappointing gross profit margin (22.9% compared with 30%) and net profit margin (7.7% compared with 12.5%). Comparator has made up for this low level of profitability by having a very high level of asset utilisation, as shown by an asset turnover ratio of 3.8 times, which is more than twice the average of 1.8 times.

There are two things that complicate the analysis above:

(i)   The age of Comparator's non-current assets, and
(ii)   The write off of inventory.

These are discussed below:

(i)   The carrying value of Comparator's non-current assets is only 15% of their cost, suggesting that these assets are quite old. This will have boosted the ROCE compared with a company with newer assets with a higher carrying value. However, there is not enough information to investigate this further. Also, these assets will probably need replacing soon, and because Comparator has no cash then it will need to borrow more money. This will be extremely difficult (and probably expensive) as Comparator's gearing ratio is already very high (90%) compared with the sector average (40%).

(ii)   Comparator's net profit margin is distorted by the $120,000 charge for writing off inventory. Without this the net profit margin would have been 12.6%, which is greater than the average of 12.5%. If this write-off really is a one-off not-to-be-repeated event then this suggests that the underlying return on capital employed is 53.5%. However, the sector averages do not include similar information on one-off costs.

Financial position

Long term

As mentioned above, Comparator's gearing ratio is already high and the need to replace old plant and equipment could push it higher. As the existing equipment cost $3.6m some years ago Comparator could expect to spend as much again today, all of it on borrowed money. This would require a gearing ratio of 1,100%, which the banks would almost certainly not tolerate. The alternative would be to raise more share capital. At the current market price of $6 a share a further 600,000 shares would need to be issued, which would double the number of shares. This also seems an unlikely prospect. However, without new loans or share capital there can be no new equipment.

Short term

Comparator's quick and current ratios are below the industry average, which suggests that there may be short term cash flow problems and poor financial management.

Although the working capital cycle is relatively good (34 days compared with 36), the individual components are worse implying that there is poor inventory control, poor credit control, and a shortage of cash to pay suppliers. Poor inventory control may have caused the build up of obsolete inventory (leading to the $120,000 write-off), and poor credit control can lead to an increase in bad debts. Delaying paying suppliers (who now have to wait 68 days to be paid) is a short term fix, but it can back-fire if suppliers lose patience with Comparator and demand cash on delivery, or refuse to deliver at all.

Interest cover, dividends, tax and overdraft

Although the interest cover of ten is good in terms of profits, there is no cash to pay the interest. Likewise there is $85,000 tax to pay. We are not told what the overdraft limit is, but it appears that Comparator can only meet its obligations if the overdraft is increased.

Investment ratios

Comparator's dividend yield of 2.5% is low compared with the average of 6%, which will dissuade many investors from subscribing to a new share issue. On the other hand it suggests that the share price is relatively high. This might be because investors are aware of additional information that promises a brighter future for Comparator, or maybe the share price will drop when these results are published.

The dividend cover of 1.07 is also worrying; Comparator is paying out almost its entire earnings at a time when it needs to generate cash to pay off its liabilities and invest in new equipment.

Summary and conclusion

At first sight Comparator's operating performance appears to be good compared with its rivals, but further analysis suggests that this might be boosted by old plant and equipment. Comparator's financial position is worrying both in the short term and the long term, and it is difficult to see how Comparator will be able to meet its obligations and invest in the future. Unless things improve Comparator's going concern status must be in doubt.

65 Breadline

Text reference. Chapter 20.

Top tips. Part (a) The question gives the game away by asking you to consider related party issues. If you mentally go through the normal consolidation adjustments you should be able to think of five ways in which they could affect the perceived performance of a subsidiary.

Part (b) Financial analysis is a key part of the syllabus and a key skill throughout your professional career. The first thing you must do is to identify who you are performing the analysis for and why. In this case you are reporting to your own Chief Executive. The purpose of the report is not so clear. The body of the question refers to the possibility of acquiring Breadline and the recoverability of the money owed to Judicious, but the requirement itself asks you to analyse the overall financial performance of Breadline. The question also reminds you to refer to areas that cause concern or require further investigation. The second thing you should do is to review the financial statements to pick out obvious changes from one year to the next. When you have identified these, then you can switch on your calculator and calculate the ratios. Finally, remember that the marks are for your comments, not for the calculations.

Easy marks. Part (a) should be 5 easy marks.

Examiner's comments. Part (a) was a discussion of issues that may arise in part (b), although several candidates failed to realise this. Part (b) was generally well answered, although far too many answers gave the movements without discussing reasons for those movements. The notes given to the financial statements contained vital information that was ignored by too many candidates.

Marking scheme

		Marks
(a)	1 mark per relevant point to a maximum of	5
(b)	Format and presentation of report	1
	Calculation of relevant ratios – up to	6
	Appropriate comments on above ratios	10
	References to areas of concern	5
	Available	22
	Maximum	20
	Maximum for question	25

(a)   **Assessing a subsidiary's performance**

The trade of a subsidiary is carried out for the benefit of the group as a whole, not for the benefit of the subsidiary itself. Therefore there will be transactions, assets and liabilities that only exist because of the subsidiary's position within the group. The value of these transactions (and the transaction itself) will not have been agreed on an 'arm's length' basis. Some typical examples are noted below:

Revenues and cost of sales

Group companies often trade between themselves at an agreed price. This price is normally above or below the market price. Either way it means that one group company will be reporting a higher gross profit at the expense of another.

Also, these transactions might not take place at all if the companies were independent. For example, a baker might buy its flour from a subsidiary, but would choose a completely different supplier if the companies were independent.

Group companies normally don't compete against each other. This means that a subsidiary might refrain from making sales that it would otherwise have made. Also, it might be protected against competition from other group companies.

Shared costs and benefits

Group companies often pool resources in order to get economies of scale. For example office buildings and administration costs can be shared, reducing the cost to each company. Marketing, distribution, research and development will also be better and cheaper if they are shared across a group.

Finance is often raised at competitive rates for the group as a whole, with the funds then being passed on to the subsidiaries. Sometimes the finance for a subsidiary will be deliberately subsidised via an inter-company loan account.

All of the above practices are legitimate and make sound business sense. However, they all distort the reported performance of an individual subsidiary company. If the subsidiary were independent its trade and its profitability would be very different.

(b)   **Report to the Chief Executive of Judicious on the financial position of Breadline**

From: Assistant Financial Controller

Introduction

This report investigates the overall financial position of Breadline with particular reference to the possibility of acquiring Breadline and the recoverability of the amounts owed to Judicious.

This report is based on the published financial statements of Breadline for the year ending 31 December 20X1. Breadline is a wholly owned subsidiary of Wheatmaster.

There are a number of areas that cause concern, or where further investigation is necessary. These are highlighted in the report.

Revenues and profitability

Breadline has **increased revenues** by 31% and increased its reported gross profit margin from 26% to 30%. On the face of it this looks like good sustainable growth.

However, the notes to the accounts report that the **profit on disposal** of the freehold premises was credited to cost of sales. This will have reduced the cost of sales and **inflated gross profit**. It is a one off profit that cannot be repeated in the future. The financial effect of this sale is not known but it can be estimated. The company's business address and trading premises have not changed; this suggests that the company is still occupying the same buildings. In 20X0 Breadline had freehold buildings valued at $1,250,000 and no leasehold buildings. In 20X1 Breadline had no freeholds but owned a leasehold costing $2,500,000. This suggests a sale and lease back arrangement. Because the proceeds of the freehold must have been greater than the cost of the leasehold this puts a minimum value on the sale proceeds of $2.5m and a minimum profit of $1.25m. If 20X1's cost of sales are adjusted for this then the gross profit in 20X1 would be $1.3m and the gross profit margin only 15%. This suggests that Breadline has boosted sales by cutting its selling price. This has reduced operating profits in the current year and is unsustainable in the long run.

Interest cover

Although the reported interest cover has dropped from 206 to 100 it is still at an **extremely safe level** (interest cover of 6 would be adequate). However, excluding the profit on disposal of the freehold reduces profit before interest in 20X1 to $740,000. Also, Breadline has taken out a $500,000 loan note at a 2% interest rate. This is below the market rate of 8%. In one way or another Breadline will have to pay the market rate of interest, either by offering a premium on redemption or conversion rights, and so the true interest charge on the loan notes will be $40,000, not $10,000. This makes the total interest charge for the year $50,000 and reduces the interest cover to 15.

Interest cover of fifteen is still good, but with the overdraft increasing and profitability declining the chances are that this is going to deteriorate further over the coming years.

Working capital management

Inventory levels have remained **steady** at about 18 days. **Receivables have increased** from 34 days to 41 days. This may have been because the credit control department has been unable to cope with the 31% increase in sales. However, 41 days is acceptable. Likewise payables have edged up from 45 days to 52 days. Overall, the working capital cycle has remained steady at 7.8 days this year compared with 7.1 days last year.

What is worrying for Judicious is that Breadline has **not been paying us as quickly** as other suppliers. Last year the balance owed to Judicious was 45.6 days old which was close to the average of 44.8 days. This year the balance is 103.4 days, which is twice the average. This difference could have been caused by increased sales by Judicious in the last two months of the year, or more likely by Breadline favouring other suppliers over Judicious. Maybe Breadline is paying amounts owing to group companies before it is paying its third party suppliers.

Financing

Breadline has received $600,000 from issuing new shares ($400,000 capital + $200,000 premium) and $500,000 from issuing a loan note. The shares were issued to Wheatmaster, its parent, and the loan note was also probably issued to a related party. (That would account for the below market rate of interest.) In total $1,100,000 has been raised, but then $900,000 has been paid out by way of dividend. It would have been much more efficient to have forgone the shares and loans and not paid a dividend either. The only explanation for this **money-go-round** is that it has transferred $900,000 of distributable profits up to the parent.

The **dividend is particularly worrying** because Breadline could only pay it by distributing the profit made on disposal of the freehold property. This is reducing Breadline's capital base.

Breadline has also received a substantial (but unknown) amount from the disposal of property. The only obvious investment during the year is the purchase of another $870,000 of plant.

Despite all this cash coming in, during the year the bank balance has fallen from $250,000 in hand to an overdraft of $220,000, a cash outflow of $470,000.

Conclusion

Breadline's apparent progress and prosperity does not survive detailed examination. Its profits and cash flows appear to have been **manipulated** for the benefit of its parent, and to inflate the reported profits before selling the business. The dividends and sale and leaseback transactions also suggest that Wheatmaster is trying to extract as much value from the business as possible before selling it. Therefore I would **not recommend that Judicious should acquire Breadline**.

Also, Judicious should seek to recover the amount owed to it for supplies, and to enforce stricter credit control in the future.

Summary of ratios

	20X1	20X0
Increase in revenues: ($8,500 – $6,500)/$6,500	31%	
Gross profit margins: $2,550/$8,500 ($1,690/$6,500)	30%	26%
Revised gross profit in 20X1: $2,550,000 – $1,250,000	$1.3m	
Revised gross profit margin in 20X1: $1.3m/$8.5m	15%	
Reported interest cover: 20X1 ($2,550 – $560)/$20	100	
20X0 ($1,690 – $660)/$5		206
Revised profit before interest 20X1: ($2,550 – $1,250 – $560)	$740K	
Revised interest 20X1: ($500,000 × 8%) + $10,000	$50K	
Revised interest cover 20X1: $740,000/$50,000	15	

Working capital management

	20X1	20X0
Inventory days		
Based on a revised cost of sales in 20X1 of $7,200 ($5,950 + $1,250)		
20X1: (370/7,200) × 365 days 20X0: (240/4,810) × 365 days	18.8	18.2
Receivable days		
20X1: (960/8,500) × 365 days 20X0: (600/6,500) × 365 days	41.2	33.7
Payable days		
Based on a revised cost of sales in 20X1 of $7,200		
20X1: (1,030/7,200) × 365 days 20X0: (590/4,810) × 365 days	52.2	44.8
Working capital cycle:	7.8	7.1
Ageing of the amounts owed to Judicious		
20X1: (340/1,200) × 365 days 20X0: (100/800) × 365 days	103.4	45.6

66 Preparation question: Dickson Co

Dickson Co
Cash flow statement for year ended 31 March 20X8

	$'000	$'000
Cash flows from operating activities		
Profit before taxation	342	
Adjustments for:		
Depreciation	57	
Amortisation (W2)	60	
Interest expense	15	
Profit on disposal of assets	(7)	
	467	
Decrease in trade receivables (274 – 324)	50	
Increase in inventories (360 – 227)	(133)	
Decrease in trade payables (274 – 352)	(78)	
Cash generated from operations	306	
Interest paid (W5)	(10)	
Income taxes paid (W4)	(256)	
Net cash from operating activities		40
Cash flows from investing activities		
Development expenditure	(190)	
Purchase of property, plant & equipment (W1)	(192)	
Proceeds from sale of property, plant & equipment	110	
Net cash used in investing activities		(272)
Cash flows from financing activities		
Proceeds from issue of shares [850 – 500 – (400 ×1/8)]	300	
Proceeds from issue of debentures	50	
Payment of finance lease liabilities (W3)	(31)	
Dividends paid	(156)	
Net cash from financing activities		163
Net decrease in cash and cash equivalents		(69)
Cash and cash equivalents at beginning of period		109
Cash and cash equivalent at end of period		40

Notes to the cash flow statement

Note 1: Property, plant and equipment

During the period, the company acquired property, plant and equipment with an aggregate cost of $248,000 of which $56,000 was purchased by means of finance leases. Cash payments of $192,000 were made to acquire property, plant and equipment.

Workings

1   *Additions to property, plant and equipment*

Property, plant and equipment

	$'000		$'000
Bal b/d	637	Depreciation	57
Revaluations (152 – 60 + 8)	100	Disposals	103
Finance leases	56		
∴ Additions	192		
		Bal c/d	825
	985		985

2   *Development expenditure amortisation*

Development expenditure

	$'000		$'000
Bal b/d	160		
Expenditure	190	∴ Amortisation	60
		Bal c/d	290
	350		350

3   *Finance lease payments*

Finance lease liability

	$'000		$'000
		Bal b/d – > 1 year	80
		– < 1 year	12
∴ Paid	31		
		New finance leases	56
Bal c/d – > 1 year	100		
– > 1 year	17		
	148		148

4   *Income taxes paid*

Income tax payable

	$'000		$'000
		Bal b/d – current	45
		– deferred	153
∴ Paid	256		
		Income statement	162
Bal c/d – current	56		
– deferred	48		
	360		360

5   *Interest paid*

Interest payable

	$'000		$'000
		Bal b/d	
∴ Paid	10	I/S	15
Bal c/d			
	15		15

67 Planter

Text reference. Chapter 21.

Top tips. An unusually straight forward cash flow question; they are normally combined with a written explanation or analysis. Any candidate who had practised this topic would score well.

Easy marks. 25 very easy marks if you work methodically through the question.

Examiner's comments. This question was popular and well answered. Common errors included:

- Wrong treatment of the interest accrual
- Failure to calculate tax correctly
- Failure to exclude non-cash items
- Inability to deal with the bonus issue

Marking scheme

	Marks
Reconciliation of operating profit to operating cash flows, one per item	8
Interest paid	2
Investment income	1
Taxation	2
Purchase of plant	2
Purchase of land and buildings	2
Sale of plant	1
Sale of investments	1
Ordinary dividend	2
Issue of ordinary shares	2
Redemption of loan notes	2
Decrease in cash	1
Available	**26**
Maximum for question	**25**

PLANTER
CASH FLOW STATEMENT FOR THE YEAR ENDED 31 MARCH 20X4

	$	$
Cash flows from operating activities		
Profit before taxation (17,900 – 1,700 + 400)		16,600
Adjustments for:		
Depreciation (W1)		28,400
Loss on disposal of PPE ($7,800 - $12,000)		4,200
Profit on disposal of investments ($11,000 - $8,700)		(2,300)
Interest expense		1,700
Investment income		(400)
Operating profit before working capital changes		48,200
(Increase) decrease in trade & other receivables (50,400 – 28,600)		(21,800)
(Increase) decrease in inventories (43,300 – 57,400)		14,100
Increase (decrease) in trade payables (26,700 – 31,400)		(4,700)
Cash generated from operations		35,800
Investment income		400
Interest paid (1,700 – 300)		(1,400)
Income taxes paid (8,900 + 1,100)		(10,000)
Net cash from operating activities		24,800
Cash flows from investing activities		
Proceeds of disposal of investments	11,000	
Proceeds of disposal of plant	7,800	
Purchase of property, plant and equipment (W1)	(45,200)	
Net cash used in investing activities		(26,400)
Cash flows from financing activities		
Proceeds from issue of share capital (W2)	28,000	
Repayment of loan (39,800 – 43,200)	(3,400)	
Dividends paid	(26,100)	
Net cash from financing activities		(1,500)
Net decrease in cash and cash equivalents		(3,100)
Opening cash and cash equivalents		1,200
Closing cash and cash equivalents		(1,900)

Workings

1   Property, plant and equipment

Summary

	Purchases	Depreciation
	$	$
Buildings	7,100	1,800
Plant	38,100	26,600
	45,200	28,400

Land and buildings

	Cost	Depreciation
	$	$
Opening	49,200	5,000
Revaluation (18,000 – 12,000)	6,000	-
Depreciation (Balancing figure)	-	1,800
Purchases (Balancing figure)	7,100	-
Closing	62,300	6,800

Plant

		Cost	Depreciation
		$	$
Opening		70,000	22,500
Disposal		(23,500)	(11,500)
		46,500	11,000
Depreciation (Balancing figure)		-	26,600
Purchases (Balancing figure)		38,100	-
Closing		84,600	37,600

2   Share issues

	Capital	Premium	Total
	$	$	$
Opening	25,000	5,000	30,000
1 for 10 bonus issue	2,500	(2,500)	-
Cash issue (balancing figure)	22,500	5,500	28,000
Closing	50,000	8,000	58,000

68 Bigwood

Text reference. Chapters 19 and 21.

Top tips. This is a typical cash flow statement question, with half the marks for preparing the statement and half for interpretation. Make sure that you ring-fence half of your time for the interpretation in Part (b). Even if you haven't finished the cash flow statement, you will have identified the key points about Bigwood's financial position and performance. Also note that the question gives you the relevant ratios; you must explain the possible causes and consequences of these ratios.

Easy marks. The cash flow statement is 12 easy marks.

Examiner's comments. This required a cash flow statement, followed by analysis.

Part (a) was generally well answered although some candidates had trouble with disposal of non-current assets and the increase in the loan.

Part (b) on interpretation was very mixed. Disappointingly, few candidates calculated extra ratios and very few commented on the cash flow statement in part (a).

Marking scheme

			Marks
(a)	Net profit before tax		1
	Depreciation		1
	Loss on disposal		1
	Working capital items		3
	Interest paid		1
	Income tax paid		1
	Capital expenditure		1
	Disposal proceeds		1
	Equity dividends		1
	Financing – equity shares		1
	– loans		1
	Decrease in cash		1
		Available	**14**
		Maximum	**12**
(b)	up to 3 marks for additional ratios		3
	1 mark per relevant point including 1 mark for format		10
		Maximum	**13**
		Maximum for question	**25**

BIGWOOD
CASH FLOW STATEMENT FOR THE YEAR ENDED 30 SEPTEMBER 20X4

	$'000	$'000
Cash flows from operating activities		
Profit before taxation (I/S)		700
Adjustments for:		
Depreciation (W1)		3,800
Loss on disposal of plant		1,250
Interest expense		300
Operating profit before working capital changes		6,050
(Increase) decrease in trade receivables (100 – 50)		(50)
(Increase) decrease in inventories (2,900 – 1,500)		(1,400)
Increase (decrease) in trade payables (3,100 – 2,150)		950
Cash generated from operations		5,550
Interest paid		(300)
Income taxes paid (450 + 250 – 220)		(480)
Net cash from operating activities		4,770
Cash flows from investing activities		
Cost of disposal of plant	(50)	
Purchase of property, plant and equipment (W1)	(10,500)	
Net cash used in investing activities		(10,550)
Cash flows from financing activities		
Proceeds from issue of share capital (5,000 + 1,000 – 3,000)	3,000	
Receipt of loan (3,000 – 1,000)	2,000	
Dividends paid (SCE)	(600)	
Net cash from financing activities		4,400
Net decrease in cash and cash equivalents		(1,380)
Opening cash and cash equivalents (B/S)		450
Closing cash and cash equivalents (B/S)		(930)

Working for property, plant and equipment

	Cost	Depreciation	Carrying Value
	$'000	$'000	$'000
Opening	9,500	3,000	6,500
Scrapped	(3,000)	(1,800)	(1,200)
Depreciation (balancing figure)	-	3,800	(3,800)
Purchases (balancing figure)	10,500	-	10,500
Closing	17,000	5,000	12,000

Loss on disposal; carrying value ($1,200,000) + disposal costs ($50,000) = $1,250,000.

Bigwood
Financial Position and Performance
Two years ending 30 September 20X4

Performance

During the year sales area increased by 35% (from 40,000m^2 to 54,000m^2), helping to increase sales by 17% (from $19.6m to $23m). The low increase in sales compared with floor space may be explained by the timing of the increase and the disruptions caused during refurbishment. The full benefit of the expansion may only be felt next year.

The relative performance of the two lines of trade suggests that the expansion has been misdirected towards clothing at the expense of food. Food floor space has increased by only 20%, but this has yielded a 75% increase in turnover accompanied by an increase in the gross profit margin from 25% to 32.1%. Clothing floor space increased by 37% but sales only rose by 2.5% and the gross profit margin halved from 18.6% to 9.4%.

The food lines are obviously popular, as sales and margins have grown. This demand for food has probably helped to decrease the stock holding period from 17 days to 15 days, which is always a good thing for perishable products like food.

The situation with clothing is the reverse; the fall in margins and barely static sales suggests that prices have had to be slashed to shift stock. This is not sustainable in the long run. Even with discounted prices, the level of unsold clothes has mounted from 39 days to 68 days. This is worrying in a seasonal and fashionable business like clothing, and may suggest that further price cuts will be needed to shift clothing before it becomes out of date.

One puzzling statistic is that the margin on food is higher than that on clothing. Normally food sells at a very low margin compensated for by high turnover. This suggests that Bigwood has specialised in high value-added foods rather than basic groceries.

The information given encourages depreciation to be apportioned between the products on the basis of floor space. This apportionment results in a loss of $1,878,000 after depreciation for clothing, wiping out the $1,828,000 profit made by food. These figures must be treated with caution because the refrigeration equipment needed to sell food will have a higher depreciation charge than the coat hangers needed to sell clothes.

Operating expenses have grown faster than sales, rising from 9.7% of revenues to 12%. Normally expenses are expected to decrease as a percentage of sales as economies of scale kick in. This increase suggests either poor cost control (which is worrying) or some one-off costs associated with the expansion and refurbishment.

The high level of investment and poor profitability is reflected by the decline in the ROCE from 33.9% to 9.3%. Hopefully next year will see a full year of profits from the enlarged and refurbished business and a reduction in costs.

Liquidity

The current ratio has deteriorated slightly from 0.77 to 0.71; however this low ratio is not unusual for retailers and is often seen as a sign of efficient working capital management. The increase in the accounts payable payment period from 50 to 59 days is not a problem as long as it does not rise further next year; a longer payment period might create bad will amongst Bigwood's suppliers.

At first glance it appears that the long-term liquidity of Bigwood gives cause for concern, with a net outflow of cash of $1.38m, an increase in gearing from 17% to 28% and a fall in interest cover from 25 times to 3.3 times. However, the situation is healthier than it looks as is explained below.

Bigwood has lost $1.38m of cash despite $3m of new share capital and $2m of new loans. But this new finance only covered half of the $10.5m of capital expenditure. This means that $4m of the expenditure came from cash generated during the year. If Bigwood takes a rest from expansion next year then it should generate another $4m of free cash which is enough to payoff the $930,000 overdraft and the $3m of loans.

Although the income statement reports a fall in interest cover from 25 to 3.3, the cash flow statement shows that cash generated from operations is 18.5 times the interest paid, which is quite comfortable.

Investor ratios

The fall in the share price from $6 to $3 shows that investors are pessimistic about Bigwood's future, although some of the fall will have been caused by the dilution from the share issue. The dividend per share will have decreased from 20 cents to 12 cents because of this issue, which will depress the share price.

The total dividend has been maintained at the cost of reducing the dividend cover from 2.33 to 0.75. Paying out dividends bigger than profits is unsustainable, but it may be intended to advertise the management's confidence in Bigwood's future. Net cash inflows from operating activities of $4.77m are about 8 times the dividend paid, and so the relatively high dividend will not be an immediate problem.

Summary

The results for 20X4 are disappointing considering the amount of investment put into the business. However, the future should be better for the following reasons:

- The business generates $4m of free cash each year. This will reduce Bigwood's debts and finance costs, and provide funds for further expansion.

- Next year should see a full year of increased profits from this year's capital expenditure, without the disruption caused by the redevelopment.

Management could help Bigwood's recovery by allocating more resources to the profitable food lines and by purchasing more popular clothing.

Additional ratios

	20X4	20X3	
Floor space			
Clothes	48,000	35,000	+ 37%
Food	6,000	5,000	+ 20%
Total	54,000	40,000	+ 35%
Sales			
Clothes	16,000	15,600	+ 2.5%
Food	7,000	4,000	+ 75%
Total	23,000	19,600	+ 17.3%

Profitability 20X4

	Clothes	Food	Total
Sales	16,000	7,000	23,000
Cost of sales	(14,500)	(4,750)	(19,250)
Gross profit	1,500	2,250	3,750
Depreciation	(3,378)	(422)	(3,800)
	(1,878)	1,828	(50)

Operating expense %

20X4	Expenses	2,750	= 12%
	Revenues	23,000	
20X3		1,900	
		19,600	= 9.7%

Interest cover in cash

Cash from operations	$5,550,000	= 18.5 times
Interest paid	$300,000	

Dividend cover

20X4	450/600	= 0.75
20X3	1,400/600	= 2.33

69 Casino

Text reference. Chapter 21.

Top tips. As always, the five easy marks in Part (b) should be won first.

The cash flow itself is reasonably straight forward, although there are small complications involving property and finance costs.

Easy marks. Part (b) is 5 easy marks.

Examiner's comments. This question was well answered. One common error was failure to deal with the recalculation of depreciation after the revaluation in part (a). Part (b) was reasonably well answered. However some candidates did not keep to the point and became repetitious. There are no marks awarded for repetition.

Marking scheme

		Marks
(a)	Cash flows from operating activities	
	Operating loss	1
	Depreciation and loss on sale adjustments	4
	Working capital terms	3
	Interest paid	1
	Income tax	2
	Investing activities	7
	Financing 1 mark per item	4
	Cash and cash equivalents b/f and c/f	1
	Available	**23**
	Maximum	**20**
(b)	1 mark per relevant point to **Maximum**	**5**
	Maximum for question	**25**

(a) CASINO
CASH FLOW STATEMENT FOR THE YEAR ENDED 31 MARCH 20X5

	$m	$m
Cash flows from operating activities		
Loss before taxation		(44)
Adjustments for:		
Depreciation (W1)		93
Amortisation (510 – 400)		110
Loss on disposal of PPE (from question)		12
Interest expense		24
Investment income		(12)
		183
(Increase) decrease in trade & other receivables (350 – 420)		70
(Increase) decrease in inventories (808 – 372)		(436)
Increase (decrease) in trade payables (530 – 515)		15
Cash used in operations		(168)
Investment income (3 + 12 – 5)		10
Interest paid		(16)
Income taxes paid (W3)		(81)
Net cash outflow from operating activities		(255)
Cash flows from investing activities		
Proceeds of disposal of plant (from question)	15	
Purchase of property, plant and equipment (W1)	(170)	
Net cash used in investing activities		(155)
Cash flows from financing activities		
Proceeds from issue of share capital [(300 + 60) – 200]	160	
Proceeds of loan (160 – 2 issue costs)	158	
Repayment of loan (150 + 6 penalty)	(156)	
Dividends paid (from question)	(25)	
Net cash from financing activities		137
Net decrease in cash and cash equivalents		(273)
Opening cash and cash equivalents		195
Closing cash and cash equivalents		(78)

[**Note**: Short term deposits are included in cash equivalents.]

Workings

1   Property, plant and equipment

Summary

	Purchases	Depreciation
	$m	$m
Buildings	110	12
Plant	60	81
	170	93

Land and buildings at carrying value

	$m
Opening	420
Revaluation (from question)	70
Depreciation (See * below)	(12)
	478
Purchases (Balancing figure)	110
Closing	588

*The revaluation will have cleared out the opening depreciation, so the charge must be the same as the closing balance.

Plant at carrying value

	$m
Opening	340
Additions (from question)	60
Disposals (see below)	(27)
	373
Depreciation (Balancing figure)	(81)
Closing	292

Carrying value of disposals; proceeds $15m, loss $12m, carrying value $27m.

2 *Tax*

TAX

C/f	Current	15	B/f	Current	110
	Deferred	90		Deferred	75
			Charge		1
Cash paid	balance	81			-
		186			186

(b) **Usefulness and reliability**

It is often said that cash flow statements are more useful and reliable than income statements. This claim is made because cash is the life blood of a business. Without cash the business cannot grow, repay its borrowings, service its finance, or pay a dividend. Without cash a business will wither and eventually fail. Therefore cash generation is more important than profitability.

Cash flow statements are also seen as being more reliable than income statements. Profit is based on the accruals concept which requires asset lives, provisions, fair values, contract profitability, impairment and so on to be estimated. Because this is subjective it is possible to have two different, but equally valid, profit figures. Cash is not subjective; cash inflows and outflows are all a question of fact.

However, the income statement is useful and cash flow statements are not as objective as they first seem. Cash inflow can be boosted by cutting back on investment and delaying paying creditors. This will give the illusion of success in the short run, but is bottling up investment expense and supplier bad will for the future. Even honest managers would be reluctant to make long-term investments if they thought that they would be judged solely on short-term cash generation. By matching income and expenditure, the income statement gives the reader a better understanding of the long term profitability of the company.

Cash flow statements and income statements are meant to complement each other. The quality of the profits claimed in the income statement can be assessed by comparing them with the cash generated from operations in the cash flow statement. The sustainability of dividends can also be assessed with reference to the cash flow statement.

70 Tabba

Text reference. Chapter 21.

Top tips. Don't forget the eight marks for interpretation in Part (b). If you are running out of time break off from the main statement to make some sensible comments about the cash flows that you have already calculated; there are good marks available for some obvious (and not so obvious) comments.

The cash flow itself is reasonably straight forward, although there are some complications involving finance leases and grants.

Easy marks. None of this question is particularly difficult. Part (b) is a possible 8 easy marks, so make sure you leave time to get them.

Examiners comments. This was a popular question and on the whole well answered. There were some examples of non-cash movements appearing as cash flows and possibly some candidates had not prepared for a cash flow question as it came up in the previous paper. Question spotting is a dangerous activity. The main errors involved depreciation calculations, the government grant, the tax calculation and the sale and leaseback transaction.

Marking scheme

		Marks
(a)	Profit before tax	½
	Depreciation	1
	Amortisation of government grant	1
	Profit on sale of factory	1
	Increase in insurance claim	1
	Working capital items 1 mark each	
	Adjustment for interest receivable/payable	½
	Interest paid	1
	Income tax paid	2
	Sale of factory	1
	Purchase of non-current assets	1
	Receipt of government grant	1
	Interest received	1
	Redemption of 10% loan	1
	Issue of 6% loan	1
	Repayment of finance lease	2
	Cash b/f and c/f	1
	Available	**20**
	Maximum	**17**
(b)	1 mark per relevant point to a	**Maximum**	**8**
	Maximum for question	**25**

(a) TABBA

CASH FLOW STATEMENT FOR THE YEAR ENDED 30 SEPTEMBER 20X5

	$m	$m
Cash flows from operating activities		
Profit before taxation		50
Adjustments for:		
Depreciation (W1)		2,200
Profit on disposal of PPE (W1)		(4,600)
Release of grant (W2)		(250)
Increase in insurance claim receivable (1,500 – 1,200)		(300)
Interest expense		260
Investment income		(40)
Operating loss before working capital changes		(2,680)
(Increase) decrease in inventories (2,550 – 1,850)		(700)
(Increase) decrease in trade & other receivables (3,100 – 2,600)		(500)
Increase (decrease) in trade payables (4,050 – 2,950)		1,100
Cash used in operations		(2,780)
Interest received		40
Interest paid		(260)
Income taxes paid (W3)		(1,350)
Net cash outflow from operating activities		(4,350)
Cash flows from investing activities		
Proceeds of grants (From question)	950	
Proceeds of disposal of plant (From question)	12,000	
Purchase of property, plant and equipment (W1)	(2,900)	
Net cash from investing activities		10,050
Cash flows from financing activities		
Proceeds of loan (6% loan received)	800	
Repayment of loan (10% loan repaid)	(4,000)	
Payments on finance leases (W4)	(1,100)	
Net cash from financing activities		(4,300)
Net increase in cash and cash equivalents		1,400
Opening cash and cash equivalents		(550)
Closing cash and cash equivalents		850

Workings

1   *Property, plant and equipment*

	Cost	Depreciation	Carrying value	Revaluation
	$'000	$'000	$'000	$'000
Opening	20,200	4,400	15,800	1,600
Finance lease additions	1,500	-	1,500	
Disposals	(8,600)	(1,200)	(7,400)	(1,600)
Subtotal	13,100	3,200		
Additions*	2,900	-	2,900	
Depreciation charge*	-	2,200	(2,200)	-
Closing	16,000	5,400	10,600	-

*Balancing figures

2   *Release of grant*

	$'000
Opening (400 + 900)	1,300
Received (from question)	950
Released (Balancing figure)	(250)
Closing (1,400 + 600)	2,000

3   TAX

C/f	Current	100	B/f	Current	1,200
	Deferred	200		Deferred	500
Credit in I/S		50			
Cash paid	balance	1,350			-
		1,700			1,700

4   MOVEMENT ON FINANCE LEASE

C/f	Current	2,000	B/f	Current	1,700
	Non-current	900		Non-current	800
			New		1,500
Cash paid	balance	1,350			-
		4,000			4,000

(b)   **Changes in Tabba's financial position**

The last section of the cash flow statement reveals a healthy increase in cash of $1.4m. However, Tabba is losing cash hand over foot and its going concern status must be in doubt.

To survive and thrive businesses must generate cash from their operations; but Tabba has absorbed $2.68m. Whereas most companies report higher operating cash inflows than profits, Tabba has reported the reverse. The only reason Tabba was able to report a profit was because of the one-off $4.6m surplus on disposal. There were two other items that inflated profits without generating cash; a $300,000 increase in the insurance claim receivable and a $250,000 release of a government grant. Without these three items Tabba would have reported a $5.1m loss before tax.

Were it not for the disposal proceeds Tabba would be reporting a $10.6m net decrease in cash. Tabba has no other major assets to sell and so the coming year will see a large outflow of cash unless Tabba's trading position improves. When the current operating lease expires in four years time there will probably be a rent hike, further damaging Tabba's profitability and cash flows.

The high tax bill for the previous year suggests that Tabba's fall from profitability has been swift and steep. Despite this downturn in trade Tabba's inventories and receivables have increased, suggesting poor financial management. This in turn damages cash flow, which is indicated by the increase in the level of payables.

There are some good signs though. Investment in non-current assets has continued, although $1.5m of this was on finance leases which are often a sign of cash shortages. Some of the disposal proceeds have been used to redeem the expensive $4m 10% loan and replace it with a smaller and cheaper $800,000 6% loan. This will save $352,000 per annum.

Tabba's recovery may depend on whether the circumstances causing the slump in profits and cash flow will either disappear of their own accord or whether Tabba can learn to live with them. The cash flow statement has however highlighted some serious issues for the shareholders to discuss with the directors at the annual general meeting.

71 Minster

Text reference. Chapters 19 and 21.

Top tips. In this question 40% of the marks were for commenting on the financial position and performance of the company. This was not that simple, and it was important not to spend too long on the cash flow statement and leave insufficient time for (b).

Easy marks. The easy marks here were the cash flow statement. There were a few complexities such as the unwinding of the discount, on which you should not have wasted much time, but it was otherwise straightforward and you should have scored good marks on it. Part (b) was not that easy because there were no obvious issues to report on. The company was not failing or overtrading or doing tremendously well either. So it was important to look at the information in the question and the cash flow statement and see what you could learn from them, rather than computing a raft of ratios.

Marking scheme

			Marks
(a)	cash flow from operating activity		
	profit before tax adjusted for investment income and finance cost		1
	depreciation/amortisation		2
	working capital items		2
	finance costs		2
	income taxes paid		2
	investing activities (including 1 for investment income)		4
	financing – issue of ordinary shares		1
	– issue of 9% loan		1
	dividend paid		1
	cash and cash equivalents b/f and c/f		1
		available	17
		maximum	**15**
(b)	1 mark per relevant point		10
		Maximum for question	**25**

(a) MINSTER
     CASH FLOW STATEMENT FOR THE YEAR ENDED 30 SEPTEMBER 2006

	$'000	$'000
Cash flows from operating activities		
Profit before tax		142
Depreciation		255
Software amortisation (180 – 135)		45
Investment income		(20)
Finance costs		40
		462
Decrease in inventories		30
Decrease in receivables		110
Decrease in payables		(205)
Increase in amounts due from construction contracts		(25)
Cash generated from operations		372
Interest paid (40 – 12 (unwinding of discount))		(28)
Income taxes paid (W1)		(54)
Net cash from operating activities		290
Cash flows from investing activities		
Property, plant and equipment (W2)	(410)	
Software	(180)	
Investments	(10)	
Investment income received (20 – 15 (investment gain))	5	
Net cash used in investing activities		(595)
Cash flows from financing activities		
Dividends paid (500 × 4 × 5c)	(100)	
9% loan note	120	
Equity share issue (125 share cap + 140 premium))	265	
Net cash from financing activities		285
Decrease in cash		(20)

Workings

1 *Income taxes paid*

	$'000
Balance b/f	50
Charge for year	57
Reduction in deferred tax provision	7
Tax paid (balancing figure)	(54)
Balance c/f	60

2 *Property, plant and equipment*

	$'000
Balance b/f	940
Environmental provision	150
Revaluation (60 – 25)	35
Depreciation	(255)
Acquisitions (balancing figure)	410
Balance c/f	1,280

(b) **Re: financial performance and position of Minster**

Minster's net assets have increased by $285,000 over the year. The company shows a gross profit percentage of 20% and a net profit percentage of 10% - both quite healthy - and its cash generated from operating activities is $372,000. However, retained earnings have decreased by $15,000 due to the payment of a dividend in excess of the net profit after tax. There has also been a bonus issue during the year, so Minster's shareholders have been well rewarded.

There are some significant changes in working capital levels over the year. Inventories and trade payables have both decreased. This could be due to more efficient purchasing and inventory control, perhaps the introduction of a JIT system. The level of trade receivables has also declined, perhaps due to more efficient credit collection. Conversely, these changes could be due to a reduction in the level of activity, rather than any increase in efficiency but, looking at the large investment in non-current assets, it appears unlikely that the business is 'winding down' to any degree. This is borne out by the increase in construction contract WIP.

The most noticeable feature in the cash flow statement is the heavy investment in non-current assets. As there are no disposals and no non-current assets were scrapped, this suggests expansion into new business activities or processes, rather than replacement of worn out or obsolete machinery. In addition to $410,000 on property, plant and equipment $180,000 has been spent on software licences, which suggests that the new non-current assets comprise equipment which will computerise some of Minster's processes. This reflects positive expectations about the future trading environment.

This investment has been funded by a 9% loan note and a share issue, presumably a rights issue. The rights issue yielded $265,000, reflecting the confidence of shareholders. The loan note issue, offset by the share issue, takes Minster's gearing to just over 7%. This is still low and the interest, while fairly high, is at least tax-deductible. There would have to be a very significant downturn in the business for it to be unable to afford the interest payments and, if the extra investment pays off and profits rise, the returns to shareholders will be greater than if more funds had been raised from another equity issue, which would have diluted shareholdings.

72 Preparation question: Changing prices

(a) CURRENT COST OPERATING PROFIT FOR 20X6

	$m	$m
Historical cost profit		15
Current cost adjustments:		
Depreciation adjustment	3	
Cost of sales adjustment	5	
		(8)
Current cost profit		7

SUMMARISED CURRENT COST BALANCE SHEET
AS AT 31 DECEMBER 20X6

	$m	$m
Property, plant & equipment		85
Current assets		
Inventories	21	
Receivables	30	
Bank	2	
		53
		138
Equity		88
Long-term liability		20
Current liabilities		30
		138

(b)   (i)   **Interest cover**

HC accounts: 15 ÷ 3 = 5 times
CC accounts: 7 ÷ 3 = 2.3 times

(ii)   **Return on shareholders' equity**

HC accounts: 12 ÷ 62 = 19.4%
CC accounts: 4 ÷ 88 = 4.5%

(iii)   **Debt/equity ratio**

HC accounts: 20 ÷ 62 = 32.3%
CC accounts: 20 ÷ 88 = 22.7%

(c)   (i)   **Interest cover**

Companies must maintain their capital base if they wish to stay in business. The significance of the interest cover calculation is that it indicates the extent to which profits after tax are being eaten into by payments to finance external capital. The figures calculated above indicate that only one-fifth of historical cost profit is being absorbed in this way, while four-fifths are being retained to finance future growth. On the face of it, this might seem satisfactory; however, the current cost interest cover is only 2.3 times indicating that, after allowing for the impact of rising prices, interest payments absorb nearly half of profits after tax.

(ii)   **Return on shareholders' equity**

This is the ratio of profits earned for shareholders (ie profits after interest) to shareholders' equity. Once again, the position disclosed by the historical cost accounts is more favourable than appears from the current cost ratio. The historical cost profit is higher than the current cost profit because no allowance is made for the adverse impact of rising prices, and, at the same time, the denominator in the historical cost fraction is lower because, shareholders' capital is stated at historical values rather than their higher current values.

The significance of the ratio is that it enables shareholders to assess the rate of return on their investment and to compare it with alternative investments that might be available to them.

(iii)   **Debt/equity ratio**

The significance of this ratio is as a measure of the extent to which the company's net assets are financed by external borrowing and shareholders' funds respectively.

In times of rising prices it can be beneficial to finance assets from loan capital. While the assets appreciate in value over time (and the gain accrues to shareholders), the liability is fixed in monetary amount. The effect of this is that current cost accounts tend to give a more favourable picture of the debt/equity ratio than historical cost accounts. In the ratios calculated above, the amount of debt is $20m in both balance sheets. This represents nearly one-third of the historical cost value of shareholders' funds, but only one-fifth of the equity calculated on a current cost basis.

73 Update

(a)   *Problems with historic cost*

Although retail price inflation has eased throughout the developed world, it is still a big issue for many businesses.

The carrying values of property and other assets with long useful lives soon become unrealistic if based on historic cost, leading to the following problems:

- Even with modest inflation, the depreciation charge on these assets will be too low in comparison with the revenues that the assets are generating, inflating operating profits.

- The return on capital employed is doubly distorted; not only are operating profits overstated, but the related net assets will be understated, resulting in a flattering and unrealistic return. This makes it difficult to compare two companies with similar assets if those assets were bought at different times.

- Low asset values reduce the net assets of a business. This exaggerates the gearing ratio, which might dissuade banks from advancing loans to the business. It might also cause the stock market to undervalue a business.

The traditional solution to these problems is to revalue certain items. However, this creates a hybrid set of financial statements, with some assets at historic cost others at valuation.

(b)   *Alternative methods*

	Historic cost $		CPP $		Current cost $
Cost / Valuation	250,000	(a)	300,000	(b)	280,000
Carrying value based on 2 years depreciation (c)	160,000		192,000		179,200
Carrying value based on 3 years depreciation (d)	128,000		153,600		143,360
Depreciation charge for this year (c − d = e)	32,000		38,400		35,840

(1)   The original cost of $250,000 will be indexed up for the change in the retail price index between the date of purchase and the balance sheet date.

$250,000 × 216 / 180 = $300,000

(2)   The current cost will be reduced to reflect the lower productivity of the old asset.

$320,000 × 420 / 480 = $280,000

(3)   The carrying value after two years depreciation at 20% reducing balance will be 64% of the gross amount (0.8 × 0.8).

(4)   The carrying value after three years depreciation at 20% reducing balance will be 51.2% of the gross amount (0.8 × 0.8 × 0.8).

(5)   This years charge will be the difference between (c) and (d).

Mock Exams

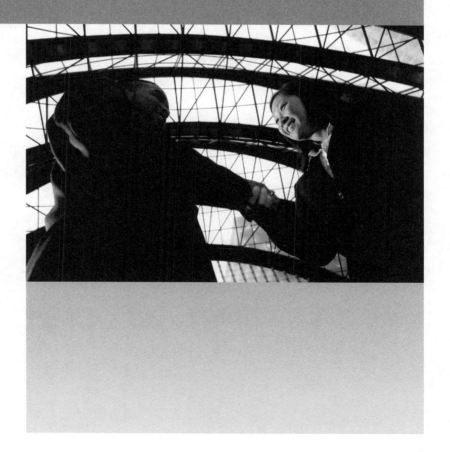

ACCA

Fundamentals

Paper F7

Financial Reporting

Mock Examination 1

Question Paper	
Time allowed	
Reading and Planning Writing	**15 minutes** **3 hours**
Answer all FIVE questions	

DO NOT OPEN THIS PAPER UNTIL YOU ARE READY TO START UNDER EXAMINATION CONDITIONS

ACCA

Fundamentals

Paper F7

Financial Reporting

Mock Examination 1

Question Paper		
Time allowed		
Reading and planning writing		15 minutes 3 hours
Answer all FIVE questions.		

DO NOT OPEN THIS PAPER UNTIL YOU ARE READY TO START UNDER EXAMINATION CONDITIONS

Question 1 Horsefield

Horsefield, a public company, acquired 90% of Sandfly's $1 ordinary shares on 1 April 20X0 paying $3.00 per share. The balance on Sandfly's retained earnings at this date was $800,000. On 1 October 20X1, Horsefield acquired 30% of Anthill's $1 ordinary shares for $3.50 per share. The balance sheets of the three companies at 31 March 20X2 are shown below.

	Horsefield		Sandfly		Anthill	
	$'000	$'000	$'000	$'000	$'000	$'000
Non-current assets						
Property, plant and equipment		8,050		3,600		1,650
Investments		4,000		910		nil
		12,050		4,510		1,650
Current assets						
Inventory	830		340		250	
Accounts receivable	520		290		350	
Bank	240		nil		100	
		1,590		630		700
Total assets		13,640		5,140		2,350
Equity and liabilities						
Equity						
Ordinary shares of $1 each		5,000		1,200		600
Reserves:						
Retained earnings b/f	6,000		1,400		800	
Profit year to 31 March 20X2	1,500		900		600	
		7,500		2,300		1,400
		12,500		3,500		2,000
Non-current liabilities						
10% loan notes		500		240		nil
Current liabilities						
Accounts payable	420		960		200	
Taxation	220		250		150	
Overdraft	nil		190		nil	
		640		1,400		350
Total equity and liabilities		13,640		5,140		2,350

The following information is relevant.

(i) *Fair value adjustments*

On 1 April 20X0 Sandfly owned a property that had a fair value of $120,000 in excess of its book value. The value of this property has not changed since acquisition.

Just prior to its acquisition, Sandfly was successful in applying for a six-year licence to dispose of hazardous waste. The licence was granted by the government at no cost. However, Horsefield estimated that the licence was worth $180,000 at the date of acquisition.

(ii) In January 20X2 Horsefield sold goods to Anthill for $65,000. These were transferred at a mark up of 30% on cost. Two thirds of these goods were still in the inventory of Anthill at 31 March 20X2.

(iii) To facilitate the consolidation procedures the group insists that all intragroup current account balances are settled prior to the year-end. However, a cheque for $40,000 from Sandfly to Horsefield was not received until early April 20X2. Intragroup balances are included in accounts receivable and payable as appropriate.

(iv) There are no indications that goodwill has been impaired.

(v) Anthill is to be treated as an associate of Horsefield.

Required

(a)   Prepare the consolidated balance sheet of Horsefield as at 31 March 20X2 in accordance with IFRS 3
      Business combinations.   **(20 marks)**

(b)   Discuss the matters to consider in determining whether an investment in another company constitutes
      associate status.   **(5 marks)**

                                                                                          (Total = 25 marks)

Question 2 Tintagel

Reproduced below is the draft balance sheet of Tintagel, a public listed company, as at 31 March 20X4.

	$'000	$'000
Non-current assets (note (i))		
Freehold property		126,000
Plant		110,000
Investment property at 1 April 20X3 (note (ii))		15,000
		251,000
Current Assets		
Inventory (note (iii))	60,400	
Trade receivables and prepayments	31,200	
Bank	13,800	105,400
Total assets		356,400
Equity and liabilities		
Equity		
Ordinary shares of 25c each		150,000
Reserves		
Share premium	10,000	
Retained earnings – 1 April 20X3	52,500	
– Year to 31 March 20X4	47,500	110,000
		260,000
Non-current liabilities		
Deferred tax – at 1 April 20X3 (note (v))		18,700
Current liabilities		
Trade payables (note (iii))	47,400	
Provision for plant overhaul (note (iv))	12,000	
Taxation	4,200	
		63,600
Suspense account (note (vi))		14,100
Total equity and liabilities		356,400

(i)   The income statement has been charged with $3·2 million being the first of four equal annual rental
      payments for an item of plant. This first payment was made on 1 April 20X3. Tintagel has been advised that
      this is a finance lease with an implicit interest rate of 10% per annum. The plant had a fair value of $11·2
      million at the inception of the lease. This is equivalent to the present value of the minimum lease payments.
      Rentals are paid in advance.

      None of the non-current assets have been depreciated for the current year. The freehold property should be
      depreciated at 2% on its cost of $130 million, the leased plant is depreciated at 25% per annum on a straight
      line basis and the sundry plant is depreciated at 20% on the reducing balance basis. The heavy excavating
      plant is being depreciated over 6 years on a straight line basis.

Plant is split as follows:

	$'000
Heavy excavating plant	40,000
Sundry plant	70,000
	110,000

(ii)   Tintagel adopts the fair value model for its investment property. Its value at 31 March 20X4 has been assessed by a qualified surveyor at $12·4 million.

(iii) During an inventory count on 31 March 20X4 items that had cost $6 million were identified as being either damaged or slow moving. It is estimated that they will only realise $4 million in total, on which sales commission of 10% will be payable. An invoice for materials delivered on 12 March 20X4 for $500,000 has been discovered. It has not been recorded in Tintagel's bookkeeping system, although the materials were included in the inventory count.

(iv)   Tintagel operates some heavy excavating plant which requires a major overhaul every three years. The overhaul is estimated to cost $18 million and is due to be carried out in April 20X5. The provision of $12 million represents two annual amounts of $6 million made in the years to 31 March 20X3 and 20X4.

This plant was purchased for $60m on 1 April 20X2 and is being depreciated over 6 years on the straight line basis.

(v)   The deferred tax provision required at 31 March 20X4 has been calculated at $22·5 million.

(vi)   The suspense account contains the credit entry relating to the issue on 1 October 20X3 of a $15 million 8% loan note. It was issued at a discount of 5% and incurred direct issue costs of $150,000. It is redeemable after four years at a premium of 10%. Interest is payable six months in arrears. The first payment of interest has not been accrued and is due on 1 April 20X4. The effective rate of interest is 12.1%.

Required

(a)   Commencing with the retained earnings figures in the above balance sheet ($52·5 million and $47·5 million), prepare a schedule of adjustments required to these figures taking into account any adjustments required by notes (i) to (vi) above.   **(11 marks)**

(b)   Redraft the balance sheet of Tintagel as at 31 March 20X4 taking into account the adjustments required in notes (i) to (vi) above.   **(14 marks)**

(Total = 25 marks)

Question 3 Nedburg

The financial statements of Nedberg for the year to 30 September 20X2, together with the comparative balance sheet for the year to 30 September 20X1 are shown below:

INCOME STATEMENT – YEAR TO 30 SEPTEMBER 20X2

	$m
Sales revenue	3,820
Cost of sales (note (1))	(2,620)
Gross Profit for the period	1,200
Operating expenses (note (1))	(300)
Interest – Loan note	(30)
Profit before tax	870
Taxation	(270)
Profit for the period	600

BALANCE SHEETS AS AT 30 SEPTEMBER

	20X2 $m	20X2 $m	20X1 $m	20X1 $m
Non-current assets				
Property, plant and equipment		1,890		1,830
Intangible assets (note (2))		650		300
		2,540		2,130
Current assets				
Inventory	1,420		940	
Trade receivables	990		680	
Cash	70	2,480	nil	1,620
Total assets		5,020		3,750
Equity and liabilities				
Ordinary Shares of $1 each		750		500
Reserves:				
Share premium		350		100
Revaluation surplus		140		nil
Retained earnings		1,890		1,600
Total equity		3,130		2,200
Non-current liabilities (note(3))		870		540
Current liabilities (note(4))		1,020		1,010
Total equity and liabilities		5,020		3,750

Notes to the financial statements

(1)   Cost of sales includes depreciation of property, plant and equipment of $320 million and a loss on the sale of plant of $50 million. It also includes a credit for the amortisation of government grants. Operating expenses include a charge of $20 million for the impairment of goodwill.

(2)   Intangible non-current assets

	20X2 $m	20X1 $m
Deferred development expenditure	470	100
Goodwill	180	200
	650	300

(3)   Non-current liabilities

	20X2 $m	20X1 $m
10% loan note	300	100
Government grants	260	300
Deferred tax	310	140
	870	540

(4)   Current liabilities

	20X2 $m	20X1 $m
Trade payables	875	730
Bank overdraft	nil	115
Accrued loan interest	15	5
Taxation	130	160
	1,020	1,010

The following additional information is relevant:

(i)   *Intangible fixed assets*

The company successfully completed the development of a new product during the current year, capitalising a further $500 million before amortisation charges for the period.

(ii)   *Property, plant and equipment/revaluation reserve*

- The company revalued its buildings by $200 million on 1 October 20X1. The surplus was credited to revaluation surplus.

- New plant was acquired during the year at a cost of $250 million and a government grant of $50 million was received for this plant.

- On 1 October 20X1 a bonus issue of 1 new share for every 10 held was made from the revaluation surplus.

- $10 million has been transferred from the revaluation surplus to realised profits as a year-end adjustment in respect of the additional depreciation created by the revaluation.

- The remaining movement on property, plant and equipment was due to the disposal of obsolete plant.

(iii) *Share issues*

In addition to the bonus issue referred to above Nedberg made a further issue of ordinary shares for cash.

(iv)   *Dividends*

Dividends paid during the year amounted to $320,000.

Required

(a)   A cash flow statement for Nedberg for the year to 30 September 20X2 prepared in accordance with IAS 7 *Cash Flow Statements*.   **(20 marks)**

(b)   Comment briefly on the financial position of Nedberg as portrayed by the information in your cash flow statement.   **(5 marks)**

(Total = 25 marks)

Question 4 Shiplake

Shiplake is preparing its financial statements to 31 March 20X2. The following situations have been identified by an impairment review team.

(a)   On 1 April 20X1 Shiplake acquired two subsidiary companies, Halyard and Mainstay, in separate acquisitions. Consolidated goodwill was calculated as:

	Halyard	Mainstay
	$'000	$'000
Purchase consideration	12,000	4,500
Estimated fair value of net assets	(8,000)	(3,000)
Consolidated goodwill	4,000	1,500

A review of the fair value of each subsidiary's net assets was undertaken in March 20X2. Unfortunately both companies' net assets had declined in value. The estimated value of Halyard's net assets as at 1 April 20X1 was now only $7 million. This was due to more detailed information becoming available about the market value of its specialised properties. Mainstay's net assets were estimated to have a fair value of $500,000 less than their carrying value. This fall was due to some physical damage occurring to its plant and machinery.

(3 marks)

(b)   Shiplake has an item of earth-moving plant, which is hired out to companies on short-term contracts. Its carrying value, based on depreciated historical cost, is $400,000. The estimated selling price of this asset is only $250,000, with associated selling expenses of $5,000. A recent review of its value in use based on its forecast future cash flows was estimated at $500,000. Since this review was undertaken there has been a dramatic increase in interest rates that has significantly increased the cost of capital used by Shiplake to discount the future cash flows of the plant.

(4 marks)

(c)   Shiplake is engaged in a research and development project to produce a new product. In the year to 31 March 20X1 the company spent $120,000 on research that concluded that there were sufficient grounds to carry the project on to its development stage and a further $75,000 had been spent on development. At that date management had decided that they were not sufficiently confident in the ultimate profitability of the project and wrote off all the expenditure to date to the income statement. In the current year further direct development costs have been incurred of $80,000 and the development work is now almost complete with only an estimated $10,000 of costs to be incurred in the future. Production is expected to commence within the next few months. Unfortunately the total trading profit from sales of the new product is not expected to be as good as market research data originally forecast and is estimated at only $150,000. As the future benefits are greater than the remaining future costs, the project will be completed, but due to the overall deficit expected, the directors have again decided to write off all the development expenditure.   **(4 marks)**

(d)   Shiplake owns a company called Klassic Kars. Extracts from Shiplake's consolidated balance sheet relating to Klassic Kars are:

	$'000
Goodwill	80,000
Franchise costs	50,000
Restored vehicles (at cost)	90,000
Plant	100,000
Other net assets	50,000
	370,000

The restored vehicles have an estimated fair value less costs to sell of $115 million. The franchise agreement contains a 'sell back' clause, which allows Klassic Kars to relinquish the franchise and gain a repayment of $30 million from the franchisor. An impairment review at 31 March 20X2 has estimated that the value of Klassic Kars as a going concern is only $240 million.   **(4 marks)**

Required

Explain, with numerical illustrations where possible, how the information in (i) to (iv) above would affect the preparation of Shiplake's consolidated financial statements to 31 March 20X2.   **(15 marks as indicated)**

Question 5 Creative accounting

(a)   Explain, with relevant examples, what is generally meant by the term 'creative accounting';   **(5 marks)**

(b)   Explain why it is important to record the substance rather than the legal form of transactions and describe the features that may indicate that the substance of a transaction is different from its legal form.   **(5 marks)**

(Total = 10 marks)

Answers

DO NOT TURN THIS PAGE UNTIL YOU HAVE
COMPLETED THE MOCK EXAM

Answers

A PLAN OF ATTACK

If this were the real Financial Reporting exam and you had been told to turn over and begin, what would be going through your mind?

Perhaps you're having a panic. You've spent most of your study time on groups and interpretation of accounts (because that's what your tutor/BPP study Text told you to do), plus a selection of other topics, and you're really not sure that you know enough. The good news is that you can always get a solid start by tackling the first question, which is **always on group accounts.** So calm down. Spend the first few moments or so **looking at the paper,** and develop a **plan of attack.**

Looking through the paper

As it will be in the real exam, Question 1 is on group accounts. Here you have a consolidated balance sheet with one subsidiary and one associate, together with a discussion of associate status. In **Section B** you have **four questions on a variety of topics:**

- Question 2 requires adjustments to draft accounts and preparing a restated balance sheet.

- Question 3 is a cash flow statement and comment on financial position.

- Question 4 is a scenario question on impairment of assets.

- Question 5 is a discussion question on creative accounting.

All of these questions are compulsory

Question 1 is straightforward as long as you are able to deal with an associate.

Question 2 looks nasty but in fact the numbers are not difficult and you should get marks for detailed workings

Question 3 is a cash flow statement. Always a good one to go for. Remember to set up your pro-forma and work logically through the points.

Question 4 requires good knowledge of IAS 36.

Question 5 requires some thought. All the points you make must be relevant.

Allocating your time

BPP's advice is always allocate your time **according to the marks for the question** in total and for the parts of the question. But **use common sense.** If you're doing Question 4 but haven't a clue how to do Part (b), you might be advised to re-allocate you time and pick up more marks on, say, Question 5, where you can always add something to your discussion.

After the exam...Forget about it!

And don't worry if you found the paper difficult. More than likely other candidates will too. If this were the real thing you would need to **forget** the exam the minute you left the exam hall and **think about the next one**. Or, if it's the last one, **celebrate**!

Question 1 Horsefield

Text reference. Chapters 9 and 11.

Top tips. Start with **Part (b)** There are five easy marks here that can be scored quickly, leaving you with ample time for the computational question. State the definition of an associate and then discuss the factors that may give rise to "significant influence but not control".

Part (a) Although there are quite a few parts to this question, each part is in itself quite straightforward. If you take a methodical approach then you should earn high marks.

(i)   Sketch out the group structure, noting percentage holdings and the date of acquisition.

(ii)   Prepare a pro-forma balance sheet for your answer, including the assets and liabilities of the parent and its subsidiary.

(iii) Note the adjustments for fair valuations, cash in transit and inter-company dividends. (In this question the unrealised profit allowance affects the investment in the associate. See below.)

(iv)   Calculate the carrying value of the goodwill in the subsidiary.

(v)   Calculate the carrying value of the associate.

(vi)   Calculate the minority interest in the subsidiary.

(vii) Calculate the balance on the consolidated retained earnings.

Easy marks. Part (b) is 5 easy marks. Do it first to give yourself confidence.

Examiner's comments. This question was generally well answered. However, the examiner was worried by the fact that some candidates did not know that associates are accounted for by the equity method. Other errors included:

- Incorrect calculation of goodwill
- No account taken of unrealised profit on inventories
- Fair value adjustments ignored or calculated incorrectly
- Addition errors
- No adjustment for cash in transit

Marking scheme

			Marks
(a)	Calculation of goodwill		3
	Licence		2
	Leasehold		1
	Property, plant and equipment		1
	Associate		4
	Other investments		2
	Inventory		1
	Accounts receivable		1
	Bank and overdraft (shown separate)		2
	Tax		1
	Minority interest		2
	Retained earnings		4
		Available	**24**
		Maximum	**20**
(b)	1 mark per relevant point to	**Maximum**	**5**
		Maximum for question	**25**

(a)   HORSEFIELD GROUP
       CONSOLIDATED BALANCE SHEET AS AT 31 MARCH 20X2

	$'000	$'000
Assets		
Non-current assets		
Property, plant and equipment (8,050 + 3,600 + 120 fair valuation)		11,770
Goodwill (W2)		1,170
Waste disposal licence (W3)		120
Investment in associate (W4)		717
Other financial assets (4,000 + 910 – 3,240 Sandfly – 630 Anthill)		1,040
		14,817
Current assets		
Inventory (830 + 340)	1,170	
Trade receivables (520 + 290 – 40 inter-company)	770	
Bank and cash (240 + nil + 40 cash in transit)	280	
		2,220
		17,037
Equity and liabilities		
Equity attributable to equity holders of the parent		
Share capital (Parent only)		5,000
Retained earnings (W6)		8,883
Shareholders' funds		13,883
Minority interest (W7)		374
		14,257
Non-current liabilities		
10% Loan Notes (500 + 240)		740
Current liabilities		
Trade payables (420 + 960)	1,380	
Bank overdraft (Nil + 190)	190	
Income tax (220 + 250)	470	
		2,040
		17,037

Workings

1   *Group Structure as at 31 March 20X2*

Horsefield	30%	Anthill
The Parent	1 October 20X1	The Associate

90%
1 April 20X0

*Recognise as an investment
using the equity method.*

Sandfly
The Subsidiary

Consolidate in full.

2   *Goodwill in Sandfly, the Subsidiary*

	$'000	$'000
Consideration: 90% of 1.2m shares @ $3 each		3,240
Fair value of the net assets acquired		
Share capital	1,200	
Retained earnings at 1 April 20X0	800	
Fair value increase for the investment property	120	
Fair value of the waste disposal licence	180	
Fair value of the net assets at acquisition	2,300	
90% Group share		(2,070)
Cost and carrying value of goodwill		1,170

3   *Waste disposal licence*

	$'000
Fair value at acquisition	180
Amortisation for a full two years 2/6 × $180,000	(60)
Carrying value of licence 31 March 20X2	120

Top tips. An intangible asset can be recognised if its value can be determined:

(i)   By reference to an active market, or

(ii)   On a basis that reflects what the entity would have paid for the asset in an arm's length transaction. However, if this basis is used it must not give rise to negative goodwill.

In this question it has been assumed (in the absence of information to the contrary) that the $180,000 valuation meets these criteria.

---

4   *Investment in associate*

	$'000	$'000
Goodwill (W5)		120
Share of net assets at 31 March 20X2		
Share capital	600	
Retained earnings at 31 March 20X2	1,400	
	2,000	
Provision for unrealised profit in associate's inventories		
65,000 × 30/130 × 2/3	(10)	
	1,990	
30% Group share		597
Carrying value of associate 31 March 20X2		717

Top tips. The provision for unrealised profit relates to items sold to and held by the associate. Therefore, the provision reduces the value of these items that in turn reduces the book value of the associate. When the group's retained earnings are calculated the parent will suffer its 30% share of this loss because it was the parent that made the sale and claimed the profit in the first place.

---

5   *Goodwill in Anthill, the associate*

		$'000	$'000
Consideration: 30% of 600,000 shares @ $3.50 each			630
Fair value of the net assets acquired at *1 October 20X1*			
Share capital		600	
Retained earnings at 1 April 20X1		800	
Time apportioned retained profit for the year:			
6/12 × $600,000		300	
Fair value of the net assets at acquisition		1,700	
30% Group share			(510)
Cost and carrying value of goodwill			120

6   *Group reserves*

	Horsefield	Sandfly	Anthill
	$'000	$'000	$'000
Per question	7,500	2,300	1,400
Less unrealised profit: 30% × $10,000	(3)		
	7,497		
Additional amortisation on licence (W3)		(60)	
		2,240	
Pre-acquisition per question		(800)	
800 + (600 × 6/12)			(1,100)
		1,440	300
Share of Sandfly: 1,440 × 90%	1,296		
Share of Anthill: 300 × 30%	90		
	8,883		

7   *Minority interest in Sandfly, the subsidiary*

	$'000
Sandfly's equity at 31 March 20X2	3,500
Add fair value increase on the investment property	120
Add carrying value of the fair value of the licence (W3)	120
	3,740
Minority's 10% interest	374

(b)   **Associate status**

IAS 28 states that an **associate** is an entity in which the investor has **significant influence** and which is neither a subsidiary nor a joint venture of the investor.

The key idea is that the investor has significant influence over the investee company. This is the power to **participate in the financial and operating policy decisions** of the investee, but not the ability to control them. (Control would make the investee company a subsidiary of the investor.)

Identifying significant influence will obviously be subjective, but the standard cites the following situations as evidence that significant influence exists:

(i)   Representation on the board of directors
(ii)   Participation in policy making decisions
(iii) Material transactions between the investor and the investee
(iv)   Interchange of management personnel
(v)   Provision of essential technical information

A typical example would be where the investor is able to **nominate a minority of the Board of Directors**. These directors would participate in Board Level discussions on the company's operating and financial policies, and so it would be able to influence the Board's decisions. However, because the investor's nominees would form a minority on the Board they would not be able to control the outcome of any vote.

IAS 28 contains a rebuttable presumption that deems an investment to be an associate if the investor's equity shareholding is between **20% and 50%**.

Question 2 Tintagel

Text reference. Chapters 3, 13 and 16.

Top tips. The balance sheet in Part (b) should be straightforward after calculating the adjustments required in Part (a), but don't underestimate the time that it will take to draft it.

The adjustments are quite straightforward; work through them methodically and keep an eye on the time. Extend your workings to show the corrected balance at the year-end.

Easy marks. There are no easy marks for this question! However, if you are very happy with double entry, you may find part (a) straightforward. If so, this is 11 easy marks.

Examiner's comments. Some candidates find it very hard to redraft financial statements instead of preparing them from scratch. However most candidates did well. Common errors included: treatment of the lease as if it were payments in arrears; treatment of the deficit on the investment property; and treatment of the loan note.

Marking scheme

		Marks
(a)	Retained earnings	2
	Reversal of cyclic repair provision	2
	Depreciation of charges	1
	Add back lease rental	1
	Lease interest	1
	Loan interest	1
	Loss on investment property	1
	Inventory write down	1
	Unrecorded creditor	1
	Deferred tax	1
	Available	**12**
	Maximum	**11**
(b)	*Balance sheet*	
	Freehold	1
	Plant	2
	Investment property	1
	Inventory	2
	Receivables and payables and bank	1
	Trade receivables	1
	Accrued lease interest	1
	Accrued loan interest	1
	Lease obligation (current liability)	1
	Taxation	1
	Lease obligation (non-current liability)	1
	8% loan note	2
	Deferred tax	1
	Ordinary shares and share premium	1
	Available	**17**
	Maximum	**14**
	Maximum for question	**25**

(a)   Schedule of Adjustments

		Opening retained earnings $'000	Profit for year $'000	Closing retained earnings $'000
	From question	52,500	47,500	100,000
(i)	Lease restated as a finance lease (W1)			
	Remove existing rental		3,200	3,200
	Interest $(11.2 - 3.2) \times 10\%$		(800)	(800)
	Depreciation $(11.2 \times 25\%)$		(2,800)	(2,800)
	Depreciation			
	Freehold property $(\$130m \times 2\%)$		(2,600)	(2,600)
	Sundry plant $(\$70m \times 20\%)$		(14,000)	(14,000)
	Heavy excavating plant (See (iv) below)			
(ii)	Investment property			
	Fall in value $(\$15m - \$12.4m)$		(2,600)	(2,600)
(iii)	Inventory			
	NRV $(\$6m - (\$4m \times 90\%))$		(2,400)	(2,400)
	GRNI accrual		(500)	(500)
(iv)	Heavy excavating plant overhaul (W2)			
	Reverse overhaul provision	6,000	6,000	12,000
	Reverse old depreciation	10,000	10,000	20,000
	Charge new depreciation	(13,000)	(13,000)	(26,000)
(v)	Deferred tax			
	Increase $(\$22.5m - \$18.7m)$		(3,800)	(3,800)
(vi)	Loan Note (W3)			
	Interest expense		(853)	(853)
	Revised balances	55,500	23,347	78,847

Workings

1   Lease restated as a finance lease

	$'000
Fair value of asset and liability	11,200
Rental paid on first day of lease	(3,200)
	8,000
Annual interest at 10%	800
Balance at year-end	8,800
Current	
Interest	800
Capital	2,400
Total	3,200
Non-current $(8,800 - 3,200)$	5,600

2   Overhaul costs

The $12m provision for plant overhaul does not meet the criteria for a liability because there is no obligation to overhaul the asset (it could be sold or abandoned instead). The provision of $12m (and this year's charge of $6m) should be reversed.

The need for a periodic overhaul will be reflected in the depreciation charge. The total cost of $60m will be apportioned between $18m which will be consumed over three years (the overhaul costs) and the balance which will last for six years.

		Total cost	Overhaul 3 years	Balance 6 years
		$'000	$'000	$'000
1/4/X2	Cost	60,000	18,000	42,000
	Depreciation	(13,000)	(6,000)	(7,000)
31/3/X3	Carrying value	47,000	12,000	35,000
	Depreciation	(13,000)	(6,000)	(7,000)
31/3/X4	Carrying value	34,000	6,000	28,000

3   *Loan Note*

The interest expense will reflect the full cost of this loan note (discount, interest, premium etc) rather than just the interest paid. The cost is then charged using the effective interest rate.

	$'000
Received	
Nominal Value	15,000
Discount (5%)	(750)
Issue costs	(150)
Net cash received	14,100

Balance outstanding on loan notes at 31 March 20X4

	$'000
Net amount received	14,100
Interest at 12.1% (14,100 × 12.1% × 6/12)	853
Interest payable 1 April 20X4 (accrual)	(600)
Balance at 31 March 20X4	14,353

Notes

The amount repayable at the end of four years is $16,500,000 ($15m + 10% premium).

The effective interest rate allocates the cost as follows:

	$'000
Net amount received 1,10,X3	14,100
Interest at 12.1%	1,706
Interest paid (15m × 8%)	(1,200)
Balance due 30.9.X4	14,606
Interest charge	1,767
Interest paid	(1,200)
Balance 30.9.X5	15,173
Interest charge	1,836
Interest paid	(1,200)
Balance at 30.9.X6	15,809
Interest charge (balancing figure)	1,891
Interest paid	(1,200)
Balance to be repaid 30.9.X7	16,500

You do not need to do this whole calculation in order to answer the question, and will probably not need to do it in an exam, but this is how it works. As we are dealing in $'000, the numbers are rounded, so the final interest charge is a balancing figure.

(b) TINTAGEL
     BALANCE SHEET AS AT 31 MARCH 20X4

	$'000
Assets	
Non-current assets	
Freehold property (126,000 – 2,600)	123,400
Heavy excavating plant (W2)	34,000
Sundry plant (70,000 – 14,000)	56,000
Leased plant (11,200 – 2,800)	8,400
Investment property	12,400
	234,200
Current assets	
Inventories (60,400 – 2,400)	58,000
Trade receivables and prepayments	31,200
Bank	13,800
	103,000
Total assets	337,200
Equity and liabilities	
Equity	
Share Capital	150,000
Share Premium	10,000
Retained earnings (Part (a))	78,847
	238,847
Non-current liabilities	
Finance lease obligations (W1)	5,600
Loan note (W3)	14,353
Deferred tax	22,500
	42,453
Current liabilities	
Trade payables (47,400 + 500)	47,900
Finance lease obligations (W1)	2,400
Accrued finance lease interest (W1)	800
Accrued Loan Note interest (W3)	600
Income Tax	4,200
	55,900
Total equity and liabilities	337,200

Question 3 Nedburg

Text reference. Chapter 21.

Top tips. Start by putting down the proforma. Then go methodically through the net cash flow from operating activities calculation. You will have to do the workings for property, plant and equipment and deferred development expenditure in order to complete it.

Easy marks. The cash flow statement is straightforward and represents 20 easy marks.

Examiner's comments. This question was generally well answered and part (a) in particular was extremely well answered. However candidates still made mistakes in including non-cash items. Part (b) was poorly answered, some candidates making no effort to answer it at all. Most answers were superficial, giving general trends without commenting on them.

			Marks
(a)	Net cash flows from operating activities		
	1 mark per item		8
	Except – loan interest		2
	– taxation		2
	Capital expenditure – proceeds from the sale of the plant		2
	– other items, 1 mark per component		3
	Financing –equity shares		2
	– loan note		2
	Equity dividends		1
	Movement in cash and cash equivalents		1
		Available	**23**
		Maximum	**20**
(b)	1 mark per relevant point to a	**Maximum**	**5**
		Maximum for question	**25**

(a)   NEDBERG
        CASH FLOW STATEMENT FOR THE YEAR ENDED 30 SEPTEMBER 20X2

	$'000	$'000
Cash flows from operating activities		
Net profit before taxation		870
Adjustments for:		
Depreciation		320
Loss on disposal of plant		50
Amortisation of development expenditure (W1)		130
Impairment of goodwill		20
Release of government grants (W2)		(90)
Interest expense		30
Operating profit before working capital changes		1,330
(Increase) decrease in trade & other receivables (990 – 680)		(310)
(Increase) decrease in inventories (1,420 – 940)		(480)
Increase (decrease) in trade payables (875 – 730)		145
Cash generated from operations		685
Interest paid (30 + 5 – 15)		(20)
Income taxes paid (W3)		(130)
Net cash from operating activities		535
Cash flows from investing activities		
Proceeds from sale of property, plant & equipment (W4)	20	
Purchase of property, plant and equipment	(250)	
Receipt of government grant	50	
Development expenditure capitalised	(500)	
Net cash used in investing activities		(680)
Cash flows from financing activities		
Proceeds from issuance of share capital (W5)	450	
Proceeds of long term borrowings (300 – 100)	200	
Dividends paid	(320)	
Net cash from financing activities		330
Net increase in cash and cash equivalents		185
Opening cash and cash equivalents		(115)
Closing cash and cash equivalents		70

Workings

1   *Development expenditure*

DEFERRED DEVELOPMENT EXPENDITURE

	$m		$m
Opening	100	Closing	470
Expenditure	500	Amortised	130
	600		600

2   *Government Grants*

GOVERNMENT GRANTS

	$m		$m
Closing	260	Opening	300
Released during year	90	Cash received	50
	350		350

3   *Tax Paid*

TAX

		$m			$m
Closing liability	Current	130	Opening liability	Current	160
	Deferred	310		Deferred	140
Cash paid		130	Charge for the year		270
		570			570

4   *Proceeds from disposals of property, plant and equipment*

	$m
Proceeds (Balancing figure)	20
Carrying value of disposals (See below)	(70)
Loss (From question)	50

	$m
Opening carrying value	1,830
Additions	250
Revaluations	200
Disposal (Balancing figure)	(70)
Depreciation	(320)
Closing carrying value	1,890

5   *Proceeds from share issues*

	20X2	20X1
	$m	$m
Share capital	750	500
Share premium	350	100
	1,100	600
Increase	500	
One for ten bonus issue	(50)	
Proceeds of cash issue	450	

(b)   Nedberg has positive cash flow, generating $685m from operations which is sufficient to cover interest ($20m), tax ($130m) and dividends ($320m).

Unusually, the cash flow from operations is less than the operating profit of $900m. The cause of this appears to be the increase in current assets; inventories have increased by 51% and receivables by 46%. Without the comparative income statement it is impossible to say whether these increases are in line with increased activity or whether it is the result of poor working capital management.

Nedberg has paid out $250m on property plant and equipment and capitalised $500m of development costs. In theory this is a good thing, as these investments will generate profits and cash flows in the future. However, Nedberg has had to raise $650m externally in order to pay for these investments, and this cannot be repeated year after year. Nedberg would be advised to reduce its capital investment for a year or two to enable it to get its finances back in order.

The financing section reveals that Nedberg has paid out in dividends half of the money it has received by issuing loans and shares. This seems pointless; the shareholders are getting back money that they have just invested (and they might have to pay tax on the dividends that they have received). The dividend for the year is also high compared with the profits after tax; Nedberg should reduce its dividends to a more modest and sustainable amount.

Overall, Nedberg has a healthy cash flow from operating activities. However, management need to:

- monitor working capital,
- scale back capital expenditure, and
- practise dividend restraint.

4 Shiplake

(a) **Halyard and Mainstay**

This relates to the rules in IFRS 3 for fair valuing assets and calculating goodwill on the acquisition of a subsidiary. Fair values are initially established at the date of acquisition. However, these values must be revised if new evidence becomes available about the values **as at the date of acquisition**. These revisions should be made up until twelve months after the date of acquisition. Changes in the fair value of the assets and liabilities acquired will change the value of any goodwill arising on consolidation.

Fair values and goodwill must not be adjusted for changes that have occurred **since** the date of acquisition.

Halyard

In this example the revision downwards of the market value of Halyard's specialised properties would be treated as a revision of the fair values at acquisition. This will increase the initial cost of goodwill by $1m to $5m ($12m consideration less $7m fair valuation). At the year-end the goodwill is reviewed for impairment, particularly in light of the fall in value of the assets. If the recoverable amount of Halyard as a whole is still greater than the $12m purchase consideration then there is no impairment.

Mainstay

The $500,000 reduction in the value of Mainstay's net assets has been caused by damage. This cannot be treated as an adjustment to the initial fair values. The $500,000 must be charged through the income statement as an impairment.

(b) **Earth moving plant**

At present the earth moving plant is not impaired. The recoverable amount is $500,000 (which is the higher of the fair value less costs to sell of $245,000 and the value in use of $500,000). This is greater than the carrying amount of $400,000.

However, an increase in interest rates will decrease the present value of future cash inflows, which in turn decreases the value in use. The affect on Shiplake will depend on the actual changes in the value in use.

If the value in use is reduced down to $400,000 or higher, then no impairment will have occurred.

If the value in use is now between $245,000 and $400,000, then the recoverable amount will be less than the carrying value and the plant will be impaired down to its value in use.

If the value in use is now less than $245,000, then the recoverable amount will be the fair value less costs to sell of $245,000. The plant will be impaired down to its fair value less costs to sell of $245,000.

(c) **Research and development**

A key point here is that at 31 March 20X1 the costs to date of $195,000 were written off. $120,000 related to research; these costs cannot be capitalised and must be expensed as incurred. The $75,000 of development costs may be capitalised, but the directors decided to write them off because of uncertainties. That was the correct decision at the time, and these costs cannot be reinstated in 20X2 when the project approached completion. Therefore, the only costs to consider at 31 March 20X2 are the $80,000 incurred during the current year and the $10,000 costs to complete.

The $80,000 consists of direct development costs and they must be capitalised. This is because the expected profits of $150,000 are greater than the $80,000 cost to date plus the $10,000 cost to complete. These costs will then be amortised over the market life of the product.

(c) **Klassic Kars**

The carrying value of Klassic Kars is $370m, whereas the value in use of the cash generating unit as a whole is only $240m. An impairment loss of $130m has occurred, and this loss needs to be apportioned between the individual assets of the unit.

The impairment loss will be allocated to the goodwill first, and then to the other assets (tangible and intangible) on a pro-rata basis. However, no asset will be reduced below:

(1)   It own fair value less costs to sell
(2)   Its own value in use
(3)   Zero

	Carrying Value $'000	Impairment $'000		Revised Value $'000
Goodwill	80,000	(80,000)		nil
Franchise costs	50,000	(16,667)	(2)	33,333
			(3)	
Restored vehicles	90,000	nil	(1)	90,000
Plant	100,000	(33,333)	(2)	66,667
Other net assets	50,000	–	(2)	50,000
	370,000	(130,000)		240,000

Notes

(1)   The restored vehicles have a fair value less costs to sell of $115m. As this is greater than cost no impairment will be recognised against these items.

(2)   The $50m balance of the impairment (after charging $80m against goodwill) will be allocated against the franchise costs and plant on a pro-rata basis as follows:

	Carrying value $'000		Impairment $'000
Franchise costs	50,000	$50,000 × 50/150	16,667
Plant	100,000	$50,000 × 100/150	33,333
	150,000		50,000

(3)   The franchise has a fair value less costs to sell of $30m. The franchise must not be reduced below this value. As the impaired value of $33.3m is greater than the fair value less costs to sell no further adjustments are needed.

5 Creative accounting

(a)   Creative accounting is the selection of accounting policies that will portray an entity's financial position and performance in the best possible light. The policies chosen will comply with all existing professional and legal standards. In itself creative accounting is not illegal, although when taken to extremes the financial statements may no longer reflect fairly the underlying financial position and performance of the business.

Creative accounting policies are normally chosen in order to boost liquidity ratios in the balance sheet, or to increase or smooth out profits in the income statement.

Modern accounting standards have reduced the number of allowed alternatives, and so the opportunities for creative accounting are being reduced. However there are still a few areas where standards offer a choice of policies and so there is some scope for creative accounting. A few examples are noted below:

•   Capitalising interest or development costs in order to boost profits in the short term.

•   Revaluing or not revaluing a class of assets. (Revaluing tends to improve gearing, but it reduces the return on capital employed.)

•   Accounting for a joint venture using the equity method, thereby hiding the impact that the joint venture has on the entity's gross profit, finance costs, capital employed and borrowings.

There are also occasions where management deliberately overestimate the useful lives of assets, or underestimate provisions, or fail to apply appropriate policies. These practices are probably closer to fraud than to creative accounting.

(b)   IAS 1 requires financial statements to reflect the substance of transactions rather than just their legal form. This improves the reliability of the financial statements.

Most of the time there is no difference between the substance of a transaction and its legal form. For example the contract date for most sales is when the exchange of goods takes place, at which point all the rights of ownership pass from the seller to the buyer. The buyer recognises the asset, and also recognises the liability to pay for it. The seller ceases to recognise the old asset, but recognises a trade receivable instead. However there are occasions when the seller retains some of the rights of ownership. This raises the question of what assets and liabilities should be recognised, and when profits can be claimed. The legal form of these transactions often tends to overstate profits and hide liabilities.

Typical features of transactions where the substance may be different from the legal form are as follows:

- The seller continues to enjoy the risks and benefits of ownership by using the asset.
- The seller has a constructive obligation to repurchase the asset sold.
- The agreed selling price is markedly different from the market price.

The substance of these transactions are often secured loans, even though the legal form is a sale. If the legal form was reported then the "seller" would claim a profit and ignore the obligation to repurchase the asset. This is obviously misleading to the user of the accounts.

ACCA

Fundamentals

Paper F7

Financial Reporting

Mock Examination 2

Question Paper	
Time allowed	
Reading and Planning Writing	**15 minutes** **3 hours**
Answer all FIVE questions	

DO NOT OPEN THIS PAPER UNTIL YOU ARE READY TO START UNDER EXAMINATION CONDITIONS

Question 1 Hanford

Hanford acquired six million of Stopple's ordinary shares on 1 April 20X1 for an agreed consideration of $25 million. The consideration was settled by a share exchange of five new shares in Hanford for every three shares acquired in Stopple, and a cash payment of $5 million. The cash transaction has been recorded, but the share exchange has not.

The draft balance sheets of the two companies at 30 September 20X1 are:

	Hanford	Hanford	Stopple	Stopple
	$'000	$'000	$'000	$'000
Assets				
Non-current assets				
Property, plant and equipment		78,540		27,180
Investment in Stopple		5,000		nil
		83,540		27,180
Current assets				
Inventories	7,450		4,310	
Trade receivables	12,960		4,330	
Cash and bank	nil		520	
		20,410		9,160
Total assets		103,950		36,340
Equity and liabilities				
Equity				
Ordinary shares of $1 each		20,000		8,000
Reserves				
Share premium	10,000		2,000	
Retained earnings:				
At 1 October 20X0	51,260		6,000	
For the year to 30 September 20X1	13,200		8,800	
		74,460		16,800
		94,460		24,800
Non-current liabilities				
8% loan notes 20X4		nil		6,000
Current liabilities				
Accounts payable and accruals	5,920		4,160	
Bank overdraft	1,700		nil	
Provision for taxation	1,870		1,380	
		9,490		5,540
Total equity and liabilities		103,950		36,340

The following information is relevant.

(a) The fair value of Stopple's land at the date of acquisition was $4 million in excess of its carrying value. Stopple's financial statements contain a note of a contingent asset for an insurance claim of $800,000 relating to some inventory that was damaged by a flood on 5 March 20X1. The insurance company is disputing the claim. Hanford has taken legal advice on the claim and believes that it is highly likely that the insurance company will settle it in full in the near future.

(b) At the date of acquisition Hanford sold an item of plant that had cost $2 million to Stopple for $2.4 million. Stopple has charged depreciation of $240,000 on this plant since it was acquired.

(c) Hanford's current account debit balance of $820,000 with Stopple does not agree with the corresponding balance in Stopple's books. Investigations revealed that on 26 September 20X1 Hanford billed Stopple

$200,000 for its share of central administration costs. Stopple has not yet recorded this invoice. Inter company current accounts are included in accounts receivable or payable as appropriate.

(d) Stopple paid a dividend of $400,000 on 30 September 20X1. The profit and dividend of Stopple are deemed to accrue evenly throughout the year. Stopple's retained profit of $8.8 million for the year to 30 September 20X1 as shown in its balance sheet is after the deduction of the dividend. Hanford's policy is to credit to income only those dividends received from post acquisition profits. Hanford has not yet accounted for the dividend from Stopple. The cheque has been received but not banked.

(e) At the year-end an impairment review was carried out on the consolidated goodwill arising on the acquisition of Stopple, and an impairment loss of $595,000 was identified. No adjustment has yet been made for this.

Required

(a) Prepare the consolidated balance sheet of Hanford at 30 September 20X1. **(20 marks)**

(b) Suggest reasons why a parent company may not wish to consolidate a subsidiary company, and describe the circumstances in which non-consolidation of subsidiaries is permitted by International Financial Reporting Standards. **(5 marks)**

(Total = 25 marks)

Question 2 Chamberlain

The following trial balance relates to Chamberlain, a publicly listed company, at 30 September 20X4:

	$'000	$'000
Ordinary share capital		200,000
Retained profits at 1 October 20X3		162,000
6% Loan note (issued in 20X2)		50,000
Deferred tax (note (v))		17,500
Land and buildings at cost (land element $163 million (note (i))	403,000	
Plant and equipment at cost (note (i))	124,000	
Accumulated depreciation 1 October 20X3 – buildings		60,000
– plant and equipment		44,000
Trade receivables	48,000	
Inventory – 1 October 20X3	35,500	
Bank	52,500	
Trade payables		45,000
Revenue		246,500
Purchases	78,500	
Construction contract balance (note (iii))	5,000	
Operating expenses	29,000	
Loan interest paid	1,500	
Interim dividend	8,000	
Research and development expenditure (note (iv))	40,000	
	825,000	825,000

The following notes are relevant:

(i) The building had an estimated life of 40 years when it was acquired and is being depreciated on a straight-line basis. Plant and equipment, other than the leased plant, is depreciated at 12·5% per annum using the reducing balance basis. Depreciation of buildings and plant and equipment is charged to cost of sales.

(ii) The construction contract balance represents costs incurred to date of $35 million less progress billings of $30 million on a two year construction contract that commenced on 1 October 20X3. All progress billings to date have been settled by the customer. The total contract price has been agreed at $125 million and Chamberlain expects the total contract cost to be $75 million. The company policy is to accrue for profit on uncompleted contracts by applying the percentage of completion to the total estimated profit. The percentage of completion is determined by the proportion of the contract costs to date compared to the total estimated contract costs. At 30 September 20X4, $5 million of the $35 million costs incurred to date related to unused inventory of materials on site.

Other inventory at 30 September 20X4 amounted to $38·5 million at cost.

(iii) The research and development expenditure is made up of $25 million of research, the remainder being development expenditure. The directors are confident of the success of this project which is likely to be completed in March 20X5.

(iv) The directors have estimated the provision for income tax for the year to 30 September 20X4 at $22 million. The deferred tax provision at 30 September 20X4 is to be adjusted to a credit balance of $14 million.

Required

Prepare for Chamberlain:

(a) An income statement for the year to 30 September 20X4; and **(11 marks)**

(b) A balance sheet as at 30 September 20X4 in accordance with International Financial Reporting Standards as far as the information permits. **(14 marks)**

Note. A Statement of Changes in equity is NOT required.

(Total = 25 marks)

Question 3 Boston

Shown below are the summarised financial statement for Boston, a publicly listed company, for the years ended 31 March 20X5 and 31 March 20X6, together with some segment information analysed by class of business for the year ended 31 March 20X6 only:

Income statements	Carpeting	Hotels	House building	Total 20X6	Total 20X5
	$m	$m	$m	$m	$m
Revenue	90	130	280	500	450
Cost of sales (note (i))	(30)	(95)	(168)	(293)	(260)
Gross profit	60	35	112	207	190
Operating expenses	(25)	(15)	(32)	(72)	(60)
Segment result	35	20	80	135	130
Unallocated corporate expenses				(60)	(50)
Profit from operations				75	80
Finance costs				(10)	(5)
Profit before tax				65	75
Income tax expenses				(25)	(30)
Profit for the period				40	45

Balance sheets

	Carpeting	Hotels	House building	Total 31 March 20X6	Total 31 March 20X5
	$m	$m	$m	$m	$m
Tangible non-current assets	40	140	200	380	332
Current assets	40	40	75	155	130
Segment assets	80	180	275	535	462
Unallocated bank balance				15	Nil
Consolidated total assets				550	462
Ordinary share capital				100	80
Share premium				20	Nil
Retained earnings				232	192
				352	272
Segment current liabilities – tax	4	9	12	25	30
– other	4	51	53	108	115
Unallocated loans				65	40
Unallocated bank overdraft				Nil	5
Consolidated equity and total liabilities				550	462

The following notes are relevant

(i)   Depreciation for the year to 31 March 20X6 was $35 million. During the year a hotel with a carrying amount of $40 million was sold at a loss of $12 million. Depreciation and the loss on the sale of non-current assets are charged to cost of sales. There were no other non-current asset disposals. As part of the company's overall acquisition of new non-current assets, the hotel segment acquired $104 million of new hotels during the year.

(ii)   The above figures are based on historical cost values. The fair values of the segment net assets are:

	Carpeting	Hotels	House building
	$m	$m	$m
At 31 March 20X5	80	150	250
At 31 March 20X6	97	240	265

(iii)   The following ratios (which can be taken to be correct) have been calculated based on the overall group results:

Year ended	31 March 20X6	31 March 20X5
Return on capital employed	18.0%	25.6%
Gross profit margin	41.4%	42.2%
Operating profit margin	15%	17.8%
Net asset turnover	1.2 times	1.4 times
Current ratio	1.3:1	0.9:1
Gearing	15.6%	12.8%

(iv)   The following segment ratios (which can be taken to be correct) have been calculated for the year ended 31 March 20X6 only:

	Carpeting	Hotels	House building
Segment return on net assets	48.6%	16.7%	38.1%
Segment asset turnover (times)	1.3	1.1	1.3
Gross profit margin	66.7%	26.9%	40%
Net profit margin	38.9%	15.4%	28.6%
Current ratio (excluding bank)	5:1	0.7:1	1.2:1

Required

(a)   Prepare a cash flow statement for Boston for the year ended 31 March 20X6.   **(10 marks)**

Note: you are not required to show separate segmental cash flows or any disclosure notes.

(b)   Using the ratios provided, write a report to the Board of Boston analysing the company's financial performance and position for the year ended 31 March 20X6.   **(15 marks)**

Your answer should make reference to your cash flow statement and the segmental information and consider the implication of the fair value information.

Note: Segmental reporting is not in your syllabus. The segment information is provided simply to give you information about the different areas of the business for use in your answer to (b).   **(Total = 25 marks)**

Question 4 Atomic Power

You are preparing a technical note to all your clients regarding the effects of IAS 37 Provisions, contingent liabilities and contingent assets, which became effective for accounting periods beginning on or after 1 July 20X0. Amongst other things, IAS 37 replaced parts of IAS 10 in respect of contingencies.

One of your clients, Atomic Power, has asked for further help in applying IAS 37 because the company is concerned that it may not be applying the standard correctly.

Atomic Power operates nuclear power stations that supply power to international, national and regional electricity companies. Environmental clear-up costs can be a substantial item of expenditure for nuclear power plant operators; in some countries Atomic Power's licences have, by law, environmental clean-up commitment written in as part of the agreement, whereas in other countries there is no legal requirement to provide for them.

Atomic Power has brought into commission, on 1 July 20X0, a new nuclear power station, built at a cost of $600m. The plant has a licence to supply electricity for 12 years, which is the estimated life of the power station. At the end of 12 years, the station must be demolished and all the waste product (ie spent fuel) buried over 100m underground in an area sealed for contamination purposes. During the station's life the company will have to pay for the clean up of any contamination leaks from the plant's water cooling system.

The company has estimated the cost of demolition and waste disposal in 12 years' time at $540m, the discounted value of which, at an appropriate rate, is $360m. Past experience suggests that there is a 30% chance of a contamination leak occurring in any 12 month period, and the cost of cleaning up will be between $60m and $120m a time, depending on its extent. The company has a legal obligation to clean-up all contamination caused by leaks.

The company has sent you extracts from its draft financial statements to 30 June 20X1 in relation to the power plant, showing the following:

INCOME STATEMENT (EXTRACTS)

	$m
Non-current asset depreciation: power station (1/12 × $600m)	50
Provision for demolition and waste disposal (1/12 × $540m)	45
Provision for contamination leak clean-up (30% × $90m (average))	27
	122

BALANCE SHEET (EXTRACTS)

	$m
Tangible non-current assets	
Power station at cost	600
Depreciation	(50)
	550
Provisions for liabilities and charges	
Environmental costs (45 + 27)	72

No contamination leaks occurred in the year ended 30 June 20X1.

Required

(a)   Draft a technical note for your clients that explains why there is a need for an accounting standard in respect of provisions.   **(2 marks)**

(b)   Advise Atomic Power on the acceptability of its current accounting policy and redraft the extracts of the financial statements for the company in line with IAS 37.   **(8 marks)**

(c)   Explain the effect it would have on your answer to (b) if Atomic Power was operating this nuclear power station in a country that does not legislate in respect of the above types of environmental costs.   **(5 marks)**

(Total = 15 marks)

Question 5 Impairment

It is generally recognised in practice that non-current assets should not be carried in a balance sheet at values that are greater then they are 'worth'. In the past there has been little guidance in this area with the result that impairment losses were not recognised on a consistent or timely basis or were not recognised at all. IAS 36 *Impairment of assets* was issued in July 1998 on this topic.

Required

(a)   Define an impairment loss and explain when companies should carry out a review for impairment of assets.   **(3 marks)**

(b)   Describe the circumstances that indicate that a company's assets may have become impaired.   **(7 marks)**

(Total = 10 marks)

Answers

DO NOT TURN THIS PAGE UNTIL YOU HAVE
COMPLETED THE MOCK EXAM

A plan of attack

Managing your nerves

As you turn the pages to start this mock exam a number of thoughts are likely to cross your mind. At best, examinations cause anxiety so it is important to stay focused on your task for the next three hours! Developing an awareness of what is going on emotionally within you may help you manage your nerves. Remember, you are unlikely to banish the flow of adrenaline, but the key is to harness it to help you work steadily and quickly through your answers.

Working through this mock exam will help you develop the exam stamina you will need to keep going for three hours.

Managing your time

Planning and time management are two of the key skills which complement the technical knowledge you need to succeed. To keep yourself on time, do not be afraid to jot down your target completion times for each question, perhaps next to the title of the question on the paper. As all the questions are **compulsory**, you do not have to spend time wondering which question to answer!

Focusing on scoring marks

When completing written answers, remember to communicate the critical points, which represent marks, and avoid padding and waffle. Sometimes it is possible to analyse a long sentence into more than one point. Always try to maximise the mark potential of what you write.

As you read through the questions, jot down on the question paper, any points you think you might forget. There is nothing more upsetting than coming out of an exam having forgotten to write a point you knew!

Structure and signpost your answers

As you read through the paper, highlight the key words and phrases in the examiner's requirements. This will help you focus precisely on what the examiner wants.

Also, where possible try to use headings and subheadings, to give a logical and easy-to-follow structure to your response. A well structured and sign-posted answer is more likely to convince the examiner that you know your subject.

Doing the exam

Actually doing the exam is a personal experience. There is not a single *right way*. As long as you submit complete answers to five questions after the three hours are up, then your approach obviously works.

Looking through the paper

Question 1, as always, is on **group accounts**. This time it requires a balance sheet for a parent company and subsidiary. Do not neglect part (b).

- Question 2 is on **preparing financial statements for an individual company**.
- Question 3 is a cash flow statement and interpretation of accounts
- Question 4 requires good understanding of provisions
- Question 5 is a discussion question on impairment

Allocating your time

BPP's advice is to always allocate your time **according to the marks for the question.** However, **use common sense.** If you're doing a question but haven't a clue how to do part (c), you might be better off re-allocating your time and getting more marks on another question, where you can add something you didn't have time for earlier on.

Question 1 Hanford

Text reference. Chapter 9.

Top tips. Candidates were asked to prepare a consolidated balance sheet incorporating some fair value adjustments, elimination of unrealised profits, recognise a contingent asset and deal with a pre-acquisition dividend. Part (b) was a 5 mark written section testing knowledge of why and when subsidiaries are not consolidated.

Examiner's comment. This was generally the best answered question. Most candidates had a good knowledge of the basic consolidation principles, but as ever some of the adjusting items caused problems. Serious errors included:

(a)   Proportionate consolidation (at 75%)

(b)   Consolidating only half of the subsidiary's balance sheet assets and liabilities. Presumably this was because the acquisition was half way through the year. This seems to indicate confusion between income statement issues and balance sheet issues.

(c)   Incorrectly including the cost (or part of it) of the investment in the subsidiary in the consolidated balance sheet.

In part (b), many candidates were aware of the regulations relating to when subsidiaries need not be consolidated, but did not consider other reasons why a parent company may not want to consolidate a subsidiary, even though it may be permitted to do so.

(a)   HANFORD GROUP
        CONSOLIDATED BALANCE SHEET AS AT 30 SEPTEMBER 20X1

	$'000	$'000
Assets		
Non current assets		
Goodwill (W2)		5,355
Property, plant and equipment (W4)		109,360
		114,715
Current assets		
Inventory 7,450 + 4,310	11,760	
Accounts receivable 12,960 + 4,330 – 820 (W7)	16,470	
Insurance claim (W5)	800	
Bank (520 + 300 dividend)	820	
		29,850
Total assets		144,565
Equity and liabilities		
Equity attributable to the equity holders of the parent		
Ordinary shares of $1 each (W9)		30,000
Share premium (W9)		20,000
Retained earnings (W8)		66,805
		116,805
Minority interests (W6)		7,350
Total equity		124,155
Non-current liabilities		
8% loan notes 20X4		6,000
Current liabilities		
Trade accounts payable (5,920 + 4,160 – 620 (W7))	9,460	
Bank overdraft	1,700	
Provision for taxation (1,870 + 1,380)	3,250	
		14,410
		144,565

Workings

1   *Group structure*

Hanford

$$\frac{6,000}{8,000} = 75\%$$

Stopple

Note. Stopple was acquired half way through the year, so the retained profit will need to be time apportioned.

2   *Goodwill*

	$'000	$'000
Cost of business combination		25,000
Less pre-acquisition dividend (W3)		(150)
		24,850
Net assets acquired		
Share capital	8,000	
Share premium	2,000	
Retained earnings (6,000 + (8,800 × 6/12)	10,400	
Fair value adjustment (W5)	4,800	
	25,200	
Group share: 75%		18,900
Goodwill		5,950
Goodwill impairment		(595)
		5,355

3   *Pre-acquisition dividend*

Total dividend: $400,000

Group share (post acquisition): $400,000 × 6/12 × 75% = $150,000

∴ Pre-acquisition group share of dividend = $150,000

4   *Property, plant and equipment*

	$'000
Hanford (per question)	78,540
Stopple (per question)	27,180
Fair value adjustment (W5)	4,000
Unrealised profit on transfer of plant*	(360)
	109,360

* *Note.* The unrealised profit on the transfer of plant was $2.4m − $2m = $400,000. However, 240,000/2,400,000 × $400,000 = $40,000 of this profit has been realised through Stopple's depreciation charge. The unrealised profit is therefore $400,000 − $40,000 = $360,000. The entries are:

DEBIT Hanford consolidated reserves	$360,000	
CREDIT Property, plant and equipment		$360,000

5   *Fair value adjustment*

	$'000
Land	4,000
Insurance claim	800
	4,800

Following IAS 37 *Provisions, contingent liabilities and contingent assets*, the contingent asset would not be recognised in the individual financial statements of Stopple. However, at the date of acquisition the receipt of the claim is 'highly likely' and so IFRS 3 requires the asset to be recognised for consolidation purposes.

6 *Minority interests*

	$'000	$'000
Share capital		8,000
Share premium		2,000
Retained earnings per question: $6m + $8.8m	14,800	
Less central admin costs	(200)	
		14,600
Fair value adjustment		4,800
		29,400

Minority interest: 25% × $29,400,000 = $7,350,000

7 *Elimination of current accounts*

	Dr $'000	Cr $'000
Intragroup charge	200	
Accounts payable	620	
Accounts receivable		820

8 *Retained earnings*

	Hanford $'000	Stopple $'000
Per question	64,460	14,800
Central admin costs		(200)
		14,600
Less pre-acquisition (6,000 + 4,400)		(10,400)
		4,200
Unrealised profit on plant sold (W4)	(360)	
Dividend from Stopple	150	
Goodwill impairment losses	(595)	
Stopple: 4,200 × 75%	3,150	
	66,805	

9 *Ordinary shares*

No of shares Hanford acquired in Stopple = 6m

$$\therefore \text{No. of shares issued} = \frac{6m \times 5}{3} = 10m$$

	$m
Proceeds of issue:	
Total consideration	25
Cash consideration	5
∴ Proceeds for shares	20

∴ Share capital and share premium both increase by $10m.

(b) There are a number of reasons why a subsidiary may **prefer not to consolidate** a subsidiary. Most of these arise where the subsidiary is performing badly and incorporation of its results would **reflect badly on the group**. Such circumstances include the following.

(i) The subsidiary has a **poor liquidity position**.

(ii) The subsidiary is **highly geared**. If a subsidiary which carries a large amount of debt can be excluded, then the gearing of the group as a whole will be improved.

(iii)   The subsidiary may simply be **unprofitable**. Substantial operating losses might leave the parent company wishing to exclude the subsidiary's results from consolidation.

Clearly, then, excluding subsidiaries from consolidation is a possible way to manipulate an entity's results. In the revision of December 2003, IAS 27 *Consolidated and separate financial statements* only allowed exclusion if **control was intended to be temporary**. There had to be evidence that the subsidiary was acquired with the intention to dispose of it within twelve months and the management must be actively seeking a buyer. However, IFRS 5, issued in March 2004, has changed the accounting treatment again. IFRS 5 treats such subsidiaries as **held for sale** and they are consolidated.

Before the 2003 revision, exclusion was allowed if the subsidiary was operating under severe long term restrictions. This exclusion is no longer allowed. Control must be lost before exclusion is allowed.

Many years ago exclusion was allowed on the basis of dissimilar activities, the argument being that the activities of the subsidiary are so different to the activities of the other companies within the group that to include its results in the consolidation would be misleading. However, IAS 27 states that exclusion on these grounds is not justified; instead, their results should be consolidated and the 'dissimilar activity' problem resolved by giving segment information.

Question 2 Chamberlain

Top tips. As well as examining you on the format and content of the income statement and balance sheet, this question also tests your knowledge of four specific situations. Work through these first, noting their effect on the income statement and balance sheet.

As always, be methodical and don't get bogged down in the detail.

Easy marks. There are no easy marks with this question. However, a methodical approach should see you through.

Examiner's comments. This was the most popular and best answered of the optional questions. Problems occurred with: construction contracts, R & D and deferred tax.

BPP
LEARNING MEDIA

Marking scheme

			Marks
(a)	*Income statement*		
	Revenue		2
	Cost of sales		6
	Operating costs		1
	Interest expense		2
	Taxation		2
		Available	**13**
		Maximum	**11**
(b)	*Balance sheet*		
	Development costs		1
	Property, plant and equipment		2
	Amounts due from construction contract customers		2
	Inventory and accounts receivable		1
	Accrued finance income		1
	Bank and trade creditors		1
	Accrued finance costs		1
	Income tax provision		1
	Non-current liabilities		2
	Share capital and reserves (including 1 mark for dividend paid)		2
		Maximum	**14**
		Maximum for question	**25**

CHAMBERLAIN
INCOME STATEMENT FOR THE YEAR ENDED 30 SEPTEMBER 20X4

	$'000
Revenue (246,500 + 50,000 (W3))	296,500
Cost of sales (W1)	(146,500)
Gross profit	150,000
Operating expenses	(29,000)
Finance costs ($50m × 6%)	(3,000)
Profit before tax	118,000
Income tax expense (22,000 – 3,500 deferred tax)	(18,500)
Profit for the year	99,500

CHAMBERLAIN
BALANCE SHEET AS AT 30 SEPTEMBER 20X4

	$'000
Assets	
Non-current assets	
Property, plant and equipment (W2)	407,000
Development expenditure (W4)	15,000
	422,000
Current assets	
Inventories	38,500
Gross amount due from customers for contract work (W3)	25,000
Trade receivables	48,000
Cash and cash equivalents	52,500
	164,000
Total assets	586,000

	$'000
Equity and liabilities	
Equity	
Share capital	200,000
Retained earnings (162,000 + 99,500 profit – 8,000 dividend)	253,500
	453,500
Non-current liabilities	
6% Loan Note	50,000
Deferred tax	14,000
	64,000
Current liabilities	
Trade payables	45,000
Accrued interest ($3,000 charge - $1,500 paid)	1,500
Income tax	22,000
	68,500
Total equity and liabilities	586,000

Workings

1   *Cost of sales*

	$'000
Opening inventory (from TB)	35,500
Purchases (from TB)	78,500
Depreciation (W2)	16,000
Construction contract costs (W3)	30,000
Closing inventory (from question)	(38,500)
Research expenditure (from question)	25,000
	146,500

2   *Property, plant and equipment*

Total depreciation ($6m + $10m = $16m)
Total carrying value ($337m + $70m = $407m)

Land & buildings	$'000	$'000
Cost		403,000
Depreciation b/f	60,000	
Charge [(403m – 163m) $\times$ $^1/_{40}$]	6,000	
		(66,000)
Carrying value		337,000
Plant and equipment		
Cost		124,000
Depreciation b/f	44,000	
Charge [(124m – 44m) $\times$ 12.5%]	10,000	
		(54,000)
Carrying value		70,000

3   *Construction contract*

Total expected profit (125 – 75)	$50m
Profit to date (50 $\times$ $\dfrac{30}{75}$)	$20m

Income statement

Revenue (125 $\times$ $\dfrac{30}{75}$)	$50m
Cost of sales (balancing figure)	($30m)
Profit to date	$20m

Balance sheet

Costs to date	$30m
Attributable profit	$20m
Costs relating to future activity	$5m
Less progress billings	($30m)
Gross amount due from customer	$25m

4   *Research and development*

	$'000
Research (Charge to I/S as incurred)	25,000
Development (Capitalise in B/S)	15,000
Total	40,000

Question 3 Boston

Text reference. Chapters 19 and 21.

Top tips. These financial statements may have looked a bit confusing to start with, which is why you must take time to go through the question carefully and make sure you understand it. Once you had found your way round the numbers, the cash flow statement was fairly simple and more marks were available for the report in (b). In this case, the ratios were already provided, so you just had to analyse the information. As this is worth 15 marks, you should have taken time to analyse the information properly and come to some useful conclusions.

Easy marks. The cash flow statement was easy but was only worth 10 marks. 15 marks were available for the report and there was no reason not to do well on this part. Make notes before you start and cover the issues methodically.

Examiner's comments. Overall, most candidates did well on the cash flow with many receiving full marks for this section, but interpretation of the company's performance was mixed. Some simply commented on whether a particular ratio had gone up or down. This is not interpretation and attracts few marks. It is necessary to suggest what the underlying causes of the changes might be.

Marking scheme

			Marks
(a)	Profit before tax	1	
	Depreciation	1	
	Loss on sale of hotel	1	
	Increase in current assets	1	
	Decrease in current liabilities	1	
	Interest paid	1	
	Income taxes paid	1	
	Purchase of non-current assets	1	
	Sale of non-current assets	1	
	Share issue	1	
	Issue of loan	1	
	Cash and cash equivalents b/f and c/f	1	
	Available	**12**	
	Maximum		**10**
(b)	One mark per valid point to maximum		**15**
	Maximum for question		**25**

(a)   BOSTON CASH FLOW STATEMENT FOR THE YEAR ENDED 31 MARCH 20X6

	$m	$m
Net cash flow from operating activities (see Note)		50
Cash flows from investing activities		
Purchase of non-current assets (W)	(123)	
Proceeds of sale of non-current assets	28	(95)
Cash flows from financing activities		
Loan issue (65 – 40)	25	
Proceeds of share issue (120 – 80)	40	
		65
Increase in cash and cash equivalents		20
Cash and cash equivalents at beginning of period (bank overdraft)		(5)
Cash and cash equivalents at end of period (bank balance)		15

Note

	$m
Net cash flow from operating activities	
Profit before tax	65
Depreciation	35
Loss on sale of non-current asset	12
Interest expense	10
Increase in current assets	(25)
Reduction in current liabilities	(7)
Cash generated from operations	90
Interest paid	(10)
Income tax paid	(30)
Net cash flow from operating activities	50

Working

	$m
Non-current assets – balance b/f	332
Depreciation	(35)
Carrying value of disposal	(40)
Purchase of non-current assets (balancing figure)	123
Balance c/f	380

(b)   **To: The Board, Boston**
      From: A N Accountant

Report on financial performance and position for the year ended 31 March 20X6

All of Boston's profitability ratios have declined between 31 March 20X5 and 31 March 20X6. The overall ROCE has fallen from 25.6% to 18%. In spite of increased revenue and a small increase in gross profit, the operating profit has fallen. This is due to a rise in operating expenses of 8% above the rise in revenue, which should be investigated. The fall in the gross profit margin can be attributed to the $12m loss on sale of non-current assets, which was charged to cost of sales. Without this, the gross profit margin would have been 43.8%.

If ROCE were to be recalculated using the fair values of the segment net assets it would be 16.7% for 20X5 and 12.5% for 20X6. Although this is much lower overall, the gap between the ROCE for 20X5 and 20X6 is much reduced. The ROCE for 20X6 has been to some extent penalised by the addition of $64m assets to the hotels segment. These assets may not yet be producing much return.

If we look at the segments individually, carpeting is the most profitable segment and the hotel segment is the least profitable. However, if the loss on sale of non-current assets were not included in cost of sales, the hotel segment would show a gross profit of 36% - not far below house building. If we adjust the segment return on net assets for fair values, we get 36% carpeting, 8% hotels and 30% house building. This narrows the gap between carpeting and house building, but makes the hotel sector look unviable. However it is worth bearing in mind that the hotel sector currently holds $120m of unrealised profit in its net assets, which could be realised if needed.

Boston's current ratio has improved in the year to 31.3.X6, but this ignores the increase of $25m in loans. The cash flow statement shows a decrease in cash before financing of $45m. This can be explained by the $123m capital expenditure in the year, mainly on hotel properties. The company's gearing has increased due to the new loans, partly offset by the share issue, and it will now be facing higher interest payments. However, its gearing level is still not high in absolute terms.

Question 4 Atomic Power

Text reference. Chapter 13.

Top tips. IAS 37 is an important 'anti-abuse' standard in the IAS repertoire. The definitions and recognition criteria you are required to discuss in (a) are fundamental to the standard; you will not be able to apply IAS 37 if you don't know them.

(a)   TECHNICAL NOTE
IAS 37 PROVISIONS, CONTINGENT LIABILITIES AND CONTINGENT ASSETS

The use of provisions has created substantial opportunities for the **manipulation of reported profits**. One reason for this is that provisions are pervasive; they may arise in relation to almost all areas of a company's operations. Both the recognition and measurement of provisions rely to a great extent on the **judgement of management**. There is thus substantial scope for adjustment of provisions.

A particular issue is the way management use provisions to **'smooth' profits;** provisions are created for future expenditure in years when profits are healthy and then released to the profit and loss account as the expenditure arises, thus reducing the volatility of reported profits over time. IAS 37 is designed to prevent this.

Another difficult area is the use of **provisions for future losses** when one business acquires another. By creating provisions for **restructuring on acquisition** as part of the fair value exercise, the acquiring business can increase the future profitability of the acquired entity, again by releasing the provisions in future periods against the expenditure. This practice has the perverse effect of increasing goodwill the greater the restructuring charges! This has been largely prevented, not only by IAS 37, but also by IFRS 3 *Business combinations*.

Note the emphasis on a 'present obligation'; it is not sufficient to determine that there may or will be some obligation in the future. Where it is unclear as to whether there is a present obligation, IAS 37 states that it should be assumed that there is one if, on the available evidence, it is **more likely than not** that one exists.

Assuming the above definitions and recognition criteria are met, IAS 37 has rules regarding **measurement** of a provision. The amount recognised as a provision should be the **best estimate** of the expenditure required to settle the present obligation at the balance sheet date. It is necessary to incorporate this notion because of the uncertainties surrounding the outcome of provisions.

(b)   Atomic Power's current accounting policies regarding accounting for provisions is **no longer acceptable** under IAS 37. Where an entity has a present obligation that will (probably) lead to a transfer of resources embodying economic benefits as a result of past events, then a provision should be made of the full amount of the expected liability. Where that amount is expressed in future prices then these must be **discounted back** at a nominal rate. Atomic Power should thus recognise $360m as a liability, not $540m, for environmental costs on 1 July 20X0.

The credit side of the accounting entry is thus to the balance sheet heading 'provisions for liabilities and charges'. The treatment of the corresponding debit entry required by IAS 37 is controversial; it must be **added in to the cost of the asset**, to be released as the asset is depreciated over its useful life. This effectively 'grosses up' the assets and liabilities of the balance sheet and has called into question the nature of the assets recognised in this way in relation to how assets are defined in the IASB's *Framework*. In Atomic Power's case (barring the error in using $540m instead of $360m), the effects on profits will not be much different under IAS 37 than the previous policy. The value of the power station plus the provision for environmental costs will be written off over its 12 year life.

The treatment of the possible costs of contamination leaks is more problematic. If there is a leak then the company will have to pay for the clean-up costs, and each leak will cost between $60m and $120m to clean-up. The main issue is whether a **'past event'** has taken place. Is the past event the leak itself, or is it the generation of the electricity that could lead to a leak? There is also the question of the **probability** of a leak. Generally, if there is a greater than 50% chance of a liability occurring, it should be provided for, but it below 50%, then presumably the liability would be classed as contingent only, and disclosed in the notes rather than provided. The probability of a leak is only 30% in any year and indeed one did not occur this year. But over 12 years of generation of electricity, probability would suggest that a leak will occur about four times (ie one year in three). It would therefore be prudent to provide on this assumption. The cost of each leak is $60m – $120m; so taking the mid-cost, the cost of four leaks will be $90m × 4 = $360m. Over 12 years, therefore, the company would provide $30m per year.

Applying the above, the revised accounts extracts are as follows.

INCOME STATEMENT (EXTRACTS)

	$m
Non-current asset depreciation: 1/12 × (600 + 360)	80
Provision for clean-up costs: 1/12 × (90 × 4)	30
	110

BALANCE SHEET (EXTRACTS)

	$m
Non-current assets	
Power station at cost	960
Depreciation (as above)	(80)
	880
Provisions for liabilities and charges	
Provision for environmental and clean up costs (360 + 30)	390

An alternative view on the cost of cleaning up after leaks would be to say that at the balance sheet date there have been no leaks and so there is no obligation to pay out any clean-up costs. Although there may be leaks in the future, these will be from future operations, and so they should not be provided for now.

(c)   In the case put where there is no statutory requirement to clean up environmental damage, one might expect IAS 37 not to require a provision because there is no obligation to transfer economic benefits. However, IAS 37 also includes the notion of a **'constructive obligation'** as discussed in (a)(ii) above.

In Atomic Power's case, if the company has a **track record** for cleaning up environmental damage or pollution, or if it has stated its intention to do so in terms of specific or general commitment then the provisions should be made as in (b) above. However, if the company has not raised any expectations that it will clean up environmental damage, then no provisions would be required and the power station would simply be recorded at a cost of $600m and depreciated by $50m a year over 12 years.

Question 5 Impairment

(a) **Definition**

An **impairment loss** is the **amount by which the carrying value of an asset exceeds its recoverable amount**. The carrying amount is the amount at which the asset is recognised in the financial statements. This will be its cost (or valuation) less any depreciation, amortisation or previous impairment losses.

The **recoverable amount is the higher of the value in use and the fair value less costs to sell**. The value in use is the present value of the future cash flows from using the asset. The fair value less costs to sell is the amount obtained by selling the asset less the costs of disposal.

Sometimes assets need to be grouped together in 'cash generating units' in order to identify any impairment.

Companies only carry out formal impairment reviews if there are indications that an asset has been impaired (see below). However, companies should assess whether there are any indications of impairment at each balance sheet date.

(b) **Indications**

An impairment may arise **if something happens to the asset** (eg it is damaged) or if there are changes in the economy as a whole (eg new technology makes an existing asset obsolete). The standard notes the following seven indicators, divided into external sources of information and internal sources of information.

External sources of information

(1) A **significant decline in the market value** of an asset, if this decline is greater than would be expected from normal use or the passage of time.

(2) **Changes in the technological, market, economic or legal environment** in which the business operates that might have an adverse affect on the business. For example there may be better or cheaper products coming onto the market, new laws may increase costs, or restrictive practices may be outlawed. These will all affect the profitability of a company's products and the recoverable amount of its assets.

(3) **Increases in interest rates**. These will reduce the present value of an asset's future cash flows, and may in turn reduce its recoverable amount.

(4) The **net assets of the company are greater than its market capitalisation**. This implies that the stock market's view of the company's future is more pessimistic than the company's own view of its future.

Internal sources of information

(5) Evidence of **obsolescence or physical damage**.

(6) Plans to **restructure or discontinue the operations** for which an asset is used. Some assets may become surplus to requirements.

(7) Evidence that an asset's **economic performance will be worse than expected**. This may be indicated by low operating profits or operating losses for a part of a business.

ACCA
Fundamentals
Paper F7
Financial Reporting (International)

Mock Examination 3

Pilot paper

Question Paper	
Time allowed	
Reading and Planning Writing	**15 minutes** **3 hours**
Answer all FIVE questions	

ALL FIVE questions are compulsory and MUST be attempted

1 On 1 October 2005 Pumice acquired the following fixed asset investments:
   – 80% of the equity share capital of Silverton at a cost of £13.6 million
   – 50% of Silverton's 10% loan notes at par
   – 1.6 million equity shares in Amok at a cost of £6.25 each.

The summarised draft balance sheets of the three companies at 31 March 2006 are:

	Pumice		Silverton		Amok	
	£'000	£'000	£'000	£'000	£'000	£'000
Tangible fixed assets		20,000		8,500		16,500
Investments		26,000		nil		1,500
		46,000		8,500		18,000
Current assets	15,000		8,000		11,000	
Creditors: amounts falling						
due within one year	(10,000)		(3,500)		(5,000)	
Net current assets		5,000		4,500		6,000
Total assets less current liabilities		51,000		13,000		24,000
Creditors: amounts falling after more than one year						
8% Loan note		(4,000)		nil		nil
10% Loan note		nil		(2,000)		nil
		47,000		11,000		24,000
Capital and reserves						
Equity shares of £1 each		10,000		3,000		4,000
Profit and loss account		37,000		8,000		20,000
		47,000		11,000		24,000

The following information is relevant:

(i) The fair values of Silverton's assets were equal to their carrying amounts with the exception of land and plant. Silverton's land had a fair value of £400,000 in excess of its carrying amount and plant had a fair value of £1.6 million in excess of its carrying amount. The plant had a remaining life of four years (straight-line depreciation) at the date of acquisition.

(ii) In the post acquisition period Pumice sold goods to Silverton at a price of £6 million. These goods had cost Pumice £4 million. Half of these goods were still in the stock of Silverton at 31 March 2006. Silverton had a balance of £1.5 million owing to Pumice at 31 March 2006 which agreed with Pumice's records.

(iii) The net profit after tax for the year ended 31 March 2006 was £2 million for Silverton and £8 million for Amok. Assume profits accrued evenly throughout the year.

(iv) Consolidated goodwill is to be written off over a five-year life using time apportionment in the year of acquisition.

(v) No dividends were paid during the year by any of the companies.

Required:

(a) Discuss how the investments purchased by Pumice on 1 October 2005 should be treated in its consolidated financial statements. (5 marks)

(b) Prepare the consolidated balance sheet for Pumice as at 31 March 2006. (20 marks)

(25 marks)

2   The following trial balance relates to Kala, a publicly listed company, at 31 March 2006:

	£'000	£'000
Land and buildings at cost (note (i))	270,000	
Plant – at cost (note (i))	156,000	
Investment properties – valuation at 1 April 2005 (note (i))	90,000	
Purchases	78,200	
Operating expenses	15,500	
Loan interest paid	2,000	
Rental of leased plant (note (ii))	22,000	
Dividends paid	15,000	
Stock at 1 April 2005	37,800	
Trade debtors	53,200	
Turnover		278,400
Income from investment property		4,500
Equity shares of £1 each fully paid		150,000
Profit and loss reserve at 1 April 2005		112,500
Investment property revaluation reserve at 1 April 2005		7,000
8% (actual and effective) loan note (note (iii))		50,000
Accumulated depreciation at 1 April 2005 – buildings		60,000
– plant		26,000
Trade creditors		33,400
Deferred tax		12,500
Bank		5,400
	739,700	739,700

The following notes are relevant:

(i)   The land and buildings were purchased on 1 April 1990. The cost of the land was £70 million. No land and buildings have been purchased by Kala since that date. On 1 April 2005 Kala had its land and buildings professionally valued at £80 million and £175 million respectively. The directors wish to incorporate these values into the financial statements. The estimated life of the buildings was originally 50 years and the remaining life has not changed as a result of the valuation.

Later, the valuers informed Kala that investment properties of the type Kala owned had increased in value by 7% in the year to 31 March 2006.

Plant, other than leased plant (see below), is depreciated at 15% per annum using the reducing balance method. Depreciation of buildings and plant is charged to cost of sales.

(ii) On 1 April 2005 Kala entered into a lease for an item of plant which had an estimated life of five years. The lease period is also five years with annual rentals of £22 million payable in advance from 1 April 2005. The plant is expected to have a nil residual value at the end of its life. If purchased this plant would have a cost of £92 million and be depreciated on a straight-line basis. The lessor includes a finance cost of 10% per annum when calculating annual rentals. (Note: you are not required to calculate the present value of the minimum lease payments.)

(iii) The loan note was issued on 1 July 2005 with interest payable six monthly in arrears.

(iv) The provision for corporation tax for the year to 31 March 2006 has been estimated at £28.3 million. The deferred tax provision at 31 March 2006 is to be adjusted to a credit balance of £14.1 million.

(v)   Stock at 31 March 2006 was valued at £43.2 million.

Required, prepare for Kala:

(a) A profit and loss account for the year ended 31 March 2006.   (9 marks)

(b) A statement of the movement in share capital and reserves for the year ended 31 March 2006.   (5 marks)

(c) A balance sheet as at 31 March 2006.   (11 marks)

(25 marks)

Note: A statement of total recognised gains and losses is NOT required.

3 Reactive is a publicly listed company that assembles domestic electrical goods which it then sells to both wholesale and retail customers. Reactive's management were disappointed in the company's results for the year ended 31 March 2005. In an attempt to improve performance the following measures were taken early in the year ended 31 March 2006:

- a national advertising campaign was undertaken,
- rebates to all wholesale customers purchasing goods above set quantity levels were introduced,
- the assembly of certain lines ceased and was replaced by bought in completed products. This allowed Reactive to dispose of surplus plant.

Reactive's summarised financial statements for the year ended 31 March 2006 are set out below:

Profit and loss account	£million
Turnover (25% cash sales)	4,000
Cost of sales	(3,450)
Gross profit	550
Operating expenses	(370)
Operating profit	180
Profit on disposal of plant (note (i))	40
Finance costs	(20)
Profit before taxation	200
Taxation	(50)
Profit for the financial year	150

Balance Sheet	£million	£million
Tangible fixed assets		
Property		300
Plant and equipment (note (i))		250
		550
Current assets		
Stock	250	
Debtors	360	
Bank	nil	
	610	
Creditors: amounts falling due within one year		
Bank overdraft	10	
Trade creditors	430	
Taxation	40	
	(480)	130
Creditors: amounts falling due after more than one year		
8% loan note		(200)
		480
Capital and reserves		
Equity shares of 25 pence each		100
Profit and loss account reserve		380
		480

Below are ratios calculated for the year ended 31 March 2005.

Return on year end capital employed (profit before interest and tax over total assets less current liabilities)	28.1%
Net asset (equal to capital employed) turnover	4 times
Gross profit margin	17 %
Net profit (before tax) margin	6.3 %
Current ratio	1.6:1
Closing stock holding period	46 days
Debtors' collection period	45 days
Creditors' payment period	55 days
Dividend yield	3.75%
Dividend cover	2 times

Notes:

(i)   Reactive received £120 million from the sale of plant that had a carrying amount of £80 million at the date of its sale.

(ii) the market price of Reactive's shares throughout the year averaged £3.75 each.

(iii) there were no issues or redemption of shares or loans during the year.

(iv) dividends paid during the year ended 31 March 2006 amounted to £90 million, maintaining the same dividend paid in the year ended 31 March 2005.

Required:

(a) **Calculate ratios for the year ended 31 March 2006 (showing your workings) for Reactive, equivalent to those provided.**   (10 marks)

(b) **Analyse the financial performance and position of Reactive for the year ended 31 March 2006 compared to the previous year.**   (10 marks)

(c) **Explain in what ways your approach to performance appraisal would differ if you were asked to assess the performance of a not-for-profit organisation.**   (5 marks)

                                                                                                              (25 marks)

4   (a)   The qualitative characteristics of relevance, reliability and comparability identified in the ASB's *Statement of principles for financial reporting* are some of the attributes that make financial information useful to the various users of financial statements.

     Required:

     Explain what is meant by relevance, reliability and comparability and how they make financial information useful.   (9 marks)

(b)   During the year ended 31 March 2006, Porto experienced the following transactions or events:

     (i)   entered into a finance lease to rent an asset for substantially the whole of its useful economic life.

     (ii)   a decision was made by the Board to change the company's accounting policy from one of expensing the finance costs on building new retail outlets to one of capitalising such costs.

     (iii) the company's profit and loss account prepared using historical costs showed a loss from operating its hotels, but the company is aware that that the increase in the value of its properties during the period far outweighed the operating loss.

     Required:

     Explain how you would treat the items in (i) to (iii) above in Porto's financial statements and indicate on which of the Statement's qualitative characteristics your treatment is based.   (6 marks)

                                                                                                              (15 marks)

5 SSAP 9 *Stocks and long-term contracts* deals with accounting for long-term contracts whose durations usually span at least two accounting periods.

Required:

(a) Describe the issues of revenue and profit recognition relating to long-term contracts. (4 marks)

(b) Beetie is a construction company that prepares its financial statements to 31 March each year. During the year ended 31 March 2006 the company commenced two construction contracts that are expected to be completed in the accounting period ended 31 March 2007. The position of each contract at 31 March 2006 is as follows:

Contract	1	2
	£'000	£'000
Agreed contract price	5,500	1,200
Estimated total cost of contract at commencement	4,000	900
Estimated total cost at 31 March 2006	4,000	1250
Certified value of work completed at 31 March 2006	3,300	840
Contract billings invoiced and received at 31 March 2006	3,000	880
Contract costs incurred to 31 March 2006	3,900	720

The certified value of the work completed at 31 March 2006 is considered to be equal to the revenue earned in the year ended 31 March 2006. The percentage of completion is calculated as the value of the work completed to the agreed contract price.

Required:

Calculate the amounts which should appear in the profit and loss account and balance sheet of Beetie at 31 March 2006 in respect of the above contracts. (6 marks)

(10 marks)

End of Question Paper

Answers

DO NOT TURN THIS PAGE UNTIL YOU HAVE
COMPLETED THE MOCK EXAM

A plan of attack

What's the worst thing you could be doing right now if this was the actual exam paper? Sharpening your pencil? Wondering how to celebrate the end of the exam in about 3 hours time? Panicking, flapping and generally getting in a right old state?

Well, they're all pretty bad, so turn back to the paper and let's sort out a **plan of attack**!

First things first

You have fifteen minutes of reading time. Spend this looking carefully through the questions and deciding the order in which you will attempt them. As a general rule you should attempt the questions that you find easiest first and leave the hardest until last.

This paper has five compulsory questions. Therefore, you do not have to spend your 15 minutes reading time working out which questions to answer. So you can use it to read the paper and get some idea of what you need to do. At this stage you can make notes on the question paper but not in the answer book. So scribble down anything you feel you might otherwise forget.

It's a good idea to just start with Question 1. Once you have the consolidation question done, you will feel more relaxed. Question 1 will have lots of information and you should read it a second time before you start. Get really clear about % shareholdings and dates on which they were acquired. In this question 1 you have an associate to deal with, so you know you have an additional working to do. Get the formats down and then proceed methodically with the workings.

Question 2 is a single company accounts preparation question. This is where the examiner can bring in leases, construction contracts, fixed/non-current asset complications and other issues he wants to examine. In this case you have a lease and some revaluations. Again, set the formats out and then tackle the workings. Make it very clear to the marker which workings belong to which question and cross-reference them.

Question 3 is on interpretation of accounts. You should not have any trouble with the ratios, but you must be able to *interpret* them. Read the answer carefully to see what this means.

Question 4 is a discussion question and you must ensure you are answering the question, not just writing down everything you know. In part (b), you have to be clear which characteristic relates to which issue.

Question 5 is a construction contract, which was straightforward if you knew what to do. This is a popular topic, so do not neglect it.

You've got spare time at the end of the exam.....?

If you have allocated your time properly then you **shouldn't have time on your hands** at the end of the exam. But if you find yourself with five or ten minutes to spare, check over your work to make sure that there are no silly arithmetical errors.

Forget about it!

And don't worry if you found the paper difficult. More than likely other candidates will too. If this were the real thing you would need to **forget** the exam the minute you leave the exam hall and **think about the next one**. Or, if it's the last one, **celebrate**!

Question 1

> **Top tips**. Part (a) provides you with important information for part (b) so make sure you do that first and get clear what the shareholdings are and how you will treat them. Note also that the investments have been held for **six months**, so take care working out the pre-acquisition profits.
>
> **Easy marks**. Most of the work in this question concerns the goodwill, the associate and non-current assets. You should be able to score easy marks on the goodwill, the non-current assets and the group retained earnings.

Marking scheme

	Marks
(a) 1 mark per relevant point	5
(b) Balance sheet	2 ½
property, plant and equipment	3 ½
goodwill	3
investments – associate	1
– other	2
current assets	1
equity shares	3
retained earnings	1 ½
minority interest	½
8% loan notes	1
10% loan notes	1
profit and loss account	
	20
Total for question	25

(a) The acquisition of an 80% holding in Silverton can be assumed to give Pumice control. Silverton should therefore be treated as a subsidiary from the date of acquisition and its results consolidated from that date.

As Silverton is being treated as a subsidiary, the investment in loan notes is effectively an intra-group loan. This should be cancelled on consolidation, leaving the remaining $1m of Silverton's loan notes as a non-current liability in the consolidated balance sheet.

The shares in Amok represent a 40% holding, which can be presumed to give Pumice 'significant influence', but not control. Amok should therefore be treated as an associate and its results brought into the consolidated financial statements using the equity method.

(b) PUMICE GROUP
CONSOLIDATED BALANCE SHEET AT 31 MARCH 2006

	$'000
Non-current assets	
Property, plant and equipment (W6)	30,300
Goodwill (W2)	3,600
Investment in associate (W3)	11,400
Investments – other (W7)	1,400
	46,700
Current assets (W8)	20,500
Total assets	67,200

Equity and liabilities
Equity

Share capital (parent)	10,000
Retained earnings (W5)	37,640
	47,640
Minority interest (W4)	2,560
	50,200
Non-current liabilities	
8% loan note	4,000
10% loan note (2,000 − 1,000 (W7))	1,000
Current liabilities (10,000 + 3,500 − 1,500 (W8))	12,000
Total equity and liabilities	67,200

Workings

1   *Group structure*

2   *Goodwill*

	$'000	$'000
Cost of investment		13,600
Less: fair value of net assets and liabilities acquired:		
Share capital	3,000	
Pre-acquisition retained earnings (8,000 − 1,000)	7,000	
Fair value adjustments: land	400	
plant	1,600	
	12,000	
Group share 80%		(9,600)
Goodwill		4,000
Impairment to date		(400)
Carrying value		3,600

3   *Associate*

	$'000
Cost of investment ($6.25 × 1.6m)	10,000
Share of post-acquisition profit (8,000 × 6/12) x 40%	1,600
	11,600
Less impairment	(200)
Carrying value	11,400

4   *Minority interest*

	$'000
Silverton – net assets at balance sheet date	11,000
Fair value adjustments (W2)	2,000
Depreciation adjustment ($1.6m/4 × 6/12)	(200)
	12,800
Minority share 20%	2,560

5   Group retained earnings

	Pumice	Silverton	Amok
	$'000	$'000	$'000
Per balance sheet	37,000	8,000	20,000
Additional depreciation (W4)		(200)	
Unrealised profit ((6,000 – 4,000) /2)	(1,000)		
Pre-acquisition retained earnings	–	(7,000) (W2)	(16,000)*
	36,000	800	4,000
Group share: 800 × 80%	640		
4,000 × 40%	1,600		
	38,240		
Impairment: Silverton	(400)		
Amok	(200)		
	37,640		

* (20,000 – (8,000 x 6/12)

6   Property, plant and equipment

	$'000
Pumice	20,000
Silverton	8,500
Fair value adjustments	2,000
Additional depreciation	(200)
	30,300

7   Investments

	$'000
Pumice – per balance sheet	26,000
Investment in Silverton	(13,600)
Investment in Amok	(10,000)
Intra-group loan note	(1,000)
Other investments	1,400

8   Current assets

	$'000
Pumice	15,000
Silverton	8,000
Unrealised profit in inventory ((6,000 – 4,000) / 2)	(1,000)
Intra-group debt	(1,500)
	20,500

Question 2

Top tips. The main issues in this question were the asset revaluations and the finance lease. Always check the **remaining** useful life of a revalued asset. With a finance lease you must note whether payments are made in advance or in arrears. In this case they are made in advance, so the amount payable with one year includes no interest relating to a future period.

Easy marks. You may have been confused by the finance lease but there were plenty of marks available for non-current assets and you could have scored a few more easy marks by dealing correctly with the tax.

Marking scheme

	Marks
(a) Income statement	½
revenue	4 ½
cost of sales	½
operating expenses	1 ½
investment income	1 ½
finance costs	1 ½
taxation	1 ½
	10
(b) Movement in share capital and reserves	
brought forward figures	1
revaluation	1
profit for period	1
dividends paid	1
	4
(c) Balance sheet	
land and buildings	2
plant and equipment	2
investment property	1
inventory and trade receivables	1
8% loan	½
deferred tax	½
lease obligation : interest and capital one year	1
capital over one year	1
trade payables and overdraft	1
accrued interest	½
income tax provision	½
	11
Total for question	**25**

KALA
INCOME STATEMENT FOR THE PERIOD ENDED 31 MARCH 2006

	$'000
Revenue	278,400
Cost of sales (W1)	(115,700)
Gross profit	162,700
Investment income (W2)	10,800
Operating expenses	(15,500)
Finance costs (W3)	(10,000)
Profit before tax	148,000
Income tax expense (W4)	(29,900)
Profit for the period	118,100

KALA

STATEMENT OF CHANGES IN EQUITY FOR THE PERIOD ENDED 31 MARCH 2006

	Share capital $'000	Revaluation surplus $'000	Retained earnings $'000	Total $'000
At 1 April 2005	150,000		119,500	269,500
Revaluation surplus (W8)		45,000		45,000
Profit for the period			118,100	118,100
Dividends paid	-	-	(15,000)	(15,000)
	150,000	45,000	222,600	417,600

KALA

BALANCE SHEET AS AT 31 MARCH 2006

	$'000	$'000
Non-current assets		
Property, plant and equipment (W5)		434,100
Investment property		96,300
		530,400
Current assets		
Inventory	43,200	
Trade receivables	53,200	
		96,400
Total assets		626,800
Equity and liabilities		
Equity		
Equity shares $1		150,000
Revaluation surplus		45,000
Retained earnings		222,600
		417,600
Non-current liabilities		
Deferred tax	14,100	
Amounts due under finance lease (W6)	55,000	
Loan note	50,000	
		119,100
Current liabilities		
Trade payables	33,400	
Loan interest payable (3,000 – 2,000)	1,000	
Amount due under finance lease (W6)	22,000	
Overdraft	5,400	
Income tax payable	28,300	
		90,100
Total equity and liabilities		626,800

Workings:

1   Cost of sales

	$'000
Opening inventory	37,800
Purchases	78,200
Depreciation (W7)	42,900
Closing inventory	(43,200)
	115,700

2   *Investment income*

	$'000
Per trial balance	4,500
Increase in value (90,000 × 7%)	6,300
	10,800

3   *Finance cost*

	$'000
Loan note (50,000 × 8% × 9/12)	3,000
Finance lease interest (W6)	7,000
	10,000

4   *Income tax*

	$'000
Provision for year	28,300
Transfer to deferred tax (14,100 – 12,500)	1,600
	29,900

5   *Property, plant and equipment*

	Land	Buildings	Plant	Leased plant	Total
	$'000	$'000	$'000	$'000	$'000
Cost	70,000	200,000	156,000	92,000	518,000
Accumulated depreciation		(60,000)	(26,000)		(86,000)
Revaluation (W8)	10,000	35,000			45,000
Current year depreciation (W7)		(5,000)	(19,500)	(18,400)	(42,900)
Carrying value	80,000	170,000	110,500	73,600	434,100

6   *Finance lease*

	$'000
Purchase price	92,000
Instalment paid 1 April 05	(22,000)
Balance 1 April 05	70,000
Interest 10%	7,000
Balance 31 March 06	77,000
Due within one year	22,000
Due after one year	55,000
	77,000

[Note that the amount due within one year will be paid on 1 April 06 ie before the accrual of any further interest. Therefore we do not need to deduct any future interest from this amount.]

7   *Depreciation*
Buildings

	$'000
Revalued amount/remaining useful life (175,000 / (50-15))	5,000

Plant

	$'000
(156,000 – 26,000) × 15%	19,500

Leased plant

	$'000
(92,000/5)	18,400
	42,900

8   *Revaluation surplus*

	$'000
Land (80m-70m)	10,000
Buildings (175m (200m-60m))	35,000
	45,000

Question 3

> **Top tips.** This is a good example of what the examiner wants to test in a interpretation question. Only 10 marks were available for the ratios. What you had to do was **explain** them and for this you must take into account any information you are given. In this case the asset disposals were very relevant.
>
> **Easy marks.** You may have had trouble with one or two of the ratios but you could still have scored marks for intelligent comment, as long as you had spotted the situation. Part (c) was easy marks.

Marking scheme

		Marks
(a) one mark per ratio		10
(b) 1 mark per valid point	maximum	10
(c) 1 mark per valid point	maximum	5
	Total for questions	**25**

(a)   ROCE = 220/680 × 100 = 32.3%

Net asset turnover = 4,000/680 = 5.9 times

Gross profit margin = 550/4,000 × 100 = 13.8%

Net profit margin = 200/4,000 × 100 = 5%

Current ratio = 610/480 = 1.3:1

Closing inventory holding period = 250/3,450 × 365 = 26 days

Trade receivables collection period = 360/3,000* ×365 = 44 days

* credit sales

Trade payables payment period = 430/3450 × 365 = 45 days

Dividend yield = 22.5/375* × 100 = 6%

* Dividend per share(90/400)/market price of share

Dividend cover = 150/90 = 1.67 times

(b)   **Analysis of the comparative financial performance and position of Reactive for the year ended 31 March 2006**

The first thing to notice about Reactive's results is that the ROCE has increased by 4.2 percentage points, from 28.1 to 32.3. On the face of it, this is impressive. However, we have to take into account the fact that the capital employed has been reduced by the plant disposal and the net profit has been increased by the profit on disposal. So the ROCE has been inflated by this transaction and we should look at what the ROCE would have been without the disposal. Taking out the effects of the disposal gives us the following ratios:

ROCE = 180/ (680 + 80) × 100 = 23.7%

Net asset turnover = 4,000/760 = 5.3 times

Net profit margin = 160/4,000 × 100 = 4%

Comparing these ratios to those for the period ended 31 March 2005 we can see that ROCE has fallen. This fall has been occasioned by a fall in the net profit margin. The asset turnover has improved on the previous year even after adding back the disposal.

The net profit margin can be analysed into two factors – the gross profit margin and the level of expenses. The **gross profit percentage is 3.2% down** on the previous year. This is probably due to the rebates offered to wholesale customers, which will have increased sales at the expense of profitability. The replacement of some production lines by bought in products will probably also have reduced profit margins. Sales may have been increased by the advertising campaign, but this has been additional expense charged against net profit. It looks as if management have sought to boost revenue by any available means. The plant disposal has served to mask the effect on profits.

Reactive's **liquidity has also declined** over the current year. The current ratio has gone down from 1.6 to 1.3. However, there has also been a sharp decline in the inventory holding period, probably due to holding less raw material for production. It could be that the finished goods can be delivered direct to the wholesalers from the supplier. This will have served to reduce the current ratio. The receivables collection period has remained fairly constant but the payables payment period has gone down by 10 days. It looks as if, in return for prompt delivery, the finished goods supplier demands prompt payment. This fall in the payables period will have served to improve the current ratio. We do not have details of cash balances last year, but Reactive currently has no cash in the bank and a $10m overdraft. Without the $120m from the sale of plant the liquidity situation would obviously have been much worse.

The **dividend yield has increased** from 3.75% to 6%, which looks good as far as potential investors are concerned. But we are told that the dividend amount is the same as last year. As there have been no share issues, this means that the dividend per share is the same as last year. Therefore the increase in dividend yield can only have come about through a fall in the share price. The market is not that impressed by Reactive's results. At the same time the dividend cover has declined. So the same dividend has been paid on less profit (last year's dividend cover was 2.0, so profit must have been $180m). Management decided it was important to maintain the dividend, but this was not sufficient to hold the share price up.

To conclude, we can say that **Reactive's position and performance is down** on the previous year and any apparent improvement is due to the disposal of plant.

(c)   A **not-for-profit organisation** needs funds to operate, just as a profit-making organisation does. It is also required to make good and sensible use of its assets and spend within its budget. To this degree, calculation of certain financial ratios and their comparison to the previous year is valid and would yield information about how well the organisation is run, and how well it manages its funds.

However, there are a number of differences between a profit-making and a not-for-profit organisation. A not-for-profit organisation does not have the basic purpose of increasing the wealth of its shareholders or of achieving a return on capital. Its success or failure is judged by the degree to which it achieves its objectives. These are laid down in a whole different set of parameters. A hospital has many different targets to meet – some of them apparently not that useful. One of its major targets will be to cut the length of its waiting lists for operations. Local government bodies may be judged on the basis of whether they have secured VFM (value for money) in spending local taxes. Schools are judged on their examination passes and their budgets may be affected by issues such as how many of their children are considered to have 'special needs'.

A charity will judge its success by the amount of work it has achieved in line with its mission statement, and by the level of funding and donations it has secured – without which nothing can be achieved.

It is worth pointing out that, just as a profit-making organisation may seek to enhance the picture given by its financial statements, not-for-profit organisations may also be driven in the same direction. It has been found in the UK that some hospitals have brought forward minor operations and delayed major ones in order to secure maximum impact on the waiting list and meet government targets. Some schools have a policy of only entering pupils for exams which they have a good chance of passing. This keeps up their pass rate and their position in the school league tables.

Question 4

Top tips. You should have had no trouble explaining the characteristics, but remember to state how they make financial information useful. Working out how the characteristics related to the scenarios took a bit more thought.

Easy marks. Part (a) was 9 easy marks.

Marking scheme

	Marks
(a) 3 marks each for relevance, reliability and comparability	9
(b) 2 marks for each transaction ((i) to (iii)) or event	6
Total for questions	**15**

(a) **Relevance**

The relevance of information must be considered in terms of the decision-making needs of users. It is relevant when it can influence their economic decisions or allow them to reassess past decisions and evaluations. Economic decisions often have a predictive quality – users may make financial decisions on the basis of what they expect to happen in the future. To some degree past performance gives information on expected future performance and this is enhanced by the provision of comparatives, so that users can see the direction in which the company is moving. The separate presentation of discontinued operations also shows how much profit or loss can be attributed to that part of the operation will be not be there in the future. This can also affect valuation of assets. One aspect of relevance is materiality. An item is material if its omission or misstatement could influence the economic decisions of users. Relevance would not be enhanced by the inclusion of immaterial items which may serve to obscure the important issues.

Reliability

Information can be considered to be reliable when it is free from error or bias and faithfully represents what it is expected to represent. The income statement must be a reliable statement of the results of the entity for the period in question and the balance sheet must faithfully represent its financial position at the end of the period. Financial statements in which provision had not been made for known liabilities or in which asset values had not been correctly stated could not be considered reliable. This also brings in the issue of substance over form. Transactions should be represented in accordance with their economic substance, rather than their legal form. This principle governs the treatment of finance leases, sale and leaseback transactions and consignment inventory. If these types of transactions are not accounted for in accordance with their economic substance, then the financial statements are unreliable.

Comparability

Comparability operates in two ways. Users must be able to compare the financial statements of the entity with its own past performance and they must also be able to compare its results with those of other entities. This means that financial statements must be prepared on the same basis from one year to the next and that, where a change of accounting policy takes place, the results for the previous year must also be restated so that comparability is maintained. Comparability with other entities is made possible by use of appropriate accounting policies, disclosure of accounting policies and compliance with International Financial Reporting Standards. Revisions to standards have to a large degree eliminated alternative treatments, so this has greatly enhanced comparability.

(b) (i) The 'substance' of a finance lease is that the lessee has acquired an asset using a loan from the lessor. Porto should capitalise the asset and depreciate it over its useful economic life (which is the same as the lease term). A finance lease liability should be set up for the same amount. The liability

BPP)))
LEARNING MEDIA

will be reduced by the lease payments, less the notional finance charge on the loan, which will be charged to the income statement. This presents the transaction in accordance with its substance, which is a key aspect of reliability.

(ii)   The Board has decided to switch to capitalisation of borrowing costs. This is a change of accounting policy and so requires retrospective adjustment. Borrowing costs expensed up to this point should be added to the carrying value of the retail outlets and credited to finance costs in the income statement and to the balance of retained earnings. A similar adjustment must be made to the previous year's financial statements. The current year's financial statements and the corresponding amounts will then appear as though this policy had always been in force, thus ensuring comparability.

(iii) This issue has to do with relevance. It could be said that the use of historical cost accounting does not adequately reflect the value of assets in this case. This can be remedied by revaluing the properties. If this is done, all properties in the category will have to be revalued. This will probably give rise to a higher depreciation charge, so it will not improve the operating loss in the income statement, but the excess can be credited back to retained earnings in the balance sheet.

Question 5

Top tips. Construction contracts appeared regularly under the old syllabus and will probably feature regularly in F7. Make sure you know how to calculate the balance sheet amounts.

Easy marks. Part (a) was 4 easy marks and you could get another 2 easy marks for getting the income statement amounts correct.

Marking scheme

		Marks
(a) one mark per valid point to	**maximum**	**4**
(b) revenue (½ mark for each contract)		1
profit/loss (½ mark for each contract)		1
amounts due from customers (contract 1)		2
amounts due to customers (contract 2)		2
		6
	Total for question	**10**

(a)   Revenue recognition is an important issue in financial reporting and it is generally accepted that revenue is earned when goods have been accepted by the customer or services have been delivered. At that stage revenue is said to have been realised. However, if this were applied to construction contracts, the effect would not necessarily be to give faithful representation.

As a construction contract can span several accounting periods, if no revenue were recognised until the end of the contract, this would certainly be prudent but would not be in accordance with the accruals concept. The financial statements would show all of the profit in the final period, when in fact some of it had been earned in prior periods. This is remedied by recognising attributable profit as the contract progresses, as long as ultimate profitability is expected. Any foreseeable loss is recognised immediately.

(b) **Income statement**

	Contract 1	Contract 2	Total
	$'000	$'000	$'000
Contract revenue	3,300	840	4,140
Contract expenses: (Contract 1: 4,000 × 60%)	(2,400)	(720)	(3,120)
Expected loss recognised (Contract 2)	-	(170)	(170)
Attributable profit/(loss)	900	(50)	850

Balance sheet

	$'000
Current assets	
Gross amount due from customers	1,800
Current liabilities	
Gross amounts due to customers	210

Workings

Contract 1

	$'000
Contract price	5,500
Costs to date	(3,900)
Costs to complete (4,000 – 3,900)	(100)
Estimated total profit	1,500
Profit to date: 1,500 × 3,300/5,500 =	900

Gross amount due from customers	
Costs to date	3,900
Profit to date	900
Less progress billings	(3,000)
	1,800

Contract 2

	$'000
Contract price	1,200
Costs to date	(720)
Costs to complete (1,250 – 720)	(530)
Expected total loss	(50)

Gross amount due to customers	
Costs to date	720
Loss to date	(50)
Less progress billings	(880)
	(210)

ACCA
Examiner's answers

1   **(a)**   As the investment in shares represents 80% of Silverton's equity, it is likely to give Pumice control of that company. Control is the ability to direct the operating and financial policies of an entity. This would make Silverton a subsidiary of Pumice and require Pumice to prepare group financial statements which would require the consolidation of the results of Silverton from the date of acquisition (1 October 2005). Consolidated financial statements are prepared on the basis that the group is a single economic entity.

The investment of 50% ($1 million) of the 10% loan note in Silverton is effectively a loan from a parent to a subsidiary. On consolidation Pumice's asset of the loan ($1 million) is cancelled out with $1 million of Silverton's total loan note liability of $2 million. This would leave a net liability of $1 million in the consolidated balance sheet.

The investment in Amok of 1.6 million shares represents 40% of that company's equity shares. This is generally regarded as not being sufficient to give Pumice control of Amok, but is likely to give it significant influence over Amok's policy decisions (eg determining the level of dividends paid by Amok). Such investments are generally classified as associates and IAS 28 *Investments in associates* requires the investment to be included in the consolidated financial statements using equity accounting.

(b)   Consolidated balance sheet of Pumice at 31 March 2006

	$'000
Non-current assets:	
Plant, property and equipment (w (i))	30,300
Goodwill (4,000 (w (ii)) – 400 impairment)	3,600
Investments – associate (w (iii))	11,400
– other ((26,000 – 13,600 – 10,000 – 1,000 intra-group loan note))	1,400
	46,700
Current assets (15,000 + 8,000 – 1,000 (w (iv)) – 1,500 current account)	20,500
Total assets	67,200
Equity and liabilities	
Equity attributable to equity holders of the parent	
Equity shares of $1 each	10,000
Reserves:	
Retained earnings (w (v))	37,640
	47,640
Minority interest (w (vi))	2,560
Total equity	50,200

Non-current liabilities		
8% Loan note	4,000	
10% Loan note (2,000 – 1,000 intra-group)	1,000	5,000
Current liabilities (10,000 + 3,500 – 1,500 current account)		12,000
		67,200

Workings in $'000

(i)   Property, plant and equipment

		$'000
Pumice		20,000
Silverton		8,500
Fair value – land	400	
– plant	1,600	2,000
Additional depreciation (see below)		(200)
		30,300

The fair value adjustment to plant will create additional depreciation of $400,000 per annum (1,600/4 years) and in the post acquisition period of six months this will be $200,000.

(ii)   Goodwill in Silverton:

	$'000	$'000
Investment at cost		13,600
Less – equity shares of Silverton (3,000 x 80%)	(2,400)	
– pre-acquisition reserves (7,000 x 80% (see below))	(5,600)	
– fair value adjustments (2,000 (w (i)) x 80%)	(1,600)	(9,600)
Goodwill on consolidation		4,000

The pre-acquisition reserves are:

At 31 March 2006	8,000
Post acquisition (2,000 x 6/12)	(1,000)
	7,000

(iii) Carrying amount of Amok at 31 March 2006

Cost (1,600 x $6.25)	10,000
Share post acquisition profit (8,000 x 6/12 x 40%)	1,600
	11,600
Impairment loss per question	(200)
	11,400

(iv) The unrealised profit (URP) in inventory is calculated as:

Intra-group sales are $6 million of which Pumice made a profit of $2 million. Half of these are still in inventory, thus there is an unrealised profit of $1 million.

(v) Consolidated reserves:

Pumice's reserves	37,000
Silverton's post acquisition (((2,000 x 6/12) - 200 depreciation) x 80%)	640
Amok's post acquisition profits (8,000 x 6/12 x 40%)	1,600
URP in inventory (see (iv))	(1,000)
Impairment of goodwill – Silverton	(400)
– Amok	(200)
	37,640

(vi) Minority interest

Equity shares of Silverton (3,000 x 20%)	600
Retained earnings ((8,000 – 200 depreciation) x 20%)	1,560
Fair value adjustments (2,000 x 20%)	400
	2,560

2 (a) Kala – Income statement – Year ended 31 March 2006

	$'000	$'000
Revenue		278,400
Cost of sales (w (i))		(115,700)
Gross profit		162,700
Operating expenses		(15,500)
		147,200
Investment income – property rental	4,500	
– valuation gain (90,000 x 7%)	6,300	10,800
Finance costs – loan (w (ii))	(3,000)	
– lease (w (iii))	(7,000)	(10,000)
Profit before tax		148,000
Income tax expense (28,300 + (14,100 – 12,500))		(29,900)
Profit for the period		118,100

(b) Kala – Statement of changes in equity – Year ended 31 March 2006

	Equity shares $'000	Revaluation reservr $'000	Retained earnings $'000	Total $'000
At 1 April 2005	150,000	nil	119,500	269,500
Profit for period (see (a))			118,100	118,100
Revaluation of property (w (iv))		45,000		45,000
Equity dividends paid			(15,000)	(15,000)
At 31 March 2006	150,000	45,000	222,600	417,600

9

(c) Kala – Balance sheet as at 31 March 2006

Non-current assets	$'000	$'000
Property, plant and equipment (w (iv))		434,100
Investment property (90,000 + 6,300)		96,300
		530,400
Current assets		
Inventory	43,200	
Trade receivables	53,200	96,400
Total assets		626,800
Equity and liabilities		
Equity (see (b) above)		
Equity shares of $1 each		150,000
Reserves:		
Revaluation	45,000	
Retained earnings	222,600	267,600
		417,600
Non-current liabilities		
8% loan note	50,000	
Deferred tax	14,100	
Lease obligation (w (iii))	55,000	119,100
Current liabilities		
Trade payables	33,400	
Accrued loan interest (w (ii))	1,000	
Bank overdraft	5,400	
Lease obligation (w (iii)) – accrued interest	7,000	
– capital	15,000	
Current tax payable	28,300	90,100
Total equity and liabilities		626,800

Workings in brackets in $'000

(i) Cost of sales:

	$'000
Opening inventory	37,800
Purchases	78,200
Depreciation (w (iv)) – buildings	5,000
– plant: owned	19,500
leased	18,400
Closing inventory	(43,200)
	115,700

(ii) The loan has been in issue for nine months. The total finance cost for this period will be $3 million (50,000 x 8% x 9/12). Kala has paid six months interest of $2 million, thus accrued interest of $1 million should be provided for.

(iii) Finance lease:

	$'000
Net obligation at inception of lease (92,000 – 22,000)	70,000
Accrued interest 10% (current liability)	7,000
Total outstanding at 31 March 2006	77,000

The second payment in the year to 31 March 2007 (made on 1 April 2006) of $22 million will be $7 million for the accrued interest (at 31 March 2006) and $15 million paid of the capital outstanding. Thus the amount outstanding as an obligation over one year is $55 million (77,000 – 22,000).

(iv) Non-current assets/depreciation:

Land and buildings:

At the date of the revaluation the land and buildings have a carrying amount of $210 million (270,000 – 60,000). With a valuation of $255 million this gives a revaluation surplus (to reserves) of $45 million. The accumulated depreciation of $60 million represents 15 years at $4 million per annum (200,000/50 years) and means the remaining life at the date of the revaluation is 35 years. The amount of the revalued building is $175 million, thus depreciation for the year to 31 March 2006 will be $5 million (175,000/35 years). The carrying amount of the land and buildings at 31 March 2006 is $250 million (255,000 – 5,000).

Plant: owned

10

The carrying amount prior to the current year's depreciation is $130 million (156,000 – 26,000). Depreciation at 15% on the reducing balance basis gives an annual charge of $19.5 million. This gives a carrying amount at 31 March 2006 of $110.5 million (130,000 – 19,500).

Plant: leased

The fair value of the leased plant is $92 million. Depreciation on a straight-line basis over five years would give a depreciation charge of $18.4 million and a carrying amount of $73.6 million.

Summarising the carrying amounts:

Land and buildings	250,000
Plant (110,500 + 73,600)	184,100
Property, plant and equipment	434,100

3 **(a)** Note: figures in the calculations are in $million

Return on year end capital employed	32.3 %	220/(1,160 – 480) x 100
Net asset turnover	5.9 times	4,000/680
Gross profit margin	13.8 %	(550/4,000) x 100
Net profit (before tax) margin	5.0 %	(200/4,000) x 100
Current ratio	1.3 :1	610:480
Closing inventory holding period	26 days	250/3,450 x 365
Trade receivables' collection period	44 days	360/(4,000 – 1,000) x 365
Trade payables' payment period (based on cost of sales)	45 days	(430/3,450) x 365
Dividend yield	6.0%	(see below)
Dividend cover	1.67 times	150/90

The dividend per share is 22.5 cents (90,000/(100,000 x 4 ie 25 cents shares). This is a yield of 6.0% on a share price of $3.75.

(b) Analysis of the comparative financial performance and position of Reactive for the year ended 31 March 2006

Profitability

The measures taken by management appear to have been successful as the overall ROCE (considered as a primary measure of performance) has improved by 15% (32.3 -28.1)/28.1). Looking in more detail at the composition of the ROCE, the reason for the improved profitability is due to increased efficiency in the use of the company's assets (asset turnover), increasing from 4 to 5.9 times (an improvement of 48%). The improvement in the asset turnover has been offset by lower profit margins at both the gross and net level. On the surface, this performance appears to be due both to the company's strategy of offering rebates to wholesale customers if they achieve a set level of orders and also the beneficial impact on sales revenue of the advertising campaign. The rebate would explain the lower gross profit margin, and the cost of the advertising has reduced the net profit margin (presumably management expected an increase in sales volume as a compensating factor). The decision to buy complete products rather than assemble them in house has enabled the disposal of some plant which has reduced the asset base. Thus possible increased sales and a lower asset base are the cause of the improvement in the asset turnover which in turn, as stated above, is responsible for the improvement in the ROCE.

The effect of the disposal needs careful consideration. The profit (before tax) includes a profit of $40 million from the disposal. As this is a 'one-off' profit, recalculating the ROCE without its inclusion gives a figure of only 23.7% (180m/(1,160 - 480m + 80m (the 80m is the carrying amount of plant)) and the fall in the net profit percentage (before tax) would be down even more to only 4.0% (160m/4,000m). On this basis the current year performance is worse than that of the previous year and the reported figures tend to flatter the company's underlying performance.

Liquidity

The company's liquidity position has deteriorated during the period. An acceptable current ratio of 1.6 has fallen to a worrying 1.3 (1.5 is usually considered as a safe minimum). With the trade receivables period at virtually a constant (45/44 days), the change in liquidity appears to be due to the levels of inventory and trade payables. These give a contradictory picture. The closing inventory holding period has decreased markedly (from 46 to 26 days) indicating more efficient inventory holding. This is perhaps due to short lead times when ordering bought in products. The change in this ratio has reduced the current ratio, however the trade payables payment period has decreased from 55 to 45 days which has increased the current ratio. This may be due to different terms offered by suppliers of bought in products.

Importantly, the effect of the plant disposal has generated a cash inflow of $120 million, and without this the company's liquidity would look far worse.

Investment ratios

The current year's dividend yield of 6.0% looks impressive when compared with that of the previous year's yield of 3.75%, but as the company has maintained the same dividend (and dividend per share as there is no change in share capital) , the 'improvement' in the yield is due to a falling share price. Last year the share price must have been $6.00 to give a yield of 3.75% on a dividend per share of 22.5 cents. It is worth noting that maintaining the dividend at $90 million from profits of $150 million gives a cover of only 1.67 times whereas on the same dividend last year the cover was 2 times (meaning last year's profit (after tax) was $180 million).

11

Conclusion

Although superficially the company's profitability seems to have improved as a result of the directors' actions at the start of the current year, much, if not all, of the apparent improvement is due to the change in supply policy and the consequent beneficial effects of the disposal of plant. The company's liquidity is now below acceptable levels and would have been even worse had the disposal not occurred. It appears that investors have understood the underlying deterioration in performance as there has been a marked fall in the company's share price.

(c) It is generally assumed that the objective of stock market listed companies is to maximise the wealth of their shareholders. This in turn places an emphasis on profitability and other factors that influence a company's share price. It is true that some companies have other (secondary) aims such as only engaging in ethical activities (eg not producing armaments) or have strong environmental considerations. Clearly by definition not-for-profit organisations are not motivated by the need to produce profits for shareholders, but that does not mean that they should be inefficient. Many areas of assessment of profit oriented companies are perfectly valid for not-for-profit organisations; efficient inventory holdings, tight budgetary constraints, use of key performance indicators, prevention of fraud etc.

There are a great variety of not-for-profit organisations; eg public sector health, education, policing and charities. It is difficult to be specific about how to assess the performance of a not-for-profit organisation without knowing what type of organisation it is. In general terms an assessment of performance must be made in the light of the stated objectives of the organisation. Thus for example in a public health service one could look at measures such as treatment waiting times, increasing life expectancy etc, and although such organisations don't have a profit motive requiring efficient operation, they should nonetheless be accountable for the resources they use. Techniques such as 'value for money' and the three Es (economy, efficiency and effectiveness) have been developed and can help to assess the performance of such organisations.

4 (a) Relevance

Information has the quality of relevance when it can influence, on a timely basis, users' economic decisions. It helps to evaluate past, present and future events by confirming or perhaps correcting past evaluations of economic events. There are many ways of interpreting and applying the concept of relevance, for example, only material information is considered relevant as, by definition, information is material only if its omission or misstatement could influence users. Another common debate regarding relevance is whether current value information is more relevant than that based on historical cost. An interesting emphasis placed on relevance within the Framework is that relevant information assists in the predictive ability of financial statements. That is not to say the financial statements should be predictive in the sense of forecasts, but that (past) information should be presented in a manner that assists users to assess an entity's ability to take advantage of opportunities and react to adverse situations. A good example of this is the separate presentation of discontinued operations in the income statement. From this users will be better able to assess the parts of the entity that will produce future profits (continuing operations) and users can judge the merits of the discontinuation ie has the entity sold a profitable part of the business (which would lead users to question why), or has the entity acted to curtail the adverse affect of a loss making operation.

Reliability

The Framework states that for information to be useful it must be reliable. The quality of reliability is described as being free from material error (accurate) and a faithful representation of that which it purports to portray (i.e. the financial statements are a faithful representation of the entity's underlying transactions). There can be occasions where the legal form of a transaction can be engineered to disguise the economic reality of the transaction. A cornerstone of faithful representation is that transactions must be accounted for according to their substance (i.e. commercial intent or economic reality) rather than their legal or contrived form. To be reliable, information must be neutral (free from bias). Biased information attempts to influence users (perhaps to come to a predetermined decision) by the manner in which it is presented. It is recognised that financial statements cannot be absolutely accurate due to inevitable uncertainties surrounding their preparation. A typical example would be estimating the useful economic lives of non-current assets. This is addressed by the use of prudence which is the exercise of a degree of caution in matters of uncertainty. However prudence cannot be used to deliberately understate profit or create excessive provisions (this would break the neutrality principle). Reliable information must also be complete, omitted information (that should be reported) will obviously mislead users.

Comparability

Comparability is fundamental to assessing an entity's performance. Users will compare an entity's results over time and also with other similar entities. This is the principal reason why financial statements contain corresponding amounts for previous period(s). Comparability is enhanced by the use (and disclosure) of consistent accounting policies such that users can confirm that comparative information (for calculating trends) is comparable and the disclosure of accounting policies at least informs users if different entities use different policies. That said, comparability should not stand in the way of improved accounting practices (usually through new Standards); it is recognised that there are occasions where it is necessary to adopt new accounting policies if they would enhance relevance and reliability.

(b) (i) This item involves the characteristic of reliability and specifically reporting the substance of transactions. As the lease agreement is for substantially the whole of the asset's useful economic life, Porto will experience the same risks and rewards as if it owned the asset. Although the legal form of this transaction is a rental, its substance is the equivalent to acquiring the asset and raising a loan. Thus, in order for the financial statements to be reliable (and comparable to those where an asset is bought from the proceeds of a loan), the transaction should be shown as an asset on Porto's balance sheet with a corresponding liability for the future lease rental payments. The income statement should be charged with depreciation on the asset and a finance charge on the 'loan'.

12

(ii)   This item involves the characteristic of comparability. Changes in accounting policies should generally be avoided in order to preserve comparability. Presumably the directors have good reason to believe the new policy presents a more reliable and relevant view. In order to minimise the adverse effect a change in accounting policy has on comparability, the financial statements (including the corresponding amounts) should be prepared on the basis that the new policy had always been in place (retrospective application). Thus the assets (retail outlets) should include the previously expensed finance costs and income statements will no longer show a finance cost (in relation to these assets whilst under construction). Any finance costs relating to periods prior to the policy change (i.e. for two or more years ago) should be adjusted for by increasing retained earnings brought forward in the statement of changes in equity.

(iii)   This item involves the characteristic of relevance. This situation questions whether historical cost accounting is more relevant to users than current value information. Porto's current method of reporting these events using purely historical cost based information (i.e. showing an operating loss, but not reporting the increases in property values) is perfectly acceptable. However, the company could choose to revalue its hotel properties (which would subject it to other requirements). This option would still report an operating loss (probably an even larger loss than under historical cost if there are increased depreciation charges on the hotels), but the increases in value would also be reported (in equity) arguably giving a more complete picture of performance.

5   (a)   The correct timing of when revenue (and profit) should be recognised is an important aspect of an income statement showing a faithful presentation. It is generally accepted that only realised profits should be included in the income statement. For most types of supply and sale of goods it is generally understood that a profit is realised when the goods have been manufactured (or obtained) by the supplier and satisfactorily delivered to the customer. The issue with construction contracts is that the process of completing the project takes a relatively long time and, in particular, will spread across at least one accounting period-end. If such contracts are treated like most sales of goods, it would mean that revenue and profit would not be recognised until the contract is completed (the "completed contracts" basis). This is often described as following the prudence concept. The problem with this approach is that it may not show a faithful presentation as all the profit on a contract is included in the period of completion, whereas in reality (a faithful representation), it is being earned, but not reported, throughout the duration of the contract. IAS 11 remedies this by recognising profit on uncompleted contracts in proportion to some measure of the percentage of completion applied to the estimated total contract profit. This is sometimes said to reflect the accruals concept, but it should only be applied where the outcome of the contract is reasonably foreseeable. In the event that a loss on a contract is foreseen, the whole of the loss must be recognised immediately, thereby ensuring the continuing application of prudence.

(b)   Beetie

Income statement	Contract 1 $'000	Contract 2 $'000	Total $'000
Revenue recognised	3,300	840	4,140
Contract expenses recognised (balancing figure contract 1)	(2,400)	(720)	(3,120)
Expected loss recognised (contract 2)		(170)	(170)
Attributable profit/(loss) (see working)	900	(50)	850

Balance sheet			
Contact costs incurred	3,900	720	4,620
Recognised profit/(losses)	900	(50)	850
	4,800	670	5,470
Progress billings	(3,000)	(880)	(3,880)
Amounts due from customers	1,800		1,800
Amounts due to customers		(210)	(210)

Workings (in $'000)

Estimated total profit:			
Agreed contract price	5,500	1,200	
Estimated contract cost	(4,000)	(1,250)	
Estimated total profit/(loss)	1,500	(50)	

Percentage complete:		
Agreed value of work completed at 31 March 2006	3,300	
Contract price	5,500	
Percentage complete at 31 March 2006 (3,300/5,500 x 100)	60%	
Profit to 31 March 2006 (60% x 1,500)	900	

At 31 March 2006 the increase in the expected total costs of contract 2 mean that a loss of $50,000 is expected on this contract. In these circumstances, regardless of the percentage completed, the whole of this loss should be recognised immediately.

13

Pilot Paper F7 (INT)
Financial Reporting (International)

Marking Scheme

This marking scheme is given as a guide in the context of the suggested answers. Scope is given to markers to award marks for alternative approaches to a question, including relevant comment, and where well-reasoned conclusions are provided. This is particularly the case for written answers where there may be more than one acceptable solution.

1	**(a)**	1 mark per relevant point	**5**
	(b)	Balance sheet:	
		property, plant and equipment	2½
		goodwill	3½
		investments – associate	3
		– other	1
		current assets	2
		equity shares	1
		retained earnings	3
		minority interest	1½
		8% loan notes	½
		10% loan notes	1
		profit and loss account	1
			20
		Total for question	**25**

2	**(a)**	Income statement	
		revenue	½
		cost of sales	4½
		operating expenses	½
		investment income	1½
		finance costs	1½
		taxation	1½
			10
	(b)	Movement in share capital and reserves	
		brought forward figures	1
		revaluation	1
		profit for period	1
		dividends paid	1
			4
	(c)	Balance sheet	
		land and buildings	2
		plant and equipment	2
		investment property	1
		inventory and trade receivables	1
		8% loan	½
		deferred tax	½
		lease obligation: interest and capital one year	1
		capital over one year	1
		trade payables and overdraft	1
		accrued interest	½
		income tax provision	½
			11
		Total for question	**25**

14

3	(a)	one mark per ratio		10
	(b)	1 mark per valid point	maximum	10
	(c)	1 mark per valid point	maximum	5
			Total for question	25

4	(a)	3 marks each for relevance, reliability and comparability		9
	(b)	2 marks for each transaction ((i) to (iii)) or event		6
			Total for question	15

5	(a)	one mark per valid point to	maximum	4
	(b)	revenue (½ mark for each contract)		1
		profit/loss (½ mark for each contract)		1
		amounts due from customers (contract 1)		2
		amounts due to customers (contract 2)		2
				6
			Total for question	10

15

Part 2 Examination – Paper 2.5(INT)
Financial Reporting (International Stream)

June 2006 Answers

1   (a)   Hydan
Consolidated income statement year ended 31 March 2006

	$'000	$'000
Revenue (98,000 + 35,200 – 30,000 intra-group sales)		103,200
Cost of sales (w (i))		(77,500)
Gross profit		25,700
Operating expenses (11,800 + 8,000 + 375 goodwill (w (ii)))		(20,175)
Interest receivable (350 – 200 intra-group (4,000 x 10% x 6/12))		150
Finance costs		(420)
		5,255
Income tax expense (4,200 – 1,000 tax relief)		(3,200)
Profit for the period		2,055
Attributable to:		
Equity holders of the parent		3,455
Minority interest (w (iv))		(1,400)
		2,055

Consolidated balance sheet as at 31 March 2006

	$'000
Non-current assets:	
Property, plant and equipment (18,400 + 9,500 + 1,200 – 300 depreciation adjustment)	28,800
Goodwill (3,000 – 375 (w (ii)))	2,625
Investment (16,000 – 10,800 – 4,000 loan)	1,200
	32,625
Current assets (w (v))	24,000
Total assets	56,625
Equity attributable to holders of the parent	
Ordinary shares of $1 each	10,000
Share premium	5,000
Retained earnings (w (iii))	17,525
	32,525
Minority interest (w (iv))	3,800
Total equity	36,325
Non-current liabilities	
7% bank loan	6,000
Current liabilities (w (v))	14,300
Total equity and liabilities	56,625

Workings in $'000
(i)   Cost of sales

Hydan	76,000
Systan	31,000
Intra-group sales	(30,000)
URP in inventories	200
Additional depreciation re fair values	300
	77,500

(ii)   Goodwill/Cost of control in Systan:

Investment at cost (2,000 x 60% x $9)		10,800
Less – ordinary shares of Systan	2,000	
– share premium	500	
– pre-acquisition reserves (6,300 + 3,000 post acq loss)	9,300	
– fair value adjustment	1,200	
	13,000 x 60%	(7,800)
Goodwill on consolidation		3,000
Goodwill is impaired by 12·5% of its carrying amount =		375

15

(iii) Consolidated reserves:

Hydan's reserves	20,000
Systan's post acquisition losses (see below) (3,500 x 60%)	(2,100)
Goodwill impairment (w (ii))	(375)
	17,525

The adjusted profits of Systan are:

Per question		6,300
Adjustments – URP in inventories (4,000 x 5%)	(200)	
– additional depreciation	(300)	(500)
		5,800

(iv) Minority interest in income statement

Systan's post acquisition loss after tax	3,000
Adjustments from (w (iii))	500
Adjusted losses	3,500 x 40% = 1,400

Minority interest in balance sheet

Ordinary shares and premium of Systan	2,500
Adjusted profits (w (iii))	5,800
Fair value adjustments	1,200
	9,500 x 40% = 3,800

(v) Current assets and liabilities
Current assets:

Hydan	18,000
Systan	7,200
URP in inventories	(200)
Intra-group balance	(1,000)
	24,000

Current liabilities:

Hydan	11,400
Systan	3,900
Intra-group balance	(1,000)
	14,300

(b) Although Systan's revenue has increased since its acquisition by Hydan, its operating performance appears to have deteriorated markedly. Its gross profit margin has fallen from 25% (6m/24m) in the six months prior to the acquisition to only 11·9% (4·2m/35·2m) in the post-acquisition period. The decline in gross profit is worsened by a huge increase in operating expenses in the post-acquisition period. These have gone from $1·2 million pre-acquisition to $8 million post-acquisition. Taking into account the effects of interest and tax a $3·6 million first half profit (pre-acquisition) has turned into a $3 million second half loss (post-acquisition). Whilst it is possible that some of the worsening performance may be due to market conditions, the major cause is probably due to the effects of the acquisition. As the question states Hydan has acquired a controlling interest in Systan and thus the two companies are related parties. Since the acquisition most of Systan's sales have been to Hydan. This is not surprising as Systan was acquired to secure supplies to Hydan. The terms under which the sales are made are now determined by the management of Hydan, whereas they were previously determined by the management of Systan. The question says sales to Hydan yield a consistent gross profit of only 5%. This is very low and much lower than the profit margin on sales to Hydan prior to the acquisition and also much lower than the few sales that were made to third parties in the post acquisition period. It may also be that Hydan has shifted the burden of some of the group operating expenses to Systan – this may explain the large increase in Systan's post acquisition operating expenses. The effect of these (transfer pricing) actions would move profits from Systan's books into those of Hydan. The implications of this are quite significant. Initially there may be a tendency to think the effect is not important as on consolidation both companies' results are added together, but other parties are affected by these actions. The most obvious is the significant (40%) minority interest, they are effectively having some of their share of Systan's profit and balance sheet value taken from them. It may also be that the management and staff of Systan may be losing out on profit related bonuses. Finally, any party using Systan's entity financial statements, for whatever purpose, would be basing any decisions they make on potentially misleading information.

16

2   (a) Darius income statement for the year ended 31 March 2006

	$'000	$'000
Revenue (w (i))		221,800
Cost of sales (w (i))		(156,200)
Gross profit		65,600
Operating expenses		(22,400)
Investment income		1,200
Loss on investment property (16,000 – 13,500 w (ii))		(2,500)
Financing cost (5,000 – 3,200 ordinary dividend (w (v))		(1,800)
Profit before tax		40,100
Income tax expense (w (iii))		(6,400)
Profit for the period		33,700

(b) Statement of recognised income and expense for the year ended 31 March 2006

Unrealised surplus on land and building	21,000
Profit for the period	33,700
Total recognised income and expense for the period	54,700

(c) Darius balance sheet as at 31 March 2006

Non-current assets		
Property, plant and equipment (w (iv))		87,100
Investment property (w (ii))		13,500
		100,600
Current assets		
Inventories (10,500 – 300 (w (i)))	10,200	
Trade receivables (13,500 + 1,500 JV)	15,000	25,200
Total assets		125,800
Equity and liabilities:		
Ordinary shares of 25c each		20,000
Reserves:		
Revaluation	21,000	
Retained earnings (w (v))	48,000	69,000
		89,000
Non-current liabilities		
Deferred tax (w (iii))	3,600	
Redeemable preference shares of $1 each	10,000	13,600
Current liabilities		
Trade payables (11,800 + 2,500 JV)	14,300	
Bank overdraft	900	
Current tax payable	8,000	23,200
Total equity and liabilities		125,800

Workings in $'000

(i)   Revenue

Per question	213,800
Joint venture revenue	8,000
	221,800

Cost of sales:

Per question	143,800
Closing inventories adjustment (see below)	300
Joint venture costs	5,000
Depreciation (w (iv)) – building	3,200
– plant	3,900
	156,200

The damaged inventories will require expenditure of $450,000 to repair them and then have an expected selling price of $950,000. This gives a net realisable value of $500,000, as their cost was $800,000, a write down of $300,000 is required.

17

(ii) The fair value model in IAS 40 *Investment property* requires investment properties to be included in the balance sheet at their fair value (in this case taken to be the open market value). Any surplus or deficit is recorded in income.

(iii) Taxation:

Provision for year	8,000
Deferred tax (see below)	(1,600)
	6,400

Taxable temporary differences are $12 million. At a rate of 30% this would require a balance sheet provision for deferred tax of $3·6 million. The opening provision is $5·2 million, thus a credit of $1·6 million will be made in the income statement.

(iv) Non-current assets
Land and building

Depreciation of the building for the year ended 31 March 2006 will be (48,000/15 years)	3,200

Plant and equipment

Per trial balance	36,000
Joint venture plant	12,000
	48,000
Accumulated depreciation 1 April 2005	(16,800)
Carrying amount prior to charge for year	31,200
Depreciation year ended 31 March 2006 at 12·5%	(3,900)
Carrying amount at 31 March 2006	27,300

Summarising:

	cost/valuation	accumulated depreciation	carrying amount
Land and building	63,000	3,200	59,800
Plant and equipment	48,000	20,700	27,300
Property, plant and equipment	111,000	23,900	87,100

(v) Retained earnings

Balance b/f	17,500
Profit for period	33,700
Ordinary dividends paid (20,000 x 4 x 4c)	(3,200)
	48,000

3 **(a)** The purpose of the Framework is to assist the various bodies and users that may be interested in the financial statements of an entity. It is there to assist the IASB itself, other standard setters, preparers, auditors and users of financial statements and any other party interested in the work of the IASB. More specifically:

– to assist the Board in the development of new and the review of existing standards. It is also believed that the Framework will assist in promoting harmonisation of the preparation of financial statements and also reduce the number of alternative accounting treatments permitted by IFRSs

– national standard setters that have expressed a desire for local standards to be compliant with IFRS will be assisted by the Framework

– the Framework will help preparers to apply IFRS more effectively if they understand the concepts underlying the Standards, additionally the Framework should help in dealing with new or emerging issues which are, as yet, not covered by an IFRS

– the above is also true of the work of the auditor, in particular the Framework can assist the auditor in determining whether the financial statements conform to IFRS

– users should be assisted by the Framework in interpreting the performance of entities that have complied with IFRS.

It is important to realise that the Framework is not itself an accounting standard and thus cannot override a requirement of a specific standard. Indeed, the Board recognises that there may be (rare) occasions where a particular IFRS is in conflict with the Framework. In these cases the requirements of the standard should prevail. The Board believes that such conflicts will diminish over time as the development of new and (revised) existing standards will be guided by the Framework and the Framework itself may be revised based on the experience of working with it.

18

BPP
LEARNING MEDIA

(b) Definitions – assets:

The IASB's Framework defines assets as 'a resource controlled by an entity as a result of past events and from which future economic benefits are expected to flow to the entity'. The first part of the definition puts the emphasis on control rather than ownership. This is done so that the balance sheet reflects the substance of transactions rather than their legal form. This means that assets that are not legally owned by an entity, but over which the entity has the rights that are normally conveyed by ownership, are recognised as assets of the entity. Common examples of this would be finance leased assets and other contractual rights such as aircraft landing rights. An important aspect of control of assets is that it allows the entity to restrict the access of others to them. The reference to past events prevents assets that may arise in future from being recognised early.

– liabilities:

The IASB's Framework defines liabilities as 'a present obligation of the entity arising from past events, the settlement of which is expected to result in an outflow from the entity of resources embodying economic benefits'. Many aspects of this definition are complementary (as a mirror image) to the definition of assets, however the IASB stresses that the essential characteristic of a liability is that the entity has a present obligation. Such obligations are usually legally enforceable (by a binding contract or by statute), but obligations also arise where there is an expectation (by a third party) of an entity assuming responsibility for costs where there is no legal requirement to do so. Such obligations are referred to as constructive (by IAS 37 *Provisions, contingent liabilities and contingent assets*). An example of this would be repairing or replacing faulty goods (beyond any warranty period) or incurring environmental costs (e.g. landscaping the site of a previous quarry) where there is no legal obligation to do so. Where entities do incur constructive obligations it is usually to maintain the goodwill and reputation of the entity. One area of difficulty is where entities cannot be sure whether an obligation exists or not, it may depend upon a future uncertain event. These are more generally known as contingent liabilities.

Importance of the definitions of assets and liabilities:

The definitions of assets and liabilities are fundamental to the Framework. Apart from forming the obvious basis for the preparation of a balance sheet, they are also the two elements of financial statements that are used to derive the equity interest (ownership) which is the residue of assets less liabilities. Assets and liabilities also have a part to play in determining when income (which includes gains) and expenses (which include losses) should be recognised. Income is recognised (in the income statement) when there is an increase in future economic benefits relating to increases in assets or decreases in liabilities, provided they can be measured reliably. Expenses are the opposite of this. Changes in assets and liabilities arising from contributions from, and distributions to, the owners are excluded from the definitions of income and expenses.

Currently there is a great deal of concern over 'off balance sheet finance'. This is an aspect of what is commonly referred to as creative accounting. Many recent company failure scandals have been in part due to companies having often massive liabilities that have not been included on the balance sheet. Robust definitions, based on substance, of assets and liabilities in particular should ensure that only real assets are included on the balance sheet and all liabilities are also included. In contradiction to the above point, there have also been occasions where companies have included liabilities on their balance sheets where they do not meet the definition of liabilities in the Framework. Common examples of this are general provisions and accounting for future costs and losses (usually as part of the acquisition of a subsidiary). Companies have used these general provisions to smooth profits i.e. creating a provision when the company has a good year (in terms of profit) and releasing them to boost profits in a bad year. Providing for future costs and losses during an acquisition may effectively allow them to bypass the income statement as they would become part of the goodwill figure.

(c) **(i)** Whilst it is acceptable to value the goodwill of $2·5 million of Trantor (the subsidiary) on the basis described in the question and include it in the consolidated balance sheet, the same treatment cannot be afforded to Peterlee's own goodwill. The calculation may indeed give a realistic value of $4 million for Peterlee's goodwill, and there may be no difference in nature between the goodwill of the two companies, but it must be realised that the goodwill of Peterlee is internal goodwill and IFRSs prohibit such goodwill appearing in the financial statements. The main basis of this conclusion is one of reliable measurement. The value of acquired (purchased) goodwill can be evidenced by the method described in the question (there are also other acceptable methods), but this method of valuation is not acceptable as a basis for recognising internal goodwill.

(ii) Accruing for future costs such as this landscaping on an annual basis may seem appropriate and was common practice until recently. However, it is no longer possible to account for this type of future cost in this manner, therefore the directors' suggestion is unacceptable. IAS 37 *Provisions, contingent liabilities and contingent assets* requires such costs to be accounted for in full as soon as they become unavoidable. The Standard says that the estimate of the future cost should be discounted to a present value (as in this example at $2 million). The accounting treatment is rather controversial; the cost should be included in the balance sheet as a provision (a credit entry/balance), but the debit is to the cost of the asset to give an initial carrying amount of $8 million. This has the effect of 'grossing up' the balance sheet by including the landscaping costs as both an asset and a liability. As the asset is depreciated on a systematic basis ($800,000 per annum assuming straight-line depreciation), the landscaping costs are charged to the income statement over the life of the asset. As the discount is 'unwound' (and charged as a finance cost) this is added to the balance sheet provision such that, at the date when the liability is due to be settled, the provision is equal to the amount due (assuming estimates prove to be accurate).

(iii) The directors' suggestion that the convertible loan should be recorded as a liability of the full $5 million is incorrect. The reason why a similar loan without the option to convert to equity shares (such that it must be redeemed by cash only) carries a higher interest rate is because of the value of the equity option that is contained within the issue proceeds of the $5 million. If the company performs well over the period of the loan, the value of its equity shares should rise and thus it would (probably) be beneficial for the loan note holders to opt for the equity share alternative. IAS 32 and 39 dealing with financial instruments require the value of the option is to be treated as equity rather than debt. The calculation of value of the equity is as follows:

	$'000
Year 1 400 x 0·91	364
Year 2 400 x 0·83	332
Year 3 5,400 x 0·75	4,050
Present value of the cash flows	4,746
Proceeds of issue	(5,000)
Difference is value of equity	254

Initially the loan would be shown at $4,746,000.

The Income statement would show:

	$'000	$'000
Loan interest paid ($5m x 8%)	400	
Accrued finance costs (balance)	75	475 (i.e. $4·746m x 10%)

At 31 March 2006 the loan would have a carrying amount of $4,821,000 ($4,746,000 + $75,000)

4   (a)   Boston – Cash Flow Statement for the year ended 31 March 2006:

Cash flows from operating activities
Note: figures in brackets are in $'000

	$'000	$'000
Profit before tax	65	
Adjustments for:		
depreciation of non-current assets	35	
loss on sale of hotel	12	
interest expense	10	
	122	
increase in current assets (155 – 130)	(25)	
decrease in other current liabilities (115 – 108)	(7)	
Cash generated from operations	90	
Interest paid (see note)	(10)	
Income taxes paid	(30)	
Net cash flow from operating activities		50
Cash flows from investing activities:		
purchase of non-current assets (see below)	(123)	
sale of non-current assets (40 – 12)	28	
Net cash used in investing activities		(95)
Cash flows from financing activities		
Issue of ordinary shares (20 + 20)	40	
Issue of loans (65 – 40)	25	
Net cash from financing activities		65
Net increase in cash and cash equivalents		20
Cash and cash equivalents at beginning of period		(5)
Cash and cash equivalents at end of period		15

Workings	$'000
Non-current assets – carrying amount	
Balance b/f	332
Disposal	(40)
Depreciation for year	(35)
Balance c/f	(380)
Cost of assets acquired	(123)

Note: interest paid may also be presented as a cash flow from financing activities.

20

(b) Report on the financial performance of Boston for the year ended 31 March 2006

To: The Board of Boston
From: A N Other
Date:

Profitability (note figures are rounded to 1 decimal place)
The most striking feature of the current year's performance is the deterioration in the ROCE, down from 25·6% to only 18·0%. This represents an overall fall in profitability of 30% ((25·6 – 18·0)/25·6 x 100). An examination of the other ratios provided shows that this is due to a decline in both profit margins and asset utilisation. A closer look at the profit margins shows that the decline in gross margin is relatively small (42·2% down to 41·4%), whereas the fall in the operating profit margin is down by 2·8%, this represents a 15·7% decline in profitability (i.e. 2·8% on 17·8%). This has been caused by increases in operating expenses of $12m and unallocated corporate expenses of $10m. These increases represent more than half of the net profit for the period and further investigation into the cause of these increases should be made. The company is generating only $1·20 of sales per $1 of net balance sheet assets this year compared to a figure of $1·40 in the previous year. This decline in asset utilisation represents a fall of 14·3% ((1·4 – 1.2)/1·4 x 100).

Liquidity/solvency
From the limited information provided a poor current ratio of 0·9:1 in 2005 has improved to 1·3:1 in the current year. Despite the improvement, it is still below the accepted norm. At the same time gearing has increased from 12·8% to 15·6%. Information from the cash flow statement shows the company has raised $65 million in new capital ($40m in equity and $25m in loans). The disproportionate increase in the loans is the cause of the increase in gearing, however, at 15·6% this is still not a highly geared company. The increase in finance has been used mainly to purchase new non-current assets, but it has also improved liquidity, mainly by reversing an overdraft of $5 million to a bank balance in hand of $15 million.

A common feature of new investment is that there is often a delay between making the investment and benefiting from the returns. This may be the case with Boston, and it may be that in future years the increased investment will be rewarded with higher returns. Another aspect of the investment that may have caused the lower return on assets is that the investment is likely to have occurred part way through the year (maybe even near the year end). This means that the income statement may not include returns for a full year, whereas in future years it will.

Segment issues
Segment information is intended to help the users to better assess the performance of an enterprise by looking at the detailed contribution made by the differing activities that comprise the enterprise as a whole. Referring to the segment ratios it appears that the carpeting segment is giving the greatest contribution to overall profitability achieving a 48·6% return on its segment assets, whereas the equivalent return for house building is 38·1% and for hotels it is only 16·7%. The main reason for the better return from carpeting is due to its higher segment net profit margin of 38·9% compared to hotels at 15·4% and house building at 28·6%. Carpeting's higher segment net profit is in turn a reflection of its underlying very high gross margin (66·7%). The segment net asset turnover of the hotels (1·1 times) is also very much lower than the other two segments (1·3 times). It seems that the hotel segment is also responsible for the group's fairly poor liquidity ratios (ignoring the bank balances) the segment current liabilities are 50% greater than its current assets ($60m compared to $40m); the opposite of this would be a more acceptable current ratio.

These figures are based on historical values. Most commentators argue that the use of fair values is more consistent and thus provides more reliable information on which to base assessments (they are less misleading than the use of historical values). If fair values are used all segments understandably show lower returns and poorer performance (as fair values are higher than historical values), but the figures for the hotels are proportionately much worse, falling by a half of the historic values (as the fair values of the hotel segment are exactly double the historical values). Fair value adjusted figures may even lead one to question the future of the hotel activities. However, before jumping to any conclusions an important issue should be considered. Although the reported profit of the hotels is poor, the market values of its segment assets have increased by a net $90 million. New net investment in hotel capital expenditure is $64 million ($104m – $40m disposal); this leaves an increase in value of $26 million. The majority of this appears to be from market value increases (this would be confirmed if the statement of recognised income and expense was available). Whilst this is not a realised profit, it is nevertheless a significant and valuable gain (equivalent to 65% of the group reported net profit).

Conclusion
Although the company's overall performance has deteriorated in the current year, it is clear that at least some areas of the business have had considerable new investment which may take some time to bear fruit. This applies to the hotel segment in particular and may explain its poor performance, which is also partly offset by the strong increase in the market value of its assets.

Yours A N other

Appendix

Further segment ratios	Carpeting	Hotels	House building
Return on net assets at fair values (35/97 x 100)	36·1%	8·3%	30·2%
Asset turnover on fair values (times) (90/97)	0·9	0·5	1·1

Note: workings have been shown for the figures for the carpeting segment only, the other segments' figures are based on equivalent calculations.

21

5   **(a)**   Income statement for the year ended 31 March 2006

	Alfa	Beta	Ceta	Total
	$m	$m	$m	$m
Revenue	8	2·0	4·8	14·8
Cost of sales	(7)	(3·5)	(4·0)	(14·5)
Profit/(loss)	1	(1·5)	0·8	0·3

Balance sheet as at 31 March 2006

	Alfa	Beta	Ceta	Total
Gross amounts due from customers (see below)	2·4		4·8	7·2
Gross amounts due to customers (see below)		(1·3)		(1·3)

Gross amounts from and to customers:

	Alfa	Beta	Ceta	Total
Contract cost incurred	12·5	3·5	4·0	20·0
Recognised profits less (losses)	2·5	(1·5)	0·8	1·8
Provision for losses to date		(1·5)		(1·5)
Payments received	(12·6)	(1·8)	(nil)	(14·4)
Due from customers	2·4		4·8	7·2
Due to customers (contract liability)		(1·3)		(1·3)

Workings (in $m):

Alfa	at 31 March 2005		at 31 March 2006	Year ended 31 March 2006
Work invoiced (5·4/90%)	6·0	(12·6/90%)	14·0	8
Cost of sales (balancing figure)	(4·5)		(11·5)	(7)
Profit (see below)	1·5		2·5	1
Percentage complete (6/20 x 100)	30%	(14/20 x 100)	70%	
Attributable profit ($5m x 30%)	1·5	(($5m x 70%) – $1m rectification)	2·5	

Prior to the rectification costs (which must be charged to the year in which they are incurred), the estimated total profit on the contract is $5 million ($20m – $15m).

Beta

Due to the increase in the estimated cost Beta is a loss-making contract and the whole of the loss must be provided for as soon as it is can be anticipated. The loss is expected to be $1·5 million ($7·5m – $6m). The sales value of the contract at 31 March 2006 is $2 million ($1·8/90%), thus the cost of sales must be recorded as $3·5 million. As costs to date are $2 million, this means a provision of $1·5 million is required.

Ceta

Based on the costs to date at 31 March 2006 of $4 million and the total estimated costs of $10 million, this contract is 40% complete. The estimated profit is $2 million ($12m – $10m); therefore the profit at 31 March 2006 is $0·8 million ($2m x 40%). This gives an imputed sales (and receivable) value of $4·8 million.

(b)   **(i)**   Savoir – EPS year ended 31 March 2004:

The issue on 1 July 2003 at full market value needs to be weighted:

	40m x 3/12 =	10m
New shares	8m	
	48m x 9/12 =	36m
		46m

Without the bonus issue this would give an EPS of 30c ($13·8m/46m x 100).

The bonus issue of one for four would result in 12 million new shares giving a total number of ordinary shares of 60 million. The dilutive effect of the bonus issue would reduce the EPS to 24c (30c x 48m/60m). The comparative EPS (for 2003) would be restated at 20c (25c x 48m/60m).

EPS year ended 31 March 2005:

The rights issue of two for five on 1 October 2004 is half way through the year. The theoretical ex rights value can be calculated as:

Holder of	100 shares worth $2·40 =	$240
Subscribes for	40 shares at $1 each =	$40
Now holds	140 worth (in theory)	$280 i.e. $2 each.

Weighting:

	60m x 6/12 x 2·40/2·00 =	36 million
Rights issue (2 for 5)	24m	
New total	84m x 6/12 =	42 million
Weighted average		78 million

EPS is therefore 25c ($19·5m/78m x 100).
The comparative (for 2004) would be restated at 20c (24c x 2·00/2·40).

(ii) The basic EPS for the year ended 31 March 2006 is 30c ($25·2m/84m x 100).

Dilution

Convertible loan stock
On conversion loan interest of $1·2 million after tax would be saved ($20 million x 8% x (100% − 25%)) and a further 10 million shares would be issued ($20m/$100 x 50).

Directors' options
Options for 12 million shares at $1·50 each would yield proceeds of $18 million. At the average market price of $2·50 per share this would purchase 7·2 million shares ($18m/$2·50). Therefore the 'bonus' element of the options is 4·8 million shares (12m − 7·2m).

Using the above figures the diluted EPS for the year ended 31 March 2006 is 26·7c ($25·2m + $1·2m)/(84m + 10m + 4·8m)).

23

Part 2 Examination – Paper 2.5(INT)
Financial Reporting (International Stream)   June 2006 Marking Scheme

This marking scheme is given as a guide in the context of the suggested answers. Scope is given to markers to award marks for alternative approaches to a question, including relevant comment, and where well-reasoned conclusions are provided. This is particularly the case for written answers where there may be more than one definitive solution.

					Marks
1	(a)	Income statement:			
		revenue			2
		cost of sales			3
		operating expenses including 1 mark for goodwill			2
		interest receivable/payable			1
		income tax			1
		minority interest			2
		Balance sheet:			
		goodwill			3
		tangible non-current assets			2
		investments			1
		current assets/current liabilities			2
		7% bank loan			1
		elimination of 10% intra group loan			1
		minority interest			2
		share capital and share premium			1
		retained earnings			1
				available	25
				maximum	20
	(b)	1 mark per relevant point to		maximum	5
				Maximum for question	**25**
2	(a)	Income statement			
		revenue			1
		cost of sales			4
		operating costs			1
		investment income			1
		loss on investment			1
		finance costs			2
		income tax			2
				available	12
				maximum	10
	(b)	Statement of recognised income and expense			
		surplus on land and buildings			1
		profit for period			1
				maximum	2
	(c)	Balance sheet			
		property, plant and equipment			4
		investment property			1
		inventories			1
		trade receivables			1
		share capital			1
		revaluation reserve			1
		retained earnings (1 for dividend deduction)			2
		overdraft			1
		trade payables			1
		current tax payable			1
		deferred tax			1
		preference shares (shown as a liability)			1
				available	16
				maximum	13
				Maximum for question	**25**

25

BPP
LEARNING MEDIA

					Marks
3	**(a)**		one mark per valid point to max		5
	(b)		one mark per valid point to max		8
	(c)	**(i)**	acceptable method to value goodwill of subsidiary		1
			although no difference in nature of goodwill;		1
			cannot use this method to value goodwill of parent		1
			IFRS specifically prohibits recognition of internal goodwill		1
			main issue is reliable measurement		1
				available	5
				maximum	4
		(ii)	IAS 37 requires immediate recognition (as a provision) of such costs		1
			future costs discounted to present value		1
			added to cost of the asset (increases depreciation)		1
			unwinding of discount is a finance cost		1
				maximum	4
		(iii)	directors' suggestion is incorrect, part of proceeds is equity		1
			IFRS require equity component to be calculated (residual equity method)		1
			Debt is $4,746,000; equity is $254,000		1
			Income statement charge is $475,000		1
			Non-current liability at 31 March 2006 $4,821,000		1
				available	5
				maximum	4
				Maximum for question	**25**
4	**(a)**		profit before tax		1
			depreciation		1
			loss on sale of hotel		1
			increase in current assets		1
			decrease in current liabilities		1
			interest paid		1
			income taxes paid		1
			purchase of non-current assets		1
			sale of non-current assets		1
			share issue		1
			issue of loan		1
			cash and cash equivalents b/f and c/f		1
				available	12
				maximum	10
	(b)		one mark per valid point to max		15
				Maximum for question	**25**

26

Marks

5 **(a)** Income statement

revenue   4

cost of sales/profit   4

balance sheet

gross amounts due from customers   4

provision   1

available   13

maximum   12

(b) **(i)** EPS – year ended 31 March 2004   4

– year ended 31 March 2004 comparative   1

– year ended 31 March 2005   4

– year ended 31 March 2005 comparative   1

available   10

maximum   9

(ii) EPS year ended 31 March 2006

– basic EPS   1

– dilution effect of options   1

– effect of convertible loan stock   1

– calculation   1

maximum   4

Maximum for question   **25**

27

Part 2 Examination – Paper 2.5(INT)
Financial Reporting (International Stream)   December 2006 Answers

1 (a) Cost of control in Sunlee:

		$'000		$'000
Consideration				
Shares (20,000 x 80% x 3/5 x $5)				48,000
Less				
Equity shares		20,000		
Pre acq reserves		18,000		
Fair value adjustments (4,000 + 3,000 + 5,000)		12,000		
		50,000	x 80%	(40,000)
Goodwill				8,000

(b) Carrying amount of Amber 30 September 2006 (prior to impairment loss):

	$'000
At cost	
Cash (6,000 x $3)	18,000
6% loan notes (6,000 x $100/100)	6,000
	24,000
Less	
Post acquisition losses (20,000 x 40% x 3/12)	(2,000)
	22,000

(c) Hosterling Group
Consolidated income statement for the year ended 30 September 2006

	$'000
Revenue (105,000 + 62,000 – 18,000 intra group)	149,000
Cost of sales (see working)	(89,000)
Gross profit	60,000
Distribution costs (4,000 + 2,000)	(6,000)
Administrative expenses (7,500 + 7,000)	(14,500)
Finance costs (1,200 + 900)	(2,100)
Impairment losses:	
Goodwill	(1,600)
Investment in associate (22,000 – 21,500)	(500)
Share of loss from associate (20,000 x 40% x 3/12)	(2,000)
Profit before tax	33,300
Income tax expense (8,700 + 2,600)	(11,300)
Profit for the period	22,000

	$'000
Attributable to:	
Equity holders of the parent	19,600
Minority Interest ((13,000 – 1,000 depreciation adjustment) x 20%)	2,400
	22,000

Note: the dividend from Sunlee is eliminated on consolidation.

	$'000
Working	
Cost of sales	
Hosterling	68,000
Sunlee	36,500
Intra group purchases	(18,000)
Additional depreciation of plant (5,000/5 years)	1,000
Unrealised profit in inventories (7,500 x 25%/125%)	1,500
	89,000

2 (a) Tadeon – Income statement – Year to 30 September 2006

	$'000	$'000
Revenue		277,800
Cost of sales (w (i))		(144,000)
Gross profit		133,800
Operating expenses (40,000 + 1,200 (w (ii)))		(41,200)
Investment income		2,000
Finance costs – finance lease (w (ii))	(1,500)	
– loan (w (iii))	(2,750)	(4,250)
Profit before tax		90,350
Income tax expense (w (iv))		(36,800)
Profit for the period		53,550

(b) Tadeon – Balance Sheet as at 30 September 2006

	$'000	$'000
Non-current assets		
Property, plant and equipment (w (v))		299,000
Investments at amortised cost		42,000
		341,000
Current assets		
Inventories	33,300	
Trade receivables	53,500	86,800
Total assets		427,800
Equity and liabilities		
Capital and reserves:		
Equity shares of 20 cents each fully paid (w (vi))		200,000
Reserves		
Share premium (w (vi))	28,000	
Revaluation reserve (w (v))	16,000	
Retained earnings (w (vii))	42,150	86,150
		286,150
Non-current liabilities		
2% Loan note (w (iii))	51,750	
Deferred tax (w (iv))	14,800	
Finance lease obligation (w (ii))	10,500	77,050
Current liabilities		
Trade payables	18,700	
Accrued lease finance costs (w (ii))	1,500	
Finance lease obligation (w (ii))	4,500	
Bank overdraft	1,900	
Income tax payable (w (iv))	38,000	64,600
Total equity and liabilities		427,800

Workings (note figures in brackets are in $'000)

(i) Cost of sales:

	$'000
Per trial balance	118,000
Depreciation (12,000 + 5,000 + 9,000 w (v))	26,000
	144,000

(ii) Vehicle rentals/finance lease:

The total amount of vehicle rentals is $6·2 million of which $1·2 million are operating lease rentals and $5 million identified as finance lease rentals. The operating rentals have been included in operating expenses.

Finance lease	$'000
Fair value of vehicles	20,000
First rental payment – 1 October 2005	(5,000)
Capital outstanding to 30 September 2006	15,000
Accrued interest 10% (current liability)	1,500
Total outstanding 30 September 2006	16,500

In the year to 30 September 2007 (i.e. on 1 October 2006) the second rental payment of $6 million will be made, of this $1·5 million is for the accrued interest for the previous year, thus $4·5 million will be a capital repayment. The remaining $10·5 million (16,500 – (4,500 + 1,500)) will be shown as a non-current liability.

(iii) Although the loan has a nominal (coupon) rate of only 2%, amortisation of the large premium on redemption, gives an effective interest rate of 5·5% (from question). This means the finance charge to the income statement will be a total of $2·75 million (50,000 x 5·5%). As the actual interest paid is $1 million an accrual of $1·75 million is required. This amount is added to the carrying amount of the loan in the balance sheet.

(iv) Income tax and deferred tax

The income statement charge is made up as follows:	$'000
Current year's provision	38,000
Deferred tax (see below)	(1,200)
	36,800

There are $74 million of deductible temporary differences at 30 September 2006. With an income tax rate of 20%, this would require a deferred tax liability of $14·8 million (74,000 x 20%). $4 million ($20m x 20%) is transferred to deferred tax in respect of the revaluation of the leasehold property (and debited to the revaluation reserve), thus the effect of deferred tax on the income statement is a credit of $1·2 million (14,800 – 4,000 – 12,000 b/f).

(v) Non-current assets/depreciation:

Non-leased plant

This has a carrying amount of $96 million (181,000 – 85,000) prior to depreciation of $12 million at 12½% reducing balance to give a carrying amount of $84 million at 30 September 2006.

The leased vehicles will be included in non-current assets at their fair value of $20 million and depreciated by $5 million (four years straight-line) for the year ended 30 September 2006 giving a carrying amount of $15 million at that date.

The 25 year leasehold property is being depreciated at $9 million per annum (225,000/25 years). Prior to its revaluation on 30 September 2006 there would be a further year's depreciation charge of $9 million giving a carrying amount of $180 million (225,000 – (36,000 + 9,000)) prior to its revaluation to $200 million. Thus $20 million would be transferred to a revaluation reserve. The question says the revaluation gives rise to $20 million of the deductible temporary differences, at a tax rate of 20%, this would give a credit to deferred tax of $4 million which is debited to the revaluation reserve to give a net balance of $16 million. Summarising:

	cost/valuation	accumulated depreciation	carrying amount
	$,000	$,000	$,000
25 year leasehold property	200,000	nil	200,000
Non-leased plant	181,000	97,000	84,000
Leased vehicles	20,000	5,000	15,000
	401,000	102,000	299,000

(vi) Suspense account

The called up share capital of $150 million in the trial balance represents 750 million shares (150m/0·2) which have a market value at 1 October 2005 of $600 million (750m x 80 cents). A yield of 5% on this amount would require a $30 million dividend to be paid.

A fully subscribed rights issue of one new share for every three shares held at a price of 32c each would lead to an issue of 250 million (150m/0·2 x 1/3). This would yield a gross amount of $80 million, and after issue costs of $2 million, would give a net receipt of $78 million. This should be accounted for as $50 million (250m x 20 cents) to equity share capital and the balance of $28 million to share premium.

The receipt from the share issue of $78 million less the payment of dividends of $30 million reconciles the suspense account balance of $48 million.

(vii) Retained earnings

	$,000
At 1 October 2005	18,600
Year to 30 September 2006	53,550
less dividends paid (w (vi))	(30,000)
	42,150

3   (a)   Most forms of off balance sheet financing have the effect of what is, in substance, debt finance either not appearing on the balance sheet at all or being netted off against related assets such that it is not classified as debt. Common examples would be structuring a lease such that it fell to be treated as an operating lease when it has the characteristics of a finance lease, complex financial instruments classified as equity when they may have, at least in part, the substance of debt and 'controlled' entities having large borrowings (used to benefit the group as a whole), that are not consolidated because the financial structure avoids the entities meeting the definition of a subsidiary.

The main problem of off balance sheet finance is that it results in financial statements that do not faithfully represent the transactions and events that have taken place. Faithful representation is an important qualitative characteristic of useful information (as described in the *Framework for the preparation and presentation of financial statements*). Financial statements that do not faithfully represent that which they purport to lack reliability. A lack of reliability may mean that any decisions made on the basis of the information contained in financial statements are likely to be incorrect or, at best, sub-optimal.

The level of debt on a balance sheet is a direct contributor to the calculation of an entity's balance sheet gearing, which is considered as one of the most important financial ratios. It should be understood that, to a point, the use of debt financing is perfectly acceptable. Where balance sheet gearing is considered low, borrowing is relatively inexpensive, often tax efficient and can lead to higher returns to shareholders. However, when the level of borrowings becomes high, it increases risk in many ways. Off balance sheet financing may lead to a breach of loan covenants (a serious situation) if such debt were to be recognised on the balance sheet in accordance with its substance.

High gearing is a particular issue to equity investors. Equity (ordinary shares) is sometimes described as residual return capital. This description identifies the dangers (to equity holders) when an entity has high gearing. The dividend that the equity shareholders might expect is often based on the level of reported profits. The finance cost of debt acts as a reduction of the profits available for dividends. As the level of debt increases, higher interest rates are also usually payable to reflect the additional risk borne by the lender, thus the higher the debt the greater the finance charges and the lower the profit. Many off balance sheet finance schemes also disguise or hide the true finance cost which makes it difficult for equity investors to assess the amount of profits that will be needed to finance the debt and consequently how much profit will be available to equity investors. Furthermore, if the market believes or suspects an entity is involved in 'creative accounting' (and off balance sheet finance is a common example of this) it may adversely affect the entity's share price.

An entity's level of gearing will also influence any decision to provide further debt finance (loans) to the entity. Lenders will consider the nature and value of the assets that an entity owns which may be provided as security for the borrowings. The presence of existing debt will generally increase the risk of default of interest and capital repayments (on further borrowings) and existing lenders may have a prior charge on assets available as security. In simple terms if an entity has high borrowings, additional borrowing is more risky and consequently more expensive. A prospective lender to an entity that already has high borrowings, but which do not appear on the balance sheet is likely to make the wrong decision. If the correct level of borrowings were apparent, either the lender would not make the loan at all (too high a lending risk) or, if it did make the loan, it would be on substantially different terms (e.g. charge a higher interest rate) so as to reflect the real risk of the loan.

Some forms of off balance sheet financing may specifically mislead suppliers that offer credit. It is a natural precaution that a prospective supplier will consider the balance sheet strength and liquidity ratios of the prospective customer. The existence of consignment inventories may be particularly relevant to trade suppliers. Sometimes consignment inventories and their related current liabilities are not recorded on the balance sheet as the wording of the purchase agreement may be such that the legal ownership of the goods remains with the supplier until specified events occur (often the onward sale of the goods). This means that other suppliers cannot accurately assess an entity's true level of trade payables and consequently the average payment period to suppliers, both of which are important determinants in deciding whether to grant credit.

(b) **(i)** Debt factoring is a common method of entities releasing the liquidity of their trade receivables. The accounting issue that needs to be decided is whether the trade receivables have been sold, or whether the income from the finance house for their 'sale' should be treated as a short term loan. The main substance issue with this type of transaction is to identify which party bears the risks (i.e. of slow and non-payment by the customer) relating to the asset. If the risk lies with the finance house (Omar), the trade receivables should be removed from the balance sheet (derecognised in accordance with IAS 39). In this case it is clear that Angelino still bears the risk relating to slow and non-payment. The residual payment by Omar depends on how quickly the receivables are collected; the longer it takes, the less the residual payment (this imputes a finance cost). Any balance uncollected by Omar after six months will be refunded by Angelino which reflects the non-payment risk.

Thus the correct accounting treatment for this transaction is that the cash received from Omar (80% of the selected receivables) should be treated as a current liability (a short term loan) and the difference between the gross trade receivables and the amount ultimately received from Omar (plus any amounts directly from the credit customers themselves) should be charged to the income statement. The classification of the charge is likely to be a mixture of administrative expenses (for Omar collecting receivables), finance expenses (reflecting the time taken to collect the receivables) and the impairment of trade receivables (bad debts).

(ii) This is an example of a sale and leaseback of a property. Such transactions are part of normal commercial activity, often being used as a way to improve cash flow and liquidity. However, if an asset is sold at an amount that is different to its fair value there is likely to be an underlying reason for this. In this case it appears (based on the opinion of the auditor) that Finaid has paid Angelino $2 million more than the building is worth. No (unconnected) company would do this knowingly without there being some form of 'compensating' transaction. This sale is 'linked' to the five year rental agreement. The question indicates the rent too is not at a fair value, being $500,000 per annum ($1,300,000 – $800,000) above what a commercial rent for a similar building would be.

It now becomes clear that the excess purchase consideration of $2 million is an 'in substance' loan (rather than sales proceeds – the legal form) which is being repaid through the excess ($500,000 per annum) of the rentals. Although this is a sale and leaseback transaction, as the building is freehold and has an estimated remaining life (20 years) that is much longer than the five year leaseback period, the lease is not a finance lease and the building should be treated as sold and thus derecognised.

The correct treatment for this item is that the sale of the building should be recorded at its fair value of $10 million, thus the profit on disposal would be $2·5 million ($10 million – $7·5 million). The 'excess' of $2 million ($12 million – $10 million) should be treated as a loan (non-current liability). The rental payment of $1·3 million should be split into three elements; $800,000 building rental cost, $200,000 finance cost (10% of $2 million) and the remaining $300,000 is a capital repayment of the loan.

(iii)   The treatment of consignment inventory depends on the substance of the arrangements between the manufacturer and the dealer (Angelino). The main issue is to determine if and at what point in time the cars are 'sold'. The substance is determined by analysing which parties bear the risks (e.g. slow moving/obsolete inventories, finance costs) and receive the benefits (e.g. use of inventories, potential for higher sales, protection from price increases) associated with the transaction.

Supplies from Monza

Angelino has, and has actually exercised, the right to return the cars without penalty (or been required by Monza to transfer them to another dealer), which would indicate that it has not 'bought' the cars. There are no finance costs incurred by Angelino, however Angelino would suffer from any price increases that occurred during the three month holding/display period. These factors seem to indicate that the substance of this arrangement is the same as its legal form i.e. Monza should include the cars in its balance sheet as inventory and therefore Angelino will not record a purchase transaction until it becomes obliged to pay for the cars (three months after delivery or until sold to customers if sooner).

Supplies from Capri

Although this arrangement seems similar to the above, there are several important differences. Angelino is bearing the finance costs of 1% per month (calling it a display charge is a distraction). The option to return the cars should be ignored because it is not likely to be exercised due to commercial penalties (payment of transport costs and loss of deposit). Finally the purchase price is fixed at the date of delivery rather than at the end of six months. These factors strongly indicate that Angelino bears the risks and rewards associated with ownership and should recognise the inventory and the associated liability in its financial statements at the date of delivery.

4 (a) Cash Flow Statement of Minster for the Year ended 30 September 2006:

	$000	$000
Cash flows from operating activities		
Profit before tax		142
Adjustments for:		
Depreciation of property, plant and equipment	255	
Amortisation of software (180 – 135)	45	300
Investment income		(20)
Finance costs		40
		462
Working capital adjustments		
Decrease in trade receivables (380 – 270)	110	
Increase in amounts due from construction contracts (80 – 55)	(25)	
Decrease in inventories (510 – 480)	30	
Decrease in trade payables (555 – 350)	(205)	(90)
Cash generated from operations		372
Interest paid (40 – 12 re unwinding of environmental provision)		(28)
Income taxes paid (w (ii))		(54)
Net cash from operating activities		290
Cash flows from investing activities		
Purchase of – property, plant and equipment (w (i))	(410)	
– software	(180)	
– investments (150 – (15 + 125))	(10)	
Investment income received (20 – 15 gain on investments)	5	
Net cash used in investing activities		(595)
Cash flows from financing activities		
Proceeds from issue of equity shares (w (iii))	265	
Proceeds from issue of 9% loan note	120	
Dividends paid (500 x 4 x 5 cents)	(100)	
Net cash from financing activities		285
Net decrease in cash and cash equivalents		(20)
Cash and cash equivalents at beginning of period (40 – 35)		(5)
Cash and cash equivalents at end of period		(25)

Note: interest paid may be presented under financing activities and dividends paid may be presented under operating activities.

Workings (in $'000)

(i) Property, plant and equipment:

carrying amount b/f	940
non-cash environmental provision	150
revaluation	35
depreciation for period	(255)
carrying amount c/f	(1,280)
difference is cash acquisitions	(410)

(ii) Taxation:

tax provision b/f	(50)
deferred tax b/f	(25)
income statement charge	(57)
tax provision c/f	60
deferred tax c/f	18
difference is cash paid	(54)

(iii) Equity shares

balance b/f	(300)
bonus issue (1 for 4)	(75)
balance c/f	500
difference is cash issue	125

Share premium

balance b/f	(85)
bonus issue (1 for 4)	75
balance c/f	150
difference is cash issue	140

Therefore the total proceeds of cash issue of shares are $265,000 (125 + 140).

(b) Report on the financial position of Minster for the year ended 30 September 2006

To:
From:
Date:

Minster shows healthy operating cash inflows of $372,000 (prior to finance costs and taxation). This is considered by many commentators as a very important figure as it is often used as the basis for estimating the company's future maintainable cash flows. Subject to (inevitable) annual expected variations and allowing for any changes in the company's structure this figure is more likely to be repeated in the future than most other figures in the cash flow statements which are often 'one-off' cash flows such as raising loans or purchasing non-current assets. The operating cash inflow compares well with the underlying profit before tax $142,000. This is mainly due to depreciation charges of $300,000 being added back to the profit as they are a non-cash expense. The cash inflow generated from operations of $372,000 together with the reduction in net working capital of $90,000 is more than sufficient to cover the company's taxation payments of $54,000, interest payments of $28,000 and the dividend of $100,000 and leaves an amount to contribute to the funding of the increase in non-current assets. It is important that these short term costs are funded from operating cash flows; it would be of serious concern if, for example, interest or income tax payments were having to be funded by loan capital or the sale of non-current assets.

There are a number of points of concern. The dividend of $100,000 gives a dividend cover of less than one (85/100 = 0·85) which means the company has distributed previous year's profits. This is not a tenable situation in the long-term. The size of the dividend has also contributed to the lower cash balances (see below). There is less investment in both inventory levels and trade receivables. This may be the result of more efficient inventory control and better collection of receivables, but it may also indicate that trading volumes may be falling. Also of note is a large reduction in trade payable balances of $205,000. This too may be indicative of lower trading (i.e. less inventory purchased on credit) or pressure from suppliers to pay earlier. Without more detailed information it is difficult to come to a conclusion in this matter.

Investing activities:
The cash flow statement shows considerable investment in non-current assets, in particular $410,000 in property, plant and equipment. These acquisitions represent an increase of 44% of the carrying amount of the property, plant and equipment as at the beginning of the year. As there are no disposals, the increase in investment must represent an increase in capacity rather than the replacement of old assets. Assuming that this investment has been made wisely, this should bode well for the future (most analysts would prefer to see increased investment rather than contraction in operating assets). An unusual feature of the required treatment of environmental provisions is that the investment in non-current assets as portrayed by the cash flow statement appears less than if balance sheet figures are used. The balance sheet at 30 September 2006 includes $150,000 of non-current assets (the discounted cost of the environmental provision), which does not appear in the cash flow figures as it is not a cash 'cost'. A further consequence is that the 'unwinding' of the discounting of the provision causes a financing expense in the income statement which is not matched in the cash flow statement as the unwinding is not a cash flow. Many commentators have criticised the required treatment of environmental provisions because they cause financing expenses which are not (immediate) cash costs and no 'loans' have been taken out. Viewed in this light, it may be that the information in the cash flow statement is more useful than that in the income statement and balance sheet.

Financing activities:
The increase in investing activities (before investment income) of $600,000 has been largely funded by an issue of shares at $265,000 and raising a 9% $120,000 loan note. This indicates that the company's shareholders appear reasonably pleased with the company's past performance (or they would not be very willing to purchase further shares). The interest rate of the loan at 9% seems quite high, and virtually equal to the company's overall return on capital employed of 9·1% (162/(1,660 + 120)). Provided current profit levels are maintained, it should not reduce overall returns to shareholders.

Cash position:
The overall effect of the year's cash flows has worsened the company's cash position by an increased net cash liability of $20,000. Although the company's short term borrowings have reduced by $15,000, the cash at bank of $35,000 at the beginning of the year has now gone. In comparison to the cash generation ability of the company and considering its large investment in non-current assets, this $20,000 is a relatively small amount and should be relieved by operating cash inflows in the near future.

Summary

The above analysis shows that Minster has invested substantially in new non-current assets suggesting expansion. To finance this, the company appears to have no difficulty in attracting further long-term funding. At the same time there are indications of reduced inventories, trade receivables and payables which may suggest the opposite i.e. contraction. It may be that the new investment is a change in the nature of the company's activities (e.g. mining) which has different working capital characteristics. The company has good operating cash flow generation and the slight deterioration in short term net cash balance should only be temporary.

Yours ....

5 **(a)** **(i)** IFRS 5 *Non-current assets held for sale and discontinued operations* defines non-current assets held for sale as those assets (or a group of assets) whose carrying amounts will be recovered principally through a sale transaction rather than through continuing use. A discontinued operation is a component of an entity that has either been disposed of, or is classified as 'held for sale' and:

(i)   represents a separate major line of business or geographical area of operations
(ii) is part of a single co-ordinated plan to dispose of such, or
(iii) is a subsidiary acquired exclusively for sale.

IFRS 5 says that a 'component of an entity' must have operations and cash flows that can be clearly distinguished from the rest of the entity and will in all probability have been a cash-generating unit (or group of such units) whilst held for use. This definition also means that a discontinued operation will also fall to be treated as a 'disposal group' as defined in IFRS 5. A disposal group is a group of assets (possibly with associated liabilities) that it is intended will be disposed of in a single transaction by sale or otherwise (closure or abandonment). Assets held for disposal (but not those being abandoned) must be presented separately (at the lower of cost or fair value less costs to sell) from other assets and included as current assets (rather than as non-current assets) and any associated liabilities must be separately presented under liabilities. The results of a discontinued operation should be disclosed separately as a single figure (as a minimum) on the face of the income statement with more detailed figures disclosed either also on the face of the income statement or in the notes.

The intention of this requirement is to improve the usefulness of the financial statements by improving the predictive value of the (historical) income statement. Clearly the results from discontinued operations should have little impact on future operating results. Thus users can focus on the continuing activities in any assessment of future income and profit.

(ii) The timing of the board meeting and consequent actions and notifications is within the accounting period ended 31 October 2006. The notification of staff, suppliers and the press seems to indicate that the sale will be highly probable and the directors are committed to a plan to sell the assets and are actively locating a buyer. From the financial and other information given in the question it appears that the travel agencies' operations and cash flows can be clearly distinguished from its other operations. The assets of the travel agencies appear to meet the definition of non-current assets held for sale; however the main difficulty is whether their sale and closure also represent a discontinued operation. The main issue is with the wording of 'a separate major line of business' in part (i) of the above definition of a discontinued operation. The company is still operating in the holiday business, but only through Internet selling. The selling of holidays through the Internet compared with through high-street travel agencies requires very different assets, staff knowledge and training and has a different cost structure. It could therefore be argued that although the company is still selling holidays the travel agencies do represent a separate line of business. If this is the case, it seems the announced closure of the travel agencies appears to meet the definition of a discontinued operation.

(iii) Partway income statement year ended:

	31 October 2006 $'000	31 October 2005 $'000
Continuing operations		
Revenue	25,000	22,000
Cost of sales	(19,500)	(17,000)
Gross profit	5,500	5,000
Operating expenses	(1,100)	(500)
Profit/(loss) from continuing operations	4,400	4,500
Discontinued operations		
Profit/(loss) from discontinued operations	(4,000)	1,500
Profit for the period	400	6,000
Analysis of discontinued operations		
Revenue	14,000	18,000
Cost of sales	(16,500)	(15,000)
Gross profit/(loss)	(2,500)	3,000
Operating expenses	(1,500)	(1,500)
Profit/(loss) from discontinued operations	(4,000)	1,500

Note: other presentations may be acceptable.

(b) (i) Comparability is one of the four principal qualitative characteristics of useful financial information. It is a vital attribute when assessing the performance of an entity over time (trend analysis) and to some extent with other similar entities. For information to be comparable it should be based on the consistent treatment of transactions and events. In effect a change in an accounting policy breaks the principle of consistency and should generally be avoided. That said there are circumstances where it becomes necessary to change an accounting policy. These are mainly where it is required by a new or revised accounting standard, interpretation or applicable legislation or where the change would result in financial statements giving a more reliable and relevant representation of the entity's transactions and events.

It is important to note that the application of a different accounting policy to transactions or events that are substantially different to existing transactions or events or to transactions or events that an entity had not previously experienced does NOT represent a change in an accounting policy. It is also necessary to distinguish between a change in an accounting policy and a change in an estimation technique.

In an attempt to limit the problem of reduced comparability caused by a change in an accounting policy, the general principle is that the financial statements should be prepared as if the new accounting policy had always been in place. This is known as retrospective application. The main effect of this is that comparative financial statements should be restated by applying the new policy to them and adjusting the opening balance of each component of equity affected in the earliest prior period presented. IAS 8 *Accounting policies, changes in accounting estimates and errors* says that a change in accounting policy required by a specific Standard or Interpretation should be dealt with under the transitional provisions (if any) of that Standard or Interpretation (normally these apply the general rule of retrospective application). There are some limited exemptions (mainly on the grounds of impracticality) to the general principle of retrospective application in IAS 8.

(ii) This issue is one of the timing of when revenue should be recognised in the income statement. This can be a complex issue which involves identifying the transfer of significant risks, reliable measurement, the probability of receiving economic benefits, relevant accounting standards and legislation and generally accepted practice. Applying the general guidance in IAS 18 *Revenue*, the previous policy, applied before cancellation insurance was made a condition of booking, seemed appropriate. At the time the holiday is taken it can no longer be cancelled, all monies would have been received and the flights and accommodation have been provided. There may be some compensation costs involved if there are problems with the holiday, but this is akin to product warranties on normal sales of goods which may be immaterial or provided for based on previous experience of such costs. The appendix to IAS 18 specifically refers to payments in advance of the 'delivery' of goods and says that revenue should be recognised when the goods are delivered. Interpreting this for Partway's transaction would seem to confirm the appropriateness of its previous policy.

The directors of Partway wish to change the timing of recognition of sales because of the change in circumstances relating to the compulsory cancellation insurance. The directors are apparently arguing that the new 'transactions and events' are substantially different to previous transactions therefore the old policy should not apply. Even if this does justify revising the timing of the recognition of revenue, it is not a change of accounting policy because of the reasons outlined in (i) above.

An issue to consider is whether compulsory cancellation insurance represents a substantial change to the risks that Partway experiences. An analysis of past experience of losses caused by uninsured cancellations may help to assess this, but even if the past losses were material (and in future they won't be), it is unlikely that this would override the general guidance in the appendix to IAS 18 relating to payments made in advance of delivery. It seems the main motivation for the proposed change is to improve the profit for the year ended 31 October 2006 so that it compares more favourably with that of the previous period.

To summarise, it is unlikely that the imposition of compulsory cancellation insurance justifies recognising sales at the date of booking when a deposit is received, and, even if it did, it would not be a change in accounting policy. This means that comparatives would not be restated (which is something that would actually suit the suspected objectives of the directors).

Part 2 Examination – Paper 2.5(INT)
Financial Reporting (International Stream)

December 2006 Marking Scheme

This marking scheme is given as a guide in the context of the suggested answers. Scope is given to markers to award marks for alternative approaches to a question, including relevant comment, and where well-reasoned conclusions are provided. This is particularly the case for written answers where there may be more than one acceptable solution.

				Marks
1	**(a)**	Goodwill of Sunlee:		
		consideration		1
		equity shares		1
		pre acquisition reserves		1
		fair value adjustments		2
			maximum	**5**
	(b)	Carrying amount and impairment of Amber:		
		cash paid		1
		6% loan note		1
		post acquisition loss		2
			maximum	**4**
	(c)	Income statement:		
		revenue		2
		cost of sales		4
		distribution costs and administrative expenses		1
		finance costs		1
		impairment of goodwill		1
		impairment of associate		1
		share of associate's loss		2
		income tax		1
		minority interests		2
		eliminate dividend from Sunlee		1
			maximum	**16**
			Maximum for question	**25**
2	**(a)**	Income statement		
		revenue		1
		cost of sales		1
		operating expenses		1
		investment income		1
		finance costs		3
		income tax expense		3
			available	**10**
			maximum	**8**
	(b)	Balance sheet		
		property, plant and equipment		3
		investment		1
		inventory and trade receivables		1
		share capital and premium		3
		revaluation reserve		2
		retained earnings (including 1 mark for the dividend)		2
		loan note		2
		deferred tax		1
		lease obligation (1 for current, 1 for long-term)		2
		trade payables and overdraft		1
		accrued lease finance costs		1
		income tax payable		1
			available	**20**
			maximum	**17**
			Maximum for question	**25**

					Marks
3	(a)		1 mark per relevant point to a	maximum	9
	(b)	(i)	1 mark per relevant point to a	maximum	5
		(ii)	sale price not at fair value raises substance issues		1
			leaseback is not a finance lease		1
			treat building as sold (derecognise) at a profit of $2·5 million		1
			rental treated as: $800,000 rental cost		1
			$200,000 finance cost		1
			$300,000 loan repayment		1
				maximum	6
		(iii)	general discussion of risks and rewards re consignment goods		2
			Issues and accounting treatment relating to supplies from Monza		2
			Issues and accounting treatment relating to supplies from Capri		2
				available	6
				maximum	5
				Maximum for question	25

4	(a)		cash flow from operating activity		
			profit before tax adjusted for investment income and finance cost		1
			depreciation/amortisation		2
			working capital items		2
			finance costs		2
			income taxes paid		2
			investing activities (including 1 for investment income)		4
			financing – issue of ordinary shares		1
			– issue of 9% loan		1
			dividend paid		1
			cash and cash equivalents b/f and c/f		1
				available	17
				maximum	15
	(b)		1 mark per relevant point		10
				Maximum for question	25

5	(a)	(i)	definitions		2
			usefulness of information		2
				maximum	4
		(ii)	discussion of whether a discontinued operation		3
			conclusion		1
				maximum	4
		(iii)	figures for revenue from continuing operations (2005 and 2006)		1
			figures for revenue from discontinued operations (2005 and 2006)		1
			figures for cost of sales from continuing operations (2005 and 2006)		1
			figures for cost of sales from discontinued operations (2005 and 2006)		1
			figures for profit from continuing operations (2005 and 2006)		1
			figures for profit from discontinued operations (2005 and 2006)		1
				maximum	6
	(b)	(i)	1 mark per relevant point	maximum	5
		(ii)	1 mark per relevant point	maximum	6
				Maximum for question	25

Review Form & Free Prize Draw – Paper F7 Financial Reporting (International) (6/07)

All original review forms from the entire BPP range, completed with genuine comments, will be entered into one of two draws on 31 July 2007 and 31 January 2008. The names on the first four forms picked out on each occasion will be sent a cheque for £50.

Name: _____   Address: _____

_____

_____

How have you used this Kit?
(Tick one box only)

☐ Home study (book only)

☐ On a course: college _____

☐ With 'correspondence' package

☐ Other _____

Why did you decide to purchase this Kit?
(Tick one box only)

☐ Have used the complementary Study text

☐ Have used other BPP products in the past

☐ Recommendation by friend/colleague

☐ Recommendation by a lecturer at college

☐ Saw advertising

☐ Other _____

During the past six months do you recall seeing/receiving any of the following?
(Tick as many boxes as are relevant)

☐ Our advertisement in *Student Accountant*

☐ Our advertisement in *Pass*

☐ Our advertisement in *PQ*

☐ Our brochure with a letter through the post

☐ Our website www.bpp.com

Which (if any) aspects of our advertising do you find useful?
(Tick as many boxes as are relevant)

☐ Prices and publication dates of new editions

☐ Information on product content

☐ Facility to order books off-the-page

☐ None of the above

Which BPP products have you used?

Text	☐	Success CD	☐	Learn Online	☐
Kit	☑	i-Learn	☐	Home Study Package	☐
Passcard	☐	i-Pass	☐	Home Study PLUS	☐

Your ratings, comments and suggestions would be appreciated on the following areas.

	Very useful	Useful	Not useful
Passing ACCA exams	☐	☐	☐
Passing P1	☐	☐	☐
Planning your question practice	☐	☐	☐
Questions	☐	☐	☐
Top Tips etc in answers	☐	☐	☐
Content and structure of answers	☐	☐	☐
'Plan of attack' in mock exams	☐	☐	☐
Mock exam answers	☐	☐	☐

Overall opinion of this Kit	Excellent ☐	Good ☐	Adequate ☐	Poor ☐

Do you intend to continue using BPP products?   Yes ☐   No ☐

The BPP author of this edition can be e-mailed at: marymaclean@bpp.com

Please return this form to: Nick Weller, ACCA Publishing Manager, BPP Learning Media Ltd, FREEPOST, London, W12 8BR

Review Form & Free Prize Draw (continued)

TELL US WHAT YOU THINK

Please note any further comments and suggestions/errors below.

Free Prize Draw Rules

1 Closing date for 31 July 2007 draw is 30 June 2007. Closing date for 31 January 2008 draw is 31 December 2007.

2 Restricted to entries with UK and Eire addresses only. BPP employees, their families and business associates are excluded.

3 No purchase necessary. Entry forms are available upon request from BPP Learning Media Ltd. No more than one entry per title, per person. Draw restricted to persons aged 16 and over.

4 Winners will be notified by post and receive their cheques not later than 6 weeks after the relevant draw date.

5 The decision of the promoter in all matters is final and binding. No correspondence will be entered into.